PROHIBITION

Also by Edward Behr

The Algerian Problem

The Thirty-Sixth Way (with Sidney Liu)

"Anyone Here Been Raped and Speaks English?"

Getting Even

The Last Emperor

Hirohito: Behind the Myth

The Complete Book of *Les Misérables*

Kiss the Hand You Cannot Bite: The Rise and Fall of
the Ceausescus

The Story of Miss Saigon (with Mark Steyn)

The Good Frenchman (The Life and Times of Maurice
Chevalier)

—

PROHIBITION

THIRTEEN YEARS THAT CHANGED AMERICA

EDWARD BEHR

ARCADE PUBLISHING • NEW YORK

FIRST NORTH AMERICAN EDITION

Library of Congress Cataloging-in-Publication Data

Behr, Edward, 1926 –
    Prohibition : thirteen years that changed America / Edward Behr. —
1st North American Ed.
      p.   cm.
    Includes bibliographical references and index.
    ISBN 1-55970-356-3
    1. Prohibition — United States — History. 2. Drinking of alcoholic
beverages — United States — History. 3. Alcoholism — United States —
History. I. Title
HV5089.B424. 1996
363.4.1.0973 — dc20   96 – 24063

Published in the United States by Arcade Publishing, Inc., New York

Distributed by Little, Brown and Company

10 9 8 7 6 5 4 3 2 1

PRINTED IN THE UNITED STATES OF AMERICA

CONTENTS

ACKNOWLEDGMENTS

Philip Guedalla once said that while history repeats itself, historians repeat each other—and all writers on Prohibition owe a huge debt to Herbert Asbury, whose *Great Illusion* remains the best record of its historical and evangelical origins. Another essential source book is *Wayne Wheeler: Dry Boss,* by Justin Stewart, Wheeler's former private secretary. I have also drawn heavily on the insider accounts of Prohibition by Roy Haynes, one of the first Prohibition Bureau commissioners, and Mabel Walker Willebrandt, who was deputy attorney general in charge of Prohibition law enforcement from 1921 to 1929.

I also want to thank the New York, St. Louis, Cincinnati, and East Hampton public libraries for their helpful cooperation, and the Library of Congress for its material on the Senate Investigative Committee on Attorney General Daugherty in 1924. I am especially beholden to a number of Cincinnati residents and experts: Jim Bruckmann, who reminisced about the pre-Prohibition fortunes of his family brewery; Jack Doll, gifted amateur photographer and organizer of a remarkable photo exhibition on George Remus; Geoffrey Giuglierino; Dr. Don H. Todzmann of the University of Cincinnati— and countless others, on Long Island and the East Coast, who were kind enough to share with me the family tales and reminiscences of not so long ago.

I would also like to thank my agent, Jean-François Samuelson, for his unfailing support, and my old friend and colleague Anthony Geffen for his constant encouragement. Thanks to him, what began as a vague telephone conversation ended up not only as a book but as an international, three-part television series.

PROHIBITION

Prohibition is better than no liquor at all.

—WILL ROGERS

INTRODUCTION

Early one fine autumn morning — October 6, 1927 — a stocky, middle-aged man named George Remus ordered George Klug, his driver, to overtake a taxi in Cincinnati's Eden Park. He had been tailing it ever since it had left the Alms Hotel with its two women passengers. After driving alongside, and motioning it to stop — it failed to do so — Remus got the driver to swerve suddenly, forcing the taxi off the road.

The cabdriver swore and hit the brakes, barely avoiding a collision, and the two women were shaken nearly off their seats. The older one, Imogene, was Remus's wife, and she was on her way to her divorce court hearing. By today's standards, she was distinctly on the stocky side, but her opulent figure, ample curves, and huge, gray-green eyes were typical beauty canons of the time, and her clothes — a black silk dress, patent leather black shoes, and black cloche hat from Paris — identified her as a woman of means. The younger woman, her daughter Ruth by an earlier marriage, was a slightly dumpy twenty-year-old.

As Ruth would later tell the court, at Remus's trial, Imogene gasped, "There's Remus," when she first spotted the overtaking car. Imogene got out of the stationary cab as Remus emerged from *his* car, a gun in his right hand (the defense later challenged this evidence, for Remus was left-handed). Ruth recounted: "He hit her on the head with his fist." Imogene said, "Oh, Daddy, you know I love you, you know I love you!" Remus turned to Ruth. "She can't get away with *that*," he snarled.

Imogene shrieked, "For God's sake, don't do it!" as Ruth, also spotting the gun, shouted, "Daddy, what are you going to do?" Then Imogene screamed, "Steve [the taxi driver], for God's sake, come over and help me!" But the driver stayed put. He heard George Remus shout, "Damn you, you dirty so-and-so bitch, *damn* you, I'll *get* you."

Imogene then rushed back into the cab, pursued by Remus. That was when he shot her, once in the stomach. She had the strength to get out of the other side of the car, running, her hands above her head, with Remus still in pursuit. She then got into another car, which had come to a halt behind the stalled taxicab, and collapsed.

Rather than confront the driver, Remus walked away. Shortly afterward, he gave himself up. As the *Cincinnati Enquirer* wrote the following day (October 7, 1927), "Thus did the much tangled domestic affairs of George Remus, once the multi-millionaire bootlegger king of Cincinnati, come to a sudden — and dramatic — climax."

The trial of George Remus for his wife's murder — and its spectacular conclusion — became the 1920s equivalent of the O. J. Simpson case. Reporters arrived from all over the United States, Canada, and even Europe — a special press room was set aside for them in the tiny courthouse. Proceedings were reported extensively in newspapers nationwide, the *Cincinnati Enquirer* running an almost verbatim account of the trial, from beginning to end.

George Remus would have remained an obscure Chicago criminal lawyer with an interest in law reform and a passionate opposition to the death penalty had Prohibition not turned him, in the space of four years, into a megastar millionaire. His *crime passionnel* stemmed not only from this sudden change in fortune, but from Imogene's sudden passion for Remus's nemesis, handsome young Justice Department agent Franklin Dodge, and her own considerable greed. Overwhelmingly, American men sided with George Remus, and even many staid, middle-class American matrons felt that Imogene "had had it coming to her."

For all the sordid details revealed during the trial, enabling Remus to present his case as an avenger rather than a murderer, Prohibition itself was the real culprit. Had there been no Volstead Act, he told the court, "I would not be here." The "greatest social experiment of modern times," as President Calvin Coolidge described it, brought with it irresistible temptations in the wake of unprecedented corruption.

The story of George and Imogene Remus is all part of that "noble experiment." George Remus's background, as a German-born "new American," was relevant to the unprecedented (and, to most Europeans, at least, deluded) attempt at the regulation of social behavior, for with hindsight, the Prohibition phenomenon can be seen not just as a well-meaning, albeit absurd, attempt to stamp out drunkenness, then regarded as society's most devastating scourge (graver even than TB, the other great affliction of the time, for it affected the mind as well as the body), but as a watershed marking the end of one American era and the beginning of another.

Beyond the debate on the rights of reformers to regulate social behavior by force, restricting individual freedom in the name of better health, morality, and godliness, Prohibition was the rearguard action of a still dominant, overwhelmingly rural, white Anglo-Saxon Protestant establishment, aware that its privileges and natural right to rule were being increasingly threatened by the massive arrival of largely despised (and feared) beer-swilling, wine-drinking new American immigrants.

Old-established Americans, most of them Protestants, of overwhelmingly British lineage, regarded themselves as the natural guardians of traditional values, and were determined to maintain their moral and religious standards by almost any means. They were also intent on preserving their own considerable privileges. As historian Andrew Sinclair later wrote,[1] the Prohibitionists' victory in 1920, turning the whole of the country dry, was "the final victory of the defenders of the American past. On the rock of the 18th Amendment, village America made its last stand."

America's Marxists, a very small minority even in the heyday of Marxism, saw Prohibition in a very different light. For them it was a deliberate attempt on the part of the "dominant bourgeoisie" to duck the *real* issues — poverty, slum housing, economic exploitation of all kinds — using the Prohibition campaign as a pretext to deflect attention from the fact that the working classes were paying a huge price for the American industrial revolution. They argued that the ideals the Prohibitionists considered most important — godliness, industry, sobriety, thrift — were deliberately, and with consummate hypocrisy, advocated to compel the underprivileged to accept their fate and inferior status. Sobriety was simply a "plutocratic weapon" employers used to make wage slaves work harder and faster on the factory assembly lines. The underlying assumption was that if the workers refrained from drink, their one easily available pleasure, they could then get by on their miserable wages.[2]

The story of Imogene and George Remus, and of their nemesis, Prohibition — in retrospect one of the greatest of American disasters, and in its day "without a doubt the most important question in American life"[3] — is oddly relevant today. In its simplistic determination to strike at the root of a "social evil" without any thought of the consequences, or of the means required to enforce it, Prohibition was a striking example of the American propensity to believe that society was infinitely malleable and that all it would take to rid America of its blemishes and turn it into a promised land would be a few well-meaning laws.

It also embodied a number of righteous beliefs — in the perfectibility of human nature and the legitimacy of the moral imperative to improve the health and well-being of the masses whether they liked it or not — that revealed a perennial American naiveté of the type embodied by successive generations of idealist-politicians.

The persistence and skill with which the architects of Prohibition pleaded their cause over most of a century, winning state after state until an overwhelming majority in Congress voted for the Eighteenth Amendment, was a textbook example of successful lobbying. All practitioners of that art have since, consciously or unconsciously, emulated the tactics of the Anti-Saloon League and its ruthless legal adviser and political power broker Wayne Wheeler. But the incompetence that followed was equally exemplary — as if the very politicians who had brought Prohibition into being were determined to do everything in their power to ensure its failure.

Despite its almost risible collapse, Prohibition's lessons are valuable — and have still not been learned. Some of its methods were strikingly similar to those used today to fight drug abuse, with equally disappointing results, and today's controversy over drugs could, with only minor semantic changes, apply to the Prohibition controversy almost a century ago. "Prohibition is what makes drugs so profitable, yet the thought of legalizing their distribution, even with rigid controls and treatment programs, arouses the fear of infecting millions of addicts," wrote Max Frankel in the *New York Times* Sunday magazine recently.[4] That fear, if valid, explains the central dilemma expressed two years ago by Senator Daniel Patrick Moynihan. "The nation's choice of policy," he wrote — legalization or prohibition — "offers a choice of outcomes." Neither alternative seemed to him entirely satisfactory: legalization entailed increased public health problems, whereas prohibition led to an enormous increase in crime. Identical concerns were expressed by equally baffled social reformers as far back as 1890.

For all its outrageously intolerant overtones, its hypocrisy and double standards, Prohibition represented a genuine attempt to better the lives of people. That it did them instead untold harm — that America has never fully recovered from the legacy of those thirteen years — should come as no surprise. As history keeps telling us — but do we ever listen? — the road to hell is paved with good intentions.

1

THE GOOD
CREATURE OF GOD

There was a time in America when liquor was regarded as God's gift to mankind and a panacea for almost every type of ailment. The last half of the eighteenth century was "the most intemperate era in American history."[1] The going price for a muscular slave was twenty gallons of whiskey; farmers found whiskey distillers gave them a far better price for grain than millers; and the "good creature of God" — *aqua vitae,* the very stuff of life — was food, medicine, and, even more than in Europe, the indispensable lubricant for civilized, enjoyable social intercourse.

From the time they were born, Americans acquired a taste for liquor: as babies, their bottles were laced with rum to keep them "pacified"; later, "able-bodied men, and women, too, for that matter, seldom went more than a few hours without a drink." Here is the *Old American Encyclopedia* (1830) describing pre-independence drinking habits:

> A fashion at the South was to take a glass of whiskey, flavored with mint, soon after waking. . . . At eleven o'clock, while mixtures, under various peculiar names — sling, toddy, flip, — solicited the appetite

at the bar of the common tippling-shop, the offices of professional men and counting rooms dismissed their occupants for a half hour to regale themselves at a neighbor's or a coffee-house with punch. . . .[2] At the dinner hour . . . whiskey and water curiously flavored with apples, or brandy and water, introduced the feast; whiskey or brandy and water helped it through; and whiskey or brandy without water secured its safe digestion. . . . Rum, seasoned with cherries, protected against the cold; rum, made astringent with peach-nuts, concluded the repast at the confectioner's; rum, made nutritious with milk, prepared for the maternal office.

Most early settlers were hard drinkers, and while the Puritans preached against every form of pleasurable self-indulgence, they outlawed drunkenness, not drinking. This would have been unthinkable, for the Bible itself was full of references to the joys, and blessings, of liquor. The Book of Proverbs contains this eulogy, that would have been in its place on the wall behind every bar in the land: "Give strong drink unto him that is ready to perish, and wine unto those that be of heavy heart. Let him drink, and forget his poverty, and remember his misery no more."

With this type of biblical *leitmotif,* it was no surprise that clergymen were among the biggest tipplers of all. At every housecall they were offered drinks, rum or cider was served almost continuously during their stay, and when they left they had to take a farewell drink for politeness' sake. Some clergymen made twenty such calls a day. No wonder a noted Temperance figure in Albany noted in 1857 that to his knowledge, "fifty percent of the clergy, within a circuit of 50 miles, died drunkards." The Reverend Leonard Woods, professor of theology at Andover Seminary, recalled in 1880 that among his acquaintances were at least forty ministers, "who were either drunkards, or so far addicted to drinking, that their reputation and usefulness were greatly impaired, if not utterly ruined."

City authorities invariably granted licenses to saloons close to churches, the rationale being that the priest and his flock would meet there between services. All ordinations, weddings, and especially funerals turned into prolonged drinking bouts, some of them phenomenal. In *The Great Illusion* Herbert Asbury cites the cost of liquid refreshment at a Virginia funeral at four thousand pounds of tobacco, and at a preacher's widow's funeral in Boston, the mourners put away over 51 gallons of Malaga. Any communal physical effort — whether harvesting, road-building, or wood-cutting — was an excuse for a binge. Workers' wages came, in part, in the form of liquor, and days off to get drunk were part of an unwritten agreement between employer and laborer.

The massive consumption of hard liquor had been a feature of "New Continent" life ever since the earliest colonization stages: as early as 1630, Peter Stuyvesant noted that "one quarter of New Amsterdam (as New York was then called) is devoted to houses for the sale of brandy, tobacco and beer." In pre-independence times, the colonies' judges were so frequently drunk at the bench that heavy fines were instituted for those proved incapable during court proceedings.

In some parts of rural America, liquor was used as currency, with prices displayed in terms of whiskey pints or gallons. Farm laborers, including slaves, got ample liquor rations. Kegs of whiskey, with tin cups attached, were at the disposal of ships' crews and passengers on flatboats on the Ohio and Mississippi Rivers. There were barrels of rum on tap in shops for favored customers, and even court sessions were an excuse for drinking: the liquor consumed by judge and jury during proceedings was a legitimate court expense. With rum, applejack, and blackstrap (rum and molasses) a few pence a quart, eighteenth-century Americans, whether rich or poor, slaves or free men and women, appear to have gone through life in a semiperpetual alcoholic haze. In the early nineteenth century, Asbury noted, "so much rum was available in the Massachusetts metropolis that it sold at retail for fourpence a quart. West Indian rum, supposed to be better than the New England product, was only twopence more."

The New Continent passion for liquor reflected the settlers' own cultural origins — in no way was it *sui generis*. The early immigrants came from a land — Britain — where eighteenth-century pub owners routinely displayed the notice "Drunk for a penny, dead drunk for twopence." Hogarth's "Gin lane" immortalized the degradation of London's wretched "lumpen proletariat." Cheap gin first made its massive appearance in London in 1724, and became an immediate addiction (much like crack or heroin today) to wretched, underpaid, unrepresented slum dwellers, so much so that the "Gin Act," passed by Parliament, attempted to contain this plague — to little effect, for, as Henry Fielding, the writer and social reformer, noted in a pamphlet published in 1751, "should the drinking of this poison be continued at its present height, during the next twenty years, there will be by that time very few of the common people left to drink it." Some at least of Fielding's "common people," intent on a different, less miserable life, must later have joined the ranks of America's eighteenth-century settlers.

The taverns where Americans did their drinking were little different in their squalor from the inns described by eighteenth- and early nineteenth-century travelers in Europe, with the exceptions that at first rum, and not gin, was the staple liquor; that hard liquor and beer (not wine) prevailed; and that it was all absurdly inexpensive. At first no licenses of any kind were required, no taxes imposed. The only proviso was that, as in Europe, saloons and bars had to be lodging houses as well — all drinking establishments were expected to provide meals and living quarters. These were, almost invariably, as in Europe, on the sordid side.

Long before the Revolution, there were big differences between European and American attitudes as far as drinking practices were concerned. Temperance — and later, Prohibition issues — from the eighteenth century on, rapidly became "the most important question in American life." The reason why is still a matter for endless debate. The puritan ethic largely explains why the Temperance issue was to become a constant religious obsession. But perhaps the simple, largely overlooked answer is that unlike Europe there were no other major issues that warranted equal concern — no wars (until the Civil War), no major social upheavals, no immediate, overwhelming cause around which public opinion might be mobilized in the interests of justice and freedom. The Prohibition issue became America's lasting preoccupation largely by default.

New Continent saloon keepers had far more clout and from the start were far more involved in the political process than their European counterparts. This, too, was an example of the idiosyncratic social context of the land, where political ideology mattered far less than in Europe.

In America, from independence onward, the saloon keeper became a key figure in local politics. He delivered the vote — usually to the highest bidder, whose political views mattered far less than his personality, his prejudices, and the amount of jobs and money at his disposal. As John Adams, America's second president, wrote of saloons in his diary in 1760:

The worst effect of all [is that] these houses are become the nurseries of our legislators. An artful man, who has neither sense nor sentiment, may, by gaining a little sway among the rabble of a town, multiply taverns and dram-shops and thereby secure the votes of taverner and retailer and all; and the multiplication of taverns will make many, who may be induced to flip and rum, to vote for any man whatever.

This lasting connection between politics and liquor, predating the Prohibition era by 150 years, was what made American drinking habits unique. In eighteenth- and nineteenth-century European literature, there are few references to the *political* clout of English publicans, or of French café or German *Bierstube* owners, though there are endless examples of European social, literary, and political groups meeting in drinking places, from Dr. Samuel Johnson's London pubs to Hitler's Munich *Bierstuben*.

The drinking habits of Americans in the eighteenth and early nineteenth centuries must be seen in this special social context. America was an overwhelmingly rural, vastly underpopulated country. Unlike Europe, it was not permanently wracked by bitter ideological conflicts (except for the issues culminating in the Civil War). The social and political life of small communities, scattered over a vast expanse of land, centered, far more than in Europe, around those twin meeting places, the church and the tavern, and it was no coincidence in an age devoid of radio, television, mass advertising, and mass-circulation newspapers that tavern keeper and preacher were key community opinion makers — influential figures whose views were taken seriously and discussed interminably. (The status of the saloon keeper would change in the second part of the nineteenth century, as increasingly they were foreign-born, reflecting the urban immigration waves that changed the composition of American society so dramatically from 1850 on.)

The early political clout of the tavern owner — and later of the brewing or liquor conglomerates that would take them over — was intolerable to idealists such as Adams. In a letter to a friend in 1811, he wrote:

I am fired with a zeal amounting to enthusiasm against ardent spirits, the multiplication of taverns, retailers, dram-shops and tippling houses, and grieved to the heart to see the number of idlers, thieves, sots and consumptive patients made for the physician in these infamous seminaries.

With time, drinking habits changed. Americans continued to drink inordinately, but, as also happened in Europe, rum and gin became working-class staples, whereas the wealthy indulged in increasingly fashionable Madeira, port, and Malaga. (Beer was not consumed in large quantities until much later, with the nineteenth-century arrival of German immigrants.) Hard cider had been a staple since the early eighteenth century, and whiskey made its first appearance about 1760 (the first distillers were in western Pennsylvania, but many farmers made their own). The Whiskey Rebellion occurred in 1794 when the federal government, discovering for the first time the *milch-cow* opportunity of liquor taxation as a source of revenue, imposed a small excise tax on distilled spirits.[3] The "whiskey war" was brutally put down by the militia. Although the farmers eventually paid the tax, "every family in Western Pennsylvania operated its own (illegal) still."[4]

In 1810, the total population of the United States was still only slightly above the 7 million mark, and though statistics were, by today's standards, primitive, they reveal that per capita consumption of liquor was huge. According to a report published in 1814 by the Massachusetts Society for the Suppression of Intemperance (one of the first of the Temperance movements), "the quantity of ardent spirits consumed in the country surpasses belief." Over 25 million gallons were consumed locally, it claimed, but

> considering the caution with which accounts of property are rendered to government through fear of taxation; considering also the quantities distilled in private families . . . there is a high probability that millions might be added to the account rendered by the marshals. Let it stand, however, as it is, and add to it eight million gallons of distilled spirits in the same year imported, and the quantity for home consumption amounts to 33,365,559 gallons (or 4.7 gallons per person).

Another Temperance society (Connecticut, May 19, 1830) reported that "in one of the most moral and regular towns of Lichtfield County, whose population is 1,586, the amount of distilled liquors retailed during the last ten years has been 36,400 gallons." Later reports from other local temperance societies claimed that the "1,900 inhabitants of Dudley, Massachusetts, drank ten thousand gallons of rum" and that "the population of Salisbury, Connecticut, consumed 29.5 gallons of rum for each of its thirty-four families" in 1827.

According to the Albany (New York) Temperance Society, its 20,000 inhabitants (in 1829) "consumed 200,000 gallons of ardent spirits" — ten gallons a head of what must have been mostly whiskey, rum, or gin. The average (white, adult, male) *yearly per capita* consumption, in the years 1750–1810, has been roughly estimated at between ten and twelve gallons of "ardent spirits."

Long before American independence, local authorities and their London masters made sporadic efforts to reduce the scale of drinking, with little success. In theory, regulations abounded: drinking shops could serve only limited quantities to each customer, who could remain there for only an hour or two (both times and quantities varied from place to place). However, the rules were rarely enforced. In Massachusetts, habitual offenders were pilloried, and made to wear hair shirts inscribed with a large D or the word *Drunkard*.

In Georgia, when drinking assumed such alarming proportions that news of it reached London, an Act of Parliament was passed in 1734 enforcing Prohibition (though beer was exempt), and a ban on exports of rum and brandy to Georgia, regarded by London's colonial authorities as the most turbulent part of the colony, was put into effect. Effective in 1735, it lasted eight years and was only rescinded in 1743 after reports reached London that Georgian farmers were abandoning their crops to concentrate on moonshining, and that contraband liquor from South Carolina was entering Georgia on a huge scale. This earliest Prohibition experiment revealed, in this Georgian microcosm, almost all of Prohibition's inherent failings: bootlegging[5] and moonshining apart, Georgian juries systematically refused to convict offenders, and some colonial enforcers of the law took bribes to look the other way. Over a century and a half later, history would repeat itself on a much vaster scale.

From the very earliest settler times, a small minority of Temperance activists tried to fight the tide. These were invariably Puritan leaders, such as Increase Mather and his more famous son Cotton, whose concern was less the physical than the religious health of their parishioners, Increase Mather preaching, for instance, in 1673, that "the flood of excessive drinking will drown Christianity." But even Cotton Mather was unable to fight the tide completely: at a "private fast" in Boston, he noted in his journal, after prayers, "some biskets, and beer, cider and wine were passed round."

The Methodists were to become the avant-garde of the Temperance movement, but their use of the word *excessive* was significant: social drinking was so prevalent that outright Prohibition was unthinkable, except to a few mavericks. So strong were the rules of social behavior that even the most abstemious preachers found it difficult to refuse a drink. Increase Mather himself put it eloquently in his sermons: "Wine is from God but the drunkard is from the devil."

The most revered American of all, George Washington, was no role model for Temperance activists. A notorious drinker — in his first few months as president, about one fourth of his household expenses were spent on liquor — he may well, if his generals' testimony is to be believed, have conducted part of the war against the British in an alcoholic haze, for, as General Marvin Kilman, a commander in the Continental Army, was to write, "Much of George Washington's continuing good cheer and famed fortitude during the long years of the war, caused to some extent by his overly cautious tactics, may have come from the bottle."

Temperance activists were still harping on the religious note seventy-one years later. Excessive drinking, they were convinced, went hand in hand with spiritual neglect — it "obliterated the fear of the Lord." In 1744, a Philadelphia grand jury, chaired by Benjamin Franklin, claimed that the greatest danger facing intemperate drinkers was "Godlessness," and that excessive drinking was responsible for the increasing evils of "swearing, poverty, *and the distaste for religion*." Thirty-five years later (February 27, 1777), a Constitutional Congress in newly independent America pressed, unsuccessfully, for a total ban on the manufacture of whiskey.

But it was Dr. Benjamin Rush, the former surgeon general of the Continental Army during the Revolution and one of the heroes of the war against the British (his signature is on the Declaration of Independence), who introduced the first scientific note in the still largely ineffective, minority campaign against excessive drinking. Rush, who had graduated from the College of New Jersey (later renamed Princeton) at the early age of fifteen, was an intellectual giant as well as the country's best-known doctor and the founder of America's first antislavery society. A Quaker, he numbered Benjamin Franklin among his close friends, and in his youth had become a disciple of another Quaker luminary, Anthony Benezet, an eccentric Temperance campaigner who was also a convinced abolitionist.

It was Benezet who aroused Rush's interest in liquor, and his later "revisionist" views. Based on his own vast medical experience, including his treatment of war casualties, his book *An Inquiry into the Effect of Spirituous Liquours on the Human Body and Mind* (published in 1785) called into question the widely held belief that alcohol was a healthy stimulant, the "good creature of God." On the contrary, he wrote, alcohol had no real food value; administered to the sick or wounded, it worsened their condition; and even moderate drinking of "ardent spirits" (by which he meant whiskey and rum, for there was little gin at the time in America) was habit-forming, leading first to memory loss, then to progressive physical and moral degradation. The addict's descent was described in Hogarthian rhetoric: "In folly it causes him to resemble a calf; in stupidity, an ass; in roaring, a mad bull; in quarreling and fighting, a dog; in cruelty, a tiger; in fetor, a skunk; in filthiness, a hog; and in obscenity, a he-goat."

Losing all moral sense, his downward path was inevitable: first came burglary, then murder, then madness and despair, and, in the end, the gallows. Rush's "Inquiry" included a chart, a "moral and physical thermometer of intemperance," that became a fixture in thousands of homes. Milk and water guaranteed "serenity of mind, reputation, long life and happiness." Wine, porter, and beer could be absorbed "only in small quantities and at meals." But the fated downward path was revealed in the following chart, on a scale of 0 to 80:

Intemperance

0		Vices	Diseases	Punishments
10	Punch	Idleness	Sickness	Debt
20	Toddy, egg rum	Gaming, peevishness	Tremors of the hands	Jail
30	Grog, brandy and water	Fighting, horse-racing	Inflamed eyes, red nose and face	Black eyes and rags
40	Flip and shrub	Lying and swearing	Sore and swelled legs	Hospital or poorhouse

50	Bitters, infused in spirits & cordials	Stealing & swindling	Jaundice, pains in hands & feet	Bridewell
60	Gin, brandy & rum in mornings	Perjury	Dropsy, epilepsy	State prison
70	The same in mornings & evenings	Burglary	Melancholy, palsy, apoplexy	Ditto for life
80	The same during day & night	Murder	Madness, despair	Gallows

The symptoms of "this odious disease" included "certain immodest actions" and other "extravagant acts: singing, hallooing, roaring, imitating the noises of brute animals, jumping, tearing off clothes, dancing naked, breaking glasses and china." The specific diseases caused by liquor were listed as follows:

1. Decay of appetite, sickness at stomach, puking of bile and discharging of frothy and viscous phlegm.
2. Obstruction of the liver.
3. Jaundice and dropping of belly and limbs, and finally every cavity of the body.
4. Hoarseness and a husky cough, leading to consumption.
5. Diabetes, i.e., a frequent and weakening discharge of pale or sweetish urine.
6. Redness and eruptions in different parts of the body, rumbuds, a form of leprosy.
7. A fetid breath.
8. Frequent and disgusting belchings.
9. Epilepsy.
10. Gout.
11. Madness — one third of patients confined owed their condition to ardent spirits. *Most of the diseases are of a mortal nature.*

Rush's renown and the apocalyptic imagery of his prose had an enormous effect on ordinary people, and on physicians and clergymen around the country, as well as on congressmen in Washington — though President James Madison continued to drink a pint of whiskey before breakfast. Rush himself was no Prohibitionist: on the contrary, the core of his argument was that consumers should be made to switch from hard liquor to wine and beer. To wean addicts, he even suggested mixing wine with opium to calm them down until they were cured — for opium then was no controlled substance but an innocuous, effective drug, almost as widespread as aspirin today.

Rush saw hard liquor as a "temporary aberration." The moderate consumption of wine and beer, ensuring health and lasting happiness, would ensure a radiant future for generations to come. Some cynics, such as Boston's Fisher Ames, who had defeated Samuel Adams for Congress in 1788, were more cynical, and realistic: "If any man supposes that a mere law can turn the taste of a people from ardent spirits to malt liquors, he has a most romantic notion of legislative power." This was a warning later Prohibition advocates would dismiss or ignore.

There was one issue that united both laissez-faire advocates and hands-on Temperance interventionists: all those in authority, in Indian territories and reservations, banned the sale of liquor to the "native American" survivors, or at least issued orders that liquor was not to be used as a medium of exchange. Earlier traders bartered cheap rum for valuable otter furs, and witnessed the consequences: Indian tribes became so addicted that their interest in trapping animals waned.

But such orders were systematically ignored. Liquor was introduced in the Northwest by John Jacob Astor's Pacific Fur Company in 1807, at first with disappointing results — to the traders. A company employee, Gabriel Franchere, noted that the "mild and inoffensive" Pacific Northwest Indians did not know how to make liquor, and despised those who drank. "These savages," he wrote, "are not addicted to intemperance, regard liquor as poison and consider drunkenness disgraceful."[6] Strong drink, noted another Northwest company trader, Ross Cox, was anathema to them: "All the Indians on the Columbia River entertain a strong aversion to ardent spirits." Liquor, they believed, was only fit for slaves.

Sir George Simpson, head of the Hudson's Bay Company in London, and a highly moral man, was aware of this and issued instructions that on no account should liquor be used as barter. But by 1824, the battle had been lost: rival traders, including Russians from across the Siberian border, had no such qualms, and although the Indian chiefs at first sent them packing, younger members of the Pacific Northwest tribes eventually challenged the elders' authority. The traders were cunning, devious — and patient. Some provided the Indian hunters with slaves, bought from other tribes, to sweeten their deals. The Hudson's Bay Company directives were still observed, at least in principle: strong drink was not used as a medium of exchange. It *was*, however, used to celebrate a deal. First the traders and the Indians drank together, to seal their contract. Then liquor became a bonus package, along with money, that accompanied every transaction. Soon afterward, this fiction went by the board, and liquor replaced money. Ten otter pelts could be had for a bottle of whiskey. Russian traders used vodka.

The result was a holocaust: liquor addiction went hand in hand with mortal disease. The Columbia River Indians died en masse, and some, such as the Chinooks, were virtually wiped out. The tragedy was recorded in extraordinarily lyrical poems, passed down from generation to generation by survivors. Here is the piteous cry of an Indian chief as he simultaneously chronicles his decay and finds solace in the whiskey that enables him to forget his plight:

> I am afraid to drink but still I like to drink.
> I don't like to drink, but I have to drink whiskey.
> Here I am singing a love song, drinking.
> I didn't know that whiskey was no good.
> And still I am drinking it.
> I found out that whiskey is no good.
> Come, come closer to me, my slaves,
> And I'll give you a drink of whiskey.
> Here we are drinking now.
> Have some more, have some more of my whiskey.
> Have a good time with it.
> Come closer to me, come closer to me, my slaves,
> We are drinking now, we feel pretty good.
> Now you feel just like me.[7]

Once the drinking habit started, Edwin Lemert,[8] a native-American specialist, noted the Indians drank until they dropped. Massacres, blood feuds, and killings all became endemic after 1820. And though the Hudson's Bay Company reiterated its instructions in 1831, unregulated competition proved too strong: the whiskey-for-skins barter continued, with fearful consequences.

Most Temperance activists, of course, were unaware of the Indians' tragic predicament. But whether as a result of Dr. Rush's writings, or because of the growing spectacle of "immoderate" drinking among increasing numbers of manual workers, Temperance societies mushroomed throughout America at the turn of the century. Active at first on the East Coast, and stimulated by campaigns conducted by puritan theologians such as the Reverend Lyman Beecher and his more famous daughter, Harriet Beecher Stowe, they formed, split, and amalgamated, but invariably thrived. *The Philanthropist*, the first Temperance newspaper, began publication in Boston in 1826. By 1829, there were a thousand Temperance societies throughout America, and *The Philanthropist* chronicled their spectacular successes: liquor dealers pledging to stop selling hard liquor and drunkards pledging no longer to drink the stuff. In 1831, Lewis Cass, a prominent Temperance advocate appointed secretary of War, put an end to the army's liquor ration, also banning the sale of "ardent spirits" in all military installations. By 1836, a web of Temperance societies — some affiliated, others single-mindedly autonomous — blanketed inhabited America. No preacher — whether Methodist, Presbyterian, or Catholic — could ignore them, and many clergymen became totally committed to these movements, providing venues, and in some cases actively using the pulpit to raise funds. They were not yet politically important, at least not in the sense that "wet" or "dry" advocacy might determine election outcomes. But they were becoming bolder, more extreme — and more intolerant. By 1836, Rush's vision of a healthy community enjoying moderate quantities of beer and wine was largely forgotten: the new Temperance leaders were on the warpath against wine, beer, and cider drinkers as well. For the first time, from the 1830s on — in pulpits, pamphlets, and medical journals — total Prohibition was being openly advocated.

2

FERVOR AND FANATICISM

A new generation of puritanical Temperance advocates, from the early nineteenth century on, discovered — and richly mined — a new theme, both simple and compelling, designed to put an end to yet another avenue of pleasure: drinking, they decided, was a mortal sin. A leading Boston preacher, the Reverend Justin Edwards, was among the first to spread this doctrine. Others quickly took it up. The evils of drink were no longer to be found, exclusively, in physical and mental deterioration: what was at stake, from the 1830s onward, was the human soul itself.

The puritan ethic has always required a "sign," an incontrovertible, *visible proof* of salvation, among its elect. In earlier days, material prosperity — as Tawney showed in *Religion and the Rise of Capitalism* — had been proof enough. But in the 1830s, it became fashionable to invoke another "sign," another kind of proof: preachers all over America began equating drunkenness with damnation, abstinence with salvation. And salvation, according to an editorial in the *Temperance Recorder,* one of a spate of new prohibitionist journals, would bring about "unprecedented peace, happiness, prosperity." Lyman Beecher, Harriet Beecher Stowe's father, repeatedly relayed the terrifying message: "Drunkards, no more than murderers, shall inherit the Kingdom of God."[1] The message became increasingly vituperative, increasingly extreme. Here, for instance, is the Reverend Mark Matthews, moderator of Seattle's First Presbyterian Church: "The saloon is the most fiendish, corrupt, hell-soaked institution that ever crawled out of the slime of the eternal pit. . . . It takes your sweet innocent daughter, robs her of her virtue, and transforms her into a brazen, wanton harlot. . . . It is the open sore of this land." It was a tone that would retain its power right up to the imposition of Prohibition in 1920.

With the new religious fervor, even Rush acknowledged that his scientific evidence had taken second place. Given that the huge majority of Americans still indulged in liquor with evident enjoyment, and little care for their health, "I am disposed to believe," he wrote, "that the business must be affected finally by religion alone."

Not that medical evidence was neglected. As so often happens, Rush's learned treatise spawned a rash of pseudoscientific, alarmist nonsense. A Dr. Thomas Sewell of Columbian College, Washington, alleged that liquor was responsible for most human afflictions: "Dyspepsia, jaundice, emaciation, corpulence, rheumatism, gout, palpitation, lethargy, palsy, apoplexy, melancholy, madness, delirium tremens, premature old age. . . ."

These were but a "small part of the endless catalogue of diseases produced by alcohol drinking." Physicians also began propagating as scientific fact a myth that became accepted, for decades, as verifiable truth: that excessive drinking could lead to the body's spontaneous combustion. Case after case, recorded not only in American but in French and British nineteenth-century medical journals, involved individuals bursting into flames from close contact with a candle, suddenly and inexplicably exploding, or even ". . . quietly simmering, while smoke poured from the apertures of the body. . . . Vivid accounts of the terrible sufferings of drunkards whose insides had been transformed into roaring furnaces were published in most of the leading temperance papers. . . . and temperance lecturers were quick to point out that such an unusual experience was but a mild foretaste of what awaited the drunkard in hell."[2] Dr. Eliphalet Nott, President of Union College,

Schenectady, New York, was an expert on this form of "spontaneous combustion," and firmly believed that

> ... these causes of death of drunkards by internal fires, kindled often spontaneously in the fumes of alcohol, that escape through the pores of the skin, have become so numerous and so incontrovertible that I presume no person of information will now be found to call the reality of their existence into question.

No one delivered these grim messages more eloquently than the Reverend Justin Edwards, a prolific writer and speaker, whose fulminating, alliterative style made him the most sought-after preacher of his day, and the Prohibitionists' chief attraction. His "Temperance Manual," originally devised as a sermon, widely distributed throughout America,[3] began with the grim premise that any human activity that did not directly involve religious worship was a misappropriation of the brief time on earth allotted to human beings, for "Ever since man turned away from God as a source of enjoyment, and from his service as a means of obtaining it, he has been prone to seek it in some improper bodily or mental gratification."

It was necessary, first of all, to demolish the theory that liquor was "the good stuff of life." Edwards ridiculed Holinshed's sixteenth-century chronicles, which claimed that

> It sloweth age; it strengtheneth youth; it helpeth digestion; it cutteth flegm; it abandoneth melancholia; it relisheth the heart; it highlighteth the mind; it quickeneth the spirits; it cureth the hydropsie; it expelleth the gravel; it puffeth away ventosity; it keepeth and preserveth the head from whirling, the eyes from dazzling, the tongue from lisping, the teeth from chattering, the hands from shivering, the sinews from shrinking, the veins from crumbling, the bones from aching, the marrow from soaking. . . .

But the core of Edwards's argument was that liquor never had been, and never could be, part of the kingdom of God, for "The ingredient [vinous fermentation] is not the product of creation, nor the result of any living process in nature. It does not exist among the living works of God." On the contrary,

. . . it is as really different from what existed before in the fruits and the grains as the poisonous miasma is different from the decomposition and decay of the vegetables from which it springs. It is as different as poison is from food, sickness from health, drunkenness from sobriety . . . they are as really different in their natures as life is from death.

He was on tricky ground here. How could God, creator of all things, not be held responsible for this "poisonous miasma"? After all, as even his most devoted parishioners must have observed, fruit and vegetables rotted with age, in a natural fermentation process.

In his zeal to deny liquor any organic authenticity whatever, his metaphors became increasingly mixed, his arguments more extreme:

To conclude that because one is good as an article of diet, and therefore the other must be good, is as really unphilosophical and false as it would be to conclude that because potatoes are good as an article of food, that therefore the soil out of which they grow is good for the same purpose.

Without a single redeeming quality, liquor

. . . has been among the more constant and fruitful sources of all our woes. Yet such has been its power to deceive men that while evil after evil has rolled in upon them, like waves of the sea, they have continued till within a few years knowingly and voluntarily to increase the cause. . . . Ministers preached against drunkenness and drank the drunkard's poison.

Conventional wisdom, in short, was that "to take a little now and then does a man good." But, Edwards continued, between 1820 and 1826 "it was realized that if drunkenness was to be done away with, men must abstain not only from abuse but from the use of what intoxicates — that is one of the first principles of moral duty." The result would be immediately forthcoming: "They will enjoy better health; *they can perform more labor;*[4] they will live longer."

Alcohol was a drug that altered perceptions. Sometimes, he admitted, "men take alcohol to drown present sorrow." Thus,

A man lost his wife, the mother of his children, and he was in great distress. He took alcohol, and under its influence grew cheerful, and seemed full of mirth. He seized the dead body of his wife, and with high glee dragged her across the room by the hair of her head, and threw her into the coffin.

Likewise, "auctioneers, merchants and others have often furnished it to their customers, gratis, to make them feel more rich, and thus induce them to purchase more goods and at higher prices, and thus cheat them." It was, of course, the Reverend Justin Edwards's intention to strike the fear of God into his listeners, and his diatribe ends with a horrific description of the impact of alcohol on the human body.

Why does alcohol cause death? Were the human body transparent, every man might answer this question. Alcohol inflames the sinews of the stomach. The surface becomes inflamed and begins to grow black. The coats become thickened. Ulcers begin to form and spread out till . . . the whole inner coat of that fundamental organ puts on an appearance of mortification, and becomes in color like the back of the chimney. Not infrequently cancers are formed and the whole surface becomes one common sore. The man cannot digest his food. The system is not nourished. Other organs become diseased, till the body itself is literally little else than a mass of putrefaction.

The "spontaneous combustion" theory was a fact.

Take the blood of a drunkard, from his head, or his liver, and distil it. You have alcohol. It has actually been taken from the brain, strong enough, on application of fire, to burn. Dr. Kirk of Scotland dissected a man who died in a fit of intoxication. From the lateral ventricles of his brain he took a fluid distinctly sensible to the smell as whiskey. When he applied a candle to it, it instantly took fire and burnt blue.

However absurd, such tales were of considerable symbolic importance to a devout Christian audience. The point was made that the drunkard was not only destroyed by fire in his own lifetime: his hideous fate reminded them of the eternal hell-fire that awaited him in the thereafter.

This, and other apocalyptic vignettes designed to strike fear in the hearts of all its readers, was the theme of an 1850s best-seller. Timothy

Shay Arthur's *Ten Nights in a Bar Room and What I Saw There* — an immensely popular, mawkish tearjerker — described the appalling fate, the "road to hell," of all those who succumbed to the temptation of ardent spirits. Interestingly, though such potboilers were dutifully written by profit-seeking hacks, no truly great American literature used the ravages of alcohol as a pretext to examine current social issues on a broader canvas.

But there was no nineteenth-century American writer comparable to Emile Zola (Jack London is his nearest equivalent, at any rate in terms of subject matter), whose favorite theme was the destruction of human lives through alcohol — the only drug that enabled the dispossessed to endure the monstrously cruel social system exploiting them. In America, alcohol was a religious rather than political or social problem. The Puritans' view of habitual drunkards was singularly uncharitable: they were perceived as weak, self-indulgent, profoundly flawed individuals, not, as in Zola, as victims of an unjust society, alcohol merely accelerating their doom.

In early nineteenth-century American literature there is almost no hint that excessive drinking may have been the only solace of desperate men and women for whom there was no other release — that for underprivileged males (women were not admitted) the saloon was at once refuge, club, library, employment agency, and sole source of local news. Jack London is an exception, but his descriptions of America's saloon culture show a mixed attitude. Although he was fascinated by the working-class companionship and sense of belonging that only the saloon could provide, he nevertheless regarded liquor as an intrinsic evil, never bothering to ask why working-class people became drunkards in the first place.

The thrust of the new, hard-line Temperance preachers was very different, and the impact of men such as the Reverend Justin Edwards was enormous because the message they imparted was far more ominous: they were convinced that the liquor industry was nothing less than a vast, godless conspiracy intended to undermine society. Their message struck an immediate chord, for any conspiracy theory — whether it has to do with witchcraft, communism, satanic child abuse, or even more recently the United Nations — has always found a ready, credulous American audience.

As the Reverend Justin Edwards constantly reminded his listeners,

Judge Jaggett says: "Over every grog shop ought to be written in great capitals: THE ROAD TO HELL, LEADING DOWN TO THE CHAMBERS OF DEATH. You sell to the healthy, and you poison them. So by the time the father is dead, the son is ready to take his place." So with men who sell poisonous drink. If they sold it to none but drunkards, they would soon kill them and the evil would cease. But the difference is: they sell to sober men. No sooner have they killed one generation than they have prepared another to be killed in the same way. That is abominable, and ought to receive universal execration.

He conceded that not *all* those involved were necessarily conscious conspirators. Some (relatively innocent) saloon keepers might plead: "But in that case I must change my business?" To which he replied, with the earnestness of the truly saved: "So must the thief, the highway robber, the murderer."

The American Temperance Society, though silent on Christian dogma, was even more intransigent. One of its booklets, *"Medico-legal Considerations upon alcoholism, and the moral and criminal responsibility of inebriates,"* by Paluel de Marmon, M.D. (reproduced in 1872 in the *Medical World*), asserted that liquor

> . . . modifies, perverts or abolishes the functions of the nerve centers. In the first stage, the drunkard is jolly good-natured, witty. His natural timidity has been changed to boldness. He is kind, generous, friendly. . . he is social and obliging. The words flow out of his mouth like a stream.

This was followed by gradual loss of physical control, ending in "brutishness and somnolence." In a tougher vein, M. W. Baker, M.D., in the *Journal of Inebriety* (April of 1887) advocated establishing

> . . . special asylums for the inebriates on a par with criminal lunatic asylums. They should resemble those provided for the insane in being under medical care; and in possessing equal powers of detention and control, and will differ from insane asylums in their stricter discipline and in the constant employment of their patients.

He recommended a mandatory one-year term for those found drunk, and a two-year term for a second offense. The magazine claimed that "300 physicians have subscribed $6300 to the U.S. inebriate asylum plan."

Ironically, as Temperance movements of all types gathered strength throughout America, the actual *consumption* of liquor decreased considerably. Data show that in 1850, per capita yearly consumption was little more than two gallons — proof that the "spiritual" health of the nation was by now a far more important consideration than the physical health originally advocated by Dr. Rush.

The growing power of church movements, especially on the East Coast, spawned a generation of new lay activists. The 1830s and 1840s saw the rise of the first great tub-thumping prohibitionist advocates — not just clergymen but men such as General James Appleton of Massachusetts, who first advocated total Prohibition in the *Salem Gazette* in 1832 and entered politics solely to further its cause, becoming a member of the Massachusetts state legislature in 1836.

There were politicians who never achieved national status but nonetheless became immensely influential in their own states: Neal Dow, a prominent Quaker, and a tanner and timber speculator from Portland (Maine), alternately cajoled and bullied his fellow citizens, lecturing them relentlessly on the evils of drink, until in 1840 this small town became America's first "dry" city (though illegal, unlicensed grog shops abounded).

In 1847, an important Maine Supreme Court ruling restricted drinking hours throughout the state, setting the scene for future legislation. This gave Dow a new importance: he had lobbied for it for years. Saloon keepers and liquor retailers argued that such measures were illegal, threatened individual liberty, and were in restraint of trade. They lost their case.

The ambitions of Neal Dow, this "pretty dapper little man," as his political opponents described him, did not stop there. Although nominally a Republican, he was no party hack, and was convinced he was if not presidential material at least qualified to be vice president of the United States, regardless of the winning party. (He partially fulfilled this goal, in 1880 becoming the tiny Prohibition party's presidential candidate.)

A brilliant lobbyist, drawing on his own considerable funds, and unfazed by repeated defeats in the Maine legislature, he constantly urged that "traffic in intoxicating drink be held and adjudged as an infamous crime."

By 1851 his persistence was rewarded, and he scored a famous victory: on June 2 that year, the Maine State Legislature finally passed the bill he had proposed so many times, making the sale of liquor illegal throughout the state. It was a law with teeth. Its provisions contained fines, prison for repeat offenders, searches, seizures, and raids on liquor stocks. Almost the entire paraphernalia of the later (1920) Eighteenth Amendment was to be found in this early Maine law.

Dow reveled in his new fame. He was now the independent mayor of Portland, welcoming Republican *and* Democratic supporters provided they held pro-Temperance views and initiating a policy that would prove so useful to the later Anti-Saloon League. He began staging much-publicized raids in his hometown, watching with evident glee as thousands of gallons of illegal liquor were poured down the gutters in front of the local town hall.

The climate of blind hate between Temperance advocates and their opponents extended to other matters. The "wets" were, by and large, dyed-in-the-wool conservatives: backed by the brewers, the distillers, and the saloon keepers, they not only opposed any form of legislation restricting drinking but were in favor of maintaining slavery. They regarded Temperance activists and abolitionists as fanatics, tarred with the same brush. This explains the violence of the attack made on Dow by his principal opponent, Democratic Senator Shepherd Cary, on the eve of the Civil War.

"I train in a different company," said Cary,

and I do not expect to have any influence in the party until the reign of niggerism and fanaticism is over. A few years ago the jackdaw Mayor of Portland, this man with the fancy vest, was at the head of the nigger movement in that city. . . . Even Abolitionism was not strong enough for his diseased palate, and he has added temperance to his former stock of humbugs. Is this Federal-abolition wringneck to be allowed to dictate to a Democratic legislation what enactments it shall pass?

For all his "liberal" antislavery convictions, Dow was also, by current standards at least, a notorious racist: he had a visceral hatred for

Irish Catholics. Their growing presence was "a permanent threat to destroy law-abiding America." After a riot in front of his town hall, in which one man was killed by the police, his first question was: "Was he an Irishman?" This atypical Quaker, who fought with his fists and flaunted his wealth, was capable of the most un-Christian callousness, happily touring the most wretched street slums of his beloved Portland with his friends, gesturing to children in rags and broken-down shacks. "Rum did that," he would say, with evident relish. Blinded by his obsession, he believed his role as mayor was to wage war not on slums but on liquor. The maniacal zeal with which his minions carried out raids on illegal liquor stocks made him so unpopular with tradespeople that he was repeatedly mugged, his windows smashed, his family threatened.

Although it banned saloons, "Dow's law" did not ban drinking: liquor could still be freely imported and consumed at home. It could also be home-brewed. The new law also proved how easily proscription could be circumvented. In Maine, as in other states with early Prohibition laws, shopkeepers started charging five cents for a soda cracker — the accompanying glass of rum was free. The early code phrase used was "Do you want to see the blind pig?" That is, do you want a glass of rum? "Blind pigs" would later become one of the slang terms for the speakeasies of the Prohibition era.

Prohibitionist fervor was not confined to Maine. In one form or another, Oregon, Minnesota, Rhode Island, Massachusetts, Vermont, and Michigan voted in *their* laws by 1852. Michigan followed in 1853, Connecticut in 1854, and Indiana, Delaware, Nebraska (a territory, not yet a state), Pennsylvania, New York, and New Hampshire in 1855.

These years coincided with the apogee of the Washingtonian Revival, a movement actually established not in Washington but in nearby Baltimore. In that town, six well-known drunkards, all of them artisans or shopkeepers, became the disciples of the Reverend Matthew Hale Smith, a noted Temperance orator. In 1840, they decided to take the pledge and campaign for abstinence, which they did with the same devotion they had previously shown for drinking.

Their movement spread, thousands of former heavy drinkers signed up, and Timothy Shay Arthur, the same potboiling author who had penned *Ten Nights in a Bar Room and What I Saw There*, praised the reformed Baltimore drunkards with his *Six Nights with the*

Washingtonians. (Another best-seller was the Reverend John Marsh's *Hannah Hawkins, or, The Reformed Drunkard's Daughter,* a tear-jerker telling the story of the conversion of Hannah's father after listening to her tearful plea "Papa, please don't send me for whiskey today!")

The Washingtonian Revival spawned a host of rival societies, such as the Independent Order of Good Templars, which increased its membership from 50,000 in 1859 to 400,000 in 1869. Some of them, somewhat condescendingly, sought out black members for the first time — segregating them in separate groups, of course. The black affiliate of the Friends of Temperance was called the Sons of the Soil.

Then, dramatically, Temperance movements all over America lost their momentum, and in time, one by one, except for Maine, state Prohibition laws were repealed. The reason was simple: for the first time since the overthrow of British rule, more pressing issues were attracting American attention.

As the abolitionist movement, leading to the Civil War, gathered momentum, priorities shifted, and for the next 25 years, all prohibitionist progress halted. The cause was also jolted by a prominent Massachusetts politician, John A. Andrew, who later became its wartime governor. Shortly before the Civil War began, he headed a legislative committee whose report totally refuted the Prohibitionists' claims. Liquor was not "sinful or hurtful in every case." More important, it was "the right of every citizen to determine for himself what he will eat or drink."

> A law prohibiting him from drinking every kind of alcoholic liquors, universally used in all countries and ages as a beverage, is an arbitrary and unreasonable interference with his rights, and is not justified by the consideration that some men may abuse their rights, and may, therefore, need the counsel and example of good men to lead them to reform.

It was an argument that "wets" would later claim to be so self-evident that they assumed, wrongly, that it must ultimately prevail. Even as the Civil War began, Maine became famous for its "temperance regiments." Neal Dow himself raised and commanded the Thirteenth Maine (Temperance) Regiment. Hundreds of families begged him to take their sons, so that they would not have to mix with volunteers of

Scottish or Irish descent, known for their hard drinking and immoral ways.

The Civil War put a stop to the onward march of the Temperance movement — it was a time of excessive alcoholic indulgence. Abraham Lincoln himself, though a temperance advocate and lifelong teetotaler, turned a blind eye to Ulysses S. Grant's excessive drinking. When called upon to remove him from his command, Lincoln replied, with his usual irony: "Can you tell me where General Grant gets his liquor? If you could, I would direct the Chief Quartermaster to lay in a large stock of the same kind of liquor, and would also direct him to furnish a supply to some of my other generals who have never yet won a victory."

But Prohibition activists would later claim that had he lived Lincoln would have proved a formidable Prohibition ally. On the very last day of his life, they recalled, it was claimed he had agreed that "after reconstruction the next great question will be the overthrow and suppression of the legalized liquor traffic."

Although Lincoln had in early life acquired a store in New Salem, Illinois, that sold liquor, he had some sympathy for the Washingtonian movement, and in his famous (1842) Temperance address, eloquently supported the Temperance cause: "We found intoxicating liquor used by everybody, repudiated by nobody. It commonly entered into the first draught of an infant, and the last thought of the dying man."

On public occasions, he noted, it was "positively insufferable" to be without it. Liquor, "the devastator, came forth in society like the Egyptian angel of death, commissioned to slay if not the first, the fairest born of every family. . . . Social and personal disasters brought by liquor come not from the abuse of a very good thing but from the use of a very bad thing."

The drys, and especially the Anti-Saloon League (ASL), would later exploit Lincoln's views with considerable effect. As the struggle for Prohibition became increasingly fierce, the ASL appropriated carefully selected Lincoln quotes. Millions of small metal buttons showed an effigy of Lincoln, circled by his words: "The legalized liquor traffic is the tragedy of civilization." A hugely popular youth movement, devised and administered by the ASL, was the Lincoln Legion for the young. Each enrolled member (and though no accurate statistics exist, they probably numbered in the millions eventually) signed a pledge and received an elaborately printed certificate. Headed "Love-Sacrifice-Service," it read:

LINCOLN LEGION

I hereby enrol in the Lincoln Legion and promise, with God's help, to keep the following pledge, written, signed and advocated by Abraham Lincoln. "Whereas the use of intoxicating liquors as a beverage is productive of pauperism, degradation and crime; and believing it is our duty to discourage that which produces more evil than good, we therefore pledge ourselves to abstain from the use of intoxicating liquors as a beverage."

What Prohibition activists conveniently ignored was that Lincoln's innate tolerance, humor, sense of irony, and, above all, concern for individual freedom would never have allowed him to support, much less impose, Prohibition legislation. In 1840, he had made his position clear when he said: "Prohibition will work great injury to the cause of temperance. It is a species of intemperance within itself, for it goes beyond the bounds of reason by legislation and makes a crime out of things that are not crime. A prohibition law strikes at the very principle upon which our Government is founded."

Even in his 1842 Temperance address he stigmatized the dogmatists' "thundering tone of anathema and denunciation." Liquor taxes were essential to pay for the huge costs of the Civil War. Reluctantly, Lincoln imposed what some regarded as crippling levies on breweries, distilleries, and saloons: a manufacturing tax of $1 per barrel of beer, 20 cents a gallon on distilled liquor, and an annual $20 tax on retail liquor outlets. To outraged Prohibitionists, Lincoln was simply perpetuating the liquor traffic.

3

THE WOMEN'S WAR

The next step in the long march toward Prohibition was very different. American women spearheaded what briefly turned into a nationwide movement, discovering their formidable power for the first time.

The Women's War against liquor was the first women's mass movement in American history. It was also the modern world's first large-scale, nonviolent protest movement. Long before Mahatma Gandhi invented the passive but effective form of protest known as Satyagraha, those waging the Women's War used their "gentle sex" and their only other weapons — passivity and Christian forbearance — to gain their ends, kindling imaginations all over America and making for compelling media coverage at a time when newspapers were assuming an increasingly influential role. Like Gandhi's followers, its "crusaders" courted arrest, welcoming blows and insults, with the deliberate intention of shaming their adversaries and turning them into guilt-ridden converts — and they succeeded, for a time, beyond their wildest dreams.

But if women were the shock troops at the forefront of this new crusade, deliberately excluding men from the actual battle, their behind-the-scenes mentors were men, and the logistics of the war were furnished by the male-dominated Protestant churches.

The Prohibition portrait gallery includes many notorious eccentrics, but few are as odd as the man who inspired the Women's War. Dr. Dioclesian Lewis was a preacher, social reformer, feminist, and health faddist whose targets included not only liquor but corsets and male chauvinism. In an age when women were still regarded as chattels, he campaigned for their freedom, not only in regard to the vote but to their physical selves. Heavy, constraining garments, he preached, were among the greatest dangers to health. In considerable advance of his time, he insisted that light clothing and short skirts were a prerequisite for better health and that "A clean tooth never decays." He advised women to walk, daily, with 20-pound sandbags perched on their heads to improve their posture.

This physical giant of a man, impervious to ridicule or threats, was a forceful personality with a distinct oratorical gift. He was also a prolific writer on hygiene and women's health problems, and was regarded by many as a charlatan because, though he used the title Doctor, he had in fact earned only a degree in "homeopathic studies" at Harvard. Although no Prohibitionist (he was too much of a libertarian for that), he was a firm believer in the evils of drink, his own father having been a notorious drunkard. It was Lewis who in the 1860s initiated the practice of walking into saloons at the head of his followers (mostly women) to pray for the souls of saloon keepers and bartenders, later lecturing in church halls on the effect of these "visitation bands," claiming that the results had been spectacular.

His message reached Elizabeth Thompson, in Hillsboro, Ohio, in 1873. Braving the sarcasm of her husband, this sixty-year-old housewife, encouraged by one of her sons, who had attended one of Dr. Lewis's meetings, summoned a group of townswomen — like her, respectable middle-class wives and mothers. After a warm-up meeting in a church hall, the women, in procession, made for Hillsboro's best-known liquor dealer, Dr. William Smith's Drug Store. After watching them picketing and praying outside his store, a contrite William Smith went up to "Mother Thompson," as she later became known, and publicly pledged to stop liquor sales, even agreeing to pour his liquor reserves into the gutter.

It was a "sign." A few days later, in the snow, Mother Thompson marshaled her troops again. This time the target was a saloon. Here too, though the wait was longer, and the praying more intense, the saloon keeper gave in to the women, and pledged to close his establishment. A beer garden run by a German, Charley Beck, was a tougher proposition. Picketing lasted two weeks, but by now the movement was in full swing, and many more volunteers were available to swell Mother Thompson's ranks and maintain a 24-hour hymn-singing marathon. "Ach, vimmins, shut up vimmins, I quits," he finally told the group.

The crusade, gathering strength all over the state, now staged more ambitious incursions further afield. In Clinton City, Ohio, the villainous John Calvin van Pelt, owner of the Dead Fall saloon, famous for its disreputable clientele, at first mobilized some of his patrons to get rid of the women by force. They remained where they were until forced to flee under a hail of stones and brickbats. Many suffered cuts and bruises, and, as a result, Pelt was jailed for a week. There he underwent a dramatic conversion, for on his release, before an audience of praying, hymn-singing crusaders, he smashed his liquor casks himself, announcing he was doing so "to sacrifice that which I fear has ruined many souls."

For several months, the "Women's Crusade" became an itinerant wonder, attracting crowds similar to those that flock to self-proclaimed saints claiming miraculous powers. On Dr. Lewis's advice, Mother Thompson restricted her activities to villages and small towns. Other, related "women crusaders" attempted, without success, to emulate her in New England (Dr. Lewis noted that this part of America was "not adapted to this new method of warfare") and in larger towns, such as Cincinnati, a liquor stronghold. Invariably in these big cities the crusade was a total failure. But though its greatest impact was on the Midwest, there were instances of successful women's crusades picketing as far away as California. Mrs. Annie Wittenmayer, a later president of the National Women's Christian Temperance Union, who was to chronicle the crusaders' movement, wrote of further "miracles." In Cleveland, a saloon keeper's wife loosed three fierce dogs on a kneeling "crusader," Mrs. Charles Wheeler, who never stopped praying but simply extended her hands to pat the animals on the head: they curled up at her feet. In Ohio, another saloon keeper's wife hurled a torrent of vile abuse at the kneeling, praying women. Their leader cried out: "Lord, silence this woman," and "immediately, the woman's mouth was shut like a steel trap, and she never spoke another word as long as she lived."

In retrospect, Mother Thompson's Women's Crusade proved to be more of a media triumph than a lasting contribution to the Prohibition cause. After its initial successes, it lost its momentum. Between 1873 and 1875, Ohio and Indiana state revenues dropped considerably. The *New York Tribune* reported that over $300,000 in liquor taxes had been forfeited because so many breweries and saloons had closed. But this proved only temporary. One by one, breweries and saloons reopened as media interest waned and the crusaders returned to their home activities.

The crusade not only brought the by-now almost moribund Temperance issue back on the front pages but kick-started the churches into a further round of activity. Presbyterian Church organizers in Cleveland, who had closely followed the crusade phenomenon from afar, were well aware that many of their parishioners had been erstwhile crusaders. They convened a meeting in the winter of 1874 that led to the establishment of the National Women's Christian Temperance Union (WCTU). Representatives came from seventeen states, and this brand-new organization was to prove far more effective than any ephemeral, emotional crusade. Crucial, too, to its success was the election as first WCTU President of the formidable Frances Elizabeth Willard — a former university professor and a born organizer (and ex-crusader) — who soon had chapters of the movement in every state. Willard herself was the child of rigidly puritan Methodist parents. On Sundays, "the activities of the otherwise industrious family slowed down almost to the point of immobility. Willard Sr. would not shave, black his boots, write or read a letter, even look up a word in a dictionary, receive or make a visit."[1]

A tomboy, she developed "wild crushes on girls" as an adolescent, and her later friendships were exclusively with the same sex (an early engagement was rapidly terminated, and she never married). Needless to say, Frances Willard was brought up to believe that liquor was evil incarnate, promoting Godlessness and the "devil's works." The notion that liquor, in moderation, could be harmless, and even beneficial, was always anathema to the WCTU. Moderation was "the shoddy life-belt, which promises safety, but only tempts into danger, and fails in the hour of need. . . . the fruitful fountain from which the flood of intemperance is fed. . . . Most men become drunkards by trying to drink moderately and failing." When she began making Temperance speeches, Willard used a bung starter from a saloon as a gavel. She almost invariably dressed as a man, and her strict, humorless abstinence and crusading zeal marked her throughout her life.

She was one of the earliest activists to work for nationwide Prohibition, and it was under her leadership in 1875 that the WCTU petitioned Congress to do so. The WCTU's leaflets were designed to teach children about the evils of drink from the earliest possible age. Sunday school literature included "Counting Fingers." Its contents may seem laughably simplistic today, but in the 1870s, at a time when the WCTU was increasing its hold on such schools all over America, it had a huge impact on children — and on all God-fearing parents. The cover was an outspread hand, with numbered fingers, and its jingle was:

One, two, three, four, five fingers on every little hand.
Listen while they speak to us; be sure we understand.

1- THERE IS A DRINK THAT NEVER HARMS It will make us strong.

2- THERE IS A DRINK THAT NEVER ALARMS Some drinks make people wicked.

3- A DRINK THAT KEEPS OUR SENSES RIGHT There are drinks that will take away our senses.

4- A DRINK THAT MAKES OUR FACES BRIGHT We should never touch the drinks that will put evil into our hearts and spoil our faces.

5- GOD GIVES US THE ONLY DRINK — 'TIS PURE, COLD WATER.

Other effective children's teaching devices were APPLES ARE GOD'S BOTTLES ("Do you want to open God's bottle? Bite the apple with your teeth and you will taste the sweet juice God has put in His bottle for you.") and GRAPES ARE GOD'S BOTTLES (in the same vein).

The WCTU's first major triumph was to compel all public schools to teach a course on the evils of drink. Standard teaching practices included demonstrations of little scientific value but of startling impact.

Teacher would place part of a calf's brain in an empty glass jar. After discoursing on the nature of the brain and the nature of alcohol, she would then pour a bottle of alcohol into the jar. The color of the calf's brain would turn from its normal pink to a nasty gray. And that, the teacher would conclude in sepulchral tones, is what would happen to her pupils' little brains if ever they drank Satan's brew.

Along with the later secular Anti-Saloon League, the WCTU would be the formidable lobbying instrument that would in time make nationwide Prohibition inevitable. It was largely due to the WCTU that the Prohibition party made its ephemeral appearance on the political scene.

But twenty-five years later, while the WCTU was already hard at work, another woman was to lead a media blitz on the "devilish forces of liquor," and for a while her exploits completely overshadowed the more serious, academically inclined WCTU.

In the portrait gallery of Prohibition eccentrics, Carry Nation, still a legend in Kansas (where a small museum commemorates her activities), stands out as the wildest, maddest, most frenzied crusader of all. Although she was nominally a member of the WCTU, hers was a one-woman war, and she was determined to wage it on her own terms.

Born Carry Moore in 1846, in Garrard City, Kentucky — a town famous for its revivalist meetings — she became a rebel and a misfit while still a child. She has been dismissed as a freak, her detractors noting her own family's insanity. Her crusade against liquor, sex, and tobacco accurately reflected the tragic circumstances of her own disturbed emotional life. So unbalanced and out of control was she that in other circumstances, like some members of her mother's family, she might well have been confined to a mental institution. Her own mother, committed to a psychiatric hospital in old age, believed she was Queen Victoria, and even had her long-suffering husband build her a gilded royal carriage, from which she airily waved a white-gloved hand at bemused slaves on her husband's near-bankrupt Kentucky plantation.

A born rebel, Carry Nation was rejected by her eccentric mother, spending most of her time with blacks and slaves, and this closeness with them would remain with her all of her life. She became a firm believer in slave folklore, with special emphasis on clairvoyance and ghosts. Her first vision — of her grandmother — occurred at the age of eight. Subsequently, as she noted in "The Use and Need of the Life of Carry Nation," a largely incoherent record of her life, she frequently conversed with Jesus Christ and claimed her powers as a rainmaker had ended many a local drought.

The Civil War ruined the Moore family, turning them into wandering refugees who eventually settled in Cass County, near Kansas City. There, Carry, now a towering but plain and excessively bony 19-year-old — subject to fits, convulsions, and bouts of manic depression — fell in love with a handsome young doctor, Charles Gloyd, who married her in 1867 after a whirlwind courtship. Gloyd, she found out only on her wedding day, was an alcoholic. After the birth of a handicapped daughter, the couple separated, and Gloyd died shortly thereafter.

It was this first husband — a heavy smoker as well as a heavy drinker, and a Freemason to boot — who fired her rage against liquor, tobacco, and Freemasonry[2], in that order. For the rest of her life she would wage a relentless campaign against all three. As she later wrote:

> I believe that, on the whole, tobacco has done more harm than intoxicating drinks. The tobacco habit is followed by thirst for drink. The face of the smoker has lost the scintillations of intellect and soul. The odor of his person is vile, his blood is poisoned. . . . The tobacco user can never be the father of a healthy child.

Despite her unfortunate marital experience — which left her with such a hatred of sex that she took to stalking terrified courting couples, cursing and lunging at them with her umbrella — she married again. This time she was convinced that "David Nation was the husband God had selected for me." His family name may have had something to do with it. Anticipating the theories of French psychiatrist Jacques Lacan concerning the hidden meaning of words, she attributed considerable significance to the fact that as a married woman she would at last be empowered to "Carry a Nation."

Her second marriage was almost as unsatisfactory, but for other reasons. A henpecked preacher, lawyer, and occasional journalist, Nation was a dismal failure. He farmed cotton for a while, then ran a small hotel. Eventually he established a small law practice in Medicine Lodge, Kansas, where Carry, by now a WCTU member, was a prison visitor. Her husband occasionally officiated as a preacher, but unsuccessfully, for his delivery was poor and his material stereotyped. His halting delivery was further marred by Carry Nation, sitting in the front row of the church, prompting, interrupting, and sometimes bringing his sermon to an end with a peremptory "That will be all for today, David."

Kansas had been an officially dry state since 1880, but the local law was a joke, the state a drinker's paradise, and the local politicians hand in glove with liquor vendors and saloon keepers. In the 1890s, the small town of Medicine Lodge had seven saloons. Periodically, the WCTU picketed them, in the manner of the former "crusaders," and Carry Nation herself composed — and delivered — poems, half songs, and half hymns as the crusaders knelt and prayed outside.[3]

But the propensity for violence in her huge frame (she was over six feet tall), together with her disturbed temperament, compelled more direct, physical action. Emulating her heroine, Joan of Arc, she claimed to have received a divine message from Jesus, the "big brother" she talked to regularly, and who now commanded her to act. Aged fifty-three, and with only one WCTU follower at her side, she burst into a Medicine Lodge drugstore illegally selling liquor, and, with a sledgehammer, smashed a keg of whiskey to smithereens, accompanying her action with a mixture of invective and appeals to the Lord. Understandably, no one dared confront her formidable, flailing rage.

It was the beginning of a whirlwind war: loading up a buggy with hammers and rocks, she drove to nearby Kiowa, another wide-open town, storming three saloons in a row in sudden hit-and-run raids. When she was through, Dobson's Saloon, its largest, most famous establishment, was completely wrecked, littered with splintered furniture, broken bottles, and shattered kegs. She lobbed billiard balls into plate glass windows and expensive mirrors with devastating effect. The bartenders and clientele were mesmerized, powerless to react.

Back in Medicine Lodge, she bought a large hatchet — an instrument of destruction that was to become her emblem, and enrich the American vocabulary with the word *hatchetization*. Her message was now painfully direct: "Smash! Smash! For Jesus' sake, smash!"

In a series of raids all over Kansas, she continued the good work, leaving in her wake wrecked cherrywood bars, smashed plate glass windows, and slashed, defaced paintings — "hatchetizing" kegs of rum and whiskey and reducing heavy barroom furniture to firewood. Her raids were so sudden, her violence so frightening, that few dared face her directly.

Local authorities were in a quandary: though she was inflicting huge losses on saloon keepers, the saloons (or "joints") were, after all, unauthorized. She was, admittedly illegally, destroying valuable property, but the property was part and parcel of an illicit activity. Consequently, she seldom spent more than one night in jail, and reveled in the publicity — posing, kneeling in her cell, conversing with Jesus, and clasping a Bible as press photographers crowded around her. The jailers became her friends, for she was also capable of considerable charm.

Kansas was soon too small for her. Soon she was showing up, always without warning, all over America, wrecking saloons in St. Louis, Cincinnati (where she refrained from hatchetization; the joints, she claimed, simply too numerous), Philadelphia, and New York. She became, overnight, a media star. Songs were written about her, and saloon keepers, dreading her hit-and-run tactics, securely padlocked their establishments until she was known to have left town.

At intervals, back in Kansas, she published "The Smasher's Mail," a wildly intemperate news-sheet full of invective against President McKinley and all other drinkers, smokers, and Freemasons. After McKinley's murder, she even wrote a disjointed editorial reviling both McKinley and his anarchist assassin. A series of lucrative lecture appearances had to be canceled because her audiences turned against her for condoning the President's murder. But she continued to raise funds, selling autographed postcards of herself by mail, as well as miniature hatchets.

Her outrageous conduct caused the WCTU, which had earlier provided her with legal and financial assistance, to keep her, increasingly, at arm's length. In the end, when her money ran out, and the media finally lost interest in her, she no longer destroyed *real* saloons but reenacted her raids on stage, reciting her poems and spouting her rage. In one play specially written for her, she "hatchetized" a bar, breaking 29 bottles.

An unscrupulous agent, who drank but concealed the fact from her, booked her for a series of appearances in England. The visit was not a success. Her lectures were ill-attended, and when she attempted to "hatchetize" some pubs, she was promptly fined. She was unaware that she had become a figure of fun — a female Professor Unrath out of Josef Von Sternberg's film classic *The Blue Angel*. After a final mental breakdown, she died in a mental institution, aged 65. As newspapers later gleefully recorded, Prohibition agents carried out a raid on a huge still that bootleggers had installed on what had once been Carry Nation's family farm.

4

THE LINEUP

Carry Nation and the Women's War had revealed the power, but also the limits, of individual emotional fervor where the war against liquor was concerned. As America slowly recovered from the physical and moral wounds of the Civil War, the lines of a new, more protracted war were slowly being drawn up. In the Reconstruction era, there was less room for individual eccentrics: society was becoming more organized, more complicated, and vested interests, on both sides, more formidable. Both the Prohibition activists and their bitterest enemies, the brewers and distillers, became increasingly institutionalized, increasingly manipulative.

The Prohibitionists' object now was not so much public opinion as the fluctuating mass of constantly wavering, opportunistic or blatantly corrupt politicians. It would be unfair to dismiss all of them as puppets in the hands of powerful vested interests. But the stakes were high, the temptations often irresistible. Most surprising of all, in retrospect, was the intensity of the battle: although Temperance issues became important in Europe, they never affected the political mainstream, except, briefly, perhaps, in Scotland and Scandinavia. In America, from 1810 on, Prohibition became a hugely important political issue, and would remain so for the next 130 years.

Prohibition illuminated the fundamental differences in political agendas on opposite sides of the Atlantic. To Europeans, the American obsession with Prohibition was — and remains — difficult to understand. European issues were very different. The failed Revolutions of 1848, the Paris Commune of 1871, the violent anarchist movements, the Marxist-Leninist explosion and the spread of communism, and the rise of fascism in the 1920s and 1930s: these were the seminal issues of the 1810–1933 period. Ironically, even America's most militant labor unions, which took their ideological cue from European events, found themselves caught up in the Prohibition dispute. At first, the only well-organized Prohibition lobby was Frances E. Willard's WCTU. Its impact, on as yet unenfranchised American women, and on all children going to Sunday schools, was huge. But the very cloistered, housewifely constraints imposed on them compelled the WCTU to strike out in many different directions. With American women enthusiastically embracing every worthy cause, from prison reform to adult education for growing numbers of foreign-born illiterates, the WCTU was compelled to extend its activities, inevitably diluting its strength with the pursuit of too many good causes. Its Department of Social Purity campaigned against prostitution and the white slave trade; the Department for the Suppression of Social Evil was intent on proving that alcohol was the cause of all major crime; and the Department of Unfermented Wine lobbied for the use of the unfermented grape in church services. The name Department for Inducing Corporations to Require Total Abstinence on Their Employees speaks for itself.

The WCTU was predominantly middle class. Its members were largely the wives of doctors, lawyers, merchants, and wealthy farmers. They wanted to better the working class economically, socially, and morally — even against its wish and inclination. They had plans (which, predictably, failed) to replace the hated saloon by the innocuous coffeehouse — a typically paternalistic, middle-class ambition that showed how out of touch they were with the working class.

There *were* a few working-class Prohibitionists, in a handful of trade unions, but they were mostly left-wingers who wanted to educate the workers politically and found that the lure of the saloon interfered with their indoctrination attempts. The International Workers of the World (IWW) did later claim that "the capitalists use saloons to tranquilize and humiliate the proletariate," but working-class Americans showed no signs that they were averse to such humiliation.[1]

Almost as worthy a cause, to WCTU members, as Prohibition was women's suffrage, and this proved a double-edged, confusing issue, for not all Prohibitionists were in favor of the vote for women, and anti-Prohibitionists were overwhelmingly against it. The Women's War triggered a fundamental change in attitudes. While it was at its height, an anonymous suffragist wrote in a letter to the New York *Herald Tribune*, which published it in 1874:

> To deny her the use of that most efficient weapon, a vote, and then urge her into contest with the liquor trade is like saying that women cannot use artillery . . . but ought to form the advance in an attack on an army well drilled in their use, sending them forward with broadswords, javelins and other implements of medieval warfare.

Much more averse to publicity than the WCTU, another lobby, established at the start of the Civil War, became increasingly active in the Reconstruction period. Understandably shocked by what they regarded as discriminatory taxes in 1862, the brewers formed the United States Brewers Association to ensure that they would never be taken by surprise again. Their dues (from $25 to $1,000, according to their size) enabled them to use considerable slush funds on cooperative politicians and consumers alike.

The most vocal opponents of Prohibition were the "new Americans." From 1840 onward, millions of Germans, Irish, and Italians entered the country, bringing their wine-, whiskey-, and beer-drinking culture with them, fueling a brewers', distillers', and winemakers' boom. At the Brewers Association's first meeting in 1862, many of its members spoke in German — the only language in which they were fluent. In increasingly expensive lobbying and newspaper campaigns, they quickly focused on the issue of women's suffrage: the brewers and distillers knew that women were the Prohibitionists' chief allies and saw the WCTU as its most formidable foe. The repeated failures of many state legislatures to bring about women's suffrage must be laid at their door. Wherever state suffrage amendments were introduced, they went into action. In Oregon in 1853, for instance, Arthur Denny, a leading Prohibitionist, introduced legislation to give the vote to (white) women. He failed by one vote. Some thirty years later, the Supreme Court of Washington State, invoking "technicalities," declared the newly passed women's suffrage law invalid. Insiders knew that the behind-the-scenes artisan of this decision was Tacoma's Harry Morgan — gambler, local political boss, and saloon supporter — an early precursor of the "mobster generation" of the 1920s and 1930s.

The Prohibition drive was mixed. Among its advocates were both "liberals" — with a left-wing political agenda that included women's suffrage, abolitionism, labor law, and other reforms, and trade unionism — and members at the opposite end of the political spectrum. These were the increasingly vocal opponents of unrestricted immigration and railroad and farm support grants; in other words, conservative (at that time) America's rural or small-town not-so-silent majority.

Because both Democratic and Republican politicians demonstrated their shifty venality, purists in both parties decided salvation lay elsewhere. The Prohibition party, established in 1869, and active in some twenty states, was by no means confined to cranks and religious fanatics. Among its members were distinguished liberals of all types, including partisans of women's franchise and of prison reform. But despite considerable media interest, and its later role as the Prohibition issue gathered momentum, this "third party" never changed American voting patterns significantly. Its first presidential nominee, James Black — a distinguished former preacher who had in earlier days been a Democrat and then a Republican, running for the presidency against Ulysses S. Grant in 1872 — made an abysmally poor showing in the election: the brewers, distillers, and saloon keepers all brought out the vote for the popular general, who was also a notorious drunkard. And though Grant's successor, Rutherford B. Hayes, was a Temperance sympathizer with a WCTU activist wife (a wit quipped that at White House state dinners, water flowed like champagne), the brewers' lobbying power made Prohibition not only unlikely but unthinkable. If Prohibition was — as the excesses of the nineteenth-century preachers showed — a confused, inchoate search for material as well as spiritual order in American life, the massive influx first of beer-drinking

Germans, then of beer- and whiskey-swilling Irish, and finally of wine-drinking Italians made it at the turn of the century look like a hopeless, long-lost cause.

But the Prohibition movement would soon develop a new, and formidable, weapon. The broad-based Anti-Saloon League (ASL), established in 1893, was dependent neither on women (though it welcomed their participation) nor on political parties. Although its board of directors consisted of leading representatives of the Protestant Church, which raised considerable funds for the ASL, church control was nominal. Decision-making was in the hands of a new breed of Americans — business-oriented, sophisticated, and almost self-consciously "modern." Religious fanatics were kept at arm's length.

The ASL's slow but inexorable Prohibition campaign, one of the most exemplary lobbying feats the world has ever seen, was enormously helped by the turn-of-the-century industrial revolution boom and its attendant communications revolution, bringing railroads to the remotest parts of the Northwest, then street-cars and electricity to the cities. With this revolutionary urban change came the predatory monopolies, and increasingly profit-oriented manufacturers. These in turn gave new strength to all those campaigning against child-labor abuses and for shorter working hours. The new breed of do-gooders also included socially conscious drys, intent on preserving both the physical and moral health of workers.

The "whiskey tents" of railroad workers; the rapid, nationwide industrial growth, especially in "new" territories, such as the Northwest, that had earlier been remote, rural settlements; and the influx of new Americans all contributed to a climate of fear caused by a sharp increase in crime of all types. America became increasingly aware in the nineteenth century of the havoc brought about by social and economic change: delinquency, poverty, prostitution, and excessive political corruption. It had long been a cliché that "liquor releases the brute nature in man." It was only too easy for the new generation of Prohibitionist activists to argue that liquor provoked and exacerbated all of these scourges. In their eagerness to put an end to them, the drys demonized not only all drinkers but all saloons that dispensed liquor.

In the pre-Prohibition era, there was a saloon for every three hundred Americans, but by no means all of them corresponded to the grim picture painted by the ASL and the WCTU. Jack London described the saloon as "a terribly wonderful place where life was different." Coming from an underprivileged background himself, and a born outsider, he saw it as a place "where men come together to exchange ideas, to laugh and boast and dare, to relax, to forget the dull toil of tiresome nights and days." More prosaically, a Washington State committee of prominent citizens in the 1890s wrote that the saloon "met the thirst for fellowship, or amusement and recreation."

In the nineteenth and early twentieth centuries, the saloon was not only the one place working-class men (the presence of women was not encouraged) got together and socialized, but it also served as their only available employment agency and club. There were newspapers, mailboxes, pencils, paper, bulletin boards advertising jobs, card tables, and sometimes bowling alleys and billiard tables. The saloons also served the much decried "free lunch," which although invariably salty to stimulate thirst was often of reasonable quality. Not all saloon keepers were ogres, throwing out those who cost more in food than they paid back in drink. And although prostitutes used some saloons to ply their trade, most saloons did not countenance their presence, and on weekends perfectly innocent social gatherings involving singing, dancing, and recitations took place. In short, the saloon was, except for the free lunch, not much different from the average English pub — except that until local "dry" restrictions started taking their toll, saloons were open seven days a week, twenty-four hours a day. This was because the saloon keepers were under considerable pressure from the brewery owners, eager to maximize their profits and recuperate their loans. Saloon keepers were also heavily taxed: just before Prohibition was introduced, they paid a yearly $1,000 fee.

The war for Prohibition was also a struggle for racial purity.

> In the North-West, local legislators knew they were moving from a frontier to an industrial society, with the construction of the Pacific Highway, the growth of the railroads. They were determined that the laborers should not be a prey to the "hell on wheels" that accompanied the workers elsewhere. . . . the feeling was strong that workers must be protected from the saloon keepers.[2]

William Newell, Governor of Washington Territory (it only became a state in 1889) denounced "the fearful destruction of property

and happiness which [liquor] occasions in its march of desolation, disease and death. . . . The vice, degeneration and crime which
it engenders . . . with no redeeming influence for the good, may well
cause it to be a subject of the greatest solicitude to our race." One of
the many nineteenth-century Temperance movements that prospered
from the Civil War days, the International Order of the Grand Templars,
also tirelessly equated Prohibition with family morality. Its message,
published in the Seattle *Mirror*,[3] was also a call to war: "The temperance war! It is coming! It is here! The issue involves the sanctity
of the home, the chastity of youth, the moral and political purity of
voters."

Class lines were increasingly drawn up. In 1890, an editorial in a
Prohibitionist paper asked: "Where else shall we look but to the farmer
to counteract the venality and corruption of the slums of our cities'
population, that seems to be so rapidly increasing by the aggregation
of alien voters, anarchists and saloon influences?" It was all part of
that constantly recurring element in American social and political life:
the "politics of virtue." But as various states, under pressure from increasingly assertive dry groups and opportunistic politicians, began to
introduce their own local laws, the battle remained fairly even-handed.

In the small town of Everett, in Washington State, where there
were forty saloons, the churches energetically campaigned for local prohibition in a 1910 election, though not all religious groups were dry.
Some Catholics, Lutherans, and Jews were in favor of "good" saloons,
and raised the issue of personal liberty and choice. The local *Labor
Journal*, a militant unionist newspaper, argued that the dramatically
lower life expectancy of working men (60 percent that of the rich) was
due not to drink but to the disastrous consequences of low wages and
working conditions generally. "Wets and drys boycotted each other's
businesses. There were street brawls, a frenzy of meetings, parades,
prayers."[4] In the event, Everett voted dry, but a subsequent state-level
vote rejected Prohibition entirely.

Thanks to men such as Newell, the Alcohol Education Act (AEA),
passed in Seattle in 1885–86, taught the evils of drink as a mandatory course in all schools. "The AEA was the compost heap that
brought the Volstead Act into being after three generations of indoctrination." But, as Norman Clark points out, "unlike the Indians, the
manual laborers who built the railroads had a common culture and

potential political clout." The short-lived Progressive party — which included among its "populists" beer-drinking first-generation German immigrants, whiskey-drinking Irish Catholics, and wine-drinking Italians — was powerful enough as the nineteenth century came to an end to equate Prohibitionists with cranks.

It was the Anti-Saloon League's sophisticated understanding of the confused, often contradictory, nature both of Prohibitionist activists and of the anti-Prohibitionist forces arrayed against them that made the ASL into the driving force that would eventually lead to the passing of the Volstead Act. Between 1893 and 1918, a handful of its leaders would bring about nothing less than a social, moral, and political revolution.

Whereas moral propagandists such as Ernest H. Cherrington brought the Prohibition message to the masses, it was Wayne Wheeler — the ASL's behind-the-scenes political manipulator ("controlling six Congresses, dictating to two Presidents" and "becoming the most masterful and powerful single individual in the United States")[5] — who, more than any other Prohibitionist activist, engineered the political change.

By all accounts, including those of his subordinates and fellow ASL executives, Wheeler was in many ways a deeply flawed, utterly ruthless manipulator of singularly limited vision. His conversion to Prohibition was not religious in origin, nor did he come from an alcoholic family. His later reminiscences about the evils of drink are curiously undramatic, though he did his best to sensationalize them: in one instance, he was forced to listen to the divagations of an " 'Old Soak' . . . acting out the story of *Ten Nights in a Bar Room* while mother and we children gasped in alarm. . . . My dreams were long colored by that scene." On another occasion, a farm laborer "stuck the tine of his fork into my bare leg while I was packing down the hay he pitched on the wagon. He had been drinking but did not believe his condition required any excuse." Wheeler's career suggests that he chose to make his mark as a Prohibitionist because he realized that with his natural talent for manipulation and intrigue this was the surest means of acquiring the behind-the-scenes power he craved.

His credentials were impeccable. The fourth of nine children of an Ohioan cattle dealer and farmer, young Wayne displayed from childhood onward the entrepreneurial skills so admired in nineteenth-

century puritan society. As a schoolboy, he earned pocket money operating a sausage-making machine in a local butcher's shop. No sooner
did he move to Oberlin College than he took a job as a dormitory
janitor. "Wherever he saw a remunerative position open, he entered
the gap," whether this meant waiting on tables, deputizing for the
college chaplain, publishing scorecards, or dealing in books, rugs, or
blackboard-desks. With this background and his trading skills, he might
well have joined the ranks of the robber barons who were already
changing the face of America.

But Wheeler also fancied himself a poet, orator, and debater, and it
was this need to thrust himself into the limelight that first attracted him
to the Prohibitionist cause. Oberlin college had been, since its early establishment as Oberlin Collegiate Institute in 1832, at the forefront of
the abolitionist battle — and abolitionists were also, overwhelmingly,
Prohibitionists. This deeply Calvinist college was a nurturing-ground
for fledgling missionaries, and Wheeler quickly started mining a rich
seam. In debates at religious meetings he began speaking out on the
plight of the African Negro — whose wretchedness, at least according
to American missionaries there, was not due to colonial abuses (about
which Wheeler was curiously silent) but to overindulgence in alcohol.

As a freshman, Wheeler's speech to the college debating society,
"Rum on the Congo," made considerable impact, and has been preserved. Based on letters to a fellow student of a missionary father, it
was a typical example of the hyperbole that passed for eloquence at the
time (1890).

> Today, the eyes of the Christian world are turned to the "Free
> State" of the Congo. Its present condition and its future is the burden
> of every philanthropist's soul!
>
> But let us for a moment turn to Germany. The representatives of
> the fourteen leading powers of the world have met in Berlin. They are
> considering the future relations of the Congo with the outside world.
>
> The earnest petition to keep rum from the savages is scarcely no-
> ticed. The rum dealer who represents Germany urges absolute free
> commerce on the Congo. Holland heartily approves and in spite of
> the slight objection of the U.S. and England, the resolution is carried.
> Their object is accomplished. Henceforth the Congo will be prey to
> the ravenous trader! . . . Its only purpose is to increase commerce, no
> matter at what expense, even of innocent life.

Wheeler went on to paint an idyllic picture of the Congo "before the liquor traffic was legalized," with lucrative trade in ivory palm oil and coffee. "A commerce was fast developing which might have been the richest in the world, had it not been for the iniquitous rum dealer." Richest for whom? Wheeler did not pursue this line of thought. Given the brutal aspects of Belgian rule in the Congo, later stigmatized obliquely by Joseph Conrad in *Heart of Darkness* and more openly by André Gide, the beneficiaries would certainly not have been the native Congolese.

Be this as it may, the Congo was paradise no longer, for "The stupefying climate of the Congo renders men an easy prey to this evil of drink. . . . The Caffirs and the Hottentots have been reduced by this poison, until they are no longer distinct tribes." Wheeler cited missionary reports of

> four hundred blacks lying drunk in the streets. . . . Thirty girls under sixteen lay drunk, even parts of their clothing bartered for drink. . . . Germany and America export eight million gallons of rum to the Congo yearly, with the result that the Negro has degenerated morally and mentally. . . . remember as you go next Sunday morn to church that the Congo native, his wife and children lie in their hovels drunk.

There were no references to heavy-drinking Belgian colonial settlers.

When the ASL turned to Oberlin College to recruit a full-time worker to help bring about "an era of clear thinking and clean living," Wheeler was an obvious choice. At first, he demurred: the pay was low, and he had "another business proposition." But the ASL's Ohio League was headed by the Reverend Howard Hyde Russell, himself an Oberlin alumnus and a powerful, persuasive preacher. "When I pointed out to him," Russell later wrote, "that a man to fill the other position could be much more easily found than one for this complex and strenuous service, he agreed to treat the matter carefully and prayerfully. We bowed together — Oberlin's training had made it easy for us to do this — and we asked God to be the guide as to the duty involved and to inspire the right conclusion."

Russell got his way. Wheeler, however, committed himself to ASL work for "one year only." His duties as a full-time "dry worker" were twofold: as a church preacher on Sundays (he was already a regular speaker, his passionate delivery much appreciated by congregations of all types) and as an "Organizer of legislative districts." The issue was the Haskell Local Option Bill, allowing counties to become dry if a majority of voters so decided. There had been 200,000 dry petitioners in favor of the bill, but only 36 state legislators had voted for it. Whether the idea came from Wheeler or from Russell is not known, but the Ohio ASL took a step that would establish the pattern for Wheeler's later lobbying tactics: it informed the legislators who had voted for the bill that the ASL would throw its weight behind them, and at the same time do its best to discredit the bill's most vocal opponents.

Wheeler was assigned the task of ensuring the political demise of John Locke of London, Madison County, a virulent anti-Prohibitionist who had told the House: "If you want to dig your political grave, vote for the Haskell [dry] bill." Locke was a candidate for the State Senate, and seemed unbeatable. But Wheeler's tactics proved dazzling. He persuaded the ASL to buy him a bicycle, to give him the required mobility. He then tirelessly lobbied clergymen and leading citizens in the three counties casting their votes in the election. His next step was to persuade a prominent dry Methodist businessman, W. N. Jones, to stand against Locke, becoming, in effect, his campaign manager. The turning point was Wheeler's use of volunteers to bring the voters to the polling booths. Jones was elected, and offered to pay Wheeler a substantial fee for his invaluable services. Wheeler refused. The League, he said, was not out to make money but to "make it safe for men to vote right."

He had found his vocation, as a brilliant, behind-the-scenes operator. There was no further talk of leaving to go into a more profitable business. Instead, Wheeler realized that the ASL badly needed a fully trained lawyer in its ranks. Studying in his spare time, he graduated from the Western Reserve University in Cleveland in 1898 and became the ASL's first full-time attorney. In his defense of local liquor laws (dry counties had made their appearance all over Ohio) he appeared in over 3,000 cases — later claiming that he won all but ten of them.

Wheeler remained poorly paid. The ASL was not yet the recipient of huge endowments, and even had difficulty raising enough money to pay Wheeler's minimal expenses. In 1901, he married Ella Bell Candy, the daughter of a leading Columbus Prohibitionist, and they soon had three sons, but his financial prospects remained grim. The ASL did not pay enough to live on, and he depended on the generosity of his wealthy father-in-law.

He continued to hone his talent for manipulation. His language in court, deliberately intemperate, infuriated those judges unsympathetic to the cause, and Wheeler in turn pursued a ceaseless campaign against those he believed to be on the side of the wets. He was sensitive to any type of anti-ASL behavior, to the point of paranoia. He turned against the mayor of Cleveland for allowing a National Retail Liquor Dealers' convention to be held there, and supported his opponent, John H. Farley, for reelection despite the fact that Farley owned two saloons. "Owning a saloon doesn't have anything to do with his official actions," Wheeler told the press with a straight face. But political expediency mattered to him more than personal convictions: His endorsement of "personal wets" who were "politically dry" (because they knew the dry issue would get them votes) was criticized in some ASL circles, as was his habit of gaining the apparent friendship of known wets solely for tactical reasons.

Wheeler claimed, with reason, that such tactics worked. From his growing web of contacts, including staunch opponents of the ASL, he was obtaining valuable information about *their* tactics. He was not the only ASL worker to use such techniques. William ("Pussyfoot") E. Johnson became an even more astute political manipulator for the ASL, specializing in "publicity and underground activities" in several states, infiltrating wet lobbies of brewers and distillers, later reaping his reward as a leading executive of the World League Against Alcoholism.

But no other ASL official achieved national prominence comparable to Wheeler's, though he was never the official leader of the ASL. Despite his meteoric rise, becoming in the space of a few years its senior attorney as well as its Ohio superintendent, he always preferred working behind the scenes, an incomparable wheeler-dealer.

In Ohio, in his early days with the ASL, he used the methods that would later prove so effective in Washington. With a complete disregard for partisan labels, the ASL systematically supported the candidate who expressed a willingness to endorse dry policies — even if it was well known that he was both a hypocrite and a toper. The ASL's refusal to enter into a political alliance with either party turned out to be one of its key assets; it was well aware of the failure of the Prohibition party to make its mark on voters, even those highly sympathetic to the cause. One of the ASL's pamphlets was its "Church in Action Against the Saloon," a question-and-answer document modeled on the catechism and devised for the guidance of ASL instructors addressing schools and meetings. One of its questions was: "May the League, at any time, be identified with any one political party for the accomplishment of its purpose?" The answer was: "No. The League is under solemn promise not to form affiliations with any political party, nor to place in nomination a ticket of its own."

This crucial ideological plank was bitterly opposed by William Jennings Bryan, the perennial Democratic presidential candidate, later President Woodrow Wilson's Secretary of State, a fanatical dry — and, in his public utterances, an unspeakably boring, flatulent windbag, who early on in his political career had made the fatal mistake of arguing that the Democratic party should become the official dry party.

Myron T. Herrick, governor of Ohio, was among the prominent politicians whose careers Wheeler destroyed virtually single-handedly. Herrick, the Republican governor of a staunchly Republican state, seemed unbeatable when he ran for reelection. But Wheeler first got the ASL to endorse the Democratic candidate, John M. Pattison, from Cincinnati, a strict churchman and dry. "We had a hard job making the people see that they were not giving up their religion when they voted Democratic," Wheeler said later.[6] "That was especially true in the rural sections, where they always voted a straight Republican ticket. I used to tell them that Lincoln wasn't running that year." Pattison won. Herrick did, subsequently, reap his reward for lifelong service to the Republican party: he was appointed U.S. ambassador in Paris, and was on hand to greet Lindbergh after his historic flight across the Atlantic (1927). Prohibition was in full swing by this time, and Wheeler wondered what Herrick and Lindbergh, a staunch Prohibitionist, had had to say to each other in private.

Soon, under Wheeler's effective direction, Ohio became — long before Prohibition — one of the driest states in the Union. As he proudly noted in 1908, 57 of its counties had gone dry under County Local Option laws. Various other dry measures instituted since he had begun working full-time for the ASL affected most of the other counties as well, so that by 1908, 60 percent of Ohio's population, and 85 percent of its territory, was under "dry legislation," though its large towns, especially Cincinnati, remained almost aggressively wet. The Ohio legislators, for all their "prohibition correctness," were well aware of the revenues liquor brought into the state coffers. Saloon licenses, introduced in 1896, first cost $350 a year, then — in 1906 — $1,000. In 1908, there were 7,050 saloons in Ohio, and 690 more opened in 1911. The ASL's position was that licensing saloons was immoral, but this challenge failed, and a licensing law gained a substantial majority. Wheeler's rearguard action was to make life more difficult for saloon keepers by prohibiting saloon operations within 300 feet of a school-house, forbidding "loitering by minors" there, compelling Sunday closings, and denying licenses to noncitizens and those of insufficiently good "moral conduct."

Wheeler was helped, indirectly, by the blatant political immorality of the times. License commissioners in Ohio and elsewhere were known to take bribes and favor friendly candidates, and many were in league with the major breweries, which in most cases were the saloons' real owners (they also maintained close relations with owners of the technically illegal speakeasies). In the course of his work, Wheeler — who in middle age bore a striking resemblance to France's elder statesman, the late Antoine Pinay — had met most of the influential figures in the business world. John D. Rockefeller, after hearing him preach, presented him with a paper vest against the cold — and $5,000 for the ASL, the first of many contributions. He was becoming an acknowledged behind-the-scenes political power in Ohio, but now he had further ambitions. Ohio was at the forefront of the war on liquor, and, in many respects, a microcosm of still overwhelmingly rural America. Wheeler was sufficiently sensitive to the public mood to know that nationwide Prohibition was becoming a distinct possibility. As a first step, he persuaded the ASL to announce that statewide Prohibition was "imminent and inevitable," introducing for the first time the notion of "a national constitutional amendment prohibiting the manufacture and sale of intoxicating liquors for beverage purposes" in the ASL's organ *The American Patriot*.

In 1913, the ASL's National Board of Trustees met in Columbus to celebrate their Jubilee Convention. Wheeler, in the wings as usual, let J. Frank Hanly, a former Governor of Indiana, make the actual call for national Prohibition, to be brought about by constitutional amendment. "For a moment there was silence, deep and tense," Wheeler recalled. "Then the convention cut loose. With a roar as wild as the raging storm outside it jumped to its feet and yelled approval. The first shot in the Eighteenth Amendment had been fired." The proposal was unanimously carried, and on December 10, 1913, a 1,000-member ASL delegation met in Washington on the steps of the Capitol, demonstrating its power and nationwide impact.

About this time, the drys were also provided with further "scientific" evidence — this time from Europe — of the ill effects of alcohol, even taken in small quantities. August Forel, a noted Swiss brain specialist, had investigated its effect on mental processes, and professed they were terrifying. So too did Emil Kraeplin, a German psychiatrist. This boosted the campaign for sobriety that was a growing feature in factories. As Norman Clark wrote, "probably even more than religion, science had prepared the public mind for complete prohibition." Ever since he began making automobiles, Henry Ford had insisted that his workers be teetotalers, and used a private police force to spy on them; anyone caught buying hard liquor in a store a second time was fired.

Throughout his subsequent dry campaign, Wheeler had systematically favored the rural dry vote. "God made the country, but man made the town" was his *leitmotif*, and, as his personal secretary noted, he viewed the cities as "un-American, lawless and wet," reserving special scorn for the "Irish, the continentals with their beer and wine, and the guzzling wet Democrats in the North and East."[7]

Even in Ohio, a model for other states, the dry vote, though effective (for the towns were underrepresented), was always a minority. He himself noted that there were only 400,000 dry voters out of a total Ohio voting population of 1,250,000. The success of ASL tactics depended to a large extent on overrepresentation in the rural areas and underrepresentation in the towns.

This led the Ohio ASL to gravely miscalculate its chances. In 1914, constitutional amendments to declare the whole of Ohio dry were defeated, and many previously dry counties returned to their wet state.

The 1914 congressional elections did, however, provide the ASL with a heaven-sent opportunity to bring the Prohibition issue to the public. In the *New York Times*,[8] Wheeler reminisced that it "mobilized 50,000 trained speakers, volunteers and regulars directing their fire

upon the wets in every village, town, city, county and state." Its literature, he wrote, "found its way to every spot in the United States. . . .
While we were fighting back in the districts, we were also bombarding
the House and Senate in Washington. . . . We kept the field workers
advised of the attitude of every individual member of Congress and
suggested ways to the local workers of winning converts."

The result, Wheeler noted, was a triumph "beyond our hopes."
The ASL knew it lacked — for the time being, at least — the votes to
push for a constitutional amendment that would make Prohibition a
reality nationwide. But it was soon to use another formidable weapon.
In March of 1917, President Woodrow Wilson called the Sixty-fifth
Congress (elected in 1916) into special session to declare war on Germany. America's entry into the war would provide a new weapon —
patriotism — to undermine the anti-Prohibitionist campaign carried
out by the saloon, liquor, and brewery vested interests.

At first the anti-Prohibitionists did not realize how effective the
jingoist campaign of the ASL would be. When they did retaliate, theirs
was a costly, bumbling, piecemeal, ineffective campaign. The brewers
and the hard liquor interests never did manage to coordinate their
efforts, for in the last resort the brewers were ready to abandon the
distillers to their fate. The brewers felt that although there was a possible case for banning hard liquor outright, beer — a benign, natural
substance — would never be banned.

The war drastically altered the picture and advanced the dry cause
beyond Wheeler's wildest hopes. After Britain and France went to war
with Germany in 1914, Wheeler, accurately gauging the feelings of his
fellow Americans, was aware that the increasingly anti-German mood,
rapidly amounting to hysteria, would be a godsend to the dry cause.
He would exploit this cynically and crudely, but with enormous effectiveness. As, in state after state, the strength of the dry vote became
increasingly apparent, it was clear to him that the Great War would
administer the final coup de grace to the opponents of Prohibition.

This was also becoming apparent to politicians all over America,
especially the most opportunistic, unscrupulous ones. In 1917, Harry
Micajah Daugherty — later to become attorney general during the
first Prohibition years and one of the most corrupt members of any
American administration — conferred with Warren Harding, then an
Ohio senator, and decided to climb on the Prohibition wagon as a

means of strengthening Republican fortunes in the state. "Prohibition," Daugherty wrote to Harding, "is going to be a movement that
has come to stay and it will be joined by the strong men of the party."[9]

In fact, Wheeler's victory was assured the day America itself
entered the war (April 6, 1917). In the last resort, it was a misguided
form of patriotism, amounting to jingoism, that would ensure the
prompt passing of the Eighteenth Amendment.

5

PROHIBITION'S FIRST VICTIMS

Although many Americans were unaware of it, a massive transformation in the ethnic mix of the United States occurred in the half-century that preceded America's entry into the First World War. Millions of Europeans, taking advantage of its ultraliberal immigration policy, settled in America, changing the country's ways.

To some Americans, steeped in the puritan culture that still centered around the farm, the family, and the church, these newly emerging ethnic patterns were deeply disturbing. As historian Dennis Brogan has noted, in New York a great and increasing part of the population was now composed of recent immigrants, usually indifferent to American issues, "having nothing to lose but their chains and little to sell but their votes."

Arguably, the single most influential group of immigrants — over eight million in the second half of the nineteenth century — came from Germany. Their culture and industriousness put an indelible stamp on the areas they settled into — and transformed American drinking habits.

The Germans had been among the earliest of America's immigrants. Germantown, Pennsylvania (now part of Philadelphia), was
founded in 1683. From 1832 onward, the trickle of German immigrants to America turned into a flood. Political unrest in Germany accelerated their departure: socialists and liberals hostile to Metternich's
policies began fleeing in large numbers after a brutally suppressed protest movement in 1832; then came the failed revolution of 1848, provoking a further flood of departures, to such an extent that by the
time the Civil War broke out there were German-speaking regiments
fighting in Lincoln's army. Bismarck's authoritarianism, especially after
1870, led to another influx. Although some of the German immigrants
were motivated by the classic hope of a better life, what set them apart
from other categories was the large proportion of highly educated,
politically sophisticated liberal intellectuals in their midst.

By 1914, they were all over America, concentrating in places
where German-Americans had already made good, such as Chicago
and Milwaukee, but nowhere was their impact greater than in Cincinnati, which became, in many ways, from the 1850s onward, almost a German city.[1] German-American historian Friedrich Gerstacker
described Cincinnati as "the Queen of the West, the Eldorado of the
German immigrant." For many years, he wrote, Cincinnati did not
even try to assimilate its German immigrants — "instead, they assimi-
lated Cincinnati." In 1820, they had been 5 percent of the population.
In 1917, 35 percent of Cincinnati was German, and almost half its inhabitants were German-speaking. German was taught in schools not as
a foreign language but as a mother tongue. Many of Cincinnati's inhabitants spoke nothing but German, and found it unnecessary to learn
English. There were German orchestras, theater groups, gymnasiums,
libraries, credit unions, and trade associations and "Vereine" (associations) of all types. In many Methodist and Lutheran churches, services
were in German. In the years 1870–1917, when the German cultural
influence was at its peak, there were twenty-seven German newspapers
and magazines in the Cincinnati area.

Cincinnati benefited enormously from the German-American
presence: they were energetic, industrious, entrepreneurial, and, above
all, civic-minded. Cincinnati's red-brick "Theatrum," said to have the
finest acoustics in the world, and now the site of the town's opera
company, is but one of their still extant landmarks. German-Americans

funded hospitals, old people's homes, cultural centers, gymnasiums, and charities of all types. In that successive immigration, waves were triggered not only by poverty and the hope of a better life but by political opposition. The town's rich cultural life reflected the diversity and intellectualism of its German-American element, including teachers, lawyers, artists, soldiers, artisans, and laborers. Tolerance prevailed: there was little or no anti-Semitism in Cincinnati — at least among its German-American element. In 1914–1915, the Mayor of Cincinnati was Frederick S. Spiegel, a Prussian-born Jew.

The German influx after 1832 made America beer-conscious. In Cincinnati especially (where beer consumption was four times the national average), beer drinking was part of the German-American way of life. There was little drunkenness; it was a social phenomenon, part of the cultural scene, on a par with oom-pah-pah brass bands, Strauss music, and choir-singing. Parties, birthdays, and commemorations of all types would have been unthinkable without the true natural tonic, the "teutonic" stein of beer. There were German-Americans all over the city, but part of Cincinnati was so German it was known as "Across the Rhine" — the "Rhine" being the old Florida-Erie Canal, since filled in. "Across the Rhine" had over a hundred cafés, *Bierstuben*, restaurants, and beer gardens with German brass bands and string orchestras. It was famous all over America: in the early 1900s, Cincinnati rivaled Niagara Falls as America's favorite honeymoon destination.

Beer-making was still a relatively small-scale business then, but in the Cincinnati area alone, in the early 1900s, there were as many breweries — all of them German-American owned — as there were German newspapers. All thrived, and all were major contributors to the local German-American League, which supported schools and charities of all kinds. They also funded their own causes. John Caspar Bruckmann had been a carpenter in his native Thuringen before coming to America in 1847, where he worked for a time as a barrel maker before establishing Bruck's, a well-known local brewery. Even as a successful entrepreneur, Bruckmann remained a farmer, growing hops in a field adjoining the Ohio-Erie Canal. On their farm, his wife Maria, herself the daughter of an inn-keeping family in Thuringen, sold homemade beer to tourists on Sundays from their front porch. Kristian Moerlein had been a blacksmith before founding Moerlein's Brewery, soon to become the biggest in Ohio. Some German-Americans also branched out into the hard liquor business: the founder of Jim Beame whiskey was Jacob Boehm.

With its beer-drinking German-Americans and its profusion of brewers on one hand, and its Prohibitionist militants on the other, Ohio became a microcosm of America as a whole: nowhere was the struggle for and against Prohibition more dramatic, and nowhere would the consequences be more tragic. Until 1914, Cincinnati's inhabitants had been a perfect illustration of melting pot virtues: though "Across the Rhine" was almost all German, there were other parts of the town in which German-Americans and Irish-Americans lived cheek-by-jowl, and if mixed marriages were rare and frowned on by both communities, altercations were even rarer. The First World War — and the growing pressures of the Prohibitionists — put an end to this halcyon period of prosperity, mutual esteem, and tolerance.

The German-American community cannot be entirely absolved from blame for what happened from 1914 onward. For all its admirable civic-mindedness, it was also deeply imbued with the notion that German cultural traditions had to be carefully preserved, that "language saves faith," and its leaders sometimes went too far, provoking charges of nationalism. Some of the decisions of the Ohio section of the German-American League, or Stadtsverband — such as choosing the twenty-fifth anniversary of the Battle of Sedan (1871) to commemorate Germany Day in 1896 — were injudicious, to say the least. It was a prickly, conservative community, highly conscious of what it regarded as particular German virtues — thrift, hard work, and godliness. It voted heavily Republican. From the moment Britain and France went to war against Germany, it also became a beleaguered minority group, preoccupied by the fate of its former compatriots (German-Americans from Cincinnati raised over $140,000 in 1914–1915 for German war victims), its loyalties to the homeland reinforced or resurrected. Early German victories were openly celebrated, both in private homes and in the columns of Cincinnati's German-language papers, the *Volksblatt* and *Freie Presse*. Ohio's German-language press constantly berated the "pro-English bias" of the *New York Times* and the Cincinnati *Times-Star* published by Charles P. Taft, a member of Ohio's most prominent family (and son of President Taft) and called for more "objective" reporting of the war. There were huge "peace demonstrations" in August of 1914 attended by Cincinnati's mayor,

Frederick Spiegel. Although he did not speak at these meetings, he had no quarrel with the *Cincinnati Enquirer*'s description of him as a "loyal German" or with gatherings of this type [the language used, of course, was German, and often ended with the singing of "Die Wacht am Rhein" ("The Watch on the Rhine") to the fury of Cincinnatians of English descent]. "A war with Germany," *Volksblatt* wrote in 1916, would be "a crime against civilization and be condemned by all fair-minded people in America." So sure were its readers of an eventual German victory that the newspaper suggested a debate on the spoils of war, also proposing both the formation of a corps of German-American volunteers to fight alongside Germany and the conquest of Canada.

Needless to say, this gave not only the xenophobic "nativists" but the drys ample anti-German ammunition. The ASL by 1914 had a hugely powerful public relations operation going (with millions of brochures distributed all over America every week), and Wheeler and his assistants lost no time reminding Americans that the brewing interests were almost all in German hands, and that at some brewers' meetings the very language used was German.

The malaise worsened with the increasing likelihood of American entry into the war. Overwhelmingly, the German-American community voted against Woodrow Wilson in the 1916 presidential election, and in turn the newly elected president stigmatized "hyphenism" — an oblique way of attacking German-Americans for their disloyalty. The German-Americans, overwhelmingly anti-Prohibitionist (though some German Methodist churches were not), also entered the fray. As early as 1914, Judge John Schwaab, president of the Ohio section of the German-American Alliance (Stadtsverband), had expressed the feelings of his community with rage bordering on paranoia: "The drink question," he thundered, "is forced upon us by the same hypocritical puritans as over there (i.e., in Europe) are endeavoring to exterminate the German nation." He was ready to fight the ASL "and the equally obnoxious advocates of female suffrage."

To their credit, when America actually entered the war (April 6, 1917) German-Americans, with very few exceptions, rallied behind the flag (Schwaab pledged his loyalty to Wilson), though there were demands (not confined to German-Americans) that conscription and the deployment of troops overseas should be determined by referendum. "Henceforth all discussion of the war and its justification must stop," said *Christliche Apologete,* the organ of the German Methodist Church in America. "Every American owes his government loyalty and obedience." A few irrepressibly vocal German-Americans who had not yet taken out U.S. citizenship returned to Germany (including the conductor of Cincinnati's symphonic orchestra); others were interned.

In Cincinnati itself, immediately after America's 1917 entry into the war, the statue of Germania, with a few minor alterations, became the statue of Columbia; Bismarck Street became Montreal Street; Frankfurt Avenue, Connecticut Avenue; Schumann Street, Meredith Street; and, significantly, German Street was changed to English Street. German was banned from schools ("Dropped! Hun language barred!" headlined the *Cincinnati Enquirer* on December 12, 1918), and books considered pro-German were removed from libraries. Vicious anti-German rumors — such as the canard that German-American meat-packing companies were deliberately putting ground glass in their hamburger — were current. The German-American Alliance was dissolved by Congress.

The German-American brewers had naively believed that even if the Prohibitionists succeeded in banning hard liquor, they themselves would remain in business. As state after state passed dry legislation, they realized they had been overly optimistic and belatedly increased their lobbying in Washington. Wheeler was quick to ride the wave of anti-German hysteria by calling attention to such "unpatriotic" practices. The United States Brewers Association, a year before America's entry into the war, came under heavy judicial scrutiny all over the country.

In Pittsburgh, a federal grand jury began investigating their political activity, and as a result scores of brewers were fined. Texas brewers were fined $281,000. Rather than have their files scrutinized and revealed to the press, the Brewers Association in New York pleaded guilty and was fined $100,000.

Without any evidence to back his charges, Wheeler claimed that not only the brewers' money but German government funds had been used to "subvert" the administration. It was Wheeler again, behind the scenes, who initiated the setting up of a Senate investigative committee, which began examining the activities of the German-American Alliance in February of 1918. In a note to the ASL, he cynically admitted that "we could not have bought for $50,000 what we have gotten on this investigation thus far, and it will continue. . . . We are not willing it to be known at present that we started the investigation." Later he wrote:

> It is a conservative statement to say that we have secured more than a million dollars worth of free advertising against the liquor traffic, through the investigation and the material that we have secured and used. There is not a week passes now but that some magazine or paper has in it a special article relating to the Alliance.

The German Alliance and its financial backers, the Brewers Association, were the "enemy in the home camp." Shortly afterward, the Alliance decided to disband, its charter was revoked, and Wayne Wheeler announced that "an active, organized opposition to Prohibition was silenced."

But as far as Wheeler was concerned, this was not sufficient. He wrote to A. Mitchell Palmer, who had been appointed Custodian of Alien Property.

> I am informed that there are a number of breweries around the country which are owned in part by alien enemies. It is reported to me that the Anheuser-Busch Company and some of the Milwaukee companies are largely controlled by alien Germans. . . . Have you made an investigation?

Palmer subsequently attacked the United States Brewers publicly for "subsidizing the press, dominating politics, being unpatriotic and preventing youth of German descent from becoming Americanized." There were "sensational" disclosures in the media. Like all good lobbyists, Wheeler never forgot a favor. In due course, he would use his influence with the Wilson Administration to get Palmer appointed attorney general.

Palmer's disclosures also enabled Wheeler to press for the first Senate investigation of the Brewers Association, and the findings, though lacking the sensational quality Wheeler had hoped for, further exacerbated ill public opinion. The fact that Arthur Brisbane — owner-publisher of the *Washington Times,* which mildly opposed total Prohibition and argued that beer should be exempt — had been loaned

$500,000 by the brewers to take control of the paper was a further triumph for the extreme drys. It was all grist to the ASL's propaganda department, by now working overtime — its printing operations working in shifts around the clock.

Wheeler also made headlines on his own. As the *éminence grise* of the Senate committee investigating the German-American Alliance, he had access to seized confidential papers. While he was on a train to Chicago to make one of his innumerable speeches to a church audience, a page fell to the floor. It was part of a compromising German-Alliance document, inciting some Germans in America to stick together and aid the Kaiser in winning the war. The alert train attendant who picked it up believed he had laid hands on an important German spy, and alerted the police. On arrival at Elizabeth, the next stop, Wheeler was arrested. As his biographer noted, "he made capital at once of the arrest by citing it as evidence of the alertness of America and the popular hatred of the Germans, especially those connected with the brewing industry."

Wheeler also used America's entry into the war to push through dry measures for the armed forces. The passing of the agricultural appropriations bill banning the sale of grain to distillers was largely his doing (to their consternation, it would remain in force after the end of the war). The measure did not, however, extend to either beer or wine, and the ASL, in a letter to President Woodrow Wilson, made its disappointment clear — adding, with surprising arrogance, that "It will be our purpose to urge the passage of the legislation prohibiting the waste of foodstuffs in the manufacture of beer and wines at the earliest date." This in turn provoked an angry editorial in the *Cincinnati Enquirer:* "for brazen effrontery, unmitigated gall, superegoism, transcendent authority, supreme impudence, commend us to the legislative committee of the Prohibition lobby. . . . Here we have the President of the United States under orders to an officious and offensive lobby."

Wheeler was delighted by attacks of this type, and pressed on. He wrote Newton D. Baker, Wilson's secretary of war, reminding him that 65 percent of the country was already dry.

> I hope you will use the weight of your influence to protect the boys in the army from the ruinous effect of liquor during the war. . . . The

parents and friends of the boys from these places especially are vitally interested in having a safe environment for them at a time when they are homesick and lonesome in the training camps. Why would it not be a good thing to establish the mobilization camps in the dry states? Several measures have already been taken in Congress to prevent the sale of liquor in or near the training camps and also the sale of liquor to persons in uniform. A bill has been introduced also to prohibit anyone from using grain in making the liquor during the war. I am sure that the people of the nation would sustain you in any effort you may make along the lines of protecting the soldiers and the resources of our nation in this hour of peril.

He even tried, but without success, to "protect the soldiers from the evils of the liquor traffic in France." In a further letter to Baker, he urged him "inasmuch as this government cannot prohibit the sale of liquor to the soldiers in France as they do in this country" to promulgate an Army order to that effect, reminding him that "this has already been done with reference to spirituous liquors." But the Army proved uncooperative, the Navy even more so. The monitoring vigilance of the ASL was such that it quickly reacted to an anti-Prohibition remark made in England by a senior U.S. Navy admiral, who had publicly referred to England's "traditions of personal liberty, where I know I could get a drink of any kind I wanted if I came to England fifty years from now." There were limits to Baker's docility, as far as the ASL was concerned: he told Wheeler that "the department is not responsible for the individual utterances of the men in the Navy."

Wheeler had discovered a rich propaganda lode and was intent on exploiting it to fullest advantage. During the war, the Prohibition cause advanced hand-in-hand with the growing wave of anti-German sentiment, and largely because of the ASL propaganda machine, anti-German hysteria did not come to an end with the Armistice but persisted in one form or another until the very end of Prohibition. In 1923, five years after the end of the war, an ASL-inspired Senate Judiciary Committee would begin hearings on "brewing and liquor interests and German and Bolshevik propaganda." It prefigured McCarthyism in action: nothing in its findings justified its title, for the only evidence Senate investigators could produce was that most breweries had contributed to various German-American associations throughout the country. There was absolutely no evidence they had financed anti-American propaganda in wartime, and the very idea that the overwhelmingly Protestant, conservative German-American brewery-owning families might be Bolshevik dupes or stalking-horses was so ridiculous that the subject was not even brought up during the proceedings.

The ASL's finest hour, in the pre-Prohibition period, came with the Worldwide Prohibition Congress, held in Columbus, Ohio, in November of 1918, only a few days after the Armistice. By this time it was clear to all that nationwide Prohibition was unstoppable. The only point at issue was when it would finally be voted in by a three-fourths majority of state votes — some observers convinced that this would happen within a year and others that the states' response would be unanimously favorable.

Representatives from all over the world attended, though, reflecting the moral as well as imperial colonialism of the times, the Indian and Chinese delegations to the Congress supposed to represent their countries consisted exclusively of American missionaries. The ASL literature distributed to delegates made somewhat inflated claims: among countries "with Prohibition" figured "300 million people, or one sixth of the world's population." These included not only Canada and Iceland, Greenland and the Faroes (the latter not really sovereign countries), but Rumania and even Russia (with the cautionary asterisk: prior to 1914). "It is significant," the ASL report added, "that they are all Christian nations." Countries with "partial prohibition" included Denmark, Sweden, Australia, New Zealand, and Scotland, and a special mention was made of France, Belgium, Switzerland, and Italy, "which outlawed absinthe." Despite the bias in favor of Christianity, countries "under the influence of so-called Prohibition religions" were China, Manchuria, Japan, India, Persia, Afghanistan, Turkey, Arabia, and some parts of North Africa and Asia, whereas there was "nominal prohibition" in Africa. Liquor was "regulated" (and taxed) "in Britain, France, Germany, Austria, Hungary, Italy, Switzerland, Belgium, Holland, Spain, Portugal and their colonial possessions."

Delegate after delegate rejoiced in (usually mercifully short) emotional addresses. The tone was set by James A. White, superintendent of the Ohio ASL (the state that witnessed the initial Oberlin College conferences that brought it into being in the first place): "God has wrought wonders in Ohio!" he proclaimed. The Reverend Sam Small,

D.D., a favorite keynote speaker, indulged in the type of oratory that had been popular in the past, but was largely irrelevant now that the United States was on the verge of nationwide Prohibition: "From the Great Lakes to the Gulf a militant majority of American people are crucifying that beastly, bloated bastard of Beelzebub, the liquor traffic. . . . Yet a few months more, and we will bury the putrid corpse of John Barleycorn."

William Jennings Bryan, the former Secretary of State and Democratic veteran — who a year later would suffer considerable embarrassment with the press revelation that he had long been on the ASL payroll (at a stipend of $11,000 a year) — intervened twice, at considerable length. By now a somewhat passé figurehead who had never recovered from his policy differences with the ASL (until he was overruled by Wheeler and the majority of his party, he had systematically opposed the ASL's "nonpolitical" policy and insisted that Prohibition should remain an exclusively Democratic issue), Bryan could not resist a sly dig at Republicans. He told the conference:

> I have a joy as a citizen and I have a joy the Democrat has, which is more than any Republican can possibly have. Now the fight is almost over, a prediction: we will have prohibition by universal assent! [He was as wrong about that, as he was about ASL nonpartisan strategy.] Is the fight ended? No. We must give the people an understanding of what alcohol means, so that back of these laws we will have a total abstinence nation and boys and girls will be taught that alcohol is a poison, for after we have won this victory, it will have to be guarded by eternal vigilance.

He did, however, accurately reflect the ASL's new internationalist militancy: in the light of its amazing successes of the last few years, it was now imperative "to export the gift of Prohibition to other countries, turning the whole world dry." In a tub-thumping speech (that fully endorsed H. L. Mencken's comment about him that "He was born with a roaring voice, and it had the trick of inflaming half-wits") he urged his fellow Prohibitionists to conquer even more distant goals.

> We must turn our energies to other countries until the whole world is brought to understand that alcohol is man's greatest enemy. Thus it is a fortunate thing that the abdication of the Kaiser and the fall of

arbitrary power came in the same year as does the fall of the brewery autocracy and that these two evils came down together. . . . Now we can go out for the evangelization of the world on the subject of intoxicating liquor.

His call was taken up by Ernest Cherrington, the ASL's president, who stigmatized "the power of the French Bourse" as an "important factor in the propagation and protection of the wine industry and traffic." He continued: "Our imperative demands are not limited to the [Versailles] Peace Conference. The important need for temperance reform must be recognized in the reconstruction program of the several nations of Europe."

What he then outlined was no less than a blueprint "for universal, world-wide prohibition . . . for now is the psychological time to strike." With considerable naiveté, the final resolutions of the conference reflected this missionary zeal.

"The time has come," they read, "for the formation of an international league for the extermination of the beverage traffic throughout the world." ASL field agents were to be stationed abroad and there was to be an international Prohibition press association, "with the launching of a prohibition periodical with a worldwide editorial policy."

The ASL was also mandated to "get in touch with American Consulates to bring directly to the attention of official foreign representatives of the U.S. government the facts as to the success and benefits of prohibition in the U.S." The ASL also pledged financial assistance to foreign temperance movements and announced that ASL lobbyists would attend the forthcoming Versailles Peace Conference.

It all reflected a new arrogance. American entry into the war had made it a world power, and the ASL delegates naively assumed that their all-powerful lobby could impose their views not only on vote-hungry American politicians but on the rest of the world. The Conference unanimously called on the governments of Great Britain and France to "issue an order prohibiting the sale of intoxicants to American soldiers and sailors in uniform. . . . We insist there should be no hesitation and no delay in issuing this order, for prompt action will prevent the formation of the wine drinking habit by our soldiers and sailors." Wheeler himself, always a political realist, doubtless knew what the Allies' answer would be, and there is no trace of an official follow-up. But with Prohibition a virtual certainty in the near future, the ASL showed it really believed — in the words of the communist hymn, the "Internationale" — that in a short space of time, Prohibition was fated to be the destiny of mankind, "Sera le genre humain."

6

AMERICA GOES DRY

Prohibition turned Andrew J. Volstead, an otherwise obscure Republican congressman from Minnesota, into a household name. It was commonly assumed that because the Eighteenth Amendment to the Constitution introducing nationwide Prohibition bore his name it was largely his doing. In fact, Volstead was its facilitator rather than its architect. Wheeler himself, as he would later boast, conceived, drafted, and copiously rewrote it. Its many weaknesses, and omissions, are largely attributable to him.

Volstead, a dour Lutheran of Norwegian origin, with a huge bristling mustache, was not even part of the hard core of dry advocates in Congress and, in his long political career, had never used the Prohibition platform as part of his election campaign strategy. On two occasions, his unsuccessful challengers to his House of Representatives seat had even been Prohibition candidates. As county prosecutor in his earlier days, he had prosecuted many cases involving illicit liquor because Minnesota had been a dry state long before 1917, but he had done so routinely, with no dogmatic belief in Prohibition's inherent virtues. It was in this same spirit, as chairman of the Senate Judiciary Committee, that he oversaw its passage, after the Supreme Court had narrowly (by five votes to four) validated its constitutionality.

Introduced on May 27, 1919, the bill was passed (255 to 166) after a three-month debate. The Senate vote followed on September 5, and, as part of routine procedure, it then went back to the House, to be adopted on October 10 by 321 to 70 votes. An already desperately ill President Wilson, further weakened by his losing fight to keep America within the League of Nations, vetoed it, on both constitutional and ethical grounds. "In all matters having to do with personal habits and customs of large numbers of our people," he wrote, "we must be certain that the established processes of legal change are followed." But that same day, the veto was overridden in Congress, and the act became law. Henceforth, the act determined, "No person shall manufacture, sell, barter, transport, import, export, deliver, furnish or possess any intoxicating liquor except as authorized in this act." The act replaced all previous dry legislation measures in force in the various states.

On the face of it, the Volstead Act was both all-encompassing and foolproof, though it did contain specific exemptions — regarding industrial alcohol, sacramental wine, certain patent medicines, doctors' prescriptions (but no more than a pint at a time per patient within a ten-day period), toilet preparations, flavoring extracts, syrups, vinegar, and cider. Brewers could remain in business provided they confined themselves to making "near-beer," with a maximum 0.5 percent alcohol content. Penalties for improper use were to be fines and prison terms — $1,000 or 30 days for the first offense, rising to $10,000 and a year for further convictions.

The act also banned liquor advertising, and the use or sale of anything that might lead to its manufacture. "Any room, house, building, boat, vehicle, structure or place where intoxicating liquor is manufactured, sold, kept or bartered in violation of this title . . . is hereby declared a common nuisance," it said, outlining the scale of fines and jail sentences for transgressors. Liquor stored for sale or vehicles used for transport were to be seized and destroyed. But the act was mute concerning the actual consumption of liquor in private homes — the one concession to individual liberty. The day before Prohibition came into effect, the New York *Daily News* gave its readers the following invaluable advice:

You may drink intoxicating liquor in your own home or in the
home of a friend when you are a bona fide guest.

You may buy intoxicating liquor on a bona fide medical
prescription of a doctor. A pint can be bought every ten days.

You may consider any place you live permanently as your home.
If you have more than one home, you may keep a stock of
liquor in each.

You may keep liquor in any storage room or club locker,
provided the storage place is for the exclusive use of
yourself, family or bona fide friends.

You may get a permit to move liquor when you change your
residence.

You may manufacture, sell or transport liquor for non-beverage
or sacramental purposes provided you obtain a Government
permit.

You cannot carry a hip flask.

You cannot give away or receive a bottle of liquor as a gift.

You cannot take liquor to hotels or restaurants and drink it in
the public dining rooms.

You cannot buy or sell formulas or recipes for homemade liquors.

You cannot ship liquor for beverage use.

You cannot manufacture anything above one half of one percent
(liquor strength) in your home.

You cannot store liquor in any place except your own home.

You cannot display liquor signs or advertisements on your
premises.

You cannot remove reserve stocks from storage.

In retrospect, the Volstead Act was hopelessly inadequate, because
it grossly underestimated the willingness of the lawbreakers to risk
conviction, the degree of human ingenuity displayed to get around
its provisions, and the ease with which the lawbreakers would be able
to subvert all those whose job was to enforce it. Above all, its failure
resulted from a naive American belief in the effectiveness of law: the
drys, whether ASL or church activists, politicians, law enforcers, or
simply individuals of strong moral convictions, were convinced that
Americans, as law-abiding citizens intensely respectful of established
authority, would obey the provisions of the Volstead Act, even if, as
drinkers and as advocates of personal, individual liberty, they deeply
resented it.

One of the few hard-headed realists who felt otherwise, immediately after the passage of the Volstead Act, was ex-President William Howard Taft. Those who thought that "an era of clear thinking and clean living" was at hand were living in a fool's paradise, he wrote. The law had been passed ". . . against the views and practices of a majority of people in many of the large cities. . . . The business of manufacturing alcohol, liquor and beer will go out of the hands of law-abiding members of the community and will be transferred to the quasi-criminal classes."

The "bond of national union" would come under severe strain, and he warned against "variations in the enforcement of the law." But even Taft scarcely foresaw the extent of the damage Prohibition would inflict on the American body politic.

To become effective, the Eighteenth Amendment required ratification by a two-thirds majority of states. The result was a foregone conclusion. Many of them were already wholly or partially dry, and Prohibition was clearly a vote-winning issue. For all that, the ASL propaganda machine moved into high gear, and a spate of songs, based on popular tunes such as "Annie Laurie" and "The Battle Hymn of the Republic," were sung in churches and Sunday schools all over America.[1] Mississippi became the first to vote for the measure. A year later, Nebraska became the thirty-sixth — and last — state whose voice was needed to make it part of the Constitution. The act prescribed a year's grace between final ratification and implementation. Twelve months later, on January 17, 1920, at the stroke of midnight, the whole of America officially went dry.

Along with the war, Prohibition had been the most talked-about issue in American homes and editorial columns. Since 1917, the debate had been so acrimonious that everyone knew what to expect. In the months leading up to January of 1920, some distillers moved large quantities of liquor abroad — the Bahamas becoming a huge storage area, which would make it, after 1920, a bootlegger's paradise. Other, less far-seeing distillers had accumulated huge stocks, for sale while purchases were still legal. But these were not as lucrative as they had expected, for prices had risen steeply, and they decided to advertise. Posters bearing the effigy of Uncle Sam appeared all over America, urging consumers to "Buy now. Uncle Sam will ENFORCE prohibition!"

Most distillers believed Prohibition would prove so unpopular and unworkable it would quickly be repealed. Hardest hit were private investors in distilleries, who held "whiskey certificates," shares measured in multigallon cases (not much different from today's coffee futures). There had been some talk of compensation, the government buying up all certificates, for eventual legal use. This was quickly dropped. By 1920, the value of whiskey certificates had plummeted to nearly nothing, their holders almost as penalized as investors holding Russian loan bonds. Failure to compensate the whiskey investors would have huge repercussions.

In the final few weeks before January 17, 1920, Americans did stock up, to the limit of their financial restrictions. Those who could afford it rented space for storage in warehouses and even in safe deposit boxes. But on January 15, 1920, two days before the act came into force, New York judge John C. Knox decreed that all liquor stocks outside the home broke the law and were liable to seizure. All across America, there was a huge panic as millions of Americans carted their liquor stocks back to their homes. The New York *Evening Post* reported a rush to "hire trucks or baby carriages or anything else on wheels." "Fair ladies sat in limousines behind alluring barricades of cases," wrote a San Francisco *Chronicle* reporter.

Surprisingly, though a phenomenal amount of drinking took place all over America on the night of January 16, the occasion failed to live up to reporters' (and saloon keepers') expectations. Whiskey had become expensive (only in one bar, the Della Robbia Room in the Hotel Vanderbilt, was it given away free), revelry was muted, and there were no great crowds on the Manhattan streets, perhaps because it was a bitterly cold night. Although mock wakes were a favorite theme (in Healey's restaurant customers were given small wooden coffins as mementos), the New York *Tribune* reported "sad scenes" on Broadway, and the *Evening Post* noted that "the big farewell failed to materialize." In somewhat hyphenated prose, the *New York Times* wrote that "the spontaneous orgies of drink that were predicted failed in large part to occur on schedule. . . . Instead of passing from us in violent paroxysms, the rum demon lay down to a painless, peaceful, though lamented, by some, death." A walk through Broadway at midnight, a *Sun* reporter observed, "revealed an almost empty thoroughfare."

There were a few exceptions: a wealthy client took over the Park Avenue Hotel for a large private party. Black cloth draped the walls; tables were covered with black crepe; waiters, musicians, and guests were dressed uniformly in black; black caviar was served; and drink came in black glasses specially ordered for the occasion. In the center of the dining room, in the place of honor, stood a black coffin filled with black bottles. The orchestra played funeral dirges, and at midnight the guests filed past the coffin as though mourning a dead person. "Lights were extinguished, and the orchestra played a few bars of dirge. Then a spotlight picked up the final spectacle — two young men and two girls, all in black, sitting at a black table and pouring the last drops from four black bottles, while they held their pocket handkerchiefs before their streaming eyes. A newspaperman who wandered into this party for a few minutes reported that it was 'the damndest thing I ever saw.' "[2] In Cincinnati, more decorously, a melancholy beerfest took place under the auspices of the old German-American Alliance, now renamed the Citizens' League.

In contrast, the following day, the Prohibitionists' self-congratulatory celebrations were awesome, their oratorical hyperbole more extravagant than ever. "They are dead, that sought the child's life," thundered the inevitable William Jennings Bryan at a huge rally in Washington attended by hundreds of Congressmen, the entire ASL establishment, and thousands of well-wishers. "They are dead! They are dead! King Alcohol has slain more children than Herod ever did. The revolution that rocked the foundation of the Republic will be felt all over the earth. As we grow better and stronger through the good influence of Prohibition, we will be in a position to give greater aid to the world."

In Norfolk, Virginia, Billy Sunday, the most famous evangelist of his day and a lifelong campaigner since his "conversion" (in earlier days he had been a noted song writer, baseball player, and an even more noted drunk), staged a mock funeral service for John Barleycorn. With his usual showmanship, he had a troupe of mimes, impersonating drunkards and devils, accompany the 20-foot-long coffin to its final resting place. "The reign of tears is over," he told a huge crowd. "The slums will soon only be a memory. We will turn our prisons into factories and our jails into storehouses and corncribs. Men will walk upright now, women will smile, and children will laugh. Hell will be forever for rent." Ominously, in Chicago, within an hour of the Volstead Act taking effect, six armed, masked men made away with whiskey earmarked for "medicinal use," worth $100,000.

The delay between the passing of the act and its implementation was no humane measure that let Americans enjoy one last year of legal drinking. The intervening year had been spent setting up some of the new law enforcement machinery, for which Congress had earmarked a meager $3 million. Some 1,500 agents of the new Prohibition Unit (soon to be called the Prohibition Bureau) were recruited, and the Coast Guard, the Customs Service, and the Internal Revenue Service trained in their new duties.

The decision to put the Prohibition Bureau under the authority of the Treasury Department — instead of the Justice Department — was Wheeler's idea, and he had personally lobbied (then) Senator Warren Harding, soon to succeed Wilson as president, to that effect. Very early on, it proved to be a disastrous decision, but not nearly as disastrous as the other decision, made concurrently, to exclude the new Prohibition agents from the Civil Service and to exempt them from its rules. In every state, their recruitment was political, an integral part of the spoils system, in the hands of local politicians whose careers depended on patronage. All that was required on the part of an aspiring Prohibition agent was the endorsement of the ASL, a congressman, or other prominent local politician. No other qualifications or character references were needed; some of the new recruits even had criminal records. The job paid a maximum salary of $2,300 a year, barely enough to live on — almost inviting corruption. The ASL later justified this decision on the grounds that had it insisted on Civil Service status for the new recruits, "to have forced the issue would have been to jeopardize the passage of the bill." But in a reply to the ASL, a National Civil Service Reform League spokesman wrote that "the plain fact is that the congressmen wanted the plunder and you let them have it." In the first few months of Prohibition, the agents were mostly Democratic appointees. When the Harding administration took over, almost all were dismissed and replaced by Republicans. The turnover was huge: in any one year, there were 10,000 applicants for 2,000 jobs, and the average length of service was only a few months — most agents being "let go" for corrupt practices that could not be satisfactorily proved or prosecuted.

Although Prohibition had been in the cards for several years, many Americans simply did not know what to expect. Whereas Colonel Daniel Porter, a New York supervising revenue agent, announced that he was confident "there will not be any violations to speak of," New Jersey Governor Edward I. Edwards said he hoped to keep New Jersey "as wet as the Atlantic ocean." In truth, the Volstead Act was flagrantly broken from the moment it became law, and continued to be flouted for the next thirteen years.

The nation's legislators and law enforcers professed to be completely taken aback, after 1920, by the extent of Prohibition-related lawbreaking — and the concomitant, almost immediate proliferation of speakeasies, bootleggers, rumrunners, moonshiners, and hijackers, all bringing violence in their wake. They need not have been so surprised. Had they bothered to look at those towns and states where Prohibition had already become law *before* 1920, they would have realized what was in store. In 1916, for instance, Prohibition had finally become a reality in Washington State, and immediately the new law there (very similar in content to the Volstead Act) had been totally ignored or subverted. A month after Spokane, then a town of 44,000 registered voters, became dry, 34,000 liquor permits had been issued, and soft-drink shops selling under-the-counter liquor were doing a roaring trade, with sixty-five brand-new drugstores — all selling liquor — competing for business. Moonshine liquor was freely available, there was a constant stream of smuggled liquor from across the nearby Canadian border, and a drugstore-owning couple whose establishment was, Carry Nation style, "hatchetized" by Prohibition vigilantes, promptly went into another line of business, running a company shipping rum from Cuba to Canada, but in fact smuggling it back into the twenty-eight dry states.

What had happened in Spokane four years before national Prohibition became law was to become the norm all over America. "A staggering increase in liquor prescribed as medicine occurred during the first five months throughout the country."[3] In Chicago alone, as soon as the Volstead Act became law, over 15,000 doctors and 57,000 retail druggists applied for licenses to sell "medicinal" liquor, and in the next three years there would be 7,000 (mostly new) "soft-drinking" parlors, actually dispensing liquor. Scores of clandestine breweries also set up shop, and small fortunes were made by printers supplying fake whiskey labels, carpenters making fake wooden crates for brand-name whiskey, and pharmacists selling ingredients for homemade stills (yeast, juniper oil, fusel oil, iodine, and caramel). Americans bought huge quantities of malt syrup, essential for turning "near-beer" into the real thing, and the Prohibition Bureau estimated that several hundred million gallons of homemade 2.5-degree beer were consumed every year. There was a run on anything containing alcohol that could be used as a basis for homemade liquor — embalming fluid, antifreeze solution, solidified and rubbing alcohol, bay rum — often with horrendous consequences, for, inexplicably, old rules requiring denatured alcohol to bear the POISON warning were discontinued.

The ingenuity of clandestine liquor manufacturers was considerable. In the Midwest, the liquid residue of silos was collected and turned into liquor. New brands sprang up: Panther Whiskey, Red Eye, Cherry Dynamite, Old Stingo, Old Horsey, Scat Whiskey, Happy Sally, Jump Steady, Soda Pop Moon, Sugar Moon, and Jackass Brandy, supposedly made of peaches. In the South, a brand called Squirrel Whiskey got its name because it was so strong it was supposed to make consumers climb trees. In the ghettos, a popular drink was known simply as nigger gin. "Sweet whiskey" was made with nitrous ether — alcohol mixed with nitric and sulfuric acid. Yack-yack Bourbon, a popular Chicago drink, was made with iodine and burnt sugar. From Mexico came "American" whiskey, made from potatoes and cactus, and from Jamaica a 90-proof alcohol concoction known as Jamaica ginger, or Jake. *Colliers* reported that victims of Jake paralysis lost control of their extremities: ". . . the victim has no control over the muscles that normally point the toes upward."

Although some Californian vineyards were ruined by Prohibition, certain Napa Valley wine-making families became exceedingly wealthy. In fact, grape production, far from declining, increased tenfold between 1920 and 1933, the main reason being the manufacture of dried grape and "raisin cakes." These were allowed, under a provision of the Volstead Act, to prevent farmers from going under entirely. The aim was, officially, to allow householders to make "nonintoxicating cider and fruit juices for home consumption to the extent of 200 gallons annually."

The raisin cakes were easily turned into something else. Wholesalers used demonstrators (often attractive, well-spoken young women) in large stores to draw attention to the wine-making possibilities of their cakes (or "bricks") while ostensibly warning against fermentation — their straight-faced cautionary patter urging buyers "not to place the liquid in a jug and put it aside for twenty-one days because it would turn into wine . . . and not to stop the bottle with a cork because this is necessary only if fermentation occurs." The bricks were sold with a label that read "Caution: will ferment and turn into wine." The biggest beneficiary of all was Beringer Vineyards in Napa Valley, whose owners, Charles and Bertha Beringer, were the first to take advantage of the obscure Volstead Act loophole. Bertha Beringer, only 32 when Prohibition began, and recently wedded to Charles, was the real brains behind the scheme, saving the family business — and inspiring countless later competitors.

The year 1917 was a record vintage year for California wines, in terms of both quality and quantity. For the first time, owing to a wartime manpower shortage, Mexican workers were recruited for the harvest. The threat of Prohibition was already very real — thanks to Wheeler, servicemen in uniform were not allowed into bars or saloons — and Bertha saw the writing on the wall. But unlike many Napa Valley owners, who ploughed up their vineyards to plant fruit trees rather than be caught with large stocks of unsellable wine, she devised the "raisin cake" *in advance of* the Volstead Act. "Instead of converting their grapes into either grape juice or sacramental wines, Beringer Brothers will dry most of them," the Saint Helena *Star* reported in September of 1919. The Charles Krug winery also beat the Volstead Act, investing in nonalcoholic grape juice and extract-making plants.

Other, less innovative vineyards went to the wall, in the first few years of Prohibition, after an initial selling spree — for in the first three months of Prohibition, the wineries were allowed to liquidate their stocks to private buyers, which they did at hugely inflated prices. But one famous Napa Valley vineyard, established in the nineteenth century by a French farmer from the Perigord, Georges de Latour (whose French vineyard had been wiped out by phylloxera), prospered for a wholly different reason.

Georges de Latour was a practicing Catholic, and an intimate friend of the archbishop of San Francisco, who instructed all the priests in his diocese to buy their sacramental wine only from him. The amounts were so huge that it is clear that most of the priests must have been bootleggers as well, for the de Latour books show that all sorts of table wines were sold to the churches. Other famous vineyards established equally lucrative contracts with Californian rabbis, many of whom became, in effect, bootleggers for their flocks — the title of rabbi guaranteeing virtual immunity from prosecution. The Prohibition Bureau's estimate was that 678 million gallons of homemade wine alone were consumed between 1925 and 1929.

In New York, whereas many great restaurants simply closed down (their owners reluctant to break the law and unwilling to provide meals without vintage wines), speakeasies proliferated on a truly startling scale. By 1922, there would be at least 5,000, and by 1927, over 30,000 — twice as many as all legal bars, restaurants, and nightclubs *before* Prohibition. Some of them — such as the Twenty-One and the Stork Club — would survive repeated closures to become fashionable post-Prohibition restaurants, just as prominent bootlegging personalities such as William "Big Bill" Dwyer and "impresario" Larry Fay would eventually become respected, adulated "café society" figures.

The career of Sherman Billingsley, the owner-founder of the Stork Club — in its day the most famous speakeasy in America — revealed the extent of Prohibition's "window of opportunity" — and how pre-1920 dry legislation provided bold entrepreneurs with valuable experience in skirting the Volstead Act's laws. Oklahoma-born Billingsley began selling bootleg liquor in a drugstore when he was twelve. He was sixteen when he was first arrested, in Seattle, for contravening the local liquor laws. Soon afterward, he was running bootleg liquor from Canada and managing three speakeasies in Detroit; at nineteen, in New York, he was running a Bronx drugstore selling medicinal whiskey.

Billingsley opened the Stork Club, with money from Frank Costello, New York's leading gangster, in 1927, and the nightly presence there of Walter Winchell, America's most famous syndicated gossip columnist (his drinks, and meals, were on the house), made it *the* place to be seen. A raid in 1931 led to its temporary closure, but the "right people" soon flocked to the new address on Fifty-third Street, undeterred by sky-high prices (a $20 cover charge, $2 for a carafe of plain water).

There were hundreds of lesser-known private drinking clubs, where affluent members could store their own liquor. According to humorist Robert Benchley (himself a serious drinker), there were thirty-eight speakeasies on East Fifty-second Street alone, and potential buyers were so convinced that every house there was a speakeasy that one householder — rather in the manner of today's New York car owners, notifying potential burglars of "no radio" — put up a notice on her front door: "This is a private residence. Do not ring." McSorley's saloon in Greenwich Village never bothered to reduce its potent beer to near beer — its popularity with the police and local politicians such that it was never raided once. A new type of nightclub became fashionable: the expensive, barely clandestine night spot run by socialites (Sherman Billingsley's Stork Club) and showbiz veterans (Belle Livingstone's Country Club on East Fifty-eighth Street and "Texas" Guinan's El Fay Club on West Forty-fifth Street). These typically included cabaret shows, dancing girls, and exotic acts. Prohibition encouraged the emergence of uniquely colorful women, whose wit and toughness attracted huge numbers of admiring customers. Belle Livingstone, a much-married ex-Broadway showgirl (her husbands included a paint salesman, an Italian count, a Cleveland millionaire, and an English engineer), charged a $5 entrance fee and $40 for a bottle of champagne. Mary Louise "Texas" Guinan was a former star of silent westerns, ex-circus rider, and vaudeville singer whose generous disposition was legendary. She even urged Walter Winchell, one of her devoted admirers, to promote, in his columns, speakeasies owned by less fortunate competitors.

The trashing of the Times Square area of New York, once the site of large numbers of respectable bars and restaurants, began with Prohibition, for not all speakeasies were furnished in the Louis XV style like the luxurious five-story Country Club. Most were dark, sordid clip joints haunted by bar girls pushing foul drinks in exchange for the promise of spurious sex to come. In Cincinnati, the attractive Across the Rhine beer gardens soon became a distant memory.

Some Prohibition advocates felt that "wide-open" towns such as New York and Chicago should be brought to heel, and called for more Prohibition agents and harsher laws (which were in fact introduced in 1925). Others became disenchanted for different reasons. Senator Thomas B. Watson (Democrat, Georgia), a lifelong dry, shocked the

Senate by drawing attention to "murder and other outrages carried out by Prohibition agents" in his state.

There was an almost immediate, nationwide change in drinking habits. It became the thing to do, among students, flappers, and respectable middle-class Americans all over the country, to defy the law — as much a manifestation of personal liberty as a thirst for alcohol.

Other changes manifested themselves. The saloon had been an almost exclusively male preserve, but the new speakeasies welcomed women. The cocktail was largely born as a result of Prohibition, because this was the only way of disguising the often horrible taste of homemade gin or flavored wood alcohol. And tens of thousands of people would die before Prohibition was over, poisoned by wood alcohol and moonshine.

7

THE PROVIDERS

With Prohibition, America was all set for a wild drinking spree that would last thirteen years, five months, and nine days. It would transform the country's morals; alter American attitudes toward law enforcers, politicians, and all those in authority; and herald a new mood of cynicism, along with an often justified conviction that the courts dispensed a form of two-tier justice based on class, wealth, and rank. And even if the Prohibition phenomenon itself, which was largely responsible for this general, unfocused resentment, was soon forgotten, for other reasons the mood of distrust has persisted to this day.

The Prohibition era has been chronicled in hundreds of films and classics, such as F. Scott Fitzgerald's *The Great Gatsby*. Underworld figures such as Al Capone, catapulted onto the world scene by Prohibition, became in time mythic heroes, as did the bootleggers' nemesis, Eliot Ness.

But the political immorality in high places that allowed the law-breakers to flourish — and that marked the 1920s in other ways — has been largely ignored or forgotten. It is as if those Americans who experienced the Prohibition years were determined to put them out of their minds as soon as it was repealed. Their reaction was understandable. Compared to the years of the Harding presidency, at the beginning of Prohibition (1920–1923), major scandals such as those that brought about the collapse of the Italian Christian Democratic hegemony looked like trifling peccadilloes.

For gangsters, bootleggers, and speakeasies to flourish, the liquor had to come from somewhere. The story of George Remus, the German-born American who became the richest bootlegger of all, shows how simple it was to lay one's hands on almost limitless quantities of whiskey without resorting to rumrunners or homemade stills — and often without even formally breaking the law.

Remus exemplified the new breed of American. His father, Franck Remus (who dropped the Germanic spelling of his first name after immigrating to America), came from Friedeberg, near Berlin. The history of the Remus family is a textbook illustration of the appalling health hazards prevalent in the nineteenth century. Franck's parents both died a few weeks after his birth, probably from cholera, and he subsequently became an apprentice in a woolen mill. There, he did well, marrying Maria Karg, the mill owner's daughter, in 1871. They had three girls, but all died in infancy. Their fourth child, George Remus, lived, and when he was four and a half years old, the three of them left for Milwaukee, then almost a German enclave, where several members of the Karg family had already settled.

In Milwaukee, tragedy continued to dog the Remus family. Maria gave birth to two more sons, who also died in infancy. She then had three more children, all girls, who lived, followed by a third son, Herman, who, as a child, was hit on the back of the head by a flying brick, and as a result became mentally unstable. He died in 1918.

Try as they might, the panel of psychiatrists who, at the request of the court, examined George Remus before his trial, and spent hours debriefing him on his antecedents, found "no record of suicidal or criminal tendencies upon the part of any member of this family." "None of the family could be called 'alcoholic,'" the panel wrote, "although many of them, as is common with their countrymen, drank considerable beer. George Remus's father drank only moderately, usually on Saturdays."

George was a good child in every way, an older sister, Mrs. Gabriel Ryerson, told the panel, "talkative, energetic, a book lover, careful in his appearance, and very seldom had to be scolded. He always looked on the bright side of things and had a sense of humor." Although Remus himself remained a lifelong teetotaler and nonsmoker, he was "fond of parties, always celebrating good news or success, dismissing discomforts of all kinds with feelings of lightheartedness. Irritations were never of long duration." Although he was quick-tempered, his sister recalled, he was affectionate, made friends easily, and had a natural sense of responsibility, even as a child. He had been confirmed in the Lutheran Church (though neither George Remus nor his family were particularly religious), but was sufficiently intrigued by the dogma of various churches to attend Catholic, Presbyterian, and occasionally Christian Science church services. Apparently, none fully satisfied him. "My religion," he told the panel, "is to pay my obligations and keep my word." He was "dubious about the hereafter and did not worry much about it." Despite his short, stocky build (in his early photographs he resembles Danny de Vito; in his later ones, Mussolini) and his one indulgence — good food — he became a strong swimmer and a much-sought-after member of the Illinois Athletic Club's water polo team. The examining psychiatrists found him "alert, friendly, courteous and perfectly willing to cooperate in every way."

As Remus told the panel, despite his mother's relatively prosperous background, his family fell on hard times shortly after settling in Milwaukee. Frank, no longer a weaver but a lumber scorer, became crippled with articular rheumatism, a virtual invalid no longer able to work.

They left for Chicago, and soon young George Remus, still in his early teens, became the family's mainstay. An uncle, George Karg, had a drugstore there, and George left school to work as his assistant. When his uncle decided to sell his shop, George obtained a bank loan and bought and ran the store himself, with a much increased profit. He was only nineteen, but had by this time become a licensed pharmacologist (by making himself out to be older than he was). He never graduated, displaying, as a student, the same headstrong qualities that were to plague him in later life. Just before his final examination, he led a student walkout to protest the behavior of an unpopular teacher, and when the teacher took his revenge, handing out punitive low grades, Remus never returned to school.

This in no way, however, prevented him from prospering. From the profits of his first shop, he bought a second drugstore near Milwaukee Avenue. He also became a certified optometrist, and his examining panel also noted that he "indulged in the practice of medicine in connection with his drug store among the people of his neighborhood." The practice was common among pharmacists; doctors were expensive, and there was no social security. Among his clients was a neighbor, Lillian Kraus. They fell in love, married, and had a daughter, Romola. In the somewhat dated jargon of the times, the panel noted that "his sexual life showed no perversities."

George Remus, in his twenties, found time not only to run two drugstores, write out prescriptions for glasses, act as an unlicensed doctor, and raise a family, but to study law at night school. At age 24 he was admitted to the Illinois Bar, and started his own practice. From the very start, he was successful. He specialized in criminal law, but also actively represented several Chicago labor unions, and made quite a name for himself as a divorce lawyer. A well-known local figure, with many Democratic connections, Remus was several times approached and asked to stand for local political office. "I could easily have become a District Attorney," he told the panel. "I was prominent enough politically to secure public office, but have never wanted to take the prosecutor's side in my life." In light of his many achievements, it is somewhat surprising that at the time of his murder trial, when they submitted him to various tests, including those standard 1920s examinations the Stanford Revision of the Binet-Simon Scale and the Otis Self-Administering Test of Mental Ability, the psychiatrists examining him found George Remus to be "of only average adult intelligence." They did add that "the possibility that this record may have been lowered by mental distraction at the time of the examination should not be overlooked."

Remus hired a legal secretary, Imogene Holmes, a young divorcée with a small daughter, Ruth. Imogene, a remarkably strong, graceful swimmer, was a voluptuous woman with somewhat extravagant tastes in clothes and unusual hats. Little is known of her family background, though she boasted to George Remus that she came "from the top drawer." Remus divorced Lillian in 1917, but continued to support her, remaining on good terms with her and their daughter, Romola, who adored him.

Chicago became dry in 1918. In this hugely corrupt city, where underworld characters immediately became bootleggers, Remus, the criminal lawyer they knew and trusted, was much in demand. Among his clients was Johnny Torrio, a nightclub and brothel owner, and one of the first Chicago bootleggers and speakeasy kings. Torrio, himself a straitlaced family man and practicing Catholic for all his many brothel ownerships, summoned one of his distant New York relatives, Alfonso Caponi, to assist him in his operations. Remus knew Capone, too, but only slightly. His acquaintanceship with the Chicago underworld was strictly professional: many of its minor members had visited his office at 167 North Clark Street, on the Chicago "Loop," some of them on murder charges. It was because as defense counsel he had been compelled to witness the capital executions of some of his clients (in the electric chair) that he came out strongly against the death penalty. Clarence Darrow, the best-known criminal lawyer in America, also a Chicago colleague, spoke highly of his abilities.

As a brilliant lawyer, and an ex-pharmacist, Remus was uniquely qualified to make a fortune out of the Volstead Act. In a series of articles about him in the St. Louis *Post-Dispatch* ("The Inside Story of the Amazing Career of George Remus, millionaire bootlegger and his band of rumrunners," St. Louis *Post-Dispatch,* January 3–20, 1926), Paul Y. Anderson wrote:

> If there has ever been a bigger bootlegger than Remus, the fact remains a secret. . . . Remus was to bootlegging what Rockefeller was to oil. In the sheer imagination of his plan, in the insolent sweep of his ambition and power with which he swept upward toward his goal, Remus can bear comparison with the captains of industry.

Remus told Anderson how the idea came to him. If gangsters of limited intelligence could make a fortune, "Remus could surely do better than they."[1]

His first step was to sell his law practice (though he remained a member of the Bar Association). He then moved, with Imogene, to Cincinnati, where they got married. It was a shrewd move: most of America's whiskey distilleries were within 300 miles of the town, and Remus knew that despite the wartime ban on grain supplies, the distilleries operating in America and producing an annual output of 286 million gallons had virtually limitless bonded stocks at their disposal. He also knew it was a seller's market: in 1917, the last "normal" year before Prohibition became law in several major states, Americans had consumed two billion gallons of hard liquor. Although some distillers sent their liquor stocks abroad before 1920, hundreds of millions of gallons remained in distilleries and government-bonded warehouses, most of them within easy reach of Cincinnati. In addition, because of Prohibition, "whiskey certificates" were worth next to nothing.

Entirely legally, using his life savings ($100,000), Remus started buying up certificates. His operations became lucrative quickly, and he was soon able to acquire entire distilleries, complete with offices, machinery, furniture, and even abandoned corner saloons, for which he did not have the slightest use. In time, Remus became the largest owner of distilleries in America, his properties including famous brand names: Fleischmann, Old Lexington Club, Rugby, Greendale, and Squibb, the largest in the country. The Fleischmann Distillery, which cost him $197,000, came with 3,100 barrels of prime rye whiskey.

The next step was to get official permission to remove the whiskey and — again quite legally — sell it to drug companies licensed to sell medicinal whiskey. "I started out buying a retail drug store in Cincinnati and converting it into a wholesale drug company," Remus told the *Post-Dispatch*. "As soon as that company had withdrawn as much liquor as possible without attracting undue attention, I organized another wholesale company, closed up the first one, and shipped the stock of drugs off to the second one. We made that carload of drugs serve as the stock for three or four wholesale companies." Surplus nonalcoholic stocks were "fired off into space" (Anderson's words) to fictitious buyers, eventually sold off as unclaimed freight. In the first few months of Prohibition, Remus set up over a dozen drug companies, closing them down when they began attracting the curiosity of enforcement agents and inventing new ones. When the regulations changed, as they soon did, to limit liquor acquisitions on the part of drug companies to 10 percent of their business, Remus simply cooked the books, showing a huge imaginary turnover.

Once in the hands of the drug companies, some of the whiskey duly ended up in pint bottles labeled "medicinal whiskey," but most of it ended up elsewhere, in the hands of bootleggers, nightclub owners, middlemen, and in exceptional cases a carefully vetted private clientele. Only a small proportion ended up as "straight" medicinal whiskey — the bootleggers and private customers a far more lucrative market. Anderson wrote that "Once out from under the eye of the government, the disposal of whiskey at fabulous prices became a simple matter. The whiskey market is always a seller's market. The supply never equals the demand. Remus's associates already had made contacts with retail bootleggers who would snap up all the good liquor that could be furnished, and would pay $80 a case and upward. There are 12 quarts, or three gallons, to a case. Remus paid from 65 cents to $4 (per case) for the certificates."

"What was wrong with that?" George Conners, Remus's closest associate, asked Anderson. "If anything was wrong it was wrong for the Government to destroy the value of those people's property without compensating them for it. If the Government wanted to abolish whiskey drinking, why didn't it buy all this whiskey and dump it in the river?" Conners told Anderson he had not intended to get into the whiskey business, "but after several of these fellows came to me, I asked Remus what he would charge me for liquor in 15 or 20 case lots." Remus suggested he think big, and quoted a price for 250-case lots. This was the start of the Remus-Conners bootleg operation on a grand scale, with Conners handling sales on a commission basis and drumming up business all over America.

"We never poisoned anybody. We sold good liquor and didn't cut it," Remus told Anderson. This and his meticulously run operation — involving shippers, drivers, bodyguards, and accountants (at his peak there were 3,000 people on his payroll) — went far to explain Remus's meteoric career. Within a few months of Prohibition, he was depositing tens of thousands of dollars a day into various bank accounts both in his own name and under aliases.

Remus had one innocuous weakness: he wanted to become a respected member of Cincinnati society. He set about it with his usual thoroughness. First he bought a huge property on Price Hill, overlooking the town, at Eighth and Hermosa Avenue, in what was then its most desirable suburb. Then, regardless of expense (it cost him $750,000, or close to several million dollars today), he had the place remodeled, furnished in somewhat garish taste, and on its extensive grounds built a greenhouse, a racing stable (he soon owned a string of racing thoroughbreds), a landscaped garden, and a series of outhouses. All but one were for his many servants, chauffeurs, and their families, but the largest housed a specially built, Olympic-size indoor swimming pool. This alone cost him another $100,000 (1920).

Much later, when Remus's mansion was demolished, two tunnels were discovered. Remus had had these built to store whiskey for his parties and as a possible getaway. "We found many empty bottles there," said Jack Doll, who, as a child, and neighbor, had played in Remus's garden, used the pool, and later was present when the mansion was pulled down. Doll would remember Remus with affection: he was friendly, welcomed poor children on his premises, and, though the property was surrounded by a chain link fence to keep the racehorses from straying, instructed his gardener to leave a space so that the local kids could squeeze under it to come and play. Doll remembers Remus playfully pushing a ten-year-old into the pool fully clothed, and then giving him a $10 bill "to buy a new suit." "You could buy a whole boy's outfit for a dollar in those days," Doll noted.

As soon as the house was ready, Remus started giving lavish parties. While Cincinnati "old money" either stayed away or made snide remarks behind his back while enjoying his hospitality, almost all found his invitations irresistible. At formal dinners (the dining room table was big enough to seat twenty in comfort), Remus slipped $100 bills under his guests' plates. On March 21, 1921, at a party staged to celebrate the completion of his swimming pool, he presented all of his guests with gold-engraved Elgin watches, as well as photographs of the occasion, taken by a specially hired photographer.

Two years later, in July of 1923, Remus, though by this time in serious trouble with the Justice Department, staged what was even by his standards an extraordinarily elaborate dancing and swimming party. The hundred guests were entertained by a fifteen-piece orchestra and a water-ballet, with Imogene Remus, herself a talented swimmer, making a guest appearance in a daringly cut swimsuit. Remus had bought up the stock of a bankrupt Cincinnati jeweler for $25,000, and upon arrival, all of the female guests got rings, and the males diamond tie-clasps. On leaving, in the early hours of the morning, there was another surprise waiting: each female guest (there were fifty in all) was presented with a brand-new 1923 Pontiac. The descendant of one of the assiduous party-goers recalled his parents saying that on these occasions Remus himself was a discreet, almost invisible host. Exploring the mansion during the 1923 extravaganza, they came across him in his library, alone, reading a book and reluctant to be disturbed.

This quest for social respectability at almost any cost was shared by many leading bootleggers elsewhere. "Lucky" Luciano (in his posthumous memoirs) recalled with obvious pride how he had mingled with Wall Street tycoons such as banker Julie Bach, attended lavish parties given on the estate of the famous Whitney family, and ingratiated himself with over a hundred top socialites, police officials, and politicians by providing them, at huge cost, with black market tickets to the 1923 Jack Dempsey–Luis Angel Firpo fight at the New York Polo Grounds.

Remus did not confine his parties to his home. There were elaborate lunch parties in his downtown Cincinnati office (on the corner of Race and Pearl Streets), with a butler and chef in constant attendance. Also in 1923, he gave a memorable birthday party for Imogene (also attended by hundreds of guests) in the ballroom of one of its most famous hotels, the Sinton.

Some of Remus's social activities were chronicled in the Cincinnati papers (though the 1923 swimming pool party was not), and he became a household name so quickly that F. Scott Fitzgerald may well have been inspired by him. In many respects, the real-life Remus and the fictional Gatsby were similar. Both were self-made men, both gave lavish parties, both despised their guests' venality, and both were low-key hosts, observing rather than dominating the party scene. There was, however, a major difference between them. Remus, in 1923, was happily married — an adoring husband and doting father who lavished every type of expensive gift on Imogene's daughter Ruth, including a gold-plated grand piano — whereas Gatsby was a loner, at heart an unrequited romantic.

It was while looking for a suitable house that Remus first met Conners, then a real-estate agent. Conners failed to sell Remus a house, but was hired by him — first as a gofer, then as a minor bootlegging partner before becoming Remus's fanatically loyal "number two." A compulsive horse-racing gambler, Conners was soon able to afford this expensive habit: working on a percentage basis, as he did from the beginning, he became a wealthy man.

Because only a small proportion of the cases removed from the distilleries ended up as medicinal whiskey, Remus needed a halfway house where the whiskey in the multigallon drums and barrels could be discreetly repackaged and bottled. Remus and Conners first went into partnership with "John Jew" Marcus, a member of the Cincinnati underworld, but this did not last. Remus wanted to preserve his respectable image, and suspected Marcus of cheating him. It was Conners who came across an isolated farmhouse in Westwood, a rural Cincinnati suburb, enabling Remus to move into the really big time, handling huge quantities of liquor while keeping everything under his personal control.

Death Valley Farm, as it was renamed, was off the beaten track, accessible by a single dirt road and virtually impossible to find unless one knew how to get there.[2] Its owner, George Dater, a bachelor, had tried his hand at making homemade wine, but nobody would buy it. Dater's assistant, hired by Remus as caretaker, was George Gehrum, "a little, rat-faced, shifty-eyed individual[3] who lived in perpetual fear of his wife, a young woman of vigorous propensities and a taste for strong drink." She had four unruly children and ran the farm.

At first Conners paid Gehrum $100 a week to store liquor there. But when the cases arrived, Gehrum panicked, and told him to clear out and take his whiskey with him. Eventually, Remus made him a rental offer he couldn't refuse. The farm was entirely remodeled. Several large cellars were built, housing storage rooms and an underground bottling plant. A block and tackle system was installed to lower barrels into the cellars. Two men were hired full-time, whose sole job was to break up the wooden cases containing the three-gallon jars that came from the distilleries.

Remus turned Death Valley Farm into a fortified enclave. He installed floodlights and hired a permanent contingent of armed men to guard it. Conners found a mobile polling booth on wheels and turned it into a sentry box at the gate entrance, staffed twenty-four hours a day by two armed men. They had a buzzer to activate a warning signal in the main building whenever anyone approached the farm. Another buzzer turned on the floodlights installed on the main building's second floor, illuminating the entire area.

These security precautions were essential. To bona fide bootleggers such as Remus and Conners, the real enemy was not the army of bureaucrats and Prohibition Bureau agents, but hijackers. Although a convoy of Remus's liquor did fall into their hands once, no "pirates" ever succeeded in breaking into Death Valley Farm, though they tried. One night in 1920, an armed gang did manage to creep up to the gate undetected. They fired volley after volley into the building, expecting its inhabitants to flee or surrender. Remus's men fired back, with devastating effect, and the gang left, taking their casualties with them. Although the battle went on for some time, no police ever showed up. There was a tacit understanding, on all sides, that encounters such as these were part of a private war between bootleggers and hijackers, not the responsibility of the police.

The sheer size of Remus's operations required him to expand in other directions. He hired a Cincinnati-based American Express employee, Harry Stratton, to act as his shipping manager, who began moonlighting for Remus while holding down what his American Express employers believed was a full-time job. It was a lucrative arrangement for all concerned: Stratton moved Remus's liquor, crated up and bearing innocuous labels, all over the United States by "American Express" for several months — until his official employers discovered what he was up to and fired him.

This compelled Remus to set up his own delivery system. He bought twenty trucks, and had them armor-plated and redesigned to carry crates securely, without risk of contents breakage. This alone cost him $20,000 — over $200,000 today. But once they left Death Valley Farm, the "pirate" predators were on the lookout for them, so he also purchased a fleet of fast cars: six armor-plated Marmots, and Packards, Locomobiles, Dodges, a Cadillac, and a Pierce-Arrow to carry squads of heavily armed men to accompany the trucks and fend off possible attacks. There were also "runners," whose fast cars were designed to carry whiskey, on a fixed-fee, per-case basis. Because Prohibition Bureau road patrols were on the lookout for sagging springs, their chassis were reinforced. At one stage, Remus even invested in some railroad cars.

Eventually, the traffic became two-way: carefully selected bootlegger middlemen from all over America (including faraway Texas, Florida, and California) were allowed to enter Death Valley Farm in their own vehicles, to carry away their merchandise themselves. The private customers even arranged for barter deals. Those driving in from the north, for instance, came with champagne and scotch whiskey smuggled in from Canada, departing with rye and bourbon. Remus's organizational talent turned Death Valley Farm into a huge liquor supermarket. Soon, he acquired five similar "halfway houses" in other parts of the country.

As a routine precaution (for he knew law enforcement patrols were watching out for suspicious-looking trucks and cars), the trucks were hosed down, washed, and waxed while the whiskey was being loaded and paid for, so that when they left the farm they looked brand new. Ever attentive to detail, and eager to keep his "respectable" bootlegger clientele, Remus provided the truck drivers with beds, meals (cooked by a reluctant Mrs. Gehrum, who complained that her employer was far too generous), and even free whiskey tots.

While at first Remus's modus operandi was so foolproof it attracted little attention, the scale of his operations was such that local and regional Prohibition directors rapidly became aware that only a fraction of the withdrawals from his newly acquired distilleries ended up as medicinal whiskey. In return for a fee — usually $3,000 per permit issue — they looked the other way. "I never handed over the money personally," Remus told the St. Louis *Post-Dispatch*.

> Usually the go-between was the politician who had got the official his job. In that case, he sometimes got more out of it than the official himself. . . . a greedier lot of parasites never existed. . . . A few men have tried to corner the wheat market only to find that there is too much wheat in the world. I tried to corner the graft market, but I learnt there isn't enough money in the world to buy up all the public officials who demand their share of it.

Among the "parasites" were many local politicians who attended his parties. Government store keepers, known as gaugers, were also systematically bribed. An unofficial "permit" market eventually sprang up all over America, with the high-level connivance of Washington-based politicians. Blank forms, already signed, made their appearance. A standard fee, Remus later reported, was $42,000, but for that money he could withdraw unlimited quantities of liquor from distilleries he did not even own, as well as government-run bonded warehouses. There was also a traffic in practically undetectable forged blank "B permits," as the authorizations were called.

The area around Death Valley Farm was regularly patrolled by mounted police, who were fully aware of its activities. "We never paid the police, there were simply too many of them," Conners told the St. Louis *Post-Dispatch,* but "a couple of mounted police came every day. We gave them a couple of quarts a week and $10 or $15 spending money. They also had a few customers of their own in town. We let them have the stuff at $80 a case."

Prohibition agents knew about Death Valley Farm, but the amount of protection paid turned it into an "off limits" area. One day, Conners later told the St. Louis *Post-Dispatch*'s Paul Anderson, two Prohibition agents blundered into the farm, apparently by mistake. They quickly realized they had made a spectacular catch. Conners immediately phoned their superior in Cincinnati, who apologized for the intrusion and asked to talk to them. "They were supposed to be looking for stills down the road," he told Conners. After the phone call, they were apologetic. Conners offered them a drink, then another. Eventually Conners sent them on their way with a thousand dollars each and a quart of rye. "They were so drunk I was afraid they wouldn't be able to drive back to town, and offered to have one of my men act as driver," he said.

The Cincinnati police were just as venal. "Several city detectives were working for us on the side," Conners told Anderson. "Each one would dig up a few customers — saloons or private parties. The detective would give us an order, tell us how much to deliver, and what to collect. Sometimes the detective would go along on the truck when the delivery was made. This would protect the truck, and assure the buyer he was getting protection and wouldn't be raided."

Altogether, Conners said, there were over a thousand salesmen on the force, working for Remus. In other cities, in other circumstances with other bootleggers, the situation was much the same.

The Cincinnati detectives did not cost Remus much, but in spite of his exceptionally well-organized legal front, his expenses were enormous. (Al Capone, a much smaller operator than Remus as far as liquor was concerned, later told investigators that bootlegging was a losing game: "Too many overheads.") At every level, in every state where his whiskey ended up, Remus parted with enormous sums to keep the government, the Prohibition Bureau, and the police off his back. He later estimated that half his gross earnings were spent in bribes. Since, at the peak of his activities, Remus was grossing about $40 million a year, this meant that $20 million went into the hands of corrupt officials. The pattern was the same all over America, whether law enforcement officials were dealing with whiskey certificate bootleggers such as Remus or with the more adventurous rumrunners. Remus told Anderson that in his entire career he only came across two people who turned down his bribes — and they were, in time, to contribute to his downfall. One was Burt Morgan, the Prohibition director of Indiana, who "could have had $250,000" to look the other way. The other was Sam Collins, the Kentucky Prohibition director, whom Remus offered $100,000 simply to quit his job and take up a far more remunerative appointment as the manager of a soft-drink plant. As state Prohibition directors, Morgan and Collins earned $4,600 a year each. With his mixture of showmanship and genuine panache, Remus would later pay tribute to the "untouchables." "You didn't sell out; I want to shake hands with you, sir," he told Collins when he met him.

Remus was not the only victim of Collins's integrity. John Langley, the Indiana State congressman who had appointed Collins Prohibition director in the first place, and expected him to be an obedient pawn, found this out to his cost. Collins had him indicted for protecting bootleggers and taking their bribes. But Morgan and Collins were remarkable exceptions to the rule.

Remus's money "sweetened" not only poorly paid officials but senior members of the Harding administration, including the very man charged at the highest level with upholding the law — the attorney general himself. Prohibition and all that went with it — corruption, bribery, the complicity of the very people supposed to fight it — can only be understood within the wider political context of 1920s America and the iniquitous Harding administration as a whole.

8

HARDING AND
THE RACKETEERS

Prohibition was part of a far larger scandal — the scandal of the Harding presidency. Warren Gamaliel Harding was, if not the worst, certainly the weakest, most indecisive president in American history. This need not have been disastrous — America faced no major external threats between 1920 and 1923 — had not the start of Prohibition coincided with the beginning of his presidency. As it was, "the Harding Administration was responsible in its short two years and five months for more concentrated robbery and rascality than any other in the whole history of Federal Government."[1]

Harding was not an evil man, nor was he, personally, exceptionally corrupt by the standards of the time. The abysmal record of his administration was partly due to a "character flaw" inherent in the man — his excessively good-natured, amicable disposition. A former colleague in his early days noted that "he wanted to be everybody's friend . . . a small town play boy." His entourage was well aware of his craving to be liked and exploited this weakness to the hilt, knowing that he was too dependent on his friends to deal with them harshly even when their corrupt practices led to public scandals. Many judges and law enforcement officers, including those dealing with Prohibition, took their cue from what they saw happening at the top.

The cronyism of the Harding administration was such that for as long as he was in office the white-collar criminals known as "the Ohio gang" who had grown up with him and become his intimate friends knew they were immune from prosecution, that Harding would protect them from the rigors of the law. Harding's own belated realization of the extent of their corruption in all likelihood contributed to a physical and mental collapse leading to his sudden, early death. His ineptitude could not possibly be ignored, even by political allies out to praise him posthumously. At a Harding Memorial Association meeting in June of 1931, President Herbert Hoover, in a singularly ambiguous eulogy, noted that

> Harding had a dim realization that he had been betrayed by a few of the men whom he had believed were his devoted friends. It was later proved in the courts of the land that these men had betrayed not only the friendship of their staunch and loyal friend but that they had betrayed their country.

Harding grew up in the small town of Marion, Ohio, where his father, an unsuccessful homeopathic doctor, earned a supplementary income as a small-time junk dealer. Even as a boy, Warren was hail-fellow-well-met, easy-going — a gregarious youngster who preferred billiards, poker, and small-town gossip to books, but was smart enough to make a good living. His first job — as editor of a small, local paper, the Marion *Star* — suited him perfectly.

He was nineteen when he first bought shares in the paper, later winning the remaining shares in a poker game. His innate deviousness made him an excellent poker player. Tall, handsome, dignified looking, he stood out in any gathering, and knew it. But he was not what he seemed: the ultimate hollow man, he looked more impressive than he was. "No man could be as much of a Roman senator as Harding looked," Mark Sullivan wrote in *Our Times*. According to the *Saturday Evening Post*, Harding "needed only a toga to complete the illusion he had come out of the ancient world."

Florence Kling was the daughter of the richest man in Marion. She was 31 and already had a daughter by a first marriage when she married Harding, then 26. His marriage was no love match but a calculated move on his part, a social as well as a financial stepping-stone. She was tall, plain, and square-jawed, "lacking any kind of charm." Although she dressed expensively, flaunting a wilting kind of femininity, she had huge hands and moved awkwardly. She had also inherited her father's dictatorial manner and "his determination to get what he wanted out of life."[2] Her household servants, and Harding himself, lived in constant terror of her incessant nagging. Because of her imperious manner, she was known in Marion as The Duchess, and the nickname stuck, right through to her White House years. Not surprisingly, the Hardings' sex life did not last long, and they had no children — for Harding, a bitter disappointment. His personal charm was considerable: in early middle age he turned into a consistent, if somewhat lazy, sentimental philanderer.

As editor and owner-publisher of a small-town paper, Harding was well placed to enter state politics. "His conception of political progress was to make no enemies," a friend noted. Partly for this reason, he became a valued member of the Republican party, then, in Ohio, dominated by forceful, unscrupulous "Tammany Hall" type personalities such as George "Boss" Cox and "Fire Engine" Joe Foraker, who ran the state like a private preserve. Harding showed little interest in the world at large: "Books did not enter into his scheme of life in any important sense. . . . He cannot fairly be called illiterate, although some of his verbiage, when he strives to attain the impressive, furnishes a sad example of the grandiloquently inept," a local newspaperman wrote. The beginning of his speech for Taft as presidential nominee in 1912 (Taft would lose to Woodrow Wilson) — "Progression is everlastingly lifting the standards that marked the end of the world's march yesterday and planting them on new and advanced heights today" — is a fair example of his rhetoric, which reminded H. L. Mencken, the great satirist and social critic of the time, of a "string of wet sponges" and "dogs barking idiotically through endless nights. . . . It is rumble and bumble. It is flap and doodle. It is balder and dash." "It is so bad," he wrote, "that a sort of grandeur creeps into it."

His amiable, conciliatory record in state politics, combined with his impressive good looks and statesmanlike (if spurious) "presence" singled him out as an above-average player, so much so that the Ohio Republican party machine encouraged him to stand as a senator. "It costs such a lot of money to live in Washington," Florence Harding told a *Marion Star* employee. "If he was only a corporation lawyer and could pick up a lot of business on the side, I'd say yes. But he couldn't do anything there. No: I don't know as we can afford it yet."[3] Harding did finally make up his mind and went to Washington in 1915, as senator for Ohio — and immediately regretted that he had not done so earlier. The Senate, as he discovered, was the most congenial club in the world for pleasure-loving, sports-loving extroverts such as himself. He enjoyed himself immensely, especially when The Duchess was not around, and failing health kept her in Marion most of the time. George B. Christian, his confidential secretary and devoted friend, writing later about these "six years of happiness," shrewdly noted that "He didn't like being a Senator, he liked being in the Senate." Voting records show his attendance was sporadic, to say the least. He was far more often on the golf course, in the Senate bar, in a poker game, or out chasing women than in the chamber itself, and "his contribution to legislation was practically nil." Like other Ohio Republicans, Harding was a consistent supporter of Prohibition only because it was a sure-fire vote-getter. But though "politically dry," he was a steady drinker.

It was during his early political apprenticeship in Ohio that two men far more flawed than he spotted his political potential, and became his faithful aides, fixers, and boon companions. The chief usefulness of Harry Micajah Daugherty, a lawyer and failed politician, was as a veteran insider, fully conversant with the devious workings of Ohio's notoriously corrupt Republican party machine. Infinitely more cynical and manipulative than Harding, and aware, after his own abortive career in state politics, that his real talent was that of a wheeling-and-dealing, back-room boy *éminence grise,* he soon became indispensable to Harding as both mentor and strategist. Jess Smith, twelve years younger than Daugherty (they came from the same home town, Washington State House), began handling Harding's financial affairs in the late 1890s. The pair would play a major role in the Prohibition saga, and the unraveling of the Harding presidency must be laid at their door.

Although both were unprincipled, utterly ruthless operators, temperamentally they were very different. Daugherty had married a beautiful local heiress, but their life together was joyless; her serious health problems soon turned him into a devoted but harassed nurse. Their son, an alcoholic, was in and out of clinics all of his adult life. A secretive political operator, quick to take advantage of the weaknesses of others, he was also on the extreme far right of his party, obsessed with the "Bolshevik peril," seeing communist conspiracies everywhere. Ideologically, he was a striking forerunner of Senator McCarthy — his smear techniques just as outrageous.

Jess Smith, a dandy, mother's boy, dilettante store-owner, man about town, and inveterate gossip, was Daugherty's devoted admirer, aide, and hireling. Almost certainly homosexual, Smith left his mother's company only once in his life, to marry Roxy Stinson, a spectacularly good-looking redhead with a showgirl's figure. It didn't last, and Smith went back to his mother, but he and Roxy remained firm friends. Smith frankly admitted his lack of manly, physical courage to her, and she, in turn, became, in time, and after his mother's death, a mother-surrogate and confidante. Smith's timorous nature made him an ideal Daugherty foil — the cringing, subservient slave-buffoon to a dominant master. The Daugherty-Smith relationship, in its brutal intimacy, is reminiscent of the protagonists in Samuel Beckett's *Waiting for Godot*. In later years, Daugherty and Smith would live together in Washington, sharing first a house, then a hotel suite, sleeping in adjoining bedrooms with the door always open, for Smith was afraid of the dark. In many respects their relations mirrored that of J. Edgar Hoover and his lifelong friend Clyde Tolson.

Daugherty and Smith were so close to Harding that he could have no secrets from them. They knew all about his philandering, including his five-year liaison with an attractive married neighbor, Carrie Phillips. They also knew about his relationship with a twenty-year-old shopgirl, Nan Britton, which began in July of 1917 (Harding was fifty-one at the time) and continued long after their child, Elizabeth Ann, was born in 1920. Harding was well aware that were this liaison to become public knowledge it would wreck his political career, and there is no doubt Daugherty and Smith took advantage of the situation, turning an already inherently weak Harding into an unwilling accomplice of their crimes.

Nan Britton wrote at length about their liaison in a book published in 1927, including a description of "the night I became his bride" that had all of the elements of a Feydeau farce.[4] They had checked into a hotel on Broadway "where his Washington friends had intimated to him that they had stopped under similar unconventional circumstances with no unpleasant consequences." But no sooner had they made love than two men — detectives on the lookout for prostitutes — burst into the room. "They've got us!" was Harding's reaction. "Let this poor little girl go," he begged them. They told him "he should have thought of that before," Britton wrote.

> I remember he told them that I was twenty-two years old and I, not realizing that he wanted to make me as old as he safely could, interrupted him and stated truthfully that I was only twenty. To almost every argument he advanced on my behalf they answered "You'll have to tell that to the judge." About that time one of the men picked up Mr. Harding's hat. Inside was his name, in gold lettering, and upon seeing the name they became calm immediately. Not only calm but strangely respectful. . . . We packed our things immediately and the men conducted us to a side entrance. On the way out Mr. Harding handed them a $20 bill. When we were in the taxi, he remarked explosively, "Gee, Nan, I thought I wouldn't get out of that under $1,000!"

In his relationship with Nan Britton, he was both infinitely devious and extraordinarily naive. He made elaborate travel arrangements for her before her pregnancy, smuggling her into his hotel room during dozens of out-of-town senatorial speaking engagements or official business trips to New York; making reservations under assumed names, but dining with her in well-known New York restaurants; going to popular New York plays with her in crowded theaters, running considerable risk of discovery — his chief concern neither the press nor public opinion but The Duchess. At the same time he wrote her forty-page love letters promising eventual marriage and an idyllic future together. He often smuggled her into his Senate office. "He told me he liked to have me be with him in his office, for then the place held precious memories and he could visualize me there during the hours he worked alone." In January of 1919, she would later write: " . . . we stayed [in his office] quite a while that evening, longer, he said, than it was wise for us to do so, because the rules governing guests in the Senate offices were rather strict. It was here, we both decided afterwards, that our baby girl was conceived. . . ."

Harding, she wrote, seemed genuinely excited by the news, and looked forward to being a father. He loved children, he said, and had always wanted a daughter. This may have been another example of Harding's deviousness, for he never allowed Nan Britton to show him their child, though once he became president she was frequently smuggled into the White House, where they made love in a broom closet adjoining his anteroom. She too obtained her share of perks: halfway through his presidency, $75,000 was appropriated to enable her, at length, to "investigate the raw silk market in the Orient."

Following Woodrow Wilson's stroke in office, both Harding's nomination as Republican presidential candidate and his subsequent election campaign also had farcical undertones. At the start of the 1919 Chicago Convention, he was no more than a favorite son, a rank outsider. There were four main contenders, all of them far more worthy presidential material. Daugherty, Harding's campaign manager, found it difficult to raise money and openly admitted, at its start, that "poor old Warren hasn't a Chinaman's chance." But during the subsequent, increasingly deadlocked convention, Daugherty worked hard in smoke-filled rooms to convince the Republican party bosses that Harding was the ideal compromise candidate. Halfway through the proceedings, George Harvey, a prominent Republican and editor of the *North American Review,* asked Harding to "tell us, in your conscience and before God, whether there is anything that might be brought up against you that would embarrass the party, any impediment that might disqualify you or make you inexpedient, as candidate or President." Harding said he needed time to consider his reply, but a short while later, almost certainly after consulting Daugherty, told him he was clean. As Harvey then told reporters covering the convention, "There ain't no first-raters this year. . . . Harding is the best of the second-raters."

By the sixth ballot, it became known on the floor that, thanks to Daugherty's efforts and patronage pledges, Harding had become the choice of the party bosses. After the eighth ballot, which showed a steep rise in the number of votes for him, the cry went up: "Climb on the bandwagon."

He finally made it on the tenth ballot, and his singularly down-to-earth reaction, on winning the nomination, was that of a born gambler, remarkable for its lack of cant or ethical content. "I feel," he said, "like a man who goes in with a pair of eights and comes out with aces full."

The party bosses were unaware of Nan Britton and her daughter, but they did know about his former mistress, Carrie Phillips. They offered her a deal: an immediate lump sum ($20,000) and a monthly allowance for as long as Harding remained president, as well as a world tour for herself and her husband. She accepted immediately.

It was Jess Smith's turn to step into the limelight. As Harding's campaign manager, he came up with two deliberately low-key, singularly uninspiring campaign slogans: "Think of America first," and "With Harding and back to normal." They proved singularly effective. After the heady interventionist days of Woodrow Wilson, the trauma of the Great War, and the unprecedentedly violent coal miners' and steel workers' strikes of the previous year (as brutally repressed as the strike of Boston's policemen, which had deeply shocked the public), America longed for a return to the good old days. The temptation to withdraw into a secure cocoon, as Charles Mee noted in *The Ohio Gang*,[5] was irresistible, and the vote for Harding, implying as it did a refusal to get involved with cynical Europeans, legitimized the American withdrawal from the League of Nations. It also explained the subliminal attraction of Prohibition, with its promise of a return not only to sobriety but to social harmony in a refreshingly simple, family-oriented, church-dominated America.

Although Jess Smith operated a campaign headquarters in Washington out of the shabby New Ebbett Hotel (Harding's penny-pinching was legendary), he believed that Harding's homespun, folksy image could best be projected by having him campaign mostly from his front porch in his home town. It was Howard Mannington, another Daugherty crony — later a notorious deal-maker, bootlegger, and shady go-between — who handled the endless stream of visitors to Marion, with Harding putting on a convincing act as a loving family man and the incarnation of small-town America's virtues and down-to-earth qualities. After visiting Harding in Marion, and watching Mrs. Harding sweep the front porch herself, Chicago Mayor "Big Bill" Thompson came away elated. "Where but in America could that happen?" he asked, prophesying that Harding would be "one of our greatest Presidents." Nan Britton was told in no uncertain terms to stay away until well after the election.

Harding may have fooled the public, but he didn't fool himself. He discovered, very soon after his election, that the United States presidency, even in the less complicated world of the 1920s, required qualities he simply did not possess. He admitted the fact, semipublicly, time and time again. "I don't think I'm big enough for the Presidency," he told a judge after a round of golf. "Oftentimes, as I sit here, I don't seem to grasp that I am President," he admitted to a newspaper columnist. "I can't make a damn thing out of this tax problem," he said to an aide. "I listen to one side and they seem right, and then, God! I talk to the other side and they seem just as right and here I am where I started. I know somewhere there is a book that will give me the truth, but Hell! I couldn't read the book!" When Arthur Draper, of the New York *Tribune*, returned from a trip abroad and sought to brief the President, Harding told him: "I don't know anything about this European stuff. You and Jud [his political secretary, Jud Welliver] get together and he can tell me later. He handles these matters for me." Harding was also famous for his malapropisms, as when, questioned about the (then alarming) 1.5-million unemployment figure, he replied that "the figures are astounding only because we are a 100 million, and this parasite percentage is always with us."

There were some able men in his administration, though on the financially archconservative side (Herbert Hoover; Andrew Mellon, a millionaire with extensive distilling interests; and an able secretary of State, Charles Evans Hughes, later to be Supreme Court chief justice, who made up for Harding's ignorance of the world at large), but they were outnumbered by mediocre Republican party hacks, dubious Ohio gang cronies, and downright crooks. Several (Secretary of War John Weeks and Labor Secretary John Davis among them) were there simply because they were poker-playing sycophants, but his most unsuitable appointment, by far, was that of Harry Daugherty as attorney general. Daugherty wanted the Justice Department and Harding owed too much to his kingmaker to refuse him anything — though he did balk at giving Jess Smith a cabinet appointment.

It didn't make any difference: Jess Smith moved into the Justice Department anyway, with an office (and a stock-market ticker-tape machine) across the anteroom from Daugherty. He had no clearly defined job, but he did have a secretary, unlimited access to Justice Department files, and a Bureau of Investigation badge, and was soon regarded as Daugherty's second in command, an unofficial deputy attorney general. There was a constant stream of shady visitors in and out of Smith's office. Thomas Felder — lobbyist, veteran member of the Ohio gang, bootlegger, and con man with underworld connections — practically used it as his own. So did Howard Mannington, now a prominent Washington bootlegger. Mannington was the Harding crony who had masterminded Harding's "front porch" election campaign in Marion with his sidekick Bill Orr, a former journalist. In a later book, *The Inside Story of the Harding Tragedy*, remarkable for its lack of substance and self-serving, mealy-mouthed ingenuity, Daugherty made almost no mention of Smith and claimed that he had known nothing of his activities until too late. But he never did explain in the book why Smith had an office in the Justice Department across from his own anteroom and what he was doing there.

Myron Herrick, the Republican party's Ohioan elder statesman, did his best to prevent Daugherty's appointment. "Harry Daugherty will wreck your administration," he told Harding — and was packed off to Paris as ambassador. Later, but only after he had been forced out of his job, the *New York Times* would belatedly write that "from the first day, Daugherty had been a gross misfit as Attorney General."

Alice Roosevelt Longworth, ex-President Teddy Roosevelt's daughter, observed the new White House social scene with patrician distaste. Under Harding, visitors came in two categories. The run-of-the-mill guests were kept downstairs, where they were served fruit juice. But Harding's cronies, and other privileged guests, were invited upstairs, where liquor flowed like water. On her first visit to Harding's study, she wrote that

> . . . no rumor could have exceeded the reality: the study was filled with cronies (Daugherty, Jess Smith), the air heavy with tobacco smoke, trays with bottles containing every imaginable brand of whiskey stood about, cards and poker chips ready at hand, an atmosphere of waistcoat unbuttoned, feet on desk, and spittoon alongside.[6]

Harding, she added, "was not a bad man. He was just a slob." Had she been allowed to visit those parts of the Senate reserved for the select few, she would have found a similar ambiance. Part of the

Senate Library had been curtained off, and had become "the best bar in town," well stocked thanks to regular visits from ingratiatingly subservient customs officials bringing with them confiscated liquor.

Harding was similarly showered with gifts of liquor. Because excessive overt flaunting of Prohibition rules was bound to attract attention, Ned McLean, the wealthy playboy son of John R. McLean, owner of the *Cincinnati Enquirer* and the *Washington Post,* provided Harding with a safe house. This was the "little green house on K Street," a short walk from the White House, where Harding's cronies met, drank, played billiards and poker, and, behind Harding's back, plotted their nefarious schemes. There was another, even safer house for Harding and his cronies outside town: a hunting lodge at Deer Park Creek, unknown even to The Duchess. All the while, the ritual of Prohibition was being ostentatiously observed. When the dreadnought *Washington* was launched in 1924, a congressman's daughter broke a bottle of river water over its bow, and Dr. Charles Foster Kent of Yale was hired to rewrite the Bible, removing all references to wine.[7]

The scandals of the Harding years came in quick succession. Under Woodrow Wilson, 13,000 post office jobs had been removed from patronage and placed under nonpolitical Civil Service regulations. Harding, under Republican pressure, annulled the ruling. The officials were fired, and the jobs parceled out to political appointees. But this was negligible compared to the scams Harding's cronies indulged in with total impunity.

Colonel "Charlie" Forbes was a close friend of Harding's — perhaps the most constant member of his poker-playing circle of intimates. Harding appointed him Health secretary and head of the Veterans Bureau, a sizeable department with a $550 million annual budget. Forbes proceeded to asset-strip his own department with all the skill of a Mafia boss. Harding's sister, Carolyn Votaw, who had married a Seventh-Day Adventist clergyman (Harding had appointed *him* federal superintendent of prisons), knew Forbes well, and introduced him to a friend of hers, a wealthy construction company executive called Elias Mortimer and his very pretty, ambitious wife Kate. There was a pressing need for veterans' hospitals, and Mortimer promised Forbes huge kickbacks for every building contract awarded to his firm. Forbes let him see the supposedly secret rival bids. For every new hospital, Forbes got a cash payment of $50,000 and up. On the pretext of looking at possible sites, the threesome took expensive trips all over America, where Forbes was lavishly entertained (and also slept with Mortimer's wife), with Mortimer footing the bill.

Forbes milked the Veterans Administration in other ways. He paid hugely inflated prices for hospital land (up to $95,000 for sites whose market value was $17,000), splitting the difference with the sellers. He disposed of brand-new hospital equipment at token prices, in return for kickbacks, then replaced what he had sold for practically nothing with brand-new items for which the Veterans Administration paid hugely inflated prices, again getting a cut. In subsequent investigations he was shown to have paid ten times the market price for 35,000 gallons of floor cleaner and 32,000 gallons of floor wax — a hundred-year supply. In all he was shown to have squandered $33 million — or several hundred million dollars in current values.

The trashing of the Veterans Administration became common knowledge. Harding duly learned of his poker buddy's practices, and flew into a rage, but protected him from the law by sending him abroad on a spurious mission. Although Forbes was eventually sentenced (in 1925) to two years in jail and fined $10,000, his real problems only began after Harding's death.

Albert Fall, secretary of the Interior, another close Harding crony, was resourceful in other, more imaginative ways. He was an intimate friend of two oil tycoons, Edward Doheny and Harry Sinclair, both, hardly coincidentally, heavy contributors to Harding's campaign fund. Before World War I, President William Howard Taft had ordered large tracts of oil-bearing land to be handed over to the U.S. Navy to ensure adequate supplies at the lowest possible cost. Thanks to a three-way scam involving Navy Secretary Edwin Dealey, Interior Secretary Albert Fall, and — in the wings — Justice Department Secretary Daugherty, the two oil tycoons ended up with most of the Navy's priceless oil-rich land.

As a first step, Navy Secretary Dealey (who later had to resign) had the site ownerships secretly transferred from the Navy to the Department of the Interior. Then Fall worked out a deal to hand them over to Doheny and Sinclair. There was a semblance of legality: in exchange for the land, Doheny and Sinclair were to build storage tanks for the Navy and provide the Department of the Interior with oil certificates (at favorable rates) to be used by U.S. Navy ships.

These arrangements were not publicized, and there were no bids from competing oilmen — Fall invoking the overriding need for secrecy in "matters affecting national defense." He himself received kickbacks amounting to several hundred thousand dollars, resigning shortly afterward to take up a well-paid sinecure in Sinclair Oil. The payoff was a tiny fraction of the hundreds of millions of dollars that Doheny and Sinclair made out of the scam, known since as the Teapot Dome scandal.

Daugherty, a later investigation showed, must have been aware of Fall's scheme (the Justice Department was required to give its stamp of approval to deals of this importance), but nothing was ever proved. Only later did it become known that he had invested in Sinclair stock before it started booming as a result of the Navy deal. Daugherty was a difficult man to catch in flagrante, operating as he did behind his front man Jess Smith. He was also utterly ruthless with the small handful of liberal Republican politicians who tried to bring him down.

Later, as investigation after investigation revealed the scandalous depths of the Harding administration, Daugherty would claim — a tactic later emulated by Senator McCarthy — that there was "abundant proof" that it was all part of "the hellish designs of the Communist International." When Senators Burton K. Wheeler and Smith W. Brookhart did succeed in launching an investigation into his Justice Department activities, he told the *New York Times* (the interview was published on April 24, 1924) that

> . . . the two senators, who spent last summer in Russia with their friends, were part of an effort to capture, by deceit and design, as many members of the Senate as possible and to spread through Washington and the cloakrooms of Congress a poison gas as deadly as that which sapped and destroyed brave soldiers in the late war. The enemy is at the gate, he [Wheeler] aims at nothing short of the overthrow of the institutions which are your protection and mine against tyranny.

Even by the lax standards of the 1920s, Daugherty's conduct while attorney general was remarkable, not just for the extent of his corruption but for its eclecticism. No transaction was too trivial for him. In the Washington brownstone on H Street Daugherty shared with Smith, the Armour meat processing company regularly delivered sides of bacon and ham, while uniformed police officers paid for past and future favors with confiscated liquor. No one, at the time, seems to have been preoccupied by the discrepancy between Daugherty's salary ($12,000 a year) and his household expenses ($50,000 at least, for he entertained heavily) — and Smith did not draw an official salary at all.

Roxy Stinson, Jess Smith's ex-wife, testifying before the Senate investigation on Daugherty, was later to be an unwilling but inexhaustible source of information. She told how Smith had boasted to her of the windfall Daugherty expected to collect from the proceeds of a pirated film of the Dempsey-Carpentier match. Smith had acquired the film on Daugherty's behalf and expected to sell it all over America. She remembered Smith telling her that Daugherty's friends had made $33 million in five days over the Sinclair Oil land deal. "Were you [i.e., Daugherty and Smith] in on it?" she asked him. "No," said Smith, "that's what we're sore about." But she also remembered how, shortly after the Sinclair Oil deal, Smith had shown up in Ohio where she lived, and proudly boasted that he had seventy-five $1,000 bills on him. She told of Daugherty and Smith's innumerable expensive junkets to New York, paid for by Joe Weber, of Weber and Fields, a big theatrical entrepreneur, who provided them with lavish accommodation, theater tickets, "and all sorts of other favors." It turned out that Weber wanted parole for his wife's brother, currently in jail. But Daugherty wanted hard cash as well as a good time in New York, and she remembered Smith telling her: "I don't know whether we'll bother with him or not. He is awful cheap and wants something for nothing."

In this immediate postwar period, there was a great deal of litigation arising out of irregular wartime contracts and seizures made under the Enemy Appropriations Act. As attorney general, Daugherty was at the center of things: he could expedite, delay, and settle cases virtually at will. In some cases, documents simply disappeared. Captain H. L. Scaife, a former Justice Department investigator, told Senator Wheeler how he had resigned in disgust after discovering that his patient investigation into the Standard Aircraft Company affair had been mysteriously "lost." The company had been paid millions of dollars during the war to provide fighter aircraft, but not a single plane had been made or delivered. It was later discovered that a representative for the Japanese Mitsui company, which had acquired the Standard Aircraft Company, had met with Jess Smith. Money had changed hands, and the proceedings just stopped.

Daugherty was equally diligent in speeding cases up, for a suitable fee. The $6 million assets of the American Metal Company, owned by the Metallgesellschaft und Metall Bank in Frankfurt, had been seized during the war. Daugherty and Fall, the secretary of the Interior, used John King, a middleman who often worked for Jess Smith, to bargain with German lawyers. $441,000 changed hands. King took a fee, with the bulk of the money going to Jess Smith. As Daugherty's bagman, he is thought to have handed over some of it to the attorney general himself.

As Senator Wheeler found out to his cost, proving Daugherty's financial involvement in these scams was not easy. There was a simple reason why Jess Smith was so invaluable to Daugherty: Smith's brother, Mal, owned the Midland National Bank of Ohio, and it was through this small bank that a lot of the money was laundered. The bank was capitalized at only $100,000, but received huge deposits regularly. When investigators finally succeeded in getting permission to look at the records, Mal Smith destroyed them, but not before Wheeler discovered that there were large fluctuating deposits there in Daugherty's name.

But Daugherty and Smith's biggest money-earner came from Prohibition. Millions of dollars passed through Jess Smith's hands provided by those shrewd enough, and wealthy enough, to buy immunity from prosecution. George Remus may not have been Smith's biggest single contributor, but he was the most notorious — for the simple reason that when, finally, his huge cash payments failed to buy him the promised exemption, he decided to spill the beans.

9

REMUS UNRAVELS

Every bootlegger, Prohibition agent, nightclub owner, and affluent private customer in the Midwest knew about Remus, his parties,
his ostentatious generosity, and his inexhaustible supply of high-quality
liquor. He was convinced he was untouchable. All of the politicians
and law enforcement agencies of the city of Cincinnati were in his
pocket, and he had what he knew was a unique relationship with the
"deputy Attorney General," Jess Smith. But his luck was not to last,
and when it went, like Job, he was assailed with every conceivable
woe.

There were a number of reasons for his downfall — his overcon-
fidence and excessive greed, to begin with. In 1922, he was well on
the way to establishing a whiskey monopoly. This was not to the liking
of other bootleggers with underworld connections, and he may well
have been the victim of a conspiracy to bring him down at all costs. His
German origins, too, were almost certainly held against him in these
hysterically anti-German years, though his immediate fall stemmed also
from the ingenuity of the two people in the world he found he could
not bribe — the Prohibition directors of Indiana and Kentucky. But

most of all his nemesis came when Jess Smith, Daugherty's front man and operative, fearful that he was about to be indicted at long last and unwilling to betray his mentor, committed suicide in December of 1923.

When, a year later, Senator Wheeler finally persuaded the Senate to look into Daugherty's record, Remus became one of the star witnesses of the investigative committee. His cross-examination explained why he had been so sure he would never come to grief, even if indicted. Remus told the committee how his lawyer, Elijah Zoline, introduced him to Smith and then "gracefully withdrew."

WHEELER: Did you know he was close to Daugherty?

REMUS: Well, having practiced criminal law, we knew these matters. It was a matter of public record that he was pretty close to the Attorney General.

WHEELER: What did he say?

REMUS: He said that for a consideration he would obtain permits, if I would pay him so much for the permits per case.

WHEELER: What did he say with reference to your being indicted in these matters, or prosecuted?

REMUS: That there would never be any conviction — maybe a prosecution, but no ultimate conviction, that no one would ever have to go to the penitentiary.

WHEELER: How much did you pay him on this first occasion?

REMUS: Fifty thousand dollars.

WHEELER: And the money paid to Jess Smith was for protection, was it not?

REMUS: Yes, he was to do what he could, to make connections as far as the withdrawal of these permits was concerned.

WHEELER: Did the payment involve him getting the permits for you?

REMUS: No, that was a different arrangement. The person withdrawing the liquor would pay $15 to $21 a case. A case contains three gallons. That you would consider overage expenses. That would be in addition to the $21 to $25 a case you would pay to the warehouseman.

WHEELER: Did Smith get any of that?

REMUS: Yes, he got about — we figured at the time he and I talked — about $1.50 to $2.50 a case.

WHEELER: Are payments of that kind included in this $250,000 to $300,000 that you paid him (for protection)?

REMUS: Oh, no, Senator.

WHEELER: That was in addition?

REMUS: Yes.

Remus told the committee of meetings with Smith in hotels in New York, Washington, Cincinnati, Indianapolis, and Columbus, Ohio (the dates, times, and places had been carefully logged), each meeting invariably concluding with cash payments, or checks made out to "pay cash." On one occasion, in Indianapolis, he saw Smith and Daugherty together but Daugherty was never directly involved in the transactions. Wheeler asked Remus whether there was any friendship between the two men, or was it "a pure-cold-blooded proposition." "Not a bit of sentiment attached to it," Remus replied. Again and again, the Senate investigators returned to the subject of Remus's promised immunity.

WHEELER: Did you discuss with him anything with reference to your indictment? [Remus was currently in jail.]

REMUS: Yes. The Department of Justice would put up a vigorous battle, but ultimately I would never see the penitentiary.

WHEELER: And that vigorous prosecution was going to be done just as a blind? Was that it?

REMUS: I am sorry to say that is not true, Senator.

WHEELER: But that is what he told you?

REMUS: Yes. He said that while there might be a conviction before the jury, the matter would go to the Court of Appeals and the case would be reversed.

WHEELER: Did Jess Smith not say to you that it did not make any difference if the Court of Appeals did confirm it, he could get you out of it?

REMUS: Yes.

WHEELER: When did he say this?

REMUS: A short time after my conviction — May 1922.

WHEELER: Even after the conviction?

REMUS: Absolutely.

WHEELER: He told you you would never serve a day, that he would see to it that you got out of it?

REMUS: Absolutely.

WHEELER: Where was this?

REMUS: At the Washington Hotel.

WHEELER: Did you pay him any money at this time?

REMUS: About twenty or thirty thousand dollars.

WHEELER: The way he would get this suspension of sentence or anything would be through the Attorney General?

REMUS: Yes. He said he was assured there would be no ultimate sending away of Remus or his men to a penitentiary.

WHEELER: And who did he say assured him of that?

REMUS: The general.

WHEELER: He called him the general, did he?

REMUS: Yes, sir.

WHEELER: How many times did he tell you that?

REMUS: I should say twice or three times.

WHEELER: Did he tell you that if the Supreme Court affirmed that decision you would still be granted a pardon, or that you would never have to serve a day in jail?

REMUS: Yes, he said that. On account of his friendship with the general, he said he would do everything he could to see that the matter would be reversed.

The indictment that Jess Smith promised would be quashed was the work of the two "untouchables": Burt Morgan, the Prohibition director of Indiana, and Sam Collins, Prohibition director of Kentucky. Luck was on their side. In 1921, a regular Death Valley Farm customer, Nathan J. Goldman, was flagged down in Indiana with cases of whiskey in his car. In court, he pleaded guilty, and received a $500 fine and a ninety-day jail sentence. In the time-honored bootlegging tradition, he had refused to say where he had obtained his liquor, but Morgan was certain it had come from Death Valley Farm, which he had heard about, though he knew nothing of its whereabouts. Since it was in another state, the chances of involving Remus seemed slim.

But Morgan went to see Goldman in jail and proposed his immediate release in return for his cooperation. Goldman accepted. He even agreed to take Morgan by car to Death Valley Farm to show him where it was. They drove there, turned around, and went back to Indiana. Unlike Cincinnati, Indiana really was a dry state, and its agents, under the "untouchable" Morgan, were less ready to be paid off, but Morgan knew he would have a hard time getting the cooperation of his Cincinnati colleagues.

Another "untouchable," Sam Collins, the Kentucky Prohibition director, was also on Remus's track. His agents had, by chance, arrested two runners from a Chicago saloon after their cargo of whiskey spilled into the street after a car crash. They too agreed to cooperate, and admitted it had come from Death Valley Farm.

Morgan and Collins got together. Since they had no jurisdiction outside their own states, they knew they would have to get the Cincinnati Bureau to issue a search warrant, and to do that they would have to trick their corrupt Cincinnati colleagues into cooperating with them. Once more, luck was on their side. Although Remus invariably insisted on cash payments so that his involvement could not be traced, he had made an exception for Goldman, who had paid for his consignment in part with a $250 check to Conners. By oversight, after Goldman's arrest, it had not been canceled, so here was invaluable proof.

Morgan and Collins, and their teams, came quietly and unannounced to Cincinnati and set up headquarters in the Sinton Hotel. They called their Cincinnati colleague, Robert E. Flora, and asked him to join them without telling him the reason for their presence. Only when Flora showed up was he told that the purpose of their visit was a raid on Death Valley Farm. After studying the evidence, he had no alternative but to issue a search warrant. Virtually under house arrest himself and unable to make a telephone call (Morgan and Collins were well aware that the Cincinnati Prohibition Bureau would tip Remus off if given the chance), Flora was compelled to go along with them on the raid.

The raiders used unmarked cars that Sunday noon, and did not have to use force, as the men at the gate assumed they were customers. Once inside, they showed their search warrant, and quickly discovered the cellars, the bottling plant, and hundreds of gallons of whiskey.

Conners and Gehrum had been to the races the day before, and did not show up at Death Valley Farm until late that Sunday afternoon. The search was still in progress. Conners pretended he was simply "looking for a friend," and he and Gehrum left in a hurry. They immediately drove to the Remus mansion to tell him of the raid.

With his extensive network of contacts, Remus had in fact heard rumors that a strange Prohibition agent was in town, but was not too concerned. Gehrum had told him there were hardly any stocks of liquor inside the farm. He had lied, it was later revealed, because he had some of his own customers lined up and wanted to make a profit on the side. Nevertheless, Remus sent a messenger down to the farm early on Sunday morning, to collect some money. The messenger was told to be sure and tell the men on duty to clear out all of the liquor, because there were strange men in town. The messenger forgot to relay the message.

Remus's first reaction, on hearing of the raid in progress, was to mount an armed expedition and rout the raiders with guns. A weeping Imogene begged him not to ("I know you'll be killed! Then what will I do?"). Remus arranged bail for those on the farm who had been arrested. Three weeks later, Conners and Remus were themselves arraigned. In May of 1922, Remus, Conners, and eleven of his staff went on trial, and were found guilty. Remus received a two-year jail sentence, and the maximum $10,000 fine. Conners and the others got sentences ranging from one year to eighteen months and fines ranging from $5,000 to $10,000. All appealed to a higher court and were allowed further bail until the next hearing.

Remus was still not overly worried, convinced that the protection money he had spent would prevent any of them from ever going to jail. "When you have Washington fixed," he told Anderson, "you don't need to go below." Even with Death Valley Farm closed, his five other halfway houses — in Reading and Hamilton, Pennsylvania; Glendale, California; Buffalo, New York; and New York City — were doing well. He carried on business almost as usual, if on a slightly smaller scale. But his extraordinary luck had deserted him, and with Smith's suicide, he had lost his expensive link to Daugherty. The Supreme Court refused to consider his case, and in January of 1924, all appeals exhausted, Remus, Conners, and his eleven subordinates began their jail sentences in Atlanta.

Remus was engaged in another major operation during the time he remained free on appeal: he had become part of a St. Louis and Indianapolis syndicate that had bought the Jack Daniel's distillery. His partners, prominent local politicians and state officials, including a congressman and the St. Louis director of Internal Revenue, assured him that their stature and influence guaranteed them all full immunity.

It was while he was in jail that this syndicate not only tricked him out of any return on his investment but behaved so ineptly that they would later be arrested, charged, and convicted. Against Remus's advice, instead of paying expensive intermediaries for withdrawal permits, and proceeding by stealth, a few cases at a time, they simply emptied the Jack Daniel's distillery of its 31,000 gallons of whiskey, replacing the barrels with water and wood alcohol. Then they committed what Remus regarded as the most unpardonable crime of all: before selling the Jack Daniel's whiskey to private customers, they watered it down — to such an extent that the purchasers demanded their money back. The case went against them, and the sensational trial that followed (Remus was originally slated to be a prosecution witness) was probably triggered by furious customers in high places.

Remus's departure from Cincinnati to an Atlanta jail was one of the highlights of the social season. Remus, in pearl-gray suit, spats, and diamond tiepin, and Imogene by his side, turned the trip into yet another party. Accompanied by federal marshals (whom he treated like honored guests), Imogene, George, Conners, and the eleven other sentenced men boarded a specially hired luxury railroad car, hitched to the regular Atlanta train. On board was a specially hired chef. Waiters served gourmet meals. On his arrival, knowing he would have to wear prison garb, Remus presented the porter with his silk shirts and reporters and photographers were on hand to interview the "Bootleg King." Remus told them he hoped to lose weight in prison.

By this time he had put his affairs in order. Imogene got a huge check to cover all expenses for the next two years. Remus also gave her power of attorney, so that she could run his business for him while he was in jail. That was to prove his biggest mistake — and the cause of even greater problems.

10

THE ADVENTURERS

Coast Guard to Long Island fisherman: "See you tonight, Charlie."
Fisherman to Coast Guard: "Not if I can help it!"[1]

While George Remus was taking advantage of loopholes in the Volstead Act to build his bootlegging empire, others, more adventurously, became smugglers — and folk heroes. The very history of the United States gave them considerable legitimacy: as lawyers constantly reminded the courts, John Hancock, a founder of the Republic and one of the signatories of the Declaration of Independence, had himself been a smuggler, openly defying the British and their hated Stamp Act at the start of the Revolutionary War. He soon became the rumrunners' patron saint. Lawyers also used to compare their clients to those heroes who had patriotically challenged the pre–Civil War Fugitive Slave Act, smuggling runaway slaves out of the South and into Canada.

In actual fact, importing liquor into America during Prohibition involved more than rum-running. It required considerable complex advance planning, usually in more than one continent, in a pre-satellite era when transatlantic communications were far more easy to monitor. Just as present-day drug traffickers constitute only part of a sophisticated organization with international ramifications — involving networks of farmers, middlemen, and money launderers from as far away as Afghanistan, Lebanon, Myanmar (ex-Burma), and Pakistan — so the rumrunners, from 1920 onward, were only bit players in a series of complicated, often European-based, operations.

But the forerunners of today's drug barons and money launderers were not underworld figures but respectable merchant banks and brokerage houses in Paris, London, Bremen, Hamburg, and Kiel, with equally respectable commission agents in Africa, Canada, Latin America, the West Indies, and the French islands of St. Pierre and Miquelon, off the Canadian coast, where liquor was exceptionally cheap (a quart of gin cost 25 cents, rum 50 cents a gallon, and a bottle of champagne $1). Prohibition would give St. Pierre and Miquelon a level of prosperity that is still remembered there with nostalgia. They are the one place in the world where their benefactor, Al Capone, even at this remove in time, remains a hero. Many of the houses still standing there are made out of the wooden cases the champagne bottles originally came in.

Increasingly, U.S. diplomats abroad were enlisted in the war against bootleggers — so much so that they began complaining that they were spending more time on anti-bootlegging activities than on their regular duties. Washington received a constant stream of information from U.S. consulates around the world relaying details of suspect ships' departures, cargoes, and probable destinations. A report from the U.S. Consulate in Copenhagen is typical of many. "The German steamer *Apis* has sailed from Copenhagen with 437,000 liters of liquor," it informed the State Department in 1923. The cargo was "falsely billed as destined for Africa but the intent is to smuggle the cargo into the United States." The reluctance of America's allies to help stamp out the liquor traffic caused diplomatic rifts similar to those that would later plague America's relations with her Latin American partners over drugs.

America's neighbors all profited from Prohibition — to the extent that European shippers of gin, whiskey and champagne began shipping stocks previously sent directly to the United States to convenient relay stations such as Mexico, Canada, and St. Pierre and Miquelon. Export records from the famous French champagne firm Moet et Chandon show that its champagne consignments to Canada increased more than tenfold from 1922 to 1929. After the end of Prohibition, exports to Canada dropped dramatically.[2]

The Bahamas became a privileged halfway house — the Medellín of the Prohibition era. Sir Harry Cordeaux, governor of the Bahamas, in a speech in Montreal in 1921, openly acknowledged that "the healthy condition of the island's finances is largely due to its liquor traffic" — so much so that 250,000 pounds were spent on harbor improvements. In the House of Commons, some teetotaling Scottish MPs criticized the British government's passivity. W. G. A. Ormsby-Gore, Colonial Office under-secretary, told the House that "practically the whole of the large increase in imports of wine and spirits into the Bahamas last year [1922] was due to Prohibition in America." Asked whether, "for the sake of friendship with America," these colonies could be rationed, Ormsby-Gore was brutally frank. "No," he said, for the traffic "would only go to Haiti or some other convenient island belonging to another nation."

To the law enforcers' fury, many prominent Americans openly aided, abetted, and praised the lawbreakers. Prohibition had only been in force eighteen months when Democratic Senator Owen Stanley broke into song on the floor of the Senate, reading into the Congressional Record the popular "Song of the Moonshiners" (to the tune of "My Country, 'Tis of Thee"):

> My country, 'tis of thee,
> Land of grape juice and tea,
> Of thee I sing.
> Land where we all have tried
> To break the laws and lied!
> From every mountain-side
> The bootlegs spring. . . .

Roy A. Haynes, the first Prohibition commissioner, wrote, in his book *Prohibition Inside Out*,[3] that "rum and narcotics smuggling, evasion of the immigration laws, and diamond smuggling run hand in hand," but that liquor was by far the most lucrative cargo. Over fifty ships of 5,000 tons and over operated out of the Bahamas in 1922, "the shippers of their lawless fleets drawn chiefly from the scum of the American waterfronts." As would be the case later with narcotics, some investments were virtually risk-free, on a "forward buying" credit plan. "If the runner is known, the local liquor importer will trust you for as many cases as you care to gamble on at $5 a case. You pay him the cost price per case until the vessel returns with the money — one of them cleared $200,000 in a few months."

Investors found as many ways of circumventing the law at sea as Remus did on land, and the methods used were strikingly similar to those used by embargo-evading arms dealers today. A Bahamian shipping owner got clearance to ship liquor to a fictitious British, Canadian, or French port. If apprehended within territorial waters, reduced in 1923 from twelve miles to three, the ship's captain simply claimed this was merely an innocent voyage between two foreign ports. After disposing of the cargo, he entered a U.S. port for clearance "on ballast," to refuel, pick up a legitimate cargo, and go on his way.

Because the U.S. Coast Guard had the right to board and search suspect vessels flying the American flag, even on the high seas, there was a rush to switch to flags of convenience — a standard procedure to get around the law. "A British merchant institutes libel proceedings against a certain (American) yacht owner who has defaulted on stores or debt, and claims he can't pay. His boat is sold. The British merchant buys it. It is now a British ship, rum-running with the same crew." Once at sea, it also became common practice to alter ships' names after a few round trips, to confuse the Coast Guard.

After the 1929 Wall Street crash, bootleggers had a huge choice of luxury yachts — the former toys of once-wealthy speculators. As Sally Rand, later the famous "fan dancer" star, recalled,

> These beautiful yachts that cost half a million dollars were sitting around (on the West Coast) with barnacles on them. These are the people who jumped out of windows. Who's gonna buy a yacht? A man came up to me and said, "Hey, any of these yachts for sale?" I said: "Are you kiddin'? They're all for sale." The guy was a bootlegger. So I sold half-million-dollar yachts to bootleggers. For five or ten thousand dollars. And took my six percent commission on them. Beautiful.[4]

The bootleggers, she said, "decorated them with pretty girls in bathing suits, like going out for a little sail. Load up and come back. . . . The interiors were done in rosewood, gold handles on the toilets and all that jazz, great oil paintings in the salons. They're now jammed up with loads and loads of wet alcohol . . . the interiors of them were gutted and ruined."

There were still easier ways of circumventing Prohibition. Just as Remus legitimately obtained B Certificates (permits) to withdraw liquor from distilleries for medicinal purposes, American distillers could, just as legitimately, export their own liquor in bulk for so-called "medicinal use" abroad. Hundreds of thousands of gallons of whiskey thus purchased, on paper at least, by businessmen in Scotland, British Columbia, New Brunswick, Germany, Cuba, and even Tijuana never reached their fictitious destinations.

> If we believed the tales of all who apply for liquor permits [wrote Haynes], we would naturally come to the absurd conclusion that the whole world is sick and desperately in need of distilled spirits. . . . Does anyone believe that Scotland, home of whiskey, is really in need of 66,000 gallons of American whiskey for non-beverage purposes? . . . It is the irony of ironies, a wet world, come to dry America to beg for liquor.

As with the later war on drugs, the goal of the law enforcers was to catch the truly major operator. "The conviction of one such," Haynes wrote, "is worth the conviction of twelve small operators. Their identities are mostly well known — but they have to be caught in the act, to establish evidence which will prove guilt in the courts." As the recent BCCI scandal showed, current drug operations have also involved at least one established bank, but during the Prohibition years the list of prestigious British and American banks providing services to rumrunners, knowingly or unknowingly, was huge. In operations involving major players, by no means confined to the underworld, money was deposited in banks in advance, held in trust, and only remitted after shipments were completed, the transactions invariably referred to as "unspecified goods or commodities."

Haynes wrote that "one finds names that once epitomized honor and power and community esteem steeped in the same befouling brew with names of thieves, thugs and murderers." Joe Kennedy, father of President John F. Kennedy, was one of those "epitomizing honor and power" who could not resist an occasional risk-free flutter, though he was careful to hide behind a screen of dummy companies.

While bankers and entrepreneurs on both sides of the Atlantic got rich on the proceeds, a new mythical hero emerged as part of Prohibition folklore: the risk-taking, devil-may-care rumrunner, even though reality seldom measured up to the legend. At least one of them was a woman. "Spanish Marie" assumed command of the boat she renamed *Kid Boots* when her husband and ship's captain fell overboard after a surfeit of cargo sampling (rumor had it that she may have given him a final push).

> She strutted about with a revolver strapped to her waist, a big knife stuck in her belt and a red bandanna tied round her head. Legend had it that she was about as tough as she looked. She was captured in March 1928 while unloading liquor at Coconut Grove, and was released on five hundred dollars bail on the plea that she must take care of her babies. The bail was increased to $3,500 when investigators found the children at home with a nurse and Spanish Marie at a speakeasy.[5]

Although millions of gallons of liquor ended up on American shores, rum-running expeditions all too often came to grief as a result of incompetence, communication failures, greed, and mutual mistrust, with expeditors and ships' captains sharing the blame.

In America's National Archives are records of several instances of undercover penetration wrecking otherwise perfect plans. Everett S. Allen, in *The Black Ships*, tells the story of a somewhat boastful London entrepreneur, Thomas Godman of the Schooners Association of London, who bragged of his unique relations with corrupt American officials. He claimed to have access to detailed Coast Guard surveillance schedules. But his letters were intercepted and his operations went terribly wrong. In 1927, he reported "a rush of orders from my friends for whiskey to meet the Christmas trade" and made plans for a $488,700 cargo to unload off Montauk Point, at the extreme tip of Long Island — a favorite landing place. But crew members deserted, fought one another, got drunk on pilfered cargo, and almost ran their boat, the *Tom August*, aground. Others went on strike or jumped ship when they learned that their wives had not been paid as promised. Godman's cargo failed to meet up with its expected customers either at sea or on shore until the crew members who remained on board began taking cases ashore themselves — and not returning. Profits on a successful run were huge, but only if it did not take too long, and the *Tom August*, cruising up and down the Long Island coast for weeks, cost Godman far more than he could afford to lose. He retired from the game a near bankrupt.[6]

Although rum-running ships such as the *Tom August* feared pirate hijackers far more than the Coast Guard, ships' officers seldom trusted even their own crews. There was always the possibility they would be tempted to themselves hijack the ship and sell the liquor. Rival syndicates also represented a constant threat. The potential rewards made for a climate aboard of distrust and permanent, brooding violence. The rumrunner *Mulhouse* was owned by a powerful French company that maintained a permanent sales representative in New York during the first few Prohibition years. It was boarded at gunpoint in Sheepshead Bay. Of its cargo of 23,000 cases of liquor, 7,000 were transferred aboard the hijacking schooner, the remaining 16,000 cases sold off to unidentified buyers in powerful speedboats as the French crew was held hostage below decks. The French syndicate's sales representative had been set up by rivals posing as respectable wholesale buyers. A mysterious bootlegger known only as "Big Eddie" was suspected of masterminding the scam.

Norwegian crews had an exceptionally bad reputation. The Coast Guard cutter *Seneca* boarded the Norwegian merchant ship *Sagatind* off the East Coast. The ship was found to be carrying 43,000 cases of liquor and $26,000 in cash. "All of *Sagatind*'s crew were stupefied with drink except for three whose jaws were broken. One man had a broken leg and many had black eyes."[7]

Although the East Coast — especially the Hamptons, Nantucket, and Martha's Vineyard — were favored off-loading areas, Puget Sound was also a favorite bootleggers' haunt, being convenient for smuggling operations initiated either in Mexico or elsewhere in the Pacific. Liquor cargoes ended up in Oregon, Washington State, and California. In some cases, Coast Guard crews responsible for policing the area actually did some rum-running themselves.

Increasingly, as the rumrunners stepped up their activities, their predators did likewise. A new breed of pirates, preying on officially commissioned smuggling ships, began intercepting cargoes, killing crews, and either sinking the vessels or leaving them disabled and motionless in the water — twentieth-century equivalents of the mysteriously abandoned *Marie Celeste*. Pirate ships operating out of Nova Scotia were particularly feared.

As with later drug operations, law enforcement agencies managed, with some success, to infiltrate the bootlegging world. One undercover agent (code name: London) surfaced in Bremen, posing as a member of a European consortium eager to invest in a rum-running operation, and managed to convince one Wilhelm Huebers, of the respectable German Products and Trade Corporation, that he was a bona fide speculator. The German firm lost its entire shipment.

The Prohibition Bureau also made considerable use of informers. Agents were authorized to pay snitches two dollars a day for information. The newly formed FBI was more generous, but the smugglers, like drug dealers later, were often one step ahead of them — they too adept at disinformation. Haynes cites the example of "Hippy" Werner, a well-known bootlegger, who told the FBI that the British trawler *Minerva*, out of Barbados, was about to land 4,000 cases of Scotch whiskey at Warwick Beach in the middle of the night, and that the landing operation would be protected by three Coast Guard boats in the smugglers' pay. A major operation was mounted, and the cargo was seized. But the *Minerva* turned out to be a decoy boat with a cargo of cheap methyl alcohol flavored with fusel oil. While the FBI and reliable Coast Guard units were busy with the *Minerva*, other boats unloaded huge amounts of valuable Scotch whiskey further down the Rhode Island coast.

The best-known, most revered rumrunner of all time was Bill McCoy, who gave rise to the well-known expression "the real McCoy," which originally referred to the high quality of his liquor. A former merchant navy first mate — who, with his brother, opened his own boatyard in Jacksonville, Florida, after the First World War, custom-building luxurious speedboats for millionaires — McCoy became a bootlegger for the money, but also out of a passion for sailing. He was fonder of the *Arethusa*, the spectacularly beautiful sloop he was able to buy with the profits of his first few runs, than he was of money, even though his returns were considerable.

McCoy made the Bahamas, where whiskey cost a mere $8 a case, his base. Total expenses for a run from the Bahamas to Martha's Vineyard and back amounted to $100,000 ($40,000 for the whiskey, $60,000 for the crew and the ship's running expenses), the average net profit per trip amounting to $300,000. The *Arethusa* (like most rum-running vessels in the West Indies area, it flew the Red Ensign) was not only a beautiful ship to look at, but was better equipped, and better run, than any other bootlegging boat. McCoy ran a tight ship. Although a reporter who went aboard later wrote that "the crew resembled as wicked a gang of cutthroats as ever bade a victim to walk the plank," they were intensely loyal to him. Pay was good, discipline stern, drinking aboard forbidden, and sales techniques highly sophisticated. McCoy's motto was "We do business day and night." Because storage space was at a premium, he packaged the liquor in pyramid-shaped, six-bottle burlap-wrapped packs rather than in wooden cases, and these were then wrapped in container-size gunnysack bales.

Others imitated him, and such was his reputation that all over America, unscrupulous domestic moonshiners, pretending that their whiskey was "straight off the boat," wrapped *their* inferior, adulterated liquor in similar burlap bags, often soaking them in salt water to give them an authentic "McCoy" appearance.

The *Arethusa* was a floating liquor store, with shelves of samples for visitors. Tasting was encouraged, but only two prospective buyers were allowed aboard at the same time — not so much to prevent law enforcement raids as to deter the hijackers, almost as numerous on the high seas as they were outside Remus's Death Valley Farm. On deck, a swiveling machine-gun emplacement was prominently in view, and every time an unidentified speedboat hove to alongside the *Arethusa,* it remained trained on the visitors throughout their shopping expedition.

Despite his precautions, McCoy's luck did not hold. He had to abandon the *Arethusa* to subordinates for a while, living as a fugitive from justice with friendly, discreet Indians on remote reservations because "they don't ask questions, they haven't any particular regard for the law."[8] Eventually his luck ran out altogether. In November of 1924, the Coast Guard cutter *Seneca* fired on the *Arethusa* off Seabright, New Jersey, and rather than risk losing his boat, McCoy surrendered, was charged, and went to jail.

Another bootlegger who achieved mythical status was Seattle-based Roy Olmstead. When Prohibition was introduced in Washington State (ahead of the Volstead Act), he was the youngest lieutenant on the Seattle police force. His superiors were unaware that their most promising detective was moonlighting as a bootlegger, using his police connections across the Canadian border to buy his supplies from trusted middlemen, some of whom were also serving or retired police officers.

He first came to prominence in March of 1920 when Prohibition agents staged an ambush on Brown's Bay, near Meadowdale, and seized a huge cargo of Olmstead's liquor. Fined and dismissed from the force, he immediately became a full-time operator, the head of an eleven-man syndicate running an operation that included not only navigators, delivery crews, and salesmen, but bookkeepers, many of them serving police officials.

The Canadian government cynically exploited the Volstead Act, officially imposing an export duty ($20 a case) on all liquor destined for the United States. Olmstead arranged for his consignments to be shipped (on paper) to Mexico, avoiding the levy. This made it possible for him to undersell his competitors, and he boasted that his brand-name Scotch and Canadian whiskey was barely more expensive in dry Seattle than in Canada. The *New York Times* described Olmstead as "the king of one of the most gigantic rum-running conspiracies in the country." The scale of his operations was huge. In 1922, the Prohibition Bureau estimated that 1.5 million gallons of bootleg whiskey came from Canada.

By 1924, Olmstead was a millionaire, dealing exclusively with wholesalers. With net profits of at least $200,000 a month, he acquired a palatial home in Mount Baker, Seattle's choicest suburb, as well as the American Radio Telephone Company, Seattle's first radio station (KFOX), which his wife Elsie ran from their home. Like Remus, Olmstead entertained on a lavish scale, and, like Remus, acquired a new glamorous companion. The elite of Seattle, including the mayor, were proud to be his friends. As a Seattle newspaper commented in 1924, "It made a man feel important to casually remark: 'as Roy Olmstead was telling me today . . .'"

His police connections were invaluable, as the following wiretap extract proves:

> Roy phoned the police station. M — came to the phone and said: "Hello, Roy, what's on your mind?" Roy said: "One of your fellows picked up one of my boys." M — replied: "Who is it?" Roy replied that it was B — "I don't give a damn what they do but I want to know before he is booked." M — replied, "I'll take care of it for you, Roy."

In another wiretapping extract, a policeman was heard telling Olmstead that he had arrested one of his men. "He was loaded clear to the axle. I could not do anything else." Olmstead quickly got to know that his phones were tapped, and exploited this to his advantage. He started giving fake orders on the phone, using an untapped telephone booth to give his staff genuine instructions.

But eventually the law caught up with him. Mabel Willebrandt, the deputy attorney general who pursued Olmstead as diligently as she did Remus, was convinced that his radio station was used to transmit coded instructions to his reception committees and wholesalers, and that key words were broadcast in specially written children's bedtime stories read on the air by Olmstead's wife. It was during one such transmission, made from Olmstead's mansion (which had its own transmitting studio) that Prohibition agents finally made their raid, and arrested him. In 1926, he stood trial for "conspiracy to possess, transport and import intoxicating liquors," and was sentenced to four years in jail.

His trial made legal history because the judge authorized hitherto illegal use of wiretaps. Olmstead's career did not end there. After his release from McNeil Island federal prison, he became a born-again Christian Scientist and devoted the rest of his life, and the remains of his considerable fortune, to charitable work with convicted prisoners. McCoy, released at the same time, retired to Florida, also with substantial funds. After the territorial waters limit was reduced to three miles, it became essential for valuable ships such as McCoy's *Arethusa* to remain at a safe distance from the coast, and a new category of player emerged — the fishermen who ferried customers to the floating liquor supermarket ships and back (also hiring themselves out to bring the liquor ashore, braving Coast Guard interception). Their exploits were celebrated in sea shanties, including these famous lines:

> Oh we don't give a damn
> For our old Uncle Sam
> Way, oh, whiskey and gin!
> Lend us a hand
> When we stand in to land,
> Just give us time
> To run the rum in!

Everett Allen, author of *The Black Ships*, grew up during Prohibition in New Bedford and remembered not only the friendly bantering between fishermen and Coast Guards but that "on most days there would be twelve to fifteen rum boats testing their engines and roaring around New Bedford harbor while a patrol boat kept an eye on them. Then, as it got later, one by one they would disappear."

Local New Bedford fishermen found rum-running far more lucrative than catching and selling fish, and many became minor dealers themselves. "You knew right away when a man stopped fishing and started running rum," a local New Bedford resident told Allen. "In the first place, his family began to eat proper and you could tell by what they bought at the grocery store, when they had had to run up a grub bill all winter." A fisherman called Manuel stored liquor in his cottage water tank, selling it to private customers by the bottle straight out of a water spigot. In wintertime, peddlers sold rubber hot water bottles containing whiskey from pushcarts in the New Bedford streets.

Freelance fishermen's "shuttle services" often operated without prior knowledge of any "floating supermarket" arrivals, for there was a constant flow back and forth. A former Coast Guard officer turned rumrunner told Everett Allen: "At night on 'rum row' [the stretch of the Atlantic nearest New Bedford] you'd think there was a city out there." Isabelle Mairs, an East Hampton teenage flapper in the 1920s, remembers watching Coast Guard vessels pursue fishing boats in spectacular chases clearly visible from East Hampton's exclusive Maidstone Club — which, though serving every conceivable type of liquor, was not raided once during the Prohibition years. Its members were far too influential, and East Hampton's police chief, a frequent guest at the club, would get so drunk that his car ended up in the lake several times.

At first, the fishermen-bootleggers used their own boats to take the liquor ashore, but as Coast Guard patrols became more experienced, and their engines faster, fishermen's boats became increasingly vulnerable. Jimmy McGhee, a motor mechanic in Manorville, near Southampton, helped save the situation for the bootleggers. His brilliant, never-patented creation was a speedboat of his own devising. It was a pared-down floating platform powered by twin watercooled airplane engines (bought cheaply from stocks of First World War surplus) and capable of speeds of up to 65 miles an hour — far faster than the fastest Coast Guard boats. McGhee's powerboats ran on aviation fuel and required skilled, cold-blooded crews, for there was a constant risk of engines overheating and blowing up at high speeds.

McGhee became a well-known figure in the Hamptons, and was in great demand not only as a mechanic but as a boat designer. Like McCoy, he was more interested in boats than in money. Although he was, in a sense, the Coast Guard's worst scourge, he never did anything illegal, consistently refused to take a cut on the liquor cargo his boats transported, and was never arrested. Long after Prohibition, this entirely self-taught mechanical genius became a well-known figure in racing car circles, and during the Second World War was hired as an adviser by Grumman, the maker of fighter aircraft.

Boats such as McGhee's, built in discreet workshops in New York and all along the East Coast, were also acquired by notorious underworld bosses whose men ran the Coast Guard gauntlet themselves. Their one-man torpedo boats were armor-plated, with bullet-proof windshields, and carried up to 400 cases and moved at 35 knots. Some of these craft have survived, including one once owned by Dutch Schultz, the notorious gangster, and are now valuable collectors' items.

The war at sea was continuous. Fishermen used their nets to foul the engines of pursuing Coast Guard boats. Regardless of the weather, veteran residents recall, there were noisy water ballets off the Hamptons coast involving fishermen's boats and their Coast Guard pursuers. In 1925, Coast Guard boats were ordered to mark suspected rum-running vessels at all times. Many of the speedboats were equipped with radios, and used codes to communicate with their land bases, even though the penalty for using an unauthorized radio on a rum-running speedboat was a $7,000 fine. The FBI knew that rumrunners ferrying liquor from parent ships to shore used accomplices, sometimes fronting as local radio station employees, to broadcast cryptic messages in Morse that only the initiated could understand.

The bootleggers' codes got increasingly sophisticated as time went on, and were not confined to radio, for they knew their mail was routinely opened, and were careful to conceal details of their shipments as best they could. As the Coast Guard's cryptanalysis improved, so did the exporters' methods. One of the biggest bootlegging conglomerates, the Consolidated Exporters' Company, hired a retired Royal Navy expert to devise and modify their codes every few weeks, paying him a $10,000 retainer.

David Kahn, in *The Code Breakers*,[9] quotes Elizabeth Smith Friedman, a senior cryptanalyst for the Coast Guard, as saying that "at no time during the [First] World War, when secret methods of communication reached their highest development, were there used such involved ramifications as are to be found in some of the correspondence of the West Coast rum-running vessels." Testifying in a New Orleans court against the Consolidated Exporters' Company, she gave this example of encoded instructions: "Anchored in harbor. Where and when are you sending fuel?" became

"MJFAK ZYWKH QATYT JSL QATS QSYGX OGTB."

Largely at her insistence, the Coast Guard eventually launched the CG-210, a patrol boat packed with high-frequency receivers and direction finders, and staffed with trained cryptanalysts that could listen in on a large number of coded messages simultaneously. It was, in a way, a high-tech breakthrough comparable to today's AWACS plane, and Kahn makes the point that without prior work on bootleggers' code-breaking, progress in World War II cryptanalysis against Germany and Japan would have been far less successful.

The Coast Guard would doubtless have gained the upper hand had it had superior craft, but when President Calvin Coolidge, Harding's successor, asked for appropriations to buy faster powerboats, legislation was often held up by wet Congressmen, including a hard-core minority known to be in the pay of rum-running financiers.

The Coast Guard was a tough adversary, but its rate of interception never rose above 5 percent of the total traffic — roughly the equivalent of law enforcement scores today involving drugs — and even this elite force of 11,000 men was by no means above suspicion. As a boy, Everett Allen recalled two uniformed Coast Guard personnel "coming into Vineyard Haven drunk enough so they tried to sell liquor in bottles right off the street."[10] On Block Island, a notoriously corrupt Coast Guard captain systematically looked the other way, and Allen remembers seeing sixty cases of whiskey awaiting collection in broad daylight within a few hundred yards of a Coast Guard station.

"It became as necessary to exercise vigilance over the Coast Guard as over the smugglers," A. Bruce Bielaski, a former federal Prohibition enforcement chief for the whole of the Atlantic seaboard, told the *Sat-*

urday Evening Post.[11] For letting fishing boats land liquor at Fort Point Bay, near Montauk, Coast Guard captain Frank J. Stuart got $2,000, the equivalent of a year's pay. Bielaski told the *Post* that some Coast Guard crews actually helped in the transfer of liquor from rum runners to speedboats. "When the schooner *Dawn*, with 2,000 cases of whiskey on board, was captured and towed into New Bedford, she suddenly sank. A report was sent through that she had gone down with 200 cases on board. We knew better. Later she had to be raised, and not a bottle of whiskey was found on her." There were also large numbers of situations in which Coast Guard crews protected the rumrunners by sending U.S. Navy destroyers trying to apprehend them off on false trails.

Because Coast Guard authorities were reluctant to admit to failings in the ranks, courts-martial were invariably held in secret, and the press was informed much later, if at all. In 1932, the Coast Guard commandant reluctantly admitted that the Coast Guard officer in charge of Georgica station, Long Island, had been sentenced to one year in the Portsmouth naval jail for "certain offenses." That same year, three boatswain's mates were convicted of "scandalous conduct" for conniving with bootleggers around Fire Island.

So incensed was one anonymous citizen that he wrote a letter to a senior Washington official asking for a loan to buy and equip "a good submarine chaser with gun, a load of torpedoes and a few machine guns. I will supply a crew. We will go to sea and sink without trace every rum boat we can find. . . . I am sick of seeing foreigners thumbing their noses at the U.S. Am I for Prohibition? Hell, no. Just tired of fiddling, fooling and graft." The writer's political agenda was clear. "I'll clean the seas of the graft as Forrest cleaned the woods of niggers." The reference was to the infamous Major General Nathan Bedford Forrest, who massacred black Union troops at Fort Pillow in 1864 — the letter itself a reminder that Prohibition supporters included not only devout Christians and moralistic Anti-Saloon Leaguers but the equivalent of today's extremist militias; that is, the then extremely powerful — and teetotal — Ku Klux Klan, which at its peak had over four million members.

Coast Guard morale was not high, even among impeccably honest crews, for several reasons. One was the grotesquely ham-handed public relations policy of the times. In January of 1923, Edward Clifford, assistant secretary of the Treasury Department, which supervised all law enforcement relating to Prohibition, recommended that "Prohibition officials be requested not to talk to newspapermen, in fact to give no publicity whatever as to what they are doing. This is also to apply to the Coast Guard. This matter cannot be handled successfully by giving out information to the press." This meant that Coast Guard exploits were seldom mentioned in the press. The consequence was that the corrupt reputation of the Prohibition Bureau spread to the far less corrupt Coast Guard.

The Coast Guard's original mission had been to ensure the safety of ships at sea, and rescue vessels in distress. But after some rum-running vessels began using fake distress signals to draw Coast Guard ships into ambushes, few humanitarian missions were attempted. As one of its supervisors, Rear Admiral Frederick C. Billard, wrote in 1927, "marked enthusiasm for this kind of operation could not be expected on the part of the average, old-time Coast Guard sailor," who felt that he was "fighting a war with one hand tied behind his back."

There were some spectacular successes. A huge rum-running vessel called the *Taboga* (which had changed its name to *Homestead* and sailed under a Costa Rican flag) surrendered at sea to two Coast Guard vessels after a running battle. It had 2,000 cases aboard — a major disappointment for the boarders, for it had enough storage space for 50,000 cases. In another case, a young Coast Guard lieutenant called Duke single-handedly boarded the *Economy* and forced its crew to surrender at revolver point. But at other times Coast Guard ships simply looked the other way as "black ships" steamed straight into New York, unloading liquor within spitting distance of Brooklyn Bridge. A black ship crew member recalled that "the wharf was full of carts and they had a gang there to unload us. All of the front street was blocked off. Cops were keeping everybody off the wharf."[12] Former Coast Guard lieutenant Joseph Slovick (who retired in 1952, having signed up as a teenager in 1928) gave a vivid description of the hazards involved. "There was no radar then, and we never knew where the ships were going to be,"[13] he said.

> Their ships were always faster than ours, and they had protection from the local community. There were spotters out there alerting

them. I remember once we were chasing a rum-running fishing vessel off Fire Island and I saw a man drop off and make for the shore. He was warning the people waiting for the consignment that they were being chased. It was a cat and mouse game, and the smugglers made great use of sandbars. We knew that within our Coast Guard station there were informers working for the bootleggers.

As seaman second class, Slovick earned $36 a month. To his knowledge, there were no black sheep among his crew mates, but there were plenty among customs officers.

A lot of the time, when we had seized some liquor, we didn't bring it into the Customs house during the daytime because we didn't want any contact with the customs men. They wore great big brown overalls and they would stash bottles of liquor in them as they carried the stuff into their trucks, as many as they could — they would keep it for their own purposes, or to sell.

11

"PROHIBITION WORKS!"

The Prohibition Department has made, and is making,
substantial progress.
— *President Warren Harding, in a preface to
Roy A. Haynes's book* Prohibition Inside Out, *1926*

Twenty months after Prohibition became effective, the Internal
Revenue Bureau, as it was then called, reckoned that bootlegging had
become a one billion dollar business, and a senior official urged the
government to take steps to recover $32 million from bootleggers in
excess profits taxes. Americans consumed 25 million gallons of illegal
liquor in 1920, the Bureau claimed, noting that another 30 million
gallons had been released to consumers for medicinal purposes by the
new Prohibition Unit.[1]

For all this disastrous beginning, Prohibition apologists felt they
had good grounds for believing that the long-awaited millennium was
at hand. Statistics could be made to prove that, at any rate in the first
few years of its existence, Prohibition worked, was indeed spectacularly
successful.

"Deaths from alcoholism took a terrific tumble in 1920," wrote
the *Literary Digest,* the best-informed, most influential American
magazine of its day. Many years later, in occupied France, when

supplies of wine and hard liquor disappeared from the shops (all stocks had been requisitioned by the Germans), there was a marked drop in cases of delirium tremens, cirrhosis of the liver, and other alcohol-related illnesses — and this was also true of America, at least until the bootleggers got organized. State budgets all over the United States, in 1921 and 1922, reflected Prohibition's impact. During those years, hospitals had fewer patients with alcohol-related illnesses; there were fewer cases of alcohol-related crimes, including street drunkenness; and there was a corresponding drop in the prison population. In Chicago, the DTs ward of Cook County Hospital was closed, as well as one wing of the Chicago City Jail.

Although Wheeler and the ASL naturally attributed the improvements exclusively to Prohibition, the Volstead Act alone was not responsible. In actual fact, as 1900–1910 statistics showed, per capita liquor consumption had steadily declined since the turn of the century, America had turned partially dry long before 1920, and in the 1917–1918 war years, many drinking American males were serving abroad.

Some health figures *were* impressive. In the years immediately before America's entry into the First World War, the death rate from alcoholism had oscillated between 4.4 and 5.8 per 100,000 people. In 1917–1918 the drop was spectacular — from 5.2 to 2.7. To Prohibitionists, this was sufficient proof that America was indeed on the threshold of the much-vaunted millennium. In 1920, the death rate from alcoholism went down still further, from over 2 per 100,000 to 1. In 1921, there was a modest rise (1.8). In 1922, the level had climbed to 2.6 — still an improvement over the 1917 figure. In 1923, it climbed still further (to 3.2), and from then on the rise became vertiginous, even if deaths caused by adulterated liquor poisoning are excluded from the count.

As late as 1925, Wayne Wheeler could, with some legitimacy, argue that the benefits of Prohibition were huge — though some of his reasoning was specious. "Prohibition is decreasing crime," the *Literary Digest* reported in January of 1925. Violent domestic crime *was* down, as were arrests for drunkenness and brawling. "Prohibition has saved a million lives," Wheeler announced that year. "The welfare of little children is too eloquent a voice to be howled down," the *Grand Rapids Herald* acknowledged.

Prohibition enthusiasts also used statistics to argue, again before bootlegging operations got into their stride, that cash once spent on liquor was now being used to buy more and better food, and that consequently people were healthier. Statistics showed that grocery stores were doing better business, and that American families were putting more money into savings accounts.

"It makes me sorry we did not have Prohibition long ago," wrote the editor-owner of the Seattle *Times,* who had originally opposed Prohibition. "Yes, sir, we have found in Seattle that it is better to buy shoes than booze."[2] The Prohibitionists naturally claimed that the Volstead Act was uniquely responsible. This was by no means certain, for the revitalized postwar economy was almost certainly a likelier reason for the new spending patterns. In any case, benefits were only temporary, and long before 1929, such claims were no longer being made.

Wheeler declared that Prohibition had "doubled the number of investors" and was fueling America's growing manufacturing boom — a "post hoc ergo propter hoc" argument, but one enthusiastically supported by most American industrialists, at least until the Great Crash of 1929.

One major but anonymous industrialist told Prohibition Commissioner Haynes that "before the Volstead Act, we had 10% absenteeism after pay day. Now it is not over 3%. The open saloon and the liquor traffic were the greatest curse to American morals, American citizenship, thrift, comfort and happiness that ever existed in the land."[3] Men such as Rockefeller (at least at first) and Edison were also Prohibition supporters. And much was made of the fact that certain skilled labor unions, such as the Brotherhood of Locomotive Engineers, had come out in favor of Prohibition.

Wheeler's most vocal and influential Prohibition ally was undoubtedly Henry Ford — a major Anti-Saloon League contributor from the start. Ford's rationale was simple: neither a principled nor a religious man (insofar as he had any moral convictions, these were based on the superiority of the white, Aryan race), his sole concern, as an innovative car manufacturer, was efficiency: hangovers slowed down the pace of the assembly line and provoked accidents. The Volstead Act did not make Henry Ford disband his private police, but their task became simpler, for they no longer had to keep watch over a multitude of saloons and liquor shops.

Halfway through Prohibition, Ford himself issued a stern warning in the *Pictorial Review*.

> For myself, if booze ever comes back to the U.S. I am through with manufacturing. I would not be bothered with the problem of handling over 200,000 men and trying to pay them wages which the saloons would take away from them. I wouldn't be interested in putting autos into the hands of a generation soggy with drink.
>
> With booze in control we can count on only two or three effective days work a week in the factory — and that would destroy the short day and the five-day week which sober industry has introduced. When men were drunk two or three days a week, industry had to have a ten- or twelve-hour day and a seven-day week. With sobriety the working man can have an eight-hour day and a five-day week with the same or greater pay. . . . I would not be able to build a car that will run 200,000 miles if booze were around, because I wouldn't have accurate workmen. To make these machines requires that the men increase their skill.

Other automobile industry tycoons shared these views, and the Carnegie Institute's tests on the effects of alcohol on human efficiency added credibility to Ford's remarks. But the arguments in favor of Prohibition were not confined to industrialists. Some of the social arguments advanced no longer used the hysterical rhetoric favored by the ASL and the WCTU, which equated Prohibition with salvation. One of the few totally honest members of the Harding administration, Mabel Willebrandt, the deputy attorney general (and the infamous Daugherty's "real" number two), argued that even if they drank in speakeasies, women were Prohibition's greatest beneficiaries.

Herself one of America's early feminists, who had defended prostitutes and victims of domestic abuse at the start of an impressive law career and had gone on to campaign for better conditions in women's prisons — scandalizing some of her more straitlaced legal colleagues by becoming an early "Murphy Brown," adopting a baby girl after her divorce — Willebrandt defended Prohibition in dispassionate, modern terms. She recognized that there was little interest in Prohibition "among those who congregate in country clubs and who have plenty of leisure and very little work." Nevertheless, speaking as a woman in a male-dominated society, she wrote that

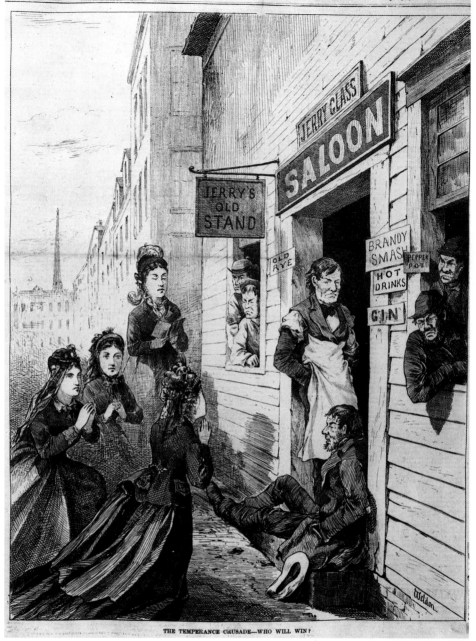

THE TEMPERANCE CRUSADE—WHO WILL WIN?

An early cartoon (1874) showing Women's Christian Temperance Union volunteers picketing a saloon full of drunks. *(Library of Congress)*

Carry Nation praying in her jail cell in Wichita, Kansas. *(Library of Congress)*

Wayne Wheeler, power broker
and Anti-Saloon League boss.
(Library of Congress)

President and
Mrs. Warren Harding.
(Library of Congress)

Andrew Volstead (1869–1947),
Minnesota congressman, author of
the Volstead Act, which brought
Prohibition into being in 1920.
(National Archives)

Warren Harding and members of his cabinet. Seated, left to right: John Weeks, Andrew Mellon, Charles Evans Hughes, Warren Harding, Calvin Coolidge, and Edwin Denby. Standing, left to right: Albert Fall, Will Hays, Harry Daugherty, Henry Wallace, Herbert Hoover, and John Davis. Daugherty was bootlegger George Remus's man in the Harding administration. *(Stock Montage, Inc.)*

Jess Smith, Harding intimate and a close friend of Attorney General Harry Daugherty, was Daugherty's bagman and effective number two in the Justice Department. *(Jack Doll/Delhi Historical Society)*

A St. Louis wine cellar chockablock with vintage French wines being inspected by a Prohibition official before it was sealed off (1920). *(National Archives)*

A Prohibition Bureau agent smashes seized liquor (1923). *(Library of Congress)*

A bootlegger's car, which crashed during a police chase
in Washington, D.C. (1926). *(Library of Congress)*

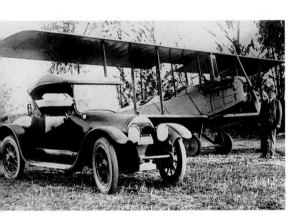

FBI agent with captured plane
and getaway car near the Mexican
border (1928). *(Library of Congress)*

Prohibition Bureau
agents raid a speakeasy in
Washington, D.C., at 922
Pennsylvania Avenue (1923).
(Library of Congress)

Special garter and miniature flask for ladies. *(Library of Congress)*

New York's largest illegal beer brewery being dismantled (1930). *(National Archives)*

An Anglo-American crew of rumrunners under arrest, posing with Prohibition agents. The top section of this composite photo shows their two-masted British schooner. *(National Archives)*

Coast guardsmen survey their latest capture in New York harbor, gunnysack-stitched whiskey bottles, like "the real McCoy," while thirsty citizens look on. *(National Archives)*

In Grosse Pointe, Michigan, a customs agent displays a long submarine cable used to pipe whiskey from Canada to the United States. *(National Archives)*

Prohibition agents breaking up New York's largest whiskey still (1927). *(National Archives)*

Inside the Remus mansion, Remus and guests pose for a photograph before a dinner given to celebrate completion of the $100,000 swimming pool. Remus is seated at the head of the table. Imogene is standing at his right. Stepdaughter Ruth is standing to his left with her arms around George's shoulders. His sister is seated at his left. *(Jack Doll/Delhi Historical Society)*

George Remus behind bars in 1924. Remus sold $75 million worth of liquor in a two-year period. At the same time he was said to have spent $20 million to pay off various federal, state, and local officials for their silence. Eventually arrested and prosecuted, he served five sentences for liquor law violations. *(Jack Doll/Delhi Historical Society)*

George Remus.
(Jack Doll/Delhi Historical Society)

The former Imogene Holmes,
Remus's second wife.
(Jack Doll/Delhi Historical Society)

Remus's adopted daughter, Ruth. She was
nineteen at the time of the murder trial.
(Jack Doll/Delhi Historical Society)

Al Capone.
(National Archives)

Free soup kitchen
in Chicago, paid for
by Al Capone (1930).
(National Archives)

Prohibition agents smashing up a bar just prior to the end of Prohibition. *(National Archives)*

"Big Bill" Thompson, mayor of Chicago during Prohibition years, and friend of gangsters. *(National Archives)*

The beginning of the end:
anti-Prohibition slogans
on cars (1930–31).
(Library of Congress)

Anti-Prohibition demonstration
in New York in 1932.
(National Archives)

In 1933, but *before* the end of Prohibition, applicants for licenses to sell draft beer line up in New York. *(National Archives)*

At Prohibition's end, there were no liquor stores, and such was the thirst for legitimate liquor that some banks turned over their premises temporarily (1933). *(National Archives)*

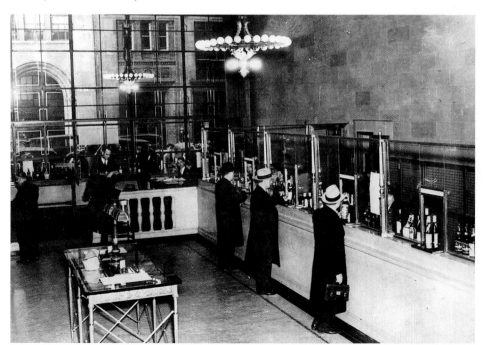

Happy workers celebrate
the reopening of their
brewery (1933).
(National Archives)

In Philadelphia,
a bar scene immediately
after Prohibition's
end (1933).
(National Archives)

Anyone who mingles freely with all classes of women is bound to discover very soon that the majority are opposed utterly and unalterably to reestablishment of open saloons. . . . Most women still lean economically upon men, their fathers or their husbands. Even if they have property they let men in the family handle it. The saloons deprived women not only of the companionship to which they thought they were entitled but absorbed money which the women felt they were entitled to share. For selfish reasons, quite as much as moral reasons, the women of the country will continue to cast their influence for prohibition. There is better furniture in the homes throughout the country than ever before, simply because a woman is able to divert a larger part of her husband's income to household uses. There are more luxuries in which the family can share: automobiles, music lessons for the children and the like.

The modern girl, who makes no protest when her escort to dinner produces a pocket flask and shares its contents with her, has no present stake in prohibition enforcement. But the moment that girl marries, she probably will, whether consciously or not, become a supporter of prohibition, because she always will be unwilling to share any part of her husband's income with either a bootlegger or a saloon-keeper operating legally. I am convinced that as far as the women of the country are concerned, prohibition has come to stay.[4]

The arguments of Roy A. Haynes, the luckless Prohibition commissioner appointed by Harding on Wheeler's recommendation (he too was part of the Ohio gang but one of the few honest ones), were far less convincing. Faced with an untenable situation, he was compelled to take an uncompromising moral stand: "It is no longer a question as to whether we are for or against that legislation, but whether we are for or against the United States Constitution."

Haynes recognized that Prohibition was hideously difficult to police. The frontier between Canada and the United States was over a thousand miles long, and Detroit was a privileged entry point. No pursuit was possible on the river separating Canada from the United States in Detroit, for spy ships "financed by Canadian brewing interests" were on a permanent lookout for Coast Guard and Prohibition Bureau craft, and the "smugglers have to be caught in the act." But his contention was that Prohibition was under control "and that control becomes more complete and more thorough every day. . . . The clamor of a dwindling clique cannot drown the voice of truth."

"The bootlegger's life is increasingly one of fear, dread and apprehension," Haynes claimed, with some truth. He failed to add that the financial rewards were such that the risks were worth taking, even if, as he noted, the bootleggers were constantly preyed on by politicians, public officials, police, and lawyers.

He was correct to say that "few men in any line or calling are subject to the temptation which besets the Prohibition enforcement agent." Bribes *were* on a phenomenal scale. A group of brewers offered some agents a monthly $300,000 retainer to look the other way. The bootleggers, Haynes wrote, regarded the agent's badge as "nothing but a license to make money. . . . Bootleggers brag of top political connections, with representatives in the Department of Justice, the Bureau of Internal Revenue and the Prohibition Unit itself." In most cases, though Haynes did not say so, such accusations were well founded.

There were indeed a few untouchables in the Prohibition Bureau, as George Remus found out to his cost. Haynes devoted a chapter to thirty "fallen heroes," agents shot and killed between 1920 and 1925, either in running gun battles, in ambushes, while searching for stills, or as a result of being lured to lonely and deserted places where they were gunned down in cold blood. These included some authentic heroes, but some "executions" involved the paying off of old scores — the price some Prohibition agents paid for failing to make good their promises to "look the other way."

Haynes could not avoid the issue of corruption within his own Prohibition Bureau. There were, he admitted, "weak men, few in number," who could not "withstand the strain of temptation placed in their way [by the bootleggers]." Invariably, Haynes wrote, Prohibition agents were advised that if they accepted bribes, they would simply be adhering to an almost official code of conduct, for "claims are made by rich and apparently influential cliques that they have connections by which they can control the action of the 'higher-ups' in the various government departments. These claims are groundless."

They were not, as he well knew. According to Haynes, only forty-three Prohibition agents were convicted in the courts between 1920 and 1925, which proved that "The force was 99% honest. . . . Let our enemies make the most of the fall of these forty-three unfortunates. I am thinking of the other 3,957 who kept the faith."

According to Haynes, of the forty-two convicted, twenty-three were found guilty of offenses involving corruption, and eight of drunkenness; one committed murder; one had a false expense account and tried to influence a grand jury; one committed theft; and the remaining eight suffered small police-court cases. "Of real corruption, therefore, the ratio stands at about one half of one per cent," Haynes claimed.

This was nonsense, even if Haynes was compelled to add that those caught "are, doubtless, but a fraction of those who are guilty," for the Prohibition Bureau's record was, on the whole, appalling. As records would later show, between 1920 and 1930, some 11,926 agents (out of a force of 17,816) were "separated without prejudice" because their criminal involvement could not be proved, and another 1,587 were "dismissed for cause," that is, for offenses that could be proved but might not warrant sentencing, or that would involve costly, publicized trials.

The discrepancy between Prohibition agents' low salaries and their life-styles was staggering — some of them even showing up for work in chauffeur-driven cars. Not just subordinate agents but senior Prohibition Bureau officials were involved in bootlegging activities. In Philadelphia in 1921, the local Prohibition director was shown to have been part of a plot to remove 700,000 gallons of whiskey (with a street value of $4 million) from government-bonded warehouses. Daugherty promptly ordered the upright local prosecuting attorney, T. Henry Walnut, who uncovered the conspiracy, to resign, and the case was dropped. And though it was reopened, thanks to Walnut's behind-the-scenes doggedness, all accused were discharged: the evidence against them in possession of the Justice Department mysteriously disappeared.

There were sufficient cases of this type to trigger a response from Harding himself. In his State of the Union message in December of 1922, he referred to "conditions relating to enforcement which savor of a nationwide scandal."

Even after 1925, when a major reorganization of the Prohibition Bureau took place under the auspices of retired general Lincoln C. Andrews, the situation hardly changed. Andrews eliminated state barriers, and did his best to make the Prohibition Bureau a part of the Civil Service, but this failed to eliminate corruption, for the simple reason that three-quarters of the Prohibition Bureau's staff failed to pass the necessary Civil Service test. By 1928, only two-thirds of the vacancies had been filled. In Pittsburgh, a congressman stood for reelection after serving a jail sentence for using his influence to allow 4,000 cases of whiskey to be released from bond into the hands of bootleggers. Not only was he reelected, but the ASL helped him win back his seat: he had always voted dry.

Haynes — who was not entirely the paragon of virtue he made himself out to be, for it was later learned that he had been paid a monthly retainer by the ASL while commissioner — preferred to lay the blame elsewhere, *outside* the Prohibition Bureau and related law enforcement agencies: "There are large communities where the entire machinery of government, municipal, county and state, is such that federal enforcement officials can get little if any cooperation whatever." In a large number of cases, judges systematically sided with the accused and against the law enforcers. "In some cases it is difficult for an observer in the courtroom to tell whether the bootlegger or the Prohibition agent is on trial." This would not be the case, he said, "if some of our better citizens would attend the courts. Friends of bootleggers throng the courtroom but friends of the law stay away."

The complicated predicament of some judges, caught between their need to be seen upholding the law and their loyalties to those who had voted for them, can be gauged from this Haynes anecdote: Some Prohibition agents were stopped for speeding while chasing a bootlegger along a highway, hauled into court, and heavily fined. The judge then called them into his chambers, returned the fine, and told them: "I'm in politics and I can't afford to let you fellows off."

Not all Prohibition agents were corrupt or intimidated by proof of collusion at the highest levels. Izzy Einstein and his partner, Moe Smith, rapidly became the two most famous Prohibition agents in America. Einstein, "the man of a thousand disguises," accounted for 20 percent of all arrests for violations of the Volstead Act in Manhattan from 1920 to 1925.

Einstein was a postal clerk on Manhattan's Lower East Side when he volunteered his services. His superior, Chief Agent James Shevlin, said he "didn't look the type." Einstein was five feet tall and weighed

225 pounds. "There might be some advantage in not looking like a detective. I could fool people better," Einstein told him. He was hired, given a gun (which he never used) and a badge, and immediately became a star.

As he later wrote,[5] he made his first arrest dressed as a working man. He went into a bar serving soft drinks and legal near beer. "The barman asked: would I like a little lollypop on the side. There was quite a laugh. I told the bartender I was a stranger who didn't know the ropes but I'd buy a pint of whiskey if it wasn't too expensive. He sold me a pint and I arrested him."

In order to keep evidence intact, Izzy invented a device, a small glass funnel easily concealed in a pencil pocket, connected by tube to a bottle hidden in the lining of his coat. Despite his unforgettable appearance and build, he fooled thousands — dedicating his book "To the 4,932 persons I arrested." His gimmicks included a straightforward proposition: "Would you like to sell a pint of whiskey to a deserving prohibition agent?" But there were also elaborate disguises involving crutches, fishing gear (in Long Island), and German, Polish, Hungarian, and Italian impersonations. Fluent in Yiddish, with unmistakably Jewish features, Einstein had great fun conning fake rabbis out of their stocks of sacramental wine.

He soon became notorious. One suspicious bartender said: "Eat this ham sandwich with the compliments of the house, and then I'll give you a drink." Izzy got rid of the ham, ate the sandwich, ordered the drink, and made the arrest. In a speakeasy with a sports clientele, he arrived in football clothes, smeared with fresh mud. In a musicians' club, he was asked to play an instrument. "I'll play you the revenue agents' march," he said. He wrote that one Pole offered him his wife in exchange for ten barrels of whiskey he had seized. He often made twenty to thirty arrests in a single day. The Brooklyn *Eagle* wrote: "Izzy does not sleep. He's on the job day and night and accomplishes more for the drys than half a dozen anti-saloon leagues." Wayne Wheeler wrote him: "The bootlegger who gets away from you has to get up early in the morning."

"By becoming a character I popularized prohibition," Einstein wrote. In fact, Izzy the showman had no strong objections to liquor. An irrepressible extrovert and a born character actor, who realized early on in life the futility of his father's ambition — that he should become a rabbi — he was never happier than when impersonating a socialite (he posed as the judge in a beauty contest before making an arrest), a southern colonel (at a Democratic convention) or a foreign dealer. So successful was he that a whole school of impersonators sprang up, pretending to be Izzy Einstein and demanding $25 shakedowns from saloon keepers.

Although Izzy later fell out with his partner, Moe, he owed much of his success to him. A favorite gimmick was for Moe Smith to pose as a rich out-of-town businessman, and Einstein as his fawning New York subordinate. The two men would sit through a meal in a fashionable New York restaurant, Einstein talking loudly about the Broadway shows Moe should see, and Moe telling him, making sure the waiter was in earshot, that what he really wanted was to find something decent to drink. Einstein would take the waiter into his confidence, the liquor would be produced, and the arrest made. Since both men were easily recognizable — Moe Smith was even fatter than Einstein, weighing in at close to 300 pounds — the naiveté of their victims seems, in retrospect, unbelievable. Their record number of arrests was due, first and foremost, to the laziness, passivity, and corruption of almost all of their Prohibition Bureau colleagues.

Izzy and Moe's out-of-town exploits were less successful. In New Orleans, a local paper carried Izzy's picture on the front page on the day of his arrival, warning that the dreaded agent provocateur was in town. Disguise apart, he and Moe Smith were capable of solid detective work. In true gumshoe fashion, they hired a room overlooking the premises of the Pure Olive Oil Company in Lower Manhattan, observing the comings and goings of its trucks for days at a time, eventually seizing a cargo of rye whiskey worth $50,000. Einstein also arrested a dealer who had imported hundreds of cases of liquor into the city who turned out to be the commercial attaché at the Peruvian consulate in New York. Because he enjoyed diplomatic immunity, Izzy recalled, "we had to give him back his liquor."

Although the Peruvian consul's dealings may have been an exception, diplomatic immunity meant that liquor could be imported for diplomats' private use, and was even served at official parties. Few ambassadors were as respectful of the law as Sir Esmé Howard, British ambassador in Washington in 1929, who not only banned the serving of wine or champagne at cocktail parties but told his staff that, out of respect for the Constitution, anyone caught ordering liquor through the "diplomatic bag" would be sent back to London in disgrace. His staff staged a huge party when his successor was named.

The trade in fake sacramental wine for religious purposes gave Izzy and Moe unlimited opportunities to perfect their provocation techniques. Practicing Jewish families were allowed one gallon per adult member per year, and sacramental wine was rationed — amounts determined by the number of registered worshippers in New York's synagogues. Needless to say, the system led to monumental abuse. As Izzy and Moe discovered, a 600-member synagogue turned out to be a laundry; a delicatessen was another. A thousand gallons of wine had been drawn for a synagogue that was no more than a postal address in a Lower East Side tenement building. They also exposed an entirely fictitious "Assembly of Hebrew Orthodox Rabbis of America," whose members consisted of one person, who, it turned out, was neither orthodox nor a rabbi, nor even Jewish, but an Irishman called Sullivan.

There were innumerable other scams. American cigar makers — among those officially entitled to alcohol for the manufacture of their products — also took advantage of the Volstead Act and the ignorance of the civil servants who administered the Bureau of Industrial Alcohol responsible for delivering it. A Philadelphia cigar maker who had spent $480 on alcohol in the previous eighteen years obtained an official permit for 420,000 gallons of alcohol a year — more than enough to soak all the cigar tobacco leaf in the world, the Prohibition Bureau later claimed. Prohibition agents also fought a losing battle with thousands of fly-by-night manufacturers of hair restorers, skin conditioners, and other toilet preparations smelling of whiskey, gin, or rum.

Hardly surprisingly, there is no mention of Izzy and Moe in Haynes's book. The reason is that their career came to an abrupt end. They had been too successful, offending too many people in the upper echelons of the police, state, and federal agencies — and in Congress. In November of 1925, pretexting an "administrative reorganization," Haynes, himself under considerable political pressure, abruptly fired them both.

For all his official optimism, Haynes's discouragement emerges in his long catalogue of prominent citizens battening onto bootleggers' bribes. In one "mid-Western industrial city" (unnamed, but probably

Cincinnati) "the mayor, the sheriff, the judge of the city court, a former prosecuting attorney, a detective sergeant, a justice of the peace, lawyers, deputy sheriffs and cabaret staffs and singers were all involved," and proprietors of places where liquor was sold illegally were "systematically protected by the police in cognizance of higher officials." A mayor of Atlanta was sentenced to eighteen months for participating in a bootlegging ring. New Jersey was "a stamping ground for bootleggers doing volume business." In a case involving 100,000 gallons of impounded wine and property worth $2 million, "the wine growers, a prominent citizen and the ex-Governor of the state of California all testified in favor of the accused." On the West Coast, one bank president, fourteen wholesalers, a lawyer, and a deputy collector of internal revenue aggregated 31 years in jail and $167,000 in fines in a case involving liquor worth $4 million.

In the face of evidence of this type, "The Federal Government," Haynes insisted, "*is* reaching big operators, the 'higher-ups,' with ever-increasing success." At the time of his writing, as later statistics would show, liquor was America's biggest industry. Americans were consuming 200 million gallons of hard liquor, 684 million gallons of malt liquor, and 118 million gallons of wine a year, and the bootleggers' overall income amounted to four billion dollars a year.

Rather than expose in detail instances of corruption among politicians, the Justice Department, the police, and the state judiciary all over America, Haynes preferred to lay the blame for his bureau's failures on a powerful international wet conspiracy. He quoted Lord Astor, who claimed in a speech in 1923 that "people are working in England to misrepresent the attitude and actions of America." He attached great importance to a (1922) "anti-Prohibition Congress" in Brussels attended by politicians from Belgium, Canada, Spain, Finland, France, Britain, Denmark, Italy, Norway, Sweden, and Switzerland, which, he said, was plotting to undermine American institutions under the pretext of "defending individual and commercial liberty." He claimed there was a powerful movement in France, headed by Count Albert de Mun, to "provide wets" with ample funds "and the active support of a hundred million European advocates." Hardly coincidentally, Haynes noted, Count de Mun was "president of one of the largest champagne companies in France and was formerly an extensive exporter to the U.S." Tourist and advertising agencies boosted France as a tourist haven and a drinker's paradise, "appealing to the comradeship that existed between Yank and poilu[6] in war days" and asserting that "in all our cities throughout our entire wine-growing region, you will not meet a drunken man."

In America itself, Haynes wrote, no fewer than forty-two organizations had been set up to fight Prohibition. The most powerful, the Association Against the Prohibition Amendment, got massive financial support from former liquor manufacturers and dealers associations. It "practically paralleled in organization method the Anti-Saloon League"; that is, it systematically backed wet congressional candidates (with considerable success, in that Volstead himself would lose his seat as a result of their efforts).

In the last resort, for all the occasional fascinating glimpses he gave of his real problems, Haynes's book never dared explore in depth the crucial problem at hand: that for all the infrequent incorruptibles, law enforcement officials' hands were tied and the Prohibition Bureau doomed because of a web of collusion — a tacit conspiracy to batten onto Prohibition involving politicians, the judiciary, the banks, and the police extending from Washington to every state of the Union and even involving the attorney general himself from 1921 to 1924.

Instead, Haynes preferred to repeat, Coué-like, the conviction that "Prohibition has come to stay" and highlight the perils of drink in any form. "Who drinks bootleg drinks with death," he wrote, citing the example of a promising actress who killed herself "because the effects of the liquor drunk at a party had caused her to seek death as a relief," and the case of the "young woman on a Hoboken ferryboat who took a drink from a flask, almost immediately staggered to the stern, plunged into the Hudson and died." That such deaths were directly attributable to Prohibition, and the nonavailability of quality liquor, seems never to have occurred to him.

But perhaps Haynes, who knew all about the drinking habits and corrupt practices of the Harding administration, deliberately wrote his book tongue in cheek. He was, after all, a Daugherty appointee, and was well aware of the latter's appalling reputation, though he did pay a somewhat ambiguous tribute to him in his book. "There can be no doubt as to the attitude of the nation's chief law enforcement officer, Attorney General Daugherty," he wrote, "to whose department is entrusted the task of prosecuting violators of the prohibition laws."

It was symptomatic of the hypocrisy of the Prohibition era that, in 1921, the American Bar Association decided to hold its annual meeting in Cincinnati — the very town where almost the entire police force was on George Remus's payroll, either as convoy guards or as salesmen on commission. In Daugherty's presence, it solemnly declared that

> The people of the United States have undertaken to suppress the age-long evil of the liquor traffic. When for the gratification of their appetites, lawyers, bankers, merchants, manufacturers and social leaders, both men and women, scoff at this law, or any other law, they are aiding the cause of anarchy, and promoting mob violence, robbery and homicide.

After hours, many of those attending the meeting were haunting the speakeasies they denounced. Every lawyer present must have been aware that "the General" was on the take, using Jess Smith as his bagman not only to dispose of controversial cases but to protect big bootleggers and even peddle B permits to them. But even the most cynical among them must have listened to Daugherty's keynote address with wry amusement.

"I do not mean to impute moral turpitude to him who is opposed to the Eighteenth Amendment," Daugherty conceded magnanimously,

> But when public sentiment has crystallized into law there can be no question as to the duty of good citizens. They may still debate as to the wisdom of the law, but there is only one course of conduct, and that is obedience to the law while it exists. . . . To refuse or to neglect to enforce a valid enactment of the legislative department of government, or to enforce it mechanically or half-heartedly, or to wink at its violation, is without justification on any sound theory of government. Those who ask or expect this not only contribute to lawlessness, but destroy the basis upon which their own security rests. Our safety and happiness lie in obedience to law by every man, woman and child.

There was loud, prolonged applause.

12

"PROHIBITION DOESN'T WORK!"

> No one who is intellectually honest will deny that
> there has not yet been effective nationwide enforcement.
> — *Mabel Willebrandt, deputy attorney general*
> *in charge of Prohibition enforcement, 1929*

Shortly after resigning her post in 1928, Mabel Willebrandt published *The Inside of Prohibition*,[1] from notes accumulated during her eight years in office as deputy attorney general in charge of Prohibition enforcement. Her book was in sharp contrast to Haynes's. Unlike him, she had no reason to pull any punches: she owed her appointment not to the Ohio gang but to former president Taft, who had strongly recommended her to Harding. And though she did pull *some* punches, (here, too, references to Daugherty are tongue-in-cheek, though criticism is clearly implied), she did not balk at allocating responsibility for failure where she felt it was due. The bootleggers and rumrunners, she made it clear, were less responsible for the Prohibition mess than the corrupt, hypocritical *system* that battened onto them.

From today's standpoint, one is tempted to ask what all the fuss was about. Who cared whether a network of speakeasies and middlemen kept Americans supplied with liquor, good or bad, while police and Prohibition agents systematically looked the other way? But the perspective was different in the twenties. The fact is that, as Willebrandt wrote, ever since the United States became a republic, "*No political, economic or moral issue has so engrossed and divided all the people of America as the Prohibition problem, except the issue of slavery.* . . . Nor will it be denied that Prohibition enforcement remains the chief, *and in fact the only real political issue of the whole nation.*"[2]

Willebrandt was one of the few in authority to point to the folly of passing a law and simply expecting it to be obeyed. Of course, such a controversial issue required teeth ("the problem of enforcement will not solve itself"), but neither the transgressors nor the corrupt Prohibition agents were really to blame. "The Federal Government's record in all these things is not such as to produce exaggerated pride in one who has been a part of it," she conceded.

Willebrandt acknowledged the quandary facing any administration, defining it as follows:

1. It was clearly impossible to prevent immense quantities of liquor from entering the country.

2. The media had perhaps exacerbated the problem, but "certainly it would be ridiculous for me to deny that liquor is sold in large and small quantities throughout the country, and that practically anyone who possesses simultaneously a thirst and as much as a quarter dollar can partly assuage that thirst."

3. At the same time, repeal of Prohibition's stricter measures, making wine and beer legal again, was "practically impossible," for she was convinced that a majority of drys would vote against any modification in the law, however much it was disobeyed. Her assessment, as a well-informed Republican, was that "Congress remains overwhelmingly dry in its votes, *whatever the personal habits of the members may be,*" and *"a Congressman who comes up for re-election every two years cannot afford to be wrong about the wet or dry sentiment of his district. He knows!*"[3]

The real culprit was the American political system itself. Traditionally, liquor interests had "financed city and state campaigns, controlled city councils, boards of commissioners, state legislatures. Through political allies they prevented enactment of early closing-hour ordinances and Sunday closing laws, the breweries and whiskey wholesalers were always willing to chip in to help elect a county or state's attorney, a member of the legislature or the city council."

Despite the swing in public opinion in favor of Prohibition — provoked by church militancy, the ASL, and, above all, America's entry
into the First World War — Willebrandt was convinced that such influence had simply passed into the hands of the bootleggers, moonshiners,
still owners, and all those with vested interests in the status quo. "The
influence of liquor in politics begins down in the City wards and often
in county districts, *but it extends if it can up to the Cabinet and the
White House in Washington.*"[4]

> After George Remus, king of the bootleggers, had been convicted
> and lost his appeals, the rumor reached me that he would never serve
> a day in Atlanta prison. I set it down as only the bragging of the
> defendant. But a few days later, a phone call came from the White
> House, stating that a respite of 60 days would be granted Remus if
> the Attorney General would send over the necessary papers. Promi-
> nent politicians . . . had intervened with the President.

She did not, of course, infer that they had, in all probability,
included the attorney general himself.

In a case involving another prominent bootlegger, "every conceivable political and personal appeal, including an appeal by a Cabinet official, was made to quash the case. Attorney General Daugherty called
me to his office and told me of the pressure that had been brought
on him to call off any further investigation into this matter." Again,
she must have known that Daugherty was playing games with her, but
chose not to mention this. Most readers, she knew, would draw their
own conclusions.

Even more damaging to those who genuinely wanted to uphold
Prohibition laws was the government's neglect of the end use of industrial alcohol. In 1926, she revealed, every month some 660,000
gallons of "denatured" alcohol were sold to a variety of customers, including pharmaceutical industries, beauticians, and drugstores — and
a tidy amount, duly flavored and sometimes lethal, had ended up in
bootleggers' whiskey bottles.

Even those relatively innocent congressmen without any bootlegging connections brought the political system into disrepute by chal-
lenging the validity of one of the laws embodied in the Constitution.
In the first place, "many originally in favor are now opposed to it," or

had become convinced that Prohibition could not be enforced, and were lobbying for its repeal.

> Many others have been antagonized by the discovery that the very men who made the Prohibition law are violating it and that many officers of the law sworn to enforce Prohibition statutes are constantly conspiring to defeat them. How can you justify prison and fines when you know for a fact that the men who make the laws and appropriate the money for Prohibition are themselves patronizing bootleggers?

It was common knowledge that "Senators and Congressmen appeared on the floor in a drunken condition," that "bootleggers infested the halls and corridors of Congress and ply their trade there," and that no attempts had ever been made to expel them. What she failed to say, but must have known, was that bootleggers kept huge stocks of liquor in the House of Representatives and Senate cellars so that orders could be met without delay. It was common knowledge that well-connected retailers had unlimited access to Senate and House of Representatives offices, with home deliveries of every conceivable type of liquor.

Congressmen and high government officials, Willebrandt noted, believed they were above the law, and customs officers were told to extend the usual courtesies and free entry privileges to them — as they would to foreign diplomats. When one congressman was caught smuggling a barrel of rum into the country after a West Indies cruise (a customs officer's attention had been drawn to a broken bottle of rum, part of thirty quarts of smuggled liquor), he was indicted but acquitted. In her book, Willebrandt failed to add that the politician concerned was Republican Congressman Everett Denison of Ohio, one of the most intransigent Prohibition propagandists in the House. Elected by rural church-going voters, like so many other publicly dry, privately wet politicians, he was compelled to toe the Prohibition line, at least in his speeches and voting record or risk losing his seat to an even more hypocritical rival. For years, men such as Denison would be the pliant tools of Wayne Wheeler's Anti-Saloon League, refusing him nothing — one of the reasons why the Prohibition albatross poisoned the political life of America for so long.

For those lacking political clout or money for lawyers there was no such leniency. In her book, Willebrandt made no mention of police persecution of small-time violators or of measures in both Michigan and New York that provided drastic mandatory sentences to those convicted for a fourth time for violations of the Volstead Act.[5]

There were some appalling travesties of justice. Both Fred Palm of Lansing and a mother of ten elsewhere in Michigan got life sentences for possession of a pint of gin. Michigan was "the wettest state in America," the *New York Herald Tribune* pointed out with heavy irony, "with tens of thousands violating the Volstead Act daily if not hourly . . . so we suggest a further simplification: instead of sentencing to life imprisonment those of its citizens who insist on harboring pints of gin in their homes, let Michigan sentence them to the chair. . . ."

"The truth is," Willebrandt wrote, "that in New York as in other cities, it is immensely profitable to the politicians to let the speakeasies flourish: politicians never lack for poll workers on election day." Prior to Prohibition, she noted,

> . . . the saloons were the assembling places and allies of crooked politicians who manipulated elections in the interests of the grabbers of franchises for street railways, electric light and gas plants and other seekers of special privilege. It is those political machines that are still functioning . . . the so-called decent citizens have done little anywhere permanently to curb the reign of the corrupt manipulators of city affairs.

Few were really prepared to fight for "decent city government." Until they did so, "there would not be honest enforcement of either Prohibition or any other laws. If the searchlight of Prohibition has revealed the city as our national shame, then it will have served more widely than the framers of the 18th Amendment ever dreamed."

But the change could not be imposed from above. Anticipating the Republican tidal wave victory in the November 8, 1995, elections, Willebrandt, in a prescient chapter titled "The Seceding States," noted that "the people of America do not want and will not permit an army of offices of the Federal Government to enforce law and order in local counties and cities. Nothing in the country is more contrary or repugnant to basic principles of our form of government."

The trouble was, as Mabel Willebrandt well knew, in some states the federal government was all that was left to enforce Prohibition — for starting with New York State (in 1923, with the assent of Democratic Governor Al Smith, an acknowledged wet), a handful of states (New Jersey, Montana, Nevada, Wisconsin) *had* repealed Prohibition, at least insofar as state law enforcement was concerned, putting the entire burden on the FBI, the Justice Department, the Treasury, the Prohibition Bureau, and the federal courts.

In New York State alone, Willebrandt pointed out, there were some 3,000 state police, a 17,000-strong city police force, 113 state supreme court judges, and 62 county prosecutors. From the end of 1923 onward, they were all ostentatiously refusing to enforce Prohibition laws. This did not mean that in these states Prohibition no longer existed; on the contrary, the introduction of the Jones Act (passed in 1925) sharply increased sentences for violations of the Volstead Act (up to five years in jail instead of two, and $10,000 fines instead of $1,000 fines, double that for recidivists), and a new "padlock" rule, admittedly only partially enforced, resulted in the permanent closure of speakeasies whose owners had come before the courts. But it did mean that federal agencies, and the highly corrupt Prohibition Bureau, could no longer enlist the aid of state authorities in their fight against bootlegging.

Furthermore, the federal judiciary, as Willebrandt well knew, was often even more reluctant to convict Prohibition offenders than the state judiciary was. Haynes had hinted that this was so, but Willebrandt gave instance after instance of federal judges and prosecutors openly mocking Prohibition law enforcement efforts, siding with the accused they were supposed to prosecute, either because they disagreed with the law, had been bought, or were actually in business partnership with the bootleggers and speakeasy operators. "With the right kind of prosecutors the bootleggers will go out of business," she wrote, but "during my eight years as Deputy Attorney General a large part of my time and energy was devoted to prosecuting prosecutors."

She cited examples of assistant attorneys responsible for enforcing the Prohibition laws being convicted of association with bootleggers, sometimes as co-owners of illicit breweries or stills, and of how judges had in court openly attacked the integrity of Prohibition Bureau officials, quoting one of them as saying: "I want to instruct the witness that a prohibition agent is not the law and most of them whom I have seen are about as far away from it as could be imagined."

There was an additional impediment to justice. U.S. commissioners were the "middlemen" who decided whether the accused should go before a grand jury. Whether they handled one case a day or ten, they were only paid a fee for the one case, which scarcely made for speedy procedures. But worse than that, many of them were unbelievably corrupt, tipping off speakeasy operators in advance so that when federal officers went on raids, all they discovered were innocuous soft drink bars with church music playing in the background. Some commissioners were known to receive monthly fees of between $50 and $75 from each speakeasy operator in town. Jury selection being their other prerogative, some deliberately selected for jury duty men and women whose anti-Prohibition bias was well known to them, or else intimidated juries to acquit accused bootleggers.

And even when speakeasy owners *were* fined, these sentences were usually excessively low (except for notoriously dry states such as Kansas), and what was even a $10,000 fine to millionaires such as George Remus and Willie Haar? In some cities and counties, bootleggers and speakeasy owners came up before local courts every month, their fines going straight into municipal accounts — barely disguised, pre-Prohibition era saloon license fees.

It was partly because state law enforcement agencies no longer handled Prohibition offenses in urban centers such as New York and actively wet states such as New Jersey that the federal authorities devised new, sophisticated techniques to convict offenders, many of them anticipating those later used by the Drug Enforcement Agency (DEA).

In 1925, for example, a speakeasy called the Bridge Whist Club opened at 14 East Forty-fourth Street in New York. It was an undercover operation, entirely financed by secret federal funds, the purpose being to obtain incriminating evidence about bootleggers and their supplies.

Surveillance techniques were primitive but effective: there were no automatic recording devices in the 1920s, but wire-linked microphones, built into the club's lampshades, were connected to the earphones of a battery of stenographers working around the clock on a shift basis. Thanks to these taps, agents did apprehend a major bootlegger, but owing to informers within its ranks, clients soon knew all about the operation. Also, much of the information gathered was deliberately planted disinformation, including references to the drinking habits of well-known politicians, clergymen, and even senior Prohibition officials.

The Justice Department also tapped Remus's phones. Many years later, in a *Collier's* article, Bill Mellin, a former agent, described how he did this. He was sent to Columbus, Ohio, where Remus had booked into a hotel suite. For nine days, Mellin waited in vain to be contacted by special agents. In the *Collier's* piece, he noted that he was probably followed during this period to make sure he was not secretly in league with Remus or his associates: "They were suspicious of some of their own agents in that city." He was given a duplicate key to Remus's suite (room 707), and a room next to it was booked for Mellin.

Mellin proceeded by stages. First, he connected the 707 extension to his own room telephone so that he could listen in on all of Remus's telephone conversations. Learning that he would be away for twenty-four hours, Mellin entered the Remus suite, picked a suitable spot on the wall and, boring a hole, inserted a mike, using soap to fill in the drill holes and painting the surface to match the wall. "It was a smooth, perfect job." In his own room, Mellin connected the wires from the mike to a handset, and installed a device that switched on a red light every time a conversation started in Remus's room. "That way, you don't have to keep the headphones on your ears all the time."

Two government stenographers were then sent in. They worked in shifts in Mellin's room, recording all of Remus's conversations with his visitors. They learned a good deal about Remus's bootlegging operations, including the fact that eighteen freight cars would soon be discharging liquor for Remus at a railroad siding in Covington, Kentucky (near Death Valley Farm).

But the operation also revealed the degree of corruption prevalent in Columbus. "One day alone, Remus had forty-four people in, and some of them were Federal prohibition agents or deputy marshals," Mellin wrote. "He paid them an average of $1,000 apiece. When I had summarized all the information, I went to a United States official in Cincinnati, and said: here's the dope. He looked at me for a full minute without talking. Then he said: 'My boy, come back tomorrow.' "

I went back the next day. He said: "Son, where is your home office?"
I told him it was in New York. He said: "Son, there are times when
a man has to be practical in this business. It's only a few weeks to
election, and the information you've dug up is political dynamite.
The men you spied on — the agents and marshals — are political appointees. Go back to New York and forget it." I didn't go back to
New York. I went to Washington and squeaked. But it didn't do me
any good. Nothing ever happened on the Remus information.[6]

There were equally flawed government-funded speakeasy operations in Washington (where a banquet for major bootleggers was
sponsored by the Prohibition Bureau in the Mayfair Hotel) and Norfolk, Virginia, and one curious aspect of the New York "Bridge Club"
operation was that long after surveillance had ceased, it continued to
function without ever being raided.

In light of all this, was Willebrandt's contention that "Congress
remained overwhelmingly dry" a tenable proposition? The answer is
that, in 1924 at any rate — for all the grotesque law enforcement failures, the open secession of New York State (the other five were still
to come), the disgust shown by honest people at blatant corruption,
and the consequent growing damage to the American body politic
itself — the mood of the country was such that repeal was not just
unlikely, but impossible.

A crucial test came that year with the Democratic presidential
nomination. Al Smith, the popular governor of New York State, was the
Democratic front-runner. Despite the fact that he was a Catholic, and
therefore deeply suspect to Southerners and the Ku Klux Klan, he was
the only candidate who stood a chance of beating Calvin Coolidge. The
latter, though Harding's vice president, had been one of the few totally
honest members of the Harding administration, and, because Harding
had died while still in office, was already a temporary White House in-
cumbent — almost always a considerable advantage for a presidential
contender.

Al Smith had the backing of Tammany Hall, that network of
largely corrupt politicians and entrepreneurs who ran the city, but
there was no hint of major scandal in his own political past — and the
fact that the 1924 Democratic Convention was being held in Madison
Square Garden was a huge plus. But convention proceedings not only

revealed an element of schizophrenia among grass-roots representatives as far as Prohibition was concerned, but dramatically underlined the veto powers of the Anti-Saloon League — its ability to ensure that any American president continued to do its bidding.

Both Wayne Wheeler and Izzy Einstein made notable appearances at the convention. It was yet another pretext for Izzy to disguise himself as a goateed Southern colonel, though by now he was so well known that his presence was not so much a disguise as a warning that those attending the convention had better moderate their drinking, at least in public. (They did not: according to witnesses, some of the delegations openly drank out of paper bags during the proceedings, and the galleries stank of whiskey.)

Wheeler had a far more serious purpose: to prevent Al Smith's nomination. As a committed Republican, he wanted Coolidge, a "sound" Prohibitionist, to become president, and knew this was a foregone conclusion unless Al Smith became a contender. Wheeler had done his homework: he controlled one-third of all the delegates (mostly from southern and midwestern states) who would never vote for a wet. But Franklin D. Roosevelt, a rising star in the Democratic party, made a keynote speech nominating Al Smith that had a galvanizing effect. "Ask your Republican friends whom they would least like to see nominated," he told the delegates, and got a huge ovation.

Al Smith himself was well aware that his real opponent was not his likeliest rival candidate William Gibbs McAdoo — a nonentity dry whose strongest credential was that he happened to be the late president Woodrow Wilson's son-in-law — but Wheeler himself. While the convention proceeded without them, the two men met secretly in a New York club.

Their long discussion was surprisingly cordial. Smith asked Wheeler why the ASL had been so adamant in banning real beer, and told Wheeler that if elected, he would probably increase its alcoholic content. But he said nothing about repealing Prohibition, hinting that he was perfectly aware of the extent of dry sentiment outside New York State, especially in the South and Midwest. He told Wheeler that "being President of the United States would be quite different from being Governor of New York." But Wheeler had the last word. When Smith made an allusion to his own possible future presidency, Wheeler told him: "Governor, you will never enter the White House."[7]

In the contest that followed, Al Smith's supporters wrecked McAdoo's chances, but Wheeler's dry delegates effectively blocked Al Smith (there were over a hundred ballots). In the end, as Wheeler had both anticipated and planned, the Democratic delegates selected a lackluster compromise candidate for the nomination — an obscure West Virginian political hack named John W. Davis. Coolidge won easily, and Prohibition was given a new lease on life.

Al Smith was not the only impeccably honest wet politician whose anti-Prohibitionist views stemmed solely from moral convictions. New York Congressman Fiorello La Guardia, who would become New York's mayor in 1929, replacing the arch-corrupt Tammany Hall figure Jimmy Walker, was another.

A brilliant media manipulator, La Guardia was almost as much of a showman as Izzy Einstein. In 1926, after tipping off the press, he marched into Room 150 of the House Office Building in bartender's uniform and proceeded to demonstrate how easy it was to make real beer, mixing near beer with malt extract, which could be bought legally. Inside Congress, he knew he was immune from prosecution, but when the news came from Albany, where the headquarters of the state's Prohibition Bureau was located, that anyone caught making "La Guardia" formula beer would be arrested, the *New York Times* announced that "Representative La Guardia will walk into a drugstore at 95 Lennox Avenue, purchase the necessary ingredients and mix his brew with a kick. Then he will stand by to be arrested." Little Flower, as he was known, was exceedingly disappointed when no Prohibition agent showed up, and a city policeman refused to arrest him. Newspapers all over America carried stories of his exploit, and one city editor wired him: "Your beer a sensation. Whole staff trying experiment. Remarkable results."[8]

Although such antics seemed at the time to make him out to be a political lightweight, his opposition to Prohibition was no mere electioneering gimmick but stemmed from his conviction that it was destroying the nation. As early as 1919, he had told Volstead that "this law will be almost impossible of enforcement. And if this law fails to be enforced — as it certainly will be as it is drawn — it will create contempt and disregard for the law all over the country." Excessive drinking, he insisted, could be curbed only by education, not legislation.

A born iconoclast, he openly proclaimed what other politicians believed but dared not even whisper. Consequently, he attracted a large number of enemies in Congress from the dry Midwest and the South. Southern congressmen, he told the House, knew full well that the moonshiners down south favored Prohibition because it increased their business ". . . if the people from the dry states would keep out of New York City, we would have no drunks there." And if they were all for Prohibition, he told a constituent, it was because Prohibition "was only enforced among the coloured population," whereas "the white gentleman openly and freely can obtain and consume all the liquor he desires." He could in fact have expanded on this theme. A detailed · survey of "police blotter" cases involving Prohibition offenses in the *Easthampton Star* from 1920 to 1933 reveals that no socialites, or even "respectable" wealthy householders, were ever arraigned in the Hamptons: the victims of local Prohibition agents' zeal were invariably working-class artisans or small potato farmers, often recent immigrants with exotic Polish names.

La Guardia returned to the theme of two-tier justice (not only concerning Prohibition enforcement) again and again. "May I remind the gentleman from Georgia," he replied to a congressman who had urged him to respect the constitutional sanctity of the law, including its Prohibition provisions, "that there is also a 14th amendment to the Constitution? The 14th Amendment deals with human rights and liberties and it is as dead as a doornail in certain sections of the country."

After a decade of Prohibition, he commented with some bitterness, ". . . politicians are ducking, candidates are hedging, the Anti-Saloon League prospering. People are being poisoned, bootleggers are being enriched, and government officials are being corrupted."

Will Rogers, the famous American humorist, may have joked that "Prohibition is better than no liquor at all," but to La Guardia, it was no laughing matter, for all its tragicomic undertones: as an Italian-American, he had a special reason to seek the end of Prohibition. He knew that the longer it lasted, the more the Italian-American image would be tarnished in the eyes of public opinion.

In fact, in New York at least, the underworld was by no means exclusively Italian-American. Frank Costello — one of its masterminds, and a brilliant businessman in his own right — took an Irish name, but he was born Francesco Castiglia, although he did his best to conceal the fact. However, his front man, "Big Bill" Dwyer; Tammany Hall operative Alfred J. Hines; and Larry Fay, owner of a taxi company that operated a mobile bootlegging operation, *were* Irish-Americans. Arnold Rothstein, one of the biggest owners of speakeasies, clip joints, and New York nightclubs (and the man who fixed the 1919 World Series), was Jewish. So were "Dutch" Schultz (Arthur Flegenheimer); Meyer Lansky, probably the most astute entrepreneur of all; and Benjamin ("Bugsy") Siegel. Nor did the Italian-American gangsters operate in a vacuum. Albert Anastasia had an official, police-approved bodyguard who was not an Italian-American. "Lucky" Luciano trusted his Jewish underworld partners more than his fellow Sicilians. A leading Mafia hit man suspected of killing the anti-fascist refugee Carlo Tresca had a direct line to the (largely Irish-American) New York police department.

Chicago was where Italian-Americans came to dominate gangland during the Prohibition years — but the problem was not simply that Al Capone, Johnny Torrio, and the infamous Genna brothers were Italian-Americans and active in the *Unione Siciliana*. In Chicago, Prohibition resulted in so blatant a collusion between underworld figures and those supposed to be fighting them that during the three terms of Chicago Mayor "Big Bill" Thompson, Capone and Torrio between them "ran and directed the political, police and federal enforcement agencies of Chicago and Cook County."[9]

13

CHICAGO

The *Untouchables,* that hugely popular TV series starring Robert Stack as Eliot Ness, with Walter Winchell's gravelly voice-over narration, gave viewers all over the world a pretty good idea of American gangland activities during Prohibition — or so they thought. In fact, the series bore as much relation to reality as a Stalinist film of the 1950s glorifying the Soviet regime. Made with the close cooperation of the FBI, under J. Edgar Hoover's supervision (he monitored the series and the FBI had censorship rights), *The Untouchables* was a complete travesty — a blatant propaganda exercise eulogizing Hoover and the FBI, bending the facts to suit him.

First shown in the early 1960s, *The Untouchables* celebrated the triumph of the forces of righteousness over absolute evil. The FBI's war on gangsters took place in a vacuum, with not the slightest hint that the underworld bosses were so aggressive because they knew they were aided and abetted by so many respectable individuals, including members of the judiciary and the police. Nor were there any references to politicians and elected officials on the take, to district attorneys and judges in collusion and even in business partnership with bootleggers, or to bribed, bent, or terrorized juries.

In fact, it can be argued that some of America's biggest villains during the Prohibition era were not the Al Capones, Johnny Torrios, Gus Morans, Dutch Schultzes, or Frank Costellos but the political bosses in New York, Chicago, and elsewhere who used the underworld to their considerable advantage, and the many venal, conniving police and law enforcement officials who supplemented their incomes with mobster money.

New York's mayor and Tammany boss James Walker — until defeated by Fiorello La Guardia in 1929 — enjoyed a cozy relationship with New York's gangland. But nowhere was the collusion between politics and organized crime more spectacularly evident than in Chicago, where Mayor "Big Bill" Thompson's three-term reign led to a virtual breakdown in law and order, and a situation in which — on a par with "Papa Doc" Duvalier's Port au Prince, Medellín (Colombia) in the 1980s, and Moscow today — gangs virtually ran the city. "Thompson," wrote Fletcher Dobyns, "made Chicago the most corrupt and lawless city in the world."[1]

It had been a wide-open town long before Prohibition became an issue. The old-time First Ward (district) Democratic bosses, "Bathhouse John" Coughlin and Michael "Hinky Dink" Kenna,[2] both sons of Irish immigrants, owed their clout, and their considerable wealth, to handouts from the brothel owners they routinely protected. "I always entertained state legislators free in the Everlight Club," Minna Everleigh, owner of Chicago's most famous and expensive brothel, told a Chicago judge after her retirement. That was the least of her favors.

"Hinky Dink" Kenna was a dour saloon owner whose generous "schooner" measures made it the most popular drinking place in town. He was also, for several decades, a hugely influential inner city Democratic party figure, who had devised a foolproof way of ensuring his partner Coughlin's reelection.

It was called chain voting: genuine ballots were spirited away and marked for "Bathhouse John." They were then distributed to floating voters, who were driven to the polling booths, where they voted, using the already marked ballots and picking up fresh ones, which they surrendered to "Hinky Dink's" henchmen, collecting a small fee in return. These were then recycled, and used with another batch of voters, ensuring that "every vote paid for was really cast for Coughlin."[3]

Long before 1920, the Chicago gangs had established a tacit but effective *modus vivendi*, sharing out their most lucrative activities — gambling, prostitution, "protection," and strike breaking — throughout the various inner city wards. Paradoxically, the fact that local politicians (including Coughlin and Kenna) were so intimately involved in the management and protection of Chicago's many brothels meant that violent crime was relatively rare. The politicians' vested interests gave Chicago's red light districts an aura of respectability — all those involved knew that bloodshed and gangland violence drove the customers away.

Prohibition brought this era to a close. The reason Chicago became synonymous with gang warfare — from 1920 to 1933, nearly eight hundred gangsters were killed in shoot-outs with other gangsters — was the irresistible profit motive. With no legitimate source of liquor left, clubs, speakeasies, and private dealers were compelled to turn to the bootleggers, and these, increasingly under the thumb of underworld bosses, became a ready prey.

From 1920 onward, a new breed of gangsters emerged to take advantage of the new situation. Underworld leaders — the term is inappropriate because they made little attempt to conceal their activities — used their links with politicians and politically appointed city officials, including the police and even the judiciary, to eliminate their rivals with virtual impunity. Given the cozy, mutually rewarding relationship that existed in Chicago between politicians and mobsters even before Prohibition, the gangland saga that followed was eminently predictable, even though the gangsters' political allegiances had always been notoriously fickle.

From 1910 onward, "Big Jim" Colosimo, the slot machine and brothel king (and owner of Chicago's celebrated saloon Diamond Jim's), had worked closely with "Hinky Dink" Kenna and "Bathhouse John" Coughlin — though he would campaign for Republican "Big Bill" Thompson for mayor in 1919. His demise, in 1920, shortly after Prohibition came into being [4] (Johnny Torrio, his bodyguard, almost certainly had him killed after "business differences" arose between them), marked the passing of an era. His was the first of the hugely expensive, ostentatious funerals that would later become a ritual. Congressmen; aldermen; members of the Chicago Opera Company; countless public officials, including district attorneys; and over a thousand First Ward Democratic party stalwarts solemnly paraded through the city behind his coffin.

In pre-Prohibition days, many brewers and distillers had behaved like loan sharks, buying up saloons and then squeezing the saloon keepers for ever-increasing profits. From 1920 on, the new, younger, greedier gangs behaved far more ruthlessly, using terror as a weapon. It was, as Remus's aide, George Conners, noted, a seller's market: with good liquor constantly in short supply, saloon keepers and nightclub and brothel owners were now compelled to buy set quantities of liquor at set prices in return for "protection." The purchasers knew that if they protested too much, the penalties could be fatal.

The police rarely intervened in such disputes, and underworld members, including those of non-Italian origin, respected a form of *omerta:* even on their deathbeds after fatal shootouts, they seldom cooperated with the police. Nor did the police intervene when rival gangs began hijacking each other's liquor. As long as no law enforcement officers got hurt, it was a private war that did not concern them. As in Cincinnati in George Remus's heyday, suitably remunerated uniformed police in Chicago even routinely escorted delivery vans belonging to specially favored bootlegging gangs.

In all fairness to Chicago, New York was not far behind. "Lucky" Luciano claimed he controlled every New York police precinct, and had a bagman deliver up to $20,000 a month to New York Police Commissioner Grover Whalen in used notes. He also maintained that after the 1929 stock market crash, he loaned Whalen $35,000 to cover his margin.[5]

Hijackings occurred with increasing frequency. The rationale was not only to acquire liquor stocks for free but to eliminate business rivals for good. "Crime," John Huston has a character say in *The Asphalt Jungle,* "is just a left-handed form of human endeavor," and in many ways there was a parallel between gangland history during the Prohibition era and that of the new industrial empires, also coming of age from 1920 onward. Gangs, like respectable conglomerates, competed for an ever larger share of the market because it was soon clear to both that they had to keep on growing or go under, gobbled up by more powerful rivals.

Chicago was unique because it became, in the early 1920s, not just a microcosm of corrupt, *affairiste* Washington under the Harding Administration but at times a virtually lawless city. "Big Bill" Thompson, its mayor, was no Daugherty. The latter was careful to maintain a respectable front while in office, using bagmen such as Jess Smith to do his dirty work.

"Big Bill" Thompson's front men tended to control *him,* for this testy, foul-mouthed tub-thumper with a child's attention span and only moderate intelligence lacked Daugherty's shrewdness, discretion, and political experience. Thompson's weapons were blustering invective, crude intimidation, and an entirely spurious, hail-fellow-well-met charm. "Big Bill" and Prohibition were certainly made for each other, and Prohibition's impact on Chicago cannot be fully explained without a closer look at one of the oddest political phenomena in American history.

In terms of damage done to Chicago's image, there was not much to choose between "Big Bill" Thompson and Al Capone. Capone was certainly by far the more sophisticated operator. He had an innate public relations sense — whether paying the hospital expenses of a middle-aged woman bystander who had been severely wounded in the eye in a shoot-out aimed at killing him in Cicero or opening soup kitchens for the destitute after the 1929 crash, even as he was about to go to jail for tax evasion. A superb media manipulator, he even convinced some respectable newsmen that he was merely a somewhat unscrupulous businessman who deplored violence and was invariably singled out as a convenient suspect even when he was totally innocent — and could prove it.

"Big Bill"'s cowboy image, popular at first, rapidly degenerated into caricatural, swaggering megalomania. Unaware of his failings, and surrounded by venal flatterers, Chicago's mayor saw himself as a pioneer, "the big builder." Although he was indeed responsible for some of Chicago's new city infrastructure, he had no real vision — he was no Robert Moses — and his anti-British, anti-Washington, anti-intellectual obsessions eventually degenerated into near-lunacy. Like Daugherty, he was an authoritarian who believed in conspiracies and favored strong-arm methods almost rivaling Capone's. Only in the Prohibition era could such a figure have dominated America's second city for so long. Without him, it's unlikely that Chicago, or Capone, would have acquired their mythic status.

William Hale Thompson's father, the scion of a wealthy Bostonian family, settled in Chicago to take advantage of the real estate boom, becoming a millionaire. "Big Bill" 's own aversion to school was such that he never graduated from high school, let alone Yale, where his overindulgent father had hoped he would follow him. From childhood, young William became obsessed with the Wild West: his single-minded passion was such that he even dressed as a cowboy, riding horses through Chicago streets. His father, in 1881, reluctantly allowed his fourteen-year-old son to "go West" and live out his fantasies at first hand instead of merely reading about them — at first as a brakeman on the Union Pacific at the height of the Gold Rush, then as a greenhorn cowboy in Cheyenne, Wyoming. At least he would no longer have to bail out his son for rowdy behavior in Chicago.

Young Thompson never became a full-fledged cowboy (he was assigned work as a camp cook), and, to please his father, continued to follow winter courses at Chicago's Metropolitan Business College, but he did acquire the brash, macho ways of the cowboys he so admired. He also learned how to run a ranch, and, in 1888, his father bought him one in Nebraska. It did well, and Thompson was all set to remain there when his father died and his mother begged him, as the oldest son, to take over the family business. Back home, his father's office more or less ran itself. Bill joined the Chicago Athletics Club, becoming one of its outstanding water polo and football stars, and making his mark as a yachtsman.

In 1900, he entered politics, as a Republican alderman in Chicago's Second Ward. He did so for a bet, but the hard-drinking, all-male world of Chicago politics, revolving around saloons and brothels, soon became a substitute for the "Wild West" of his youth, and he never looked back. A playboy who continued to devote more time to sports than to his alderman's job, he quickly acquired the tricks of the politician's trade, and his tub-thumping speeches, though at first barely literate, proved effective.

His local standing as a member of a prominent, wealthy family and his popularity as an athlete, along with his shallow, lazy approach to politics, convinced a small caucus of unscrupulous businessmen that he was an ideal front man behind whom tidy fortunes could be made. They got together to sell "Big Bill" Thompson to Chicagoans as candidate for mayor. Among them was William Lorimer, a prominent Chicago

Republican. As he put it, Thompson "may not be too much on brains, but he gets through to the people."

The career of "Blond Boss" Lorimer, his earliest patron, had already unraveled. Although the former streetcar conductor had had a meteoric rise, becoming, briefly, senator for Illinois, he had not remained one for long. In return for large campaign funds from a local lumber company, Lorimer, whose bristly mustache made him look like a Mack Sennett cop, had voted in favor of high lumber tariffs, and this came to the attention of the Chicago press, forcing his resignation. Thompson, who remained loyal to Lorimer, never lost his hatred of the *Chicago Tribune* and other Chicago papers responsible for destroying Lorimer's political career.

Another even more valuable mentor was Congressman "Poor Swede" Fred Lundin, an ex-shoeshine turned street hustler who had peddled homemade "juniper ade" on the streets of Chicago, and still invariably wore his hustler's outfit — a long black frock coat, Windsor tie, plains hat, and huge gold watch — as a trademark.

Lundin applied the same brash organizational talent to "selling" Thompson he had shown parlaying his juniper ade tonic into a profitable company. He worked the streets, recruiting local "street captains" as election agents, leaving cards behind to be filled in with names and numbers of likely Thompson voters. "On each card was a space for a notation of what kind of job the precinct captain wanted in case of victory."[6]

Although "Big Bill" campaigned only intermittently — at one crucial stage he left for Cowes to race his motor launch *Disturber III*, making a gracious speech after losing (his anti-British sentiments not yet to the fore) — his oratory was that of an earnest reformer. "I am going to clean up the dirt of the rotten administration in power," Thompson promised. "No policeman will be sent to the cabbage patch if he offends some politician; not while Bill Thompson is your mayor." For all his expressed good intentions, some of his most assiduous campaigners were gangsters; men such as Jake "Greasy Thumb" Guzik and Jimmy Mondi, owner of the Sportsman's Club, an underworld hangout.

Thompson also undertook to "protect the fair womanhood of Chicago." On a more practical note, he promised to introduce cheaper streetcar fares, improve public transportation, and build more and better schools. To Chicago blacks, arriving in large numbers from the South, he said: "I'll give you people the best opportunities you've ever had." He seems to have been genuinely anti-racist at a time when this was relatively rare in mainstream Chicago politics, but was also aware that the black vote would be crucial in several wards.

With the start of the First World War, Thompson also realized the importance of gaining the support of another minority group: Chicago's 600,000 Germans and Austrians. His anti-British, anti-Royalist bias, later to become an obsession, first became apparent as his campaign for mayor got under way in 1914. An honorary member of Chicago's German-American Alliance, he delighted in quoting excerpts from the articles of another even more pro-German Thompson — who happened to have been, until recently, U.S. consul in Berlin, and who had written extensively about the "hysterical" anti-German campaign in the British and American press. Most listeners assumed the quotes were his own. So rabid did Thompson's anti-British rhetoric become that many Chicagoans started calling him "Kaiser Bill."

The Prohibition issue was crucial, and Thompson's rival, Democrat Robert M. Sweitzer, had the support of the drys. "Ice cream, soda water, ginger ale and pop! Sweitzer, Sweitzer always on top!" was his opponent's ringing, singularly apolitical slogan. A dry Chicago parade saw a turnout of 12,000 marchers carrying appropriate banners, such as "Booze brutalizes" and "Boozers are losers." But they were vastly outnumbered, shortly afterward, by 40,000 wets, organized by the saloon and liquor lobby, the United Societies for Local Self-Government whose secretary was Anton J. Cermak, later a Thompson rival who would become mayor himself. With the help of the wets, and the support of the German, Austrian, and Afro-American minorities, Thompson won handsomely.

His reformer image did not last long. Although he did bow to dry opinion by promising to implement the Sunday closure laws, favored saloons (including "Big Jim" Colosimo's establishments) were never raided, and city workers hired on a patronage basis found they had to kick back part of their salaries to a William Hale Thompson Republican Fund (each new garbage team contributed $5 per horse and cart).

Lorimer had rightly surmised that Thompson was no intellectual giant, and that his clique of helpers would be free to plunder the city. With "Big Bill"'s tacit consent, "Poor Swede" Lundin virtually ran

Chicago, and the misrule began. Violent crime increased by 50 percent in a single year, and Colosimo's vice empire — and that of other underworld barons — flourished, in part as a result of the men Thompson chose to fill the unenviable post of police chief. The new chief of detectives, Nicholas Hunt, was a dandy with an expensive life-style and abysmal reputation, who had already been compelled to resign from the force in 1912 for protecting brothels in the Hyde Park district. So had another prominent Chicago detective, Mike Ryan, once on Colosimo's payroll.

One of Thompson's many police chiefs, Charles Healey, came to trial in 1917, and his "little green book," produced in court, showed weekly cash payments from brothels and saloons and lists of places not on the take that "can be raided." Despite overriding evidence of corruption, Clarence Darrow, the famous Chicago lawyer, won him an acquittal, thanks to a singularly understanding, appropriately selected jury.

Even before gangsters became Chicago's real masters, thanks to Prohibition, citizens were complaining that the police consistently looked the other way. John A. Carroll, head of the Hyde Park State Bank, told reporters that in order to get results, he had been compelled to hire private detectives to investigate a $272,000 bank robbery. The police were "simply not interested."

The escalating breakdown in law and order, even before Prohibition, was largely Thompson's doing. He ordered the scaling-down, then the demise, of Chicago's Morals Division, and introduced a zoning system, devised by "Poor Swede" Lundin, that made independent police work virtually impossible. In each of the city's wards, a suitably pliant police captain was selected to act as a liaison man, routinely receiving orders from a ward committeeman relaying "guidance" from Thompson and Lundin. A number of honorary precinct captaincies were created. One of them went to "Big Jim" Colosimo shortly before he was gunned down.

There were rumors, later substantiated, of payoffs and illegal profits in almost every field of city activity — school and hospital construction, public works, tramway and bus concessions. Able, honest administrators were systematically removed, and — in at least one case — driven to suicide as a result of campaigns against them. City departments were run by political hacks, whose personal loyalty to

Thompson was the sole prerequisite. The Lundin fund-raising techniques anticipated those of Colonel Charlie Forbes, soon to become the Harding administration Health secretary and prime asset-stripper. But the "Big Bill" electoral magic still worked, and he was elected for a second term in 1919.

Shortly afterward, the choice of Chicago as the site of the Republican Convention was a further boost to his career. Thompson enthusiastically endorsed Harding as candidate — like Thompson an isolationist "America firster" — but Harding's victory mattered less to him than that of his candidate for governor of Illinois, Len Small, a benign-looking farmer and unprincipled political hack. During his own campaign meetings, Small, aware of his mediocre oratorical talent, invariably cut short his own speech with groveling humility. "I'm sorry to be taking up your time," he told the crowds, "for I know you want to hear the greatest mayor Chicago ever had — the greatest man in the United States."

Until they fell out, several years later, Governor Small would protect Thompson and his clique from trouble of all types, granting pardons not only to Thompson appointees but to gangland members. Thompson's first political eclipse, in 1923, was largely the consequence of Governor Small's appearance before a grand jury for corruption. Although Thompson was acquitted (later there was ample evidence that the jury had been tampered with), their friendship did not survive. The law also caught up with Fred Lundin, who promptly left town. He too was subsequently acquitted on corruption charges, in one of the murkiest trials Chicago had yet seen. Lundin too, in later years, would turn against the man whose career he had fashioned.

In his early days, Johnny Torrio, who inherited the Colosimo empire of speakeasies, breweries, and brothels — and who was soon in partnership with *his* bodyguard, the youthful, up-and-coming New York Lower East Side expatriate Al Capone — had relied more on Democrats than on Republicans to expand his business empire — men such as Morris Eller, a trustee of the Chicago sanitary department and a prominent figure in local Democratic politics, as well as respectable attorneys and at least one former U.S. deputy marshal. But with Thompson's election as mayor, the Torrio-Capone gangs established close ties with Republican ward-heelers, aldermen, and the new Thompson political appointees.

Thompson's second spell as mayor was plagued with scandal from the start. The removal of honest city officials had taken its toll: the city was sliding into bankruptcy. Thompson knew that if he wanted a third term, his election campaign would be an expensive one. In 1921, he raised the money in ways that would later become standard practice among politicians hard pressed for cash from Grenoble to Valparaiso. He hired experts, at a cost of $3 million, to carry out a number of urban planning studies. After receiving their commissions, they discreetly turned the money over to his secret campaign fund. These funds remained unused for a long time. As Chicago's problems worsened, Thompson tried to shore up his waning popularity in increasingly demagogic ways, but was sufficiently astute to see the writing on the wall, and in 1923 announced he would not seek a third term. Chicagoans elected William E. Dever, an upright, Democratic judge — and committed dry.

Without entirely loosening their hold on Chicago — Dever's attempts to enforce Prohibition would in any case be a resounding failure — Torrio and Capone promptly shifted their activities to Cicero, a small, hitherto peaceful Chicago suburb in Cook County.

That they were able to do so was directly attributable to the local Republican party machine. Ed Konvalinka, a soda fountain owner and rising star of the local Republican party, struck a deal with Torrio and Capone: if they would work for the election of the Republican candidates in Cicero, the Republican political bosses, if elected, promised not to interfere with their activities. Torrio-Capone speakeasies, brothels, and greyhound racing tracks there were soon bringing in hundreds of thousands of dollars a month. Lauterback's, one of Capone's many Cook County investments, was both a saloon openly serving whiskey (at 75 cents a shot), beer (35 cents a stein), and wine (30 cents a glass), and a casino whose roulette stakes were almost certainly the highest in the world, often amounting to over $100,000 worth of chips on the table per spin of the wheel. "Overnight," wrote Fred D. Pasley in his *Life of Al Capone,* "Cicero seceded from the Volstead United States and went wilder West, and wilder wet, than Chicago [itself]."

The 1924 Cicero election was a textbook example of gangsterdom in action. It did not have to be rigged. Voters known to be opposition Democrats were hijacked and driven out of town, and voters were forced to cast Republican votes at gunpoint. When, alerted by outraged citizens, police arrived on the scene, there were gunfights. Among the dead was Frank Capone, one of Al's brothers.

The results were never challenged, and consequently, under nominal Republican leadership, Torrio and Capone virtually ran Cicero — its puppet mayor, Joseph Z. Klenha, soon living in mortal fear of the gang he had ushered into power.

In Chicago itself, even during Thompson's temporary eclipse, collusion between politicians and gangsters was almost as blatant. Dan O'Banion, its most powerful, colorful gangland boss, had long had a working relationship with the Democratic party. A former choirboy and lifelong devout Catholic, he had started out in life as a professional killer and strong-arm enforcer, and by the time of his violent death was accredited with twenty-five murders, though he was never brought to trial for any of them. But there was another side to this teetotaling, devoted family man, with an impeccable, Irish lace-curtain private lifestyle: he loved flowers and was the proud owner of a fashionable flower shop, which was both his official place of business and his "front." The elaborate bouquets he put together for selected clients were highly prized.

Shortly before the 1924 elections, both to reward O'Banion for past services and to remind him where his future interests lay, the Democratic party staged a testimonial dinner for him, attended by scores of gangland figures. Also present were prominent Chicago policemen such as Chief of Detectives Michael Hughes, a former prominent DA; County Clerk Robert M. Sweitzer (the same Sweitzer who had been Chicago's leading dry protagonist in 1915); and Colonel Albert A. Sprague, commissioner of public works in the Dever Administration and Democratic nominee for the Senate. After keynote speeches by Sprague and Sweitzer, O'Banion was presented with a platinum watch set in rubies and diamonds. All of this did not prevent him, weeks later, from throwing his weight behind the Republicans, in exchange for a more lucrative deal.

Law enforcement agencies and the judiciary were almost equally corrupt, and ineffective. Out of 136 gangland murders that took place in Chicago during the first five years of Prohibition, only six led to trials, and of these, all but one ended in acquittals (the sixth involved a gangster who had blown off the head of a rival inside a police precinct during an official inquest on the latter's brother's death). In a three-

year period, the Board of Pardons and Paroles freed 950 felons. Illinois Governor Len Small personally intervened to pardon professional
killer Walter Stevens (in return for some strong-arm work on a grand
jury looking into his own questionable activities). O'Banion himself,
caught red-handed robbing a labor office safe in 1921, was acquitted
by a bribed and otherwise terrified jury. Al Capone proudly displayed
a gun permit delivered by a Chicago magistrate in 1923.

But perhaps the most flagrant example of police collusion had to
do with the infamous Sicilian Genna brothers. In the first five years of
Prohibition they were Chicago's biggest bootleggers. Although their
criminal record was a long one, they had obtained a license to make
large quantities of industrial alcohol, farming the job out to slum-based
Sicilian families using primitive home stills, who delivered the liquor to
a Genna-owned warehouse factory within four blocks of the Maxwell
Street police station, one of the largest in town.

Here the raw alcohol was turned into whiskey and gin — 40,000
quarts of alcohol at about 50 cents a quart producing 120,000 quarts
of bootleg "ersatz" whiskey and gin costing anything from $15 to $60
a bottle.

No attempt was made at concealment. In any case, the factory ingredients — creosote, iodine, burnt sugar, fusel oil, cane sugar, oil of
juniper — gave off considerable telltale odors, which only the Maxwell
Street policemen seemed unable to detect.

A former manager later told investigators the factory operated on
shifts, twenty-four hours a day, with heavy trucks constantly parked
outside.

> The warehouse was run openly and in full view of everybody, un-
> molested by the State authorities other than an occasional raid. But
> notification of 24 hours was always given to the Gennas. Sometimes
> the very letters sent out by the police ordering the raid were shown to
> them. There would be a clean-up, then a raid, then a re-opening. . . .
> During all the period that I worked there the entire Genna enter-
> prise was done with the full knowledge, consent and approval of the
> Chicago police.[7]

Needless to say, the Genna brothers spent a great deal on such
protection. They maintained payroll records, not just of police but of

Cook County DA representatives, checking their identities when they showed up for their money, making sure they were paying the right people. The Maxwell Street station also routinely provided uniformed police to protect truck convoys of liquor. When proof of the pay-offs reached public prosecutors, all that happened was that some 187 uniformed policemen were transferred elsewhere.

The Genna brothers were prominent members of the Italian Republican Club, and in 1924 staged a banquet at the Morrison Hotel for their friends. Those attending included a prominent DA, a clerk of the Circuit Court, a county recorder, the head of the Cook County Republican party, and friends and cronies of an Illinois senator.

The Gennas' influence did not last. One by one, they were killed off, eliminated by Capone's gunmen as he moved in on his rivals. Although such killings invariably made front-page news, only one of the many violent deaths of 1926 became a cause célèbre. William McSwiggin, twenty-six, a police sergeant's son and prominent Cook County DA, was shot dead from a moving car outside the Pony Inn, a well-known Cicero saloon. Two other people, Jim Doherty and Tom Duffy, both well-known underworld figures and Capone rivals, died with him. A third, Myles O'Donnell, escaped.

Although McSwiggin's office claimed he had only been "trying to obtain information" at the time of his death, it was soon clear that the ambitious, up-and-coming DA had been far closer to the three men than he should have been. He was probably killed accidentally, simply because he happened to be in their company, but the testimony of Al Capone illustrated his contempt for all those connected with law enforcement. A leading suspect, Capone told the press: "Of course I didn't kill him. Why should I? I liked the kid. Only the day before he got killed he was up at my place and when he went home I gave him a bottle of Scotch for his old man. I paid McSwiggin and I paid him plenty, and I got what I was paying for." There was no trial, and the murder was never solved.

Even out of office, Thompson was seldom far from the public eye. His isolationist, anti-British, anti-Prohibition rhetoric invariably gained him media attention, as did his campaign against city school officials responsible for "tainted," insufficiently patriotic school books. He also showed an imaginative flair for publicity, as when he embarked on a highly publicized expedition to the South Seas aboard his yacht

Big Bill to bring back a mythic tree-climbing fish to a Chicago zoo — a voyage that petered out in New Orleans.

In 1927, he decided the time was ripe for a comeback. Dever tried to put Thompson on the defensive, focusing his campaign on "Big Bills"'s appallingly corrupt, gangster-ridden record.

Thompson presented himself as "Billy the Builder." His campaign was based on a vague anti-Prohibitionist, "America First," "Make Chicago Hum" program, and he answered none of Dever's specific charges of mismanagement or corruption. He made it perfectly clear he intended to defy the Eighteenth Amendment rules. "If I catch a policeman crossing the threshold of a man's home or place of business, I will fire that policeman right off the force" he told his supporters. "When I'm elected, we will not only reopen places these people have closed, but we'll open up ten thousand new ones."

Not only Capone but the fast-diminishing band of anti-Capone rivals were quick to respond, openly supporting Thompson for a third term. As Frank J. Loesch, president of the Chicago Crime Commission, noted at the time: "It did not take me long to discover that Al Capone ran the city. His hand reached into every department of city and county government." Over Capone's desk, Loesch noted, were three large oil portraits, of George Washington, Abraham Lincoln, and "Big Bill" Thompson.

A Capone campaign contribution (later estimated at $260,000) reached Thompson's headquarters through a local Republican ward-heeler, Daniel A. Serritella, known to be on Capone's payroll. Another gangster, Jack Zuta, who ostentatiously flaunted his William Hale Thompson Republican Club membership card, contributed $50,000. "Big Tim" Murphy; Abie Arends, the former manager of "Big Jim" Colosimo's nightclub; and Vincent "The Schemer" Drucci (he had been one of O'Banion's men, but had rallied Capone since his master's death) also became Thompson campaigners. Drucci distinguished himself by raiding (and wrecking) the offices of Alderman Dorsey R. Crowe, a leading Dever supporter, a week before the election, and on polling day, Capone's men patrolled polling booths as they had in Cicero in 1924. Thompson won, but with a diminished majority.

His third term unraveled more quickly than his second. There was an ominous presage on election night itself: the overcrowded yacht belonging to his "Fish Fans Club," aboard which he and some 1,500 supporters were celebrating his victory, slowly sank, settling on a sand-bank. There was no loss of life, but the proceedings were considerably dampened.

Thompson was no longer, as he had been for so long, the maverick, slick populist athlete-turned-politician whose turn of phrase galvanized unsophisticated crowds. Except for his own Chicago *Journal,* he was now anathema to the press, not only in Chicago but all over America. He himself had changed, physically and mentally. The once tall, trim athlete had become jowly and overweight, his public appearances now often downright embarrassing, revealing a growing confusion of mind.

His gangland supporters duly reaped their rewards: one of Thompson's first moves, after his election, was to appoint Daniel A. Serritella city sealer, or official verifier of shopkeepers' weights and measures. Not that Serritella did much checking: he simply haunted City Hall, unofficial ambassador to the "Mayor of Crook County," as Capone was called, conveying his master's requests.

Thompson's reelection marked the apogee of Capone's power. He began spending less time in Cicero and more in Chicago itself, renting fifty rooms, including a large conference hall, on two floors of the Hotel Metropole. Jake Guzik and Harry Mondi, Thompson's underworld campaigners during his first campaign for mayor, also became key figures in the Capone gang, running his gambling empire.

Capone had good reason to congratulate himself on his judicious funding. Shortly after his reelection, Thompson told a crowd: "We'll throw every damn dry (Prohibition) agent in jail." "I will do all in my power," he pledged, "to save Chicago citizens from any more suffering at the hands of thugs and gunmen sent here by the Federal Government."

Against all evidence, he claimed that Chicago was no more gangster-prone than any other large American city. "Sure we have crime here," he told reporters. "We will always have crime. Chicago is just like any other big city. You can get a man's arm broken for so much, a leg for so much, or beaten up for so much. Just like New York, except we print our crime and they don't."

Despite Thompson's now abysmal reputation as far as many Chicagoans were concerned, he was deluded enough to believe he might win the next Republican presidential nomination (Coolidge had let it be known he would not run for a second term) and embarked on a 10,000-mile trip through the United States to gauge his chances, on the pretext of raising funds for flood control. In a series of banquets and meetings, Thompson was suitably coy. "There are a lot of reports I want to be president," he told a San Francisco audience. "That's not true. My one ambition is to protect the people of the Mississippi valley from the floods of the future." But this denial was belied by the pamphlets handed out by his aides. The cover was a red-white-and-blue target whose bull's-eye was "America First." Inside, Thompson asked Americans to "shoot at the bull's-eye for American prosperity" through "united action," urging delegates to the next Republican Convention to work for the four "Thompsonian principles": America First, farm relief, island waterways, and national flood control.

Like an earlier attempt to sound out his chances of gaining a seat in the Senate, his presidential ambitions did not last. On his return to Chicago, he faced deep trouble. An election for state's attorney was due in 1928 and the front-runner, John A. Swanson, a "clean government" advocate and ally of Thompson's archenemy, Senator Charles S. Deneen, seriously threatened his power base.

The Swanson campaign was marked by a new gangland terrorist weapon, the pineapple bomb — so much so that it became known as the "pineapple primary." There were sixty-two bomb outrages in six months, two of them wrecking Deneen's and Swanson's homes. Thompson blamed it all on Prohibition "agents provocateurs." "There'll always be bombing as long as there is Prohibition," he told the press. Campaigning against Deneen's man, he gave his anti-Prohibition rhetoric a new twist: if whiskey was now so costly, he told crowds, it was "all the fault of King George and his rum-running fleet." Once more, he resurrected the campaign slogan "Whack King George on the snoot." Thompson also repeatedly threatened to resign if his archenemy Swanson was elected. Swanson won, and Thompson changed his mind.

With many former friends leaving the bandwagon, he now faced another calamity: a much-delayed investigation into his campaign finances had revealed irregularities on a huge scale, and a judge ordered him to pay $2,245,000 back to the city. A shocked Thompson suffered a nervous breakdown and went on a prolonged vacation. His influence further diminished as his minions got used to running the town without him. On his return, he appeared to have lost his taste for political infighting. Increasingly frail and confused, he was now little more than a figurehead.

Two sets of killings brought Chicago — and its mayor — into further disrepute. The first was the Saint Valentine's Day massacre (February 14, 1929), which would inspire countless Hollywood movies, including the unforgettable beginning of Billy Wilder's *Some Like It Hot.*

Although it was to become a mythic event, it is worth recalling that the Saint Valentine's Day massacre was nothing more than the routine settling of a banal commercial dispute. "Bugs" Moran — prominent gangster, owner of speakeasies, and would-be Capone challenger — received his regular consignments of whiskey from the Detroit Purple Gang, a bootlegging organization under Capone's control. Although the Old Log Cabin brand Moran purchased was popular with drinkers, it was expensive, and he let Capone know he would seek supplies elsewhere.

Capone did not react when Moran switched to another brand, but Moran's customers did: they hated the stuff. Moran asked Capone to resume supplies, and was shown the door. Good whiskey was in short supply, and Capone had found more lucrative customers.

Moran's men retaliated by hijacking Old Log Cabin consignments, until Capone decided something had to be done. Moran received a message that a consignment of hijacked Old Log Cabin whiskey was for sale, and could be picked up at the North Clark Street garage on the following day. At the appointed time, the killers (including two men in police uniform) entered the garage, gunning down all those inside. (The only reason Moran survived was that he was late for his appointment.) Capone had a cast-iron alibi: not only was he in his Miami home on the day of the massacre, but he had been on the telephone to a Miami district attorney at the very time of the killings. There were no convictions.

Sixteen months later, another killing again made headlines around the world. This time the victim was Alfred J. ("Jake") Lingle, thirty-eight, a *Chicago Tribune* police reporter.

Although his editors at first portrayed him as a martyr, fallen in the course of duty while on a secret investigation, this did not last. As rival newspapers soon pointed out, "Jake" Lingle, on a weekly salary of $65, had a millionaire life-style, gambled heavily, and had been very close to Capone (he died wearing a diamond-studded belt Capone had given him). They also revealed he had acted as intermediary between the police and the underworld for almost as long as he had been a reporter. The *Tribune* was compelled to acknowledge he had "engaged in practices contrary to the code of its honest reporters." Although the motive for the killing was never proved, the likeliest explanation was that Lingle had arranged for police protection of Capone-controlled greyhound racing tracks and speakeasies but had failed to pass on underworld funds, gambling with them instead. It was also believed that Capone, by this time under belated investigation by the IRS, feared that Lingle might give investigators details of Capone's financial empire, about which he knew a great deal. A minor gunman, who may or may not have been responsible for his murder, was sentenced to fourteen years in jail.

Thompson responded to the Lingle scandal by firing his police chief, but his cry to "drive the crooks and criminals out of Chicago" was singularly ill-timed. Shortly afterward, "Big Bill" Thompson's wife was attacked while in her chauffeur-driven car, and relieved of jewelry worth $10,000.

Thompson failed to secure a fourth term in office, and lived on in relative obscurity until his death on March 19, 1944, when he made headlines one last time. Although he left an estate worth only $150,000 and no will, safe deposit boxes in his name were found to contain cash, stocks, and gold certificates worth over two million dollars.

14

REMUS ON TRIAL

When last in the news, George Remus was in Washington, providing the Senate Investigative Committee on former attorney general Daugherty with startling examples of corruption at the highest levels of the Harding administration. Remus became an Atlanta penitentiary inmate in January of 1924, along with his twelve-man team and several other noted bootlegger millionaires. By this time, the drop in America's prison population that had so encouraged the drys was over. Numbers had risen sharply — in all, between 1920 and 1933, some 500,000 people would go to prison for offenses against the Volstead Act — and Atlanta, like all other American jails, was overcrowded.

But Remus was no ordinary prisoner. Money talked. His cell was a small but comfortable apartment, with its own kitchen and bathroom, in a separate building known to the inmates as "millionaire's row." Imogene, who helped him furnish it, and made arrangements for his privileged treatment with John Sartain, the prison governor, regularly visited him, bringing him delicacies, cooking and cleaning for him, and occasionally spending the night. She also acted as his business courier. In her absence, Remus took most of his meals with the governor or the chaplain. These arrangements — which also included the right to unlimited phone calls (Remus called his wife almost daily for 15 to 30 minutes at a time) and permission to go on shopping trips, even spending occasional nights out with Imogene in luxurious Atlanta hotels when she tired of the prison apartment — cost him $1,000 a month.

Franklin N. Dodge was a Justice Department agent working directly for Deputy Attorney General Willebrandt on Prohibition cases of exceptional importance, infiltrating bootlegging rings, posing as a wealthy potential investor. Despite his outstanding record, Remus's friend Willie Haar, another millionaire row inmate, thought that Dodge might be persuaded to use his influence to get Willebrandt to grant them both a pardon. Dodge, he told Remus, would certainly be a useful man to know — and who could sound him out more effectively than Imogene? Remus wrote her (sometime between March 16 and May 1, 1925): "Why do you not look up Dodge?"

Dodge came regularly to Atlanta to debrief other prisoners on separate cases (he had not been involved in the Remus case). Imogene got in touch with him, and it was in Atlanta, but outside the jail, that she and Dodge first met.

It was an immediate "fatal attraction." Imogene fell head over heels in love with the tall, handsome agent. Whether Dodge, a known womanizer, fell for her too, or simply used her, remains unclear. Nor is it clear whether, subsequently, Imogene initiated some of the moves against Remus herself, or blindly followed Dodge's instructions. In any event, shortly after that first meeting, Imogene started playing a devious, dangerous game.

Coached by Dodge, who abruptly resigned from the Justice Department shortly after Imogene became his mistress, she kept up her visits to Atlanta — ever the loyal, loving wife — but now did so on Dodge's instructions. Behind Remus's back, Imogene and Dodge embarked on a perfect crime. Not only did they set about appropriating his fortune (this was relatively easy, in that Imogene had power of attorney), but plotted to have him deported as an illegal alien. If that failed, they even considered having him murdered.

Given the straitlaced atmosphere of the time, their behavior was singularly careless. Not only did they travel together, staying in hotel rooms with communicating doors, sometimes even in the same room as a married couple under an assumed name, but Dodge moved into the Price Hill mansion with Imogene for weeks at a time, sleeping in Remus's bed, even appropriating Remus's hats, tiepins, and cufflinks — everything but his suits and shoes, which did not fit.

While Remus was serving the last months of his Atlanta sentence, Imogene, by stages, emptied his bank accounts, transferring the money into four separate accounts in Dodge's name in Lansing, Michigan, Dodge's home town. She also made over some of Remus's distillery certificates to Dodge, selling the rest at a loss and transferring the money into the Lansing accounts.

Imogene's infatuation with Dodge was total. Remus maintained charge accounts in various Cincinnati stores, and here Imogene bought Dodge clothes and jewelry, also making him a gift of Remus's personal jewelry, worth $100,000. Some of her tokens of love were childishly romantic. As George Remus's housekeeper, William Mueller, would later testify in court, Imogene had the initial R removed from the silver cutlery in the Remus mansion, substituting a D, similarly changing the initials G. R. on the door of Remus's Lincoln to F. D.

Shortly before Remus was released from jail, she stripped the mansion of all its valuable contents, leaving behind only some basic furniture. The costly paintings, and Remus's collection of George Washington's letters, of which he was inordinately proud, were discreetly sold or pawned. All of the valuable fittings and furniture, including the chandeliers, were stored in Cincinnati warehouses and garages.

While dismantling the Price Hill mansion, Imogene ordered Mueller to take a clock down from a sitting room wall. Mueller refused. "That's the master's clock," he said.

"Why, don't be afraid," Imogene told him. "Mr. Remus will never come back. We're going to have him deported. We have it all arranged. He'll go back the same as he came, with a little bundle." All this would eventually come out in court.

When Remus had testified against Daugherty in Washington, Imogene had been in the audience, very much the loyal, supportive wife. But two days before his release from jail, a lawyer he had never previously heard of came to see him, notifying him of Imogene's demand for divorce proceedings on the grounds of "cruelty." Remus would find out later that he was her third choice: two lawyers, consulted earlier, had refused to take her case, saying there were no grounds for divorce.

It was his first intimation of her betrayal — and its impact was devastating. He flew into a blind rage, smashing up the cell furniture until restrained by guards. Subsequently, between catatonic spells, the outbursts returned, to begin with, several times a day. "She's driving me mad," Remus told the *Post-Dispatch*'s John Rogers shortly after his release. "She has outraged me. After all I've done for her." He burst into uncontrollable sobs, shrieking that he was "being persecuted beyond endurance." George Conners, his trusted aide, and John Rogers, who were with him a great deal of the time, would later tell the court that it was their conviction that Imogene's conduct had driven Remus insane.

His rage returned when, in the company of a newspaper cartoonist, he came back to the now empty Price Hill mansion. Its windows and doors were boarded up, and Remus had to break in. As he surveyed the stripped, dilapidated rooms, he became aware of his full predicament for the first time. Entering the swimming pool compound, he shouted "She hasn't taken the water, I've still got the water!" bursting into a fit of hysterical laughter.

He was soon to learn that Imogene had planned everything extremely thoroughly. Her last fifteen affectionate letters to him in jail prior to the lawyer's visit had been written at one sitting, then posted at intervals by a friend, while she and Dodge were in Lansing and meeting with immigration authorities in Atlanta — all part of their plan to get Remus deported. Dodge, though no longer a member of the Justice Department, used his influence to get Remus returned to prison for another year, on other charges related to his original conviction. Remus served this extra term not in Atlanta, but in Troy, near Dayton, Ohio, where, for the first time, he was treated like an ordinary inmate.

Mabel Walker Willebrandt agreed to his eventual release but extracted a singularly vengeful price: she compelled him to testify that he had paid large sums of money to prison governor John Sartain. Millionaire's row was closed down and Sartain eventually went to jail. Under pressure from her peers, she also threatened to send him back to jail unless he withdrew his charges (made before the Senate Investigating Committee) concerning Daugherty. Remus would later confess his shame at having done so, but there were so many other independent witnesses (including Jess Smith's ex-wife) with lurid accounts of Daugherty's corrupt, predatory ways that this vindictive measure was virtually ignored. In the media and in Senate circles, no one doubted that Remus had told the truth.

It was Imogene's betrayal that led him, shortly after his release from Troy, to cooperate with prosecutors in the Jack Daniel's case. Accompanied by the faithful Conners, and John Rogers, who was researching the series about him in the St. Louis *Post-Dispatch,* he went to Indianapolis with one purpose in mind: to reveal Imogene's part in the conspiracy. Not only had she invested $20,000 of her own money in Jack Daniel's whiskey certificates, but had been influential in persuading the rogue syndicate to empty the Jack Daniel's warehouse fast — and cut the whiskey with water. To Remus — ruined, disgraced, and betrayed — this was the ultimate perfidy: not only was he a cuckold, but — through sheer greed — Imogene had destroyed his reputation as America's finest quality bootlegger.

To his dismay, the charges against Imogene were dropped. Although she had filed papers for a divorce, she was still legally his wife and he was unable to testify against her. While the Jack Daniel's case proceeded with the other accused, Imogene and Dodge even showed up in Indianapolis as interested spectators, living in a hotel as man and wife. There was one unexpected confrontation, witnessed by Rogers. A scared Imogene threw up her hands, shouting "Daddy, don't kill me, don't hurt me." Remus ignored her and turned away.

It was in Indianapolis that Remus learned that Imogene — who had found proof of his entry into the United States and of his citizenship in the Price Hill mansion and destroyed them — was trying to have him deported. While in Indianapolis, Remus also discovered that his life was in danger. Rogers learned that Dodge had contacted some gunmen in St. Louis, members of a gang called the Regan Rats, and promised them $15,000 to have him killed. Remus applied for, and received, a gun permit.

At the Indianapolis railway station, Conners caught sight of one of the gang, and persuaded Remus to take a later train. The gunmen, Conners found out later, intended to take Remus's train, stage a brawl, and kill him on board. Conners too was in danger, he would later tell the court, for Dodge and Imogene had also taken out a contract on him.

At times, Remus's attitude toward Imogene was ambiguous. Although his outbursts of rage remained an almost daily occurrence, he sometimes found excuses for her. "I knew the little woman wouldn't do this of her own free will," he told Conners on one occasion. Most of the time he was in a less forgiving mood. "I picked her out of the gutter and tried to make a lady out of her, but she didn't have it in her," he said. He would ask Conners repeatedly: "Did you think she was doing anything like this?" Conners replied that "everyone in Cincinnati was expecting something like this to happen." "My God, I must have been blind," Remus replied.

Conners had also been present when Imogene had telephoned Remus, listening in on their conversation. Imogene asked him: "You won't hurt me if I come in to see you?" Remus told her she had nothing to fear, adding: "You know I would have done the right thing by you if you had let me know." Remus asked if she was still seeing Dodge. "I've been going around with Mr. Dodge, Daddy," she said, "but there's nothing wrong morally. I've got to see him again because he has something very valuable and I must get that."

But later she called to taunt him. "Hello, Daddy, still waiting? You certainly are a mighty good waiter. I may be in tomorrow." Remus had had enough. "You aren't Mrs. Remus any more," he told her. "I'll file a cross-petition, and if you think you're going to get my property, I'll follow you to China if necessary." Rogers had been with Remus when Imogene had phoned once more. Remus asked her to name a single instance of his mistreatment of her. There was a pause, and then she said: "Your kind treatment of Romola" (her step-daughter). Remus replied: "Well, she *is* my daughter."[1]

Because Conners and Remus were convinced their lives were in danger in the Price Hill mansion, they moved into a downtown Cincinnati hotel, the Sinton. Apart from Conners, two of Remus's former staff had remained close to him: George Klug, his driver, and his secretary, Blanche Watson. All four had dinner together on the evening of October 5, 1927 — the eve of Imogene's divorce proceedings, and, as it turned out, her death.

On the morning of October 6, Remus ordered Klug to drive him to the Alms Hotel, where Imogene was staying. "There's something I want to discuss with her before we go before the judge," Remus told him. It was a ruse, to allay any suspicions Klug might have, for he did not attempt to talk to her as she left the hotel. According to a later police report, when he shot and killed her she was wearing "a black silk dress, silk stockings and a small black hat from Paris."

The meeting with Judge Dixon was at eight A.M. While he waited in vain in his chambers for them to show up, a dying Imogene was on her way to Bethesda Hospital, and Remus, having given himself up, was in police custody. The police asked him if he wanted to make a statement. "I'm at peace now after two years of hell. I'm satisfied I've done right," he told them.

In the Hamilton County Jail, Remus got special treatment once again. He kept a sizeable wardrobe (twenty suits, according to the *Cincinnati Enquirer*), and was allowed unlimited visitors, including reporters and photographers — cooperative wardens even brought him liquor for his "hospitality bar." He was photographed doing his morning exercises on the prison rooftop, and was given an additional cell, which he used as an office.

Charged with first-degree murder, which carried the death penalty, Remus was determined to defend himself. Surprisingly, for his conviction should by rights have disbarred him, Judge Chester R. Shook agreed to let Remus act as co-counsel to Robert Elston, an aristocratic-looking former district attorney and the best legal talent in Cincinnati.

This in itself ensured that the Remus trial would be a cause célèbre. Even before it began, it was attracting considerable media attention. Reporters were expected from all over America, as well as from Canada, London, and Berlin. At the Hamilton County courthouse, a courtroom was earmarked for the press. A note to them from County Clerk Frank Lewis banned the use of "artificial lights" but stated that "within reasonable limits, hand cameras can be used."

By today's standards, preliminary procedures were remarkably swift: jury selection took only four days, and a mere thirty-nine days after the murder, the Remus trial began. If it failed to make headline news that day, this was only because of an even more compelling story: the day Remus's trial began — November 14, 1927 — was also the day Charles Lindbergh was given a hero's welcome in Washington after his Atlantic crossing.

The prosecution team was an almost caricatural illustration of the gulf between America's patrician establishment and "new Americans" such as Remus. The chief prosecutor, Charles P. Taft II, whose brother ran the *Cincinnati Enquirer*, was a member of Ohio's most famous political family. Their father, former United States President William

Howard Taft, was currently serving his country in another prestigious capacity, as chief justice of the Supreme Court. In an early altercation with prosecutor Taft, Remus pointedly referred to "this young man's father." "It has been the pleasure of this defendant to appear before the High Chief Justice, but the specimen as given by the offshoot of that great renowned character is pitiful, if the Court please."

The other prosecutors, though from less prestigious backgrounds, were also from well-connected Ohio families. Taft let Walter K. Sibbald do the bulk of the talking, while Remus reserved much of his venom for Harold Basler, the most aggressive member of the prosecution team.

As is often the case in American jury trials, jury selection marked the first clash between prosecution and defense. Remus, a convicted bootlegger, was eager to discover whether any of the potential jurors were fanatical drys or otherwise prejudiced against him. The prosecutors objected to a defendant cross-examining them at all. As they knew he would, Remus lost his temper, alleging harassment.

Remus particularly resented the prosecution's attempt to discredit him as a lawyer. Basler based his allegations on an incident in Chicago years ago, in a case opposing employers and the Chicago Machinists' Union. Remus had acted for the unionists, and his court opponents had appealed to the Chicago Bar Association in an unsuccessful effort to have him disbarred. This led to the first of his many violent clashes with Basler and Taft.

> REMUS: Five hundred judges and members of the Chicago Bar have volunteered to come down here as character witnesses, and just because the son of the Chief Justice in this wonderful United States makes that kind of assertion — man, if I had you in the corridor, I would wreck you physically.
>
> BASLER: How much of this stuff is the court going to stand, this personal vilification? There is absolutely no excuse for it.
>
> REMUS (to Basler): When you were on the Eastern trip you drank two pints of whiskey — you did so!
>
> BASLER: Is that so?
>
> REMUS: That will be shown. Yes, sir, I will show you up.
>
> BASLER: Now then, your Honor sees what kind of vilification is going to be permitted here if this man indulges in such liberties as this.

REMUS: Murder is the charge. My life is at stake, and I will show that you drank liquor by the pint, not by the ounce.

BASLER: There is no occasion for this, as you can see.

REMUS: My life is at stake, not yours.

BASLER: He is turning around to talk to the newspapermen and it is not for the benefit of the court at all.

JUDGE SHOOK: I am ready to pass on the matter. Sit down, Mr. Remus. The court will disregard everything stated by Mr. Remus of any personal character.

The clash had been more violent than the official court proceedings inferred. At one point, Remus rose and strode menacingly over to Basler, waving his fists. Basler (overheard by newsmen, but not, apparently by the court stenographer) hissed: "Get back to your side, or I'll punch you."

Judge Shook allowed Remus to continue cross-examining potential jurors, but cautioned him against any more "spectacular outbursts." It was widely assumed that Remus knew so much about Basler's drinking habits because back in 1921 he had regularly supplied him with liquor.

As it turned out, most of the excused jury members were dismissed because they opposed the death penalty, not because of their attitude toward Prohibition. One juror was excused because he was a machinist, and might therefore be prejudiced in Remus's favor. Another Afro-American juror, described as "Ben Boner, negro," was also dismissed for prejudice of a different type. "I had a wife who ran away with my money too," he told the courtroom, to loud laughter, in which Remus did not join. The twelve-person jury ended up all-white. Ten were men. Its youngest female member, Mrs. Ruth Cross, was twenty-three; the oldest, Mrs. Anna Ricking, sixty-three.

Remus had rashly announced before the trial that he would not plead temporary insanity, but changed his mind after a talk with Elston, who also persuaded him not to intervene too often in the course of the trial. His more dispassionate, polished co-counsel dominated the proceedings from the very start. This was, to a large extent, the prosecution's own fault.

In his opening statement, Walter Sibbald not only accused Remus of "cold-blooded, deliberate and premeditated murder," but claimed "Remus had the assistance and the encouragement of others of the Remus gang," and that even his secretary, Blanche Watson, "was in on the conspiracy." Remus's prompt objection to the word gang was sustained.

Why the prosecution advanced the conspiracy theory is a mystery. It certainly added nothing to the case against Remus, for a conspiracy was not required to prove his own premeditation. Perhaps Taft assumed that with Remus's conviction practically a foregone conclusion, this would enable him, in a subsequent trial, to indict Conners and Klug as well. Instead, he only weakened what, on the face of it, appeared to be an open and shut case.

Subsequently, the Remus trial was scrutinized almost as relentlessly as the O. J. Simpson proceedings some seventy years later, and in retrospect it was clear the conspiracy charge harmed the prosecution's case by detracting from Remus's own dramatic role as executioner. It was in any case impossible to sustain, for there was not a shred of evidence to back it up. Conners, Klug, and Blanche Watson all insisted, in court, that there had been nothing at their dinner with him the night before to indicate that Remus intended to kill his wife. They also recalled their shock at the news of Imogene's death with such conviction the jury clearly believed them.

More damaging still to the prosecution was its unsuccessful attempt to dismiss as irrelevant any of Imogene's behavior prior to her murder. "The State doesn't think that the evidence should go back further than twenty-four hours," Sibbald said in his opening statement.

Elston, in *his* opening statement, argued against this. "Insanity is our defense," he announced, "and insanity that dates back two years, brought about by a conspiracy on the part of his wife and this Franklin L. Dodge — a conspiracy to divorce Remus, keep him in jail, get his property and then deport him." He outlined a conspiracy of a very different type — "a conspiracy to deprive the defendant of every last cent of the fortune he possessed, to keep him in prison as long as possible, and when all his sentences had been served, to deport him." Imogene Remus

. . . used the defendant's money to hire assassins to take his life. . . . Insanity may show itself in different ways. We will show that after his spell in Atlanta penitentiary there was a very great deterioration in his mental faculties. We expect to show his mind snapped because these things bore down so heavily on him, because, after all, he is only human.

Judge Shook decided evidence of this type was relevant, and would be heard. Remus had requested that all of Dodge's and Imogene's financial records be produced as evidence, and this too was granted — a huge advantage for the defense, though no reporters, at this stage, were prepared to bet on the trial's outcome.

The facts themselves were beyond dispute, for Remus had indeed gone straight to the police after the shooting, and other direct evidence was overwhelming. But, from the start, the prosecution behaved with singular incompetence. Ruth, Remus's stepdaughter, was questioned about his attitude toward her after his release from Atlanta — and although she referred to his "disagreeableness," she admitted under cross-examination by Elston that Remus was only trying to recover his property, including Ruth's car — which he had paid for.

The prosecution was equally inept in its handling of George Klug, Remus's driver. Under cross-examination by Elston, Klug told the court that he had been threatened with jail unless he confessed to his part in the conspiracy, but was told "You won't go to jail if you admit to driving Remus to the railway station." Klug, treated like a hostile witness, admitted that prior to driving Remus to the Alms Hotel, he had spent the entire night gambling, only returning to the hotel at five thirty in the morning.

The absurdity of the conspiracy allegation became apparent when another witness, William Hulvershorn, took the stand. Hulvershorn told the court how, at the wheel of his car in Eden Park, "I saw this man hurrying in the park like he was trying to make a train or something and I gave him a lift." The man jumped in, and asked to be taken to the central station. On the way, he said: "You don't know who I am?" Hulvershorn said no, and he replied "I'm George Remus." "The famous George Remus?" Hulvershorn asked. "Glad to know you." When the car arrived at the railway station, Remus appeared disconcerted. "I meant the central police station," he said, adding, "I shot someone in the park." A titter ran through the courtroom when

Hulvershorn added: "I didn't believe him when he told me who he was."

Witness after witness came forward with descriptions of Remus's hysterical grief after his return from Atlanta. Mueller told the court of the clock incident. Rogers recalled Remus's phone conversation with Imogene. He had also, in the course of his reporting, met with Imogene on her own. Imogene had told him: "Remus will never hurt me, but please don't let him hurt Mr. Dodge."

"Remus's conduct convinced me he was insane," Rogers told the court. "I went so far as to report to my managing editor, in the summer of 1926, that he had lost his mind." Another defense witness was Judge Beston S. Oppenheimer, who had earlier been involved in Imogene's divorce, but had handed the case over to another judge at an early stage. He had come to the conclusion, after hearing Remus in his chambers, that the man was "crazy." Rogers also told the court that the U.S. commissioner of immigration in Atlanta "told me that Remus was an alien, which was the reason for seeking deportation."

Although the prosecution did its best to discredit the testimony of Willie Haar, the millionaire's row convict and bootlegger, he too made an impact on the jury. In Indianapolis after his release during the Jack Daniel's trial, he told the court of parties he had attended. "Dodge and Imogene Remus were fondling, hugging and caressing one another and using profane language." In an aside, he added: "It was funny that a lot of Prohibition officials supposed to be enforcing the laws were having liquor themselves."

Thomas Berger, no ex-bootlegger but a wealthy industrial fair organizer (and a boyhood friend of Remus), was another valuable defense witness. He testified how, some months before the murder, Remus had asked him to act as mediator. He began an account of their conversation: "I said to Remus," Berger recounted, "your wife wants nothing whatever to do with you. She is in love with Franklin Dodge. She would not refund to you any of the property. . . . She didn't want a few hundred thousand dollars, but wanted to keep all she had." The judge asked Berger whether, in his opinion, Remus was sane "despite the fact that Dodge was still alive." "He ought to be where she is," Berger replied, to loud, appreciative laughter. He also confirmed that Imogene had tried to have Remus deported.

"I told Remus that the chief immigration officer at St. Louis had told me the department wanted to deport Remus," he continued. "I told Remus I asked the immigration officer to find out who was back of it, and two weeks later I told Remus the officer came to see me and said that Uncle Sam would not be a party to deport an individual for private gain of individuals like Dodge and Mrs. Remus." Again, Remus had flown into such a rage that "I thought he was going to tear one of his ears off. He wanted to go after Dodge and his wife."[2]

George Conners described his first visit to Price Hill mansion after Remus's release. "The only thing in the house was a bed and a pair of shoes, which didn't belong to Remus."[3]

By this time it was clear to reporters that the jury was on Remus's side, but if any doubt remained, it vanished on December 8, when Elston called a surprise witness, Harry Truesdale. It was to be the turning point of the trial.

15

REMUS REDUX

Elston's purpose in calling the witness, he told the judge, was to establish whether Remus had been insane. But it became increasingly clear, as Truesdale's story unfolded, that his real purpose was very different.

Truesdale's voice was so low that the court stenographer had to repeat some of his statements to the jurors. Only a verbatim account can adequately convey the tense drama of those few minutes.[1]

TRUESDALE: I followed him [Remus] several times and talked to him on October 5. [The day before the murder.]

ELSTON: When was the first time you saw him?

TRUESDALE: Sometime during the latter part of the summer. A man called Marcus pointed him out to me. [Marcus's name had already come up. Conners had alleged that Marcus had been offering $15,000 to anyone who would kill Remus]. I saw him around four-five P.M. on October 5.

ELSTON: Did you talk to him?

TRUESDALE: I went there for that purpose.

ELSTON: Did you form an opinion about sanity or insanity?

TRUESDALE: I did, on that afternoon, when I told him what I knew.

ELSTON: Now tell us what you said to him and what he said and did that causes you to form that opinion.

TRUESDALE: I told him that out at Springdale dog track a man by the name of John Marcus told me he knew how I could make $10,000 and I asked him how it would be and he told me that if I would kill a man I could get that much money.

JUDGE SHOOK: Did you tell this to Mr. Remus?

TRUESDALE: Exactly. Marcus told me he would introduce me to the party that would give me the money.

BASLER: *Did* you tell Mr. Remus this?

TRUESDALE: Exactly. Marcus said he could not take me up right away so Marcus went over to see her and came back and said she would not see me right away.

ELSTON: Who?

TRUESDALE: Mrs. Remus. Three or four days later, in Cincinnati, Marcus told me she would see me and took me to the Alms Hotel, room 708.

He introduced me to Mrs. Remus by the name of Charles and we didn't stay there long that afternoon, because she had people in the next room.

But she told me to come back the next day at three, which I did. She then told me that I would get $10,000 if I would kill Remus. She told me she would give me $5,000 and another person would give me $5,000.

I wanted some kind of surety but she would not give it me. I asked her who the other party was. She said "I will vouch for him, his money is all right."

She didn't state his name right at the time, but after a while she said his name was Franklin Dodge. She was very bitter against Remus and said she wished someone would beat his brains out.

She gave me $250 for expenses. Mrs. Remus told me Remus was at the Sinton Hotel, room 327. I went to the hotel and sat on the left side of the elevator.

Once I passed his room which was open — one time I thought of killing him in his room, but too many people went in and out. He always had a lot of callers. I kept on following him till a few days before the Dempsey-Tunney fight.

It was at this juncture that Remus burst into a flood of tears. His sobs got louder and louder until Truesdale could no longer be heard.

His daughter Romola, by his side that day, was also in tears. So was Mrs. Gabriel Ryerson, Remus's sister, and several other spectators. Both women jurors started crying too. "The jurors," the *Cincinnati Enquirer* noted, "were highly sympathetic." All eyes were on Remus, shaking spasmodically, bent over his desk, head in hands.

Between sobs, Remus asked the judge: "Will you adjourn the court for a minute, Your Honor?" Judge Shook ordered Remus removed from the courtroom. He was still sobbing as marshals escorted him out, brushing away photographers. "No, no," he told them. Turning to the judge, he said: "I am sorry, Your Honor, I . . . cannot . . . help . . . it."

The court remained in session for another thirty minutes, with Truesdale impassive in the witness box. Remus's sobs could be heard from behind the door leading to the judge's quarters. Finally Judge Shook adjourned the court.

The following morning a perfectly composed Remus entered the courtroom. "I wish to apologize, Your Honor, to you and the jury, for my unmannish [sic] conduct yesterday," he said, and Truesdale resumed his testimony.

> She said she wanted to see me at her hotel. Her bags were packed. She said she was going away. She told me I would have to hurry as it wouldn't be long before the divorce case. She said she would be gone for ten days to two weeks. After this I saw Remus in Hamilton but had no opportunity to kill him.
>
> Then on October 2 I called at the Alms Hotel. Mrs. Remus said she had been in Chicago for the Dempsey-Tunney fight. She said she was very anxious as the time was running short. She said she would meet me at midnight at the Rentschler building. I noticed a man on the corner and she said he was Dodge, the man who would give me the other $5,000.

Truesdale said Imogene and he walked to the Grand Hotel. She wanted to find out whether Remus was registered there under his name. There was a car outside, with three men inside, one of them Dodge, and Imogene and Truesdale followed at walking pace. "I was a little afraid of this," Truesdale told the court. Imogene said: "If I see him tonight, I'll kill him myself," and showed him a pearl-handled revolver in her bag. By this time Truesdale had had enough. He left. "I never got in touch with Mrs. Remus again."

When he finally met Remus, the following day — October 5 — and told him what he had just told the court, Remus broke down. "I felt he was insane." Truesdale added he had sought out Remus "because I feared I was being set up and would go to jail for something."

The prosecution did its best to discredit his story. Truesdale had a "Bertillon" — that is, a major criminal record — and Sibbald made the most of it.

> SIBBALD: You're just a petty thief. You'd do anything if you got your price, right?
>
> TRUESDALE: Yes, I would if I got the money for it.
>
> SIBBALD: You'd come here and give perjured testimony if you got enough money out of it?
>
> TRUESDALE: No, I don't give perjured testimony.
>
> SIBBALD: You'd commit murder for money but you wouldn't commit perjury for money?
>
> TRUESDALE: That's a different thing.
>
> SIBBALD: You know the woman is dead.
>
> TRUESDALE: She must be. [laughter in court]

The prosecution tried to show that Imogene had never asked him to kill Remus, but simply to set him up with a woman, so that Imogene could burst in on him in flagrante.

Truesdale denied this. Sibbald abruptly changed his line of questioning.

> SIBBALD: Did you divide the two hundred dollars with your partners?
>
> TRUESDALE: No.
>
> SIBBALD: Who were your partners?

TRUESDALE: Who were my partners? I don't see why it's necessary to bring . . .

Elston objected to the question.

TRUESDALE: I have no partners.

Truesdale denied he had been paid to testify, but, under further questioning, admitted staying at the Grand Hotel under the name of Harry Truelabe. Truesdale's appearance had been carefully planned. Just prior to his testimony, William A. Hoefft, the cigar stand manager of the Sinton Hotel, had taken the stand. Hoefft had been seen with Remus the day before the murder.

"My God, Hoefft," Remus told him, "I just had information I was going to be killed." Hoefft told the court: "He sat with his head in his hands. I stayed with him for forty-five minutes. After quieting him down, Remus apologized. . . . In my opinion he was insane."

Afterward, Elston told reporters Truesdale had agreed to testify because "he adhered to an underworld code that you make a clean breast of things when capital punishment is involved." "I've checked his story," Elston said. "There are witnesses, we can verify it."

Elston was now quietly confident. Truesdale's testimony, he believed, had made a huge impact on the jurors, turning Remus into the victim and Imogene into the executioner. The prosecution did its best to fight the tide, with evidence that relations between George Remus and Imogene had been far from idyllic long before Remus was released from jail, but their witnesses — Imogene's daughter Ruth and Elizabeth Felix, a friend of Imogene's — failed to shake the jury, in that they recalled instances of minor spats that occur among the most devoted couples. Ruth said Imogene had often been in tears after seeing Remus in Atlanta jail "because he had been brutal and unkind." In the light of the earlier testimony, Felix's claim that Imogene had been "morally irreproachable" was, to say the least, unconvincing.

Remus's character witnesses had far greater impact. The most prominent was Clarence Darrow, the criminal lawyer whose brilliant advocacy and showmanship had long turned him into a superstar. Slipping into his co-counsel role, Remus could not resist making the most of this, referring to Darrow as "the sage of the twentieth century. . . . How proud am I to know that this great humanitarian takes up his time to testify for me." Judge Shook cut him short with a curt "That's enough."

Darrow praised Remus as a man and as a lawyer, and said he knew nothing of his investigation by a grievance committee of the Chicago Bar Association, but "if he was investigated, I would not regard an indictment as affecting peace and quiet."

Taft did his best to turn Remus's emotional outburst to the prosecution's advantage. "Don't you know he was known [in Chicago legal circles] as the weeping, crying Remus?" he asked. "I knew he was a very emotional fellow, somewhat unstable," Darrow said.

Taft tried again. "Would you regard Remus as characteristic of a law-abiding citizen?" Elston objected, and the question was withdrawn.

The jury probably missed the point. In legal circles, Darrow's anti-Prohibitionist views were well known, and almost certainly explained his presence in court.

Taft brought up Remus's bootlegging past with another character witness, also a well-known Chicago attorney, Thomas S. Hogan. Again, his questions backfired.

Had Hogan been aware of Remus's conviction on liquor charges? "That's a moot question, whether it's moral turpitude," Hogan replied, anticipating Taft's next question. "While I'm a dry myself I wouldn't consider that a heinous offense against the law."

Remus could not resist making himself heard. "The defendant has never hijacked liquor," he told the court, "and the defendant has no apologies to make for having sold good liquor since 1919."

At the close of the trial, Dr. E. A. Baber, superintendent of Cincinnati's Longview psychiatric hospital and one of the panel of psychiatrists who had examined Remus, testified that he was sane. Remus subjected him to repeated questioning. It was "the peculiar situation of a man claiming insanity for his defense, cross-examining an expert on insanity" the *Cincinnati Enquirer* noted, adding that Remus "gave Dr. Baber some uncomfortable moments," as when

Remus asked him: "Sanity is the reverse of insanity, is it not, Dr. Baber?"

BABER: Yes.

REMUS: Insanity is an abnormal condition of the mind, isn't it?

BABER: Not necessarily.

Elston delighted the audience with excerpts of some of the inane tests the panel had subjected Remus to. "Didn't he say at the time that he was on trial for murder, and didn't have time to bother with this nonsense?" he reminded the court.

Taft's lackluster summing up differed little from the prosecution's opening statement, though he did his best to portray "the weeping, whining Remus" as a cynical play-actor. He also reminded the jurors that Truesdale, a convicted felon, must have known that he was immune from prosecution. Under the Ohio state laws, it was not a punishable offense to conspire to commit a crime if no crime was subsequently committed.

Remus came into his own on December 19 with an emotional summing up. "Here before you stands Remus the lawyer. In the chair there [gesturing] is Remus the defendant, charged with murder. Remus the defendant does not desire any sympathy or compassion in any shape or form whatsoever. If you feel the defendant should go to the electric chair, do not flinch. The defendant will not flinch. He stands before you in the defense of his honor and the sanctity of his home."[2]

Thanking the judge for his "fairness and squareness," Remus reminded the jury that insanity [Dr. Baber notwithstanding] in his opinion was "nothing more than the abnormal condition of the mind." He also reminded the court that Franklin Dodge, "that ace of the Prohibition department, that deuce with women, that moral leper, this human parasite with whom County Prosecutor Charles Taft traveled the country" had not been called on to testify. He made a final crack at prosecutor Basler ("Look at his profile and say whether it has the look of hypocrisy?"), ending with a reference to the Volstead Act, " . . . one of the greatest criminal and legal abortions of all time. Why, but for the act, the defendant would not have been here!" Whatever the outcome, Remus told them, "I thank you. Happy Christmas to you."

Elston's summing up was equally passionate, but on a different note.

> Was there ever a woman in history, in fiction, who treated a man worse or more shamefully than Imogene Remus? Was there ever a woman who had less reason for doing so? And yet they say he was in a normal state of mind, that October 6 when he had the faith of a little child. . . . Turn him loose for Christmas. Bring peace of mind to the man who has suffered the tortures of hell for more than two years. We are not asking for mercy, we say this man is not guilty.

Just before the jury retired, on December 20, Judge Shook took the unusual step of reminding them that outright acquittal would be "against the law," but the jury was almost certainly more receptive to his ambiguous acknowledgment of Imogene's behavior. "The law," Shook went on, "does not justify one person taking the life of another because the latter may be of a bad character."

As reporters later ascertained, their verdict was determined within two minutes, on a single ballot, but the jurors stayed out for three hours after informing the judge they had come to a decision, enjoying a long, celebratory lunch — aware that the bulk of the press would not be back in the courtroom until four P.M. As a juror later told the *Cincinnati Enquirer*, "We felt: let's go out and give him a Christmas present. He has been persecuted long enough."

"We find the defendant not guilty on the sole ground of insanity," Harry G. Byrd, the jury foreman, announced, to wild cheering, when the court reconvened. "That's American justice!" Remus shouted. Surrounded by reporters in the hubbub that followed, he extended his "deepest appreciation" to the jury, the court, the prosecutors, the sheriff and jailer. "God knows what is in my heart at the moment. The rest of my life I will dedicate to stifle the insult that is upon our statutes, known as the National Prohibition Act." Had there been no Prohibition law "to fill the coffers of a class that seeks and practices only venality," he would not have been in court in the first place, he said.

There was a party in his cell suite that night, attended by Elston, his close circle of friends, his daughter Romola, and two of the jurors.

The following day, the jury presented a unanimous petition to Judge Shook, asking him to free Remus, "if possible, in time for Christmas." A furious Judge Shook promptly ordered them to apologize to the court, which they did. But for a long time afterward, at Taft's instigation, they remained under investigation for improper conduct, facing possible jail sentences.

Remus's troubles were not over either. Taft told the press that despite the verdict, which had been "a gross miscarriage of justice . . . , [we] are not through with all the angles in this case."

A more skillful behind-the-scenes manipulator than prosecutor, Taft worked relentlessly to have Remus committed for life to an insane asylum. He successfully petitioned for a "lunacy hearing" before a probate judge. Remus was confident he would emerge a free man. Had not a panel of psychiatrists, chosen by the prosecution, proclaimed him sane?

But Taft also persuaded two members of the panel to change their minds. A Dr. David A. Wolfstein now determined that Remus was "ruthless, reckless, selfish, eccentric — the kind of man who takes the law into his own hands. . . . He has shown he can be dangerous." Over Dr. Baber's objections, the judge ruled that a two-to-one opinion was sufficient to have Remus confined to the Lima insane asylum. On January 6, 1928, an ambulance took a strait-jacketed Remus to the dreaded Kentucky "prison-hospital."

Elston promptly appealed for a habeas corpus writ on the grounds of illegal confinement, and to the Ohio Supreme Court, while Remus — for all his alleged emotional instability — displayed singular resilience in Lima, soon becoming a hero to the warders there. As reported in the *Cincinnati Post* on January 28, "Wife-slayer George Remus saved the life of a hospital guard who had been overpowered by a giant negro patient."

An appeals court was now convened to review the case, and a fresh panel of six psychiatrists again submitted him to extensive tests, which he passed with flying colors. "Remus is sane beyond a doubt," said Dr. Shelby Mumaugh, a former Longview consultant. "He is not a psychopath." "I wish I had his brain," said Dr. W. L. Neville, a Florida specialist.

Two Lima officials disagreed. A supervisor told the appeals court that Remus had "recently violated standing orders." His offense was "having in his possession a book on insanity." Lima's superintendent, W. H. Vorbau, in frequent touch with prosecutor Sibbald, cited as evidence of Remus's insanity "his persistent refusal to wear underwear."

A more insidious attempt to brand him as insane was disclosed by the *Cincinnati Post*. Prosecutor Sibbald, sent by Taft to Lima to argue in favor of his continued incarceration, intended citing Franklin Dodge as witness at the new hearing — almost certainly to provoke Remus and cast his sanity in doubt. Cornered, Sibbald admitted as much. "We want to see how Remus acts when he meets Dodge" he was foolish enough to admit to the *Post*. Dodge denied his visit had anything to do with the Remus case. He was only in Lima to sell distributors an automatic cigarette lighter whose patent he had acquired, he told the press. The judge decided Dodge's presence was not relevant to the case.

The hearing did not go Sibbald's way. Remus was the calm, dispassionate one, refusing to rise to the prosecutor's bait, and the judge ended up reprimanding Sibbald for his "intemperate language." In many respects, his cross-examination of Remus was a rehash of the murder trial, with Sibbald embarking on a scathing, interminable review of Remus's past, alleging he had always had criminal tendencies. He conspicuously failed to prove his case, succeeding only in antagonizing the court — and revealing his anti-German bias. Remus came across as an archetypal example of the new American in search of the American Dream — a compulsive workaholic and a loving, caring son, as Remus's old mother, seventy-eight, speaking in German through a translator, confirmed. (She had been called as a witness on the spur of the moment after Sibbald alleged that, after becoming rich, Remus had neglected his family). On March 30, the court declared Remus sane.

Taft did not give up even then. Invoking "irregularities," he announced he would appeal to the Ohio Supreme Court to get the decision annulled. A motion for a new trial was denied, but the Ohio Supreme Court took an inordinately long time to make up its mind while Remus appealed for release from what he described as "this dumping-ground of hell."

Finally, on June 20, 1928, he arrived at Cincinnati's Union Station, a free man at last. A small crowd of well-wishers, including some members of the jury, was there to greet him. So were Elston and

Conners. He looked tanned and fit from his work on the Lima farm, and seemed no worse for his six months there. "I shall remain in the city where people have been so kind to me," he told the *Cincinnati Post*.

Remus never returned to bootlegging, and never salvaged his fortune. He sold the Price Hill mansion (it was later pulled down), married Blanche Watson, his former secretary, and tried — but failed — to make another fortune, first in patent medicine, then in real estate.

His death, on January 20, 1952, was the occasion for a series of obituaries recalling a fabulous era. In 1995, the Cincinnati Historical Society staged a Remus exhibit. Among the memorabilia: a photograph of the party he gave to celebrate the opening of his $125,000 swimming pool, with Imogene — the glamorous bathing belle — demurely by Remus's side, and the revolver he used to kill her.

16

A FATAL TRIUMPH

While Remus remained in Lima "criminal lunatic" hospital awaiting the Ohio Supreme Court's decision on his sanity, a medical controversy of another type gripped America: for the first time, the Volstead Act was being blamed for huge numbers of deaths from poisoned liquor.

It all began on New Year's Day, 1927, with scores of emergency admissions to New York's Bellevue Hospital. There were forty-one deaths there that day, and the Department of Health announced there had been 750 such deaths in New York alone during 1926.

Although no entirely accurate nationwide statistics are available, it is probable that by 1927 such deaths may have exceeded the 50,000 mark — to say nothing of hundreds of thousands more nonfatal cases resulting in blindness or paralysis. In 1930, the Prohibition Bureau reported that in a single, small county in Kansas — an exceptionally dry state — there had been over 15,000 victims of adulterated liquor.

Bootleggers like Remus, Olmstead, and McCoy, who refused to deal in adulterated liquor, were extremely rare. In Roy Haynes's day, fifteen chemists were on hand to examine samples of all seized liquor. In very few cases did they discover genuine brand whiskey, gin, or wine.

At their most harmless, the bootleggers' wares were diluted; in the majority of cases, the chemists found liquor made of pure grain to which coloring and flavoring had been added; moonshine — from corn meal, molasses, fruit, vegetables or sugar — presented graver risks. In some cases denatured alcohol had been redistilled to remove the poison. But in others the hooch was outright poison — wood alcohol. "Of 480,000 gallons of confiscated booze analyzed in New York in 1927, 98 percent contained poisons," said a Prohibition Bureau report. The New York *Telegram* collected over 500 samples of liquor from four hundred speakeasies. Fifty-five of them were found to contain significant traces of wood alcohol, and lesser poisons were found in seventy more.

Under Volstead Act provisions, the manufacture of denatured alcohol was not only legal, but tax exempt. The denaturing substance was usually methanol, and methanol was extremely poisonous. Three glasses could be lethal, explaining the steady rise in the death toll from 1920 onward. The Volstead Act's provisions that industrial alcohol should be made undrinkable included no proviso that its contents should be labeled "poison," and this was nothing more than "legalized murder," wrote Dr. Nicolas Murray Butler of Columbia University.

So, for the first time, in early 1927, Wayne Wheeler, that master manipulator and moral scourge of godless drinkers, found himself on the defensive. Although he denied any liability, it was a fact that the ASL had originally sanctioned the use of methanol when Volstead Act provisions were being drawn up, and had lobbied against any mandatory "poison" labels on denatured alcohol. Wheeler had boasted of the ASL's key role in drafting the act so loudly, and so frequently, that he lacked all credibility now that he denied responsibility for some of its provisions.

In 1927 cartoons and editorials he was depicted as a poisoner, and a callous one at that, for his response to the attacks against him was surprisingly inept. At first he claimed that only one such death had occurred since 1920; then, when this was ridiculed by experts, he suggested, in a press statement, that "the government is under no obligation to furnish people with alcohol that is drinkable when the Constitution prohibits it. The person who drinks this industrial alcohol is a deliberate suicide."[1] This was a monstrously hard-hearted reaction from the leader of an organization heavily subsidized by the Protestant church, leading to further press attacks on him in an admittedly overwhelmingly wet press.

His clumsiness reflected not only his increasingly precarious health but his loosening grip on Congress — and the ASL itself, for Wheeler's prickly arrogance had made him many enemies within the organization. His loss of face, and clout, had begun in 1925: in a move intended to curb Wheeler's inordinate political powers, and his hold on Congress, President Coolidge appointed Lincoln C. Andrews, a forceful retired brigadier general, as assistant secretary of the Treasury, with overall responsibilities for Customs, the Coast Guard, and the Prohibition Bureau.

The nomination undermined the position of Prohibition Commissioner Haynes, a Wheeler appointee and his pliant stooge, but it also eroded some of Wheeler's own authority, for Andrews himself began keeping Wheeler at arm's length, and a number of congressmen, past victims of Wheeler's strong-arm tactics, now began an open revolt against him. And as his own power declined, a number of new, or long-dormant, anti-Prohibition associations began gathering strength.

By 1926, several articulate and increasingly powerful lobbies had emerged, campaigning for a return to pre-1920 state liquor laws and even for outright repeal. These were no easily dismissed lobbies sponsored by former brewing and distilling vested interests. The Association Against the Prohibition Amendment, the Crusaders, and the Moderation League, mostly composed of middle-class professionals, lawyers, and businessmen, had all been in existence since the early 1920s, had no connections with the liquor industry, and were now attracting considerable media attention for the first time — with prominent personalities joining their ranks. Various state bar associations, as well as the powerful American Bar Association, were now also daring to challenge the legality of the Volstead Act, drawing attention to the abuses it occasioned; the American Federation of Labor (AFL), representing the views of all but a tiny minority of factory workers, had never given up the struggle for legal 2.5-proof beer, and in 1927 was making its influence felt in Congress as never before. Anti-German sentiment was receding at last: the American Legion, to which millions of First World War veterans belonged, was also turning against the ASL, and would soon urge an end to Prohibition.

But what worried Wheeler most in 1927 was another "women's war" phenomenon, waged this time by the wets, and headed by America's most prominent female Republican. Pauline Morton Sabin, granddaughter of a Republican governor and daughter of President Theodore Roosevelt's secretary of the Navy, was a dyed-in-the-wool, mainstream Republican. After marrying a wealthy banker (himself a prominent anti-Prohibition campaigner), she had risen through the Republican ranks to become president of the Women's National Republican Club and the first female ever appointed to the previously all-male Republican National Committee. As a vocal anti-Prohibitionist, she sacrificed her long-standing Republican convictions for her new cause, exploiting the growing, nationwide resentment at corruption and two-tier justice, displaying formidable debating and organizing skills.

Wheeler was by now a very sick man, with severe heart and kidney afflictions, but was refusing to let up. On April 23, 1927, he confronted Clarence Darrow in a contradictory debate on Prohibition at Carnegie Hall. So weak was he that his opening statement had to be read by an underling, and the audience, overwhelmingly pro-Darrow, interrupted him with cruel catcalls. Wheeler responded with considerable bravado. "According to the wets I am dangerously ill and about to quit prohibition work," he told them. "This is unmitigated bunk. My health is better than the wets wish it was and it is getting better every week." In fact, he only had another five months to live, and in the brief period left would face increasingly serious challenges.

That same April, Wheeler had advance warning that Andrew Mellon, Coolidge's closest cabinet colleague, intended letting both Haynes and Andrews go, and the following month, though in constant pain, he lobbied Congress and the White House to get the decision overthrown. But he was no longer the dreaded "big boss," and Coolidge ignored his entreaties, replacing Haynes with James M. Moran, who was no friend of Wheeler's.

The ASL was now in danger of splitting into pro-Wheeler and pro-Moran factions, and had lost the cohesion that had made it so powerful. The crisis was compounded by a growing cash crisis: affluent sympathizers were now more reluctant to give as much to the ASL as they had in the past. For the first time, the league's public relations and publishing budget had to be trimmed.

Wheeler returned one last time to Oberlin, his alma mater, for graduation exercises, to bask in the adulation he knew he would always find there. This was where his ASL career had begun, and he was still an icon to present and past students. He then decided to rest up in his small summer house in Little Point Sable, Michigan, to prepare for the grueling 1928 presidential campaign that lay ahead.

Tragedy continued to dog him. A few weeks after his holiday began, a gasoline stove exploded in the kitchen, inflicting horrible, lethal burns on his wife. At the sight of her in flames, his father-in-law, Robert Candy, dropped dead of a heart attack. Wheeler attempted to resume his ASL career, but he was a broken man.

In early September Wheeler lapsed into a coma and died. The "dry boss" was duly eulogized by the very ASL personalities who had turned against him. There would be "no successor to Wheeler," the ASL pledged. This was deliberately ambiguous praise, for though it consecrated his role in bringing the Volstead Act into being in the first place, it also implied that Wheeler, especially in the last few years, had misused his powers, overstepped his role, and offended too many people. Bishop James Cannon, the head of the Methodist Church and a prim hypocrite who had frequently clashed behind the scenes with Wheeler, immediately did his best to assume the "big boss" mantle.

Wheeler had been looking forward to the 1928 presidential nomination campaigns. He wanted to make sure that — as in 1924 — he would prevent Al Smith, still the veteran governor of New York State, from gaining the nomination. But times were changing, and so had the party's mood. Its delegates to the 1928 Democratic Convention in Houston were well-behaved, with not a drunkard in sight. William Jennings Bryan, the indefatigable Democratic Prohibitionist, was dead, and Cannon lacked Wheeler's political skills.

In a series of ASL meetings and press articles just before the convention, Cannon did his best to imply that Al Smith, if elected, would turn out to be a "cocktail President." Again and again, he quoted an article in the *Nation*. "Do you believe in electing to the Presidency a man who drinks too much for his own good, and is politically a rampant wet? Does Al drink, and does he drink too much? I am reliably informed that he drinks every day, and the number of his cocktails and highballs is variously estimated at from four to eight."[2]

Slurs of this type were only moderately effective: public opinion was now far more blasé. Besides, though it was known that Al Smith was no teetotaler, he had been a popular, competent governor, and unlike many politicians — some of them toeing the dry line — had never been seen the worse for drink.

With the support of up-and-coming Democratic personalities such as Franklin D. Roosevelt and Henry Morgenthau, to say nothing of Tammany Boss George Olvany — a rough, tough, hard-drinking Irish thug — Smith easily won the nomination.

Almost half of his telegram accepting the Democratic nomination dealt with Prohibition — proof that it remained America's most crucial political issue. Whoever won, he wrote, would have to deal with a situation "entirely unsatisfactory to the great mass of our people." Without formally calling for its repeal, he urged a return to "democratic principles of local self-government and state's rights" — in other words, a return to pre-1920 local option laws. There were reports that Smith himself would have preferred a stronger statement but was advised against it by Roosevelt, aware of the lasting importance, especially in rural areas and in the South, of the dry vote.

Once the presidential contest between Herbert Hoover and Al Smith began, Bishop Cannon concentrated all his efforts on another issue he knew prejudiced, narrow-minded (and as they were then called) "nativist" voters would respond to — the Democratic candidate's Catholic faith.

Because the Vatican's *Observatore Romano* had referred in an editorial to Prohibition's ineffectiveness ("it has become so useless not to say dangerous that it would be better to abolish it"), Cannon argued — first in an article for *Outlook* magazine, then in innumerable speeches around the country — that should Smith become president, "he is likely to be tremendously influenced by the views of the Pope and the Romish cardinals," even suggesting that, if elected, he would turn part of the White House into a permanent guest house for the Pope.

His blatant bigotry emphasized the gulf between "old" and "new" Americans and the latent hostility of the former. In Cambridge, Maryland, he told a rally that Smith courted

. . . the Italians, the Sicilians, the Poles and the Russian Jews. That kind has given us a stomach-ache. We have been unable to assimilate such people in our national life, so we shut the door on them. But Smith says "give me that kind of people." He wants the kind of dirty people that you find today on the sidewalks of New York.[3]

Mabel Willebrandt also joined in the fray, though she avoided any racist invective. Addressing mass meetings of her own Methodist Episcopal church, she urged Protestants to show their support for Hoover by writing in and pledging their vote to him.[4]

Prohibition and the Catholic issue dogged Al Smith's campaign from start to finish. In Oklahoma City, a dry stronghold, he expected a hostile reception, for Ku Klux Klan crosses had lined the railroad tracks of his campaigning train. The KKK was almost as anti-Catholic as it was anti-black, and was one of the most uncompromising advocates of a dry America.

Decidedly nervous, he met the challenge directly. "An effort has been made to distract the attention of the electorate and fasten it on malicious and un-American propaganda; I specifically refer to the question of my religion," he told a large crowd inside the Oklahoma City Coliseum. "I can think of no greater disservice to this country than to have the voters of it divide upon religious lines. It is not only contrary to the spirit of the Declaration of Independence, but of the Constitution itself."

Referring to Mabel Willebrandt's canvassing of Methodist voters, he asked the overwhelmingly Protestant crowd: "What would the effect be upon these people if a prominent official of the government of the State of New York under me suggested to a gathering of the pastors of my church that they do for me what Mrs. Willebrandt suggests be done for Hoover?" Contrary to his expectations, he got a rousing reception from the Oklahomans present.

In cities with large ethnic minorities, especially where Prohibition had made brewery and distillery workers obsolete, the public response to Smith was ecstatic. In Milwaukee, his last major electioneering venue, he focused almost exclusively on Prohibition. "If there is any one subject above all others concerning which the welfare of the country requires plain speech and constructive leadership, it is the Volstead Act," he told the crowd. He not only suggested that it be amended "to allow each state to determine for itself what it wants to do about the question of local habits," but for the first time proposed a referendum on Prohibition. "The cure for the ills of democracy," he told them, "is more democracy. Hand this back to the people. Let them decide it."

He also got in a sly dig at Mabel Willebrandt. "I shall let the Republican campaign managers worry about her. From comments in the public press all over the country, they have abundant reason to do so. We all have something to be grateful for. I haven't got Mabel on my hands."[5]

Herbert Hoover, in his memoirs published twenty-three years later, claimed that "the Prohibition issue was forced into the campaign by Governor Al Smith" but made no reference to the religious polarization that was its most distinctive feature. Whatever his private misgivings may have been (in his memoirs he also claimed, with hindsight, "a reverse of enthusiasm" for the Volstead Act), he knew that in the eyes of the dry rural voters he was one of them — he had spoken out often enough on the evils of alcohol ("one of the curses of the human race") to gain their lasting support.

In the last resort, the anti-Catholic, anti-minority, nativist themes proved compelling. Hoover won by 22 million votes to Al Smith's 15.5 million, and by 444 electoral votes to 87. The election also resulted in the highest percentage of acknowledged drys ever returned to Congress. Even in New York, America's wettest state, up-and-coming Democratic star Franklin D. Roosevelt only won the New York governorship (which Al Smith had vacated) by a small (25,000) majority.

Mabel Willebrandt was right: once again, the Prohibition issue had proved a deciding factor in politics. For all the needless tragedies it provoked, the corruption and damage to the body politic it generated, the myth of a God-fearing, prosperous, hard-working dry America was more attractive to a majority of voters than Al Smith's realistic, more tolerant approach.

There were other reasons for Smith's defeat. Hoover had been a popular secretary of Commerce, untainted by scandal. America was unprecedentedly prosperous, riding a stock market boom. More important, as Al Smith himself noted shortly afterward, "the time hasn't yet come when a man may say his Rosary beads in the White House."

Not only was the leading anti-Prohibitionist contender beaten, and removed from the presidential race for all time, but dry advocates were able to claim that a new millennium was at hand, that after nine fumbling years the Volstead Act would at last come into its own.

Newly elected President Hoover did nothing to disappoint them. "I do not favor the repeal of the 18th Amendment," he said in his acceptance speech. "I stand for the efficient enforcement of the laws enacted thereunder." He described Prohibition as

> a great social and economic experiment, noble in motive and far-reaching in purpose. It must be worked out constructively. Common-sense compels us to realize that grave abuses have occurred — abuses which must be remedied. . . . There are those who do not believe in the purposes of several provisions of the Constitution. No one denies their right to seek to amend it. . . . But the Republican Party does deny the right of anyone to seek to destroy the purposes of the Constitution by indirection.

The day after Hoover's victory, anti-Prohibitionist Pauline Sabin resigned from the Republican party. In fact, repeal was only four years away.

Although the grounds for this dramatic change in mood would be overwhelmingly economic, one reason for the continued decline of the ASL involved Wheeler's self-appointed propagandizing successor and perennial rival for ASL leadership, Bishop James Cannon. Doubts began to be cast on his fitness for the role even before Hoover became president.

A Virginian, nominal Democrat, prominent member of the Methodist Episcopal church, and member of the ASL executive since 1902, Bishop Cannon was a difficult man to like. Even his closest Methodist colleagues considered him a cold fish who had never been known to laugh and seldom smiled. This puritanical Protestant Ayatollah disapproved of most if not all pleasurable activities, including gambling. He was against dancing, theatricals, and any games, sports, or art that provided glimpses of "the female person." He inveighed against Sarah Bernhardt ("an actress of brilliant powers but unsavory moral ideals") when she came to America to perform *Camille,* and against Marie Curie, the world-famous physicist, for allegedly living in sin with her equally famous scientist companion (to whom she was in fact married), claiming that "she has lost forever her claim to a place among the great men and women of the world." And, of course, he

considered Roman Catholicism "the mother of ignorance, superstition, intolerance and sin." New York, his pet hate, was "Satan's beat."[6]

A scrutiny of Bishop Cannon's financial dealings, begun in the press almost accidentally following routine inquiries into the failure of a brokerage firm with which he was associated, revealed questionable, and perhaps indictable, practices on his part. The firm, a bucket shop, had bought $477,000 worth of stocks for him, selling them for $486,000, and Cannon's profit — $9,000 — had been nearly four times what he had actually invested ($2,500). In pre-crash America, this would normally have attracted little attention — but Bishop Cannon was one of the nation's foremost anti-gambling scourges, and his own investment had been nothing less than a prodigious gamble.

As always in America, once the media had trained their sights on a target, they started delving into his past. Reporters discovered that while administering a girls' school during the First World War, Bishop Cannon had hoarded flour, then sold it on the black market at a considerable profit, narrowly escaping prosecution. His biographer, Virginius Dabney, the Richmond *Times-Dispatch* editor, would also show that he had made false income tax returns to conceal the transaction.

Reporters now embarked on a full-scale investigation of his private life, and what they found was hilarious: the narrow-minded bigot turned out to have feet of clay. The scourge of innocent pleasure-lovers was a modern equivalent of Molière's *Tartuffe*.

On one of his frequent trips to New York during the presidential campaign, Cannon had made the acquaintance of Helen McCallum and Joan Chapman in the lobby of the McAlpin Hotel in New York, where he was staying. He introduced himself as "Stephen Trent, writer," gave McCallum twenty dollars, and would subsequently pay her rent.

It was the beginning of a beautiful friendship. Despite the fact that Bishop Cannon's wife was terminally ill with cancer, he came to New York to see McCallum with increasing frequency, even leaving Washington on November 25, 1928, the day after his wife suffered a paralytic (and eventually lethal) stroke, to be with his new friend, spending the night in New York. He returned just in time for his wife's death, and funeral, but returned to New York — and McCallum — the following day.

Subsequently, Helen McCallum became an almost, but not quite, constant companion: she was with him in Jerusalem in 1929, and during an extensive trip to Europe in 1930, both times masquerading as his secretary on all-expenses-paid junkets. Rumors that Bishop Cannon was also dating a friend of McCallum's, Cary McTroy, and might even have married her secretly, made Helen seek out the press and show them some of the bishop's intimate letters to her.

Bishop Cannon and McCallum would eventually marry, but in the meantime he got into trouble of another type: this time he was charged with mishandling Republican campaign funds. He had allegedly received $65,000 but had accounted for only $17,000. Cannon dismissed the allegations as a "popish plot," but never offered a satisfactory explanation to the investigating Senate Lobby Committee. Nor did its members press hard for an answer: a majority were prominent drys, and several were on the ASL payroll.

A final indignity was in store: on their honeymoon in Brazil, after a hasty wedding in London, Bishop Cannon learned that members of his own Methodist church had formally accused him of "gross moral turpitude." He managed to overcome this hurdle as well, but only by invoking irregularities in the way his accusers had invoked the "Methodist Discipline."

The Cannon story became a favorite ongoing topic in the American press, and the ASL's reputation suffered in consequence. An unrelated, but devastating ASL scandal broke with the indictment of the league's New York state superintendent William Hamilton Anderson, eventually convicted for embezzlement.

Another prominent Prohibition personality, the incorruptible Mabel Walker Willebrandt, was also very much in the news just after Hoover's election. For all the new president's public praise (he kept her on as deputy attorney general), she resigned her post in May of 1929.

Although there were rumors she had fallen foul of her new boss, Attorney General William D. Mitchell, and that congressmen with bootlegging connections and prominent Catholics had also lobbied for her removal, the truth was far simpler: after eight years on an inadequate government salary as the single mother of an adopted daughter, the "Prohibition Portia," as Al Smith called her, craved a more financially rewarding life.

Fruit Industries, Inc., a conglomerate representing most of the California grape growers, promptly hired her as its legal counselor on a huge retainer. It proved a wise move. Thanks to Willebrandt's Washington connections, grape farmers, in the first year of Hoover's presidency, obtained large government subsidies and federal loans.

Willebrandt was useful to her new employers in other ways. Fruit Industries manufactured raisin cakes called Vine-glo, a popular raw material ingredient for homemade wine. Willebrandt's appointment was sufficient to deter Prohibition agents from prosecuting the company for infringing the Volstead Act, and Vine-glo sales boomed. A direct competitor — Vino-Sano Inc. — was not as fortunate. Its warehouses were raided and its raisin cakes confiscated, to such an extent that its president asked Willebrandt to be *its* legal counsel as well. She primly refused.

Although there was never any proof that Willebrandt herself encouraged her former Prohibition agents to persecute a business rival, she had shown, in her dealings with Remus, a ruthlessness that was peculiarly suited to the business world. She was also among the first of America's top government servants to set a much-abused precedent: crossing over into a lucrative private sector job to take advantage of expertise acquired in government service.

For all his public support of the Prohibition status quo, Hoover was fully aware of its destructive potential. To give the impression that he was sensitive to advocates of change, he did what all governments do to avert criticism: he set up a nongovernmental organization to deal with it.

The Wickersham Commission, named after its president, a distinguished lawyer, was supposed to assess the worth of the Volstead Act. Its terms of reference were, however, deliberately vague, and by the time its ambiguous findings were published, in 1931, America had been shaken by a cataclysmic event that would leave its imprint on the country right up to entry into the Second World War — the stock market crash of October 1929, triggering the Depression.

It was not just that disposable income shrank to such an extent that people could no longer afford bootleg liquor prices, and that many speakeasies lost their clients — though fashionable clubs such as the Twenty-One and the Stork Clubs still enjoyed affluent show business crowds. Far more important was the growing awareness among economists and business leaders, as well as private citizens, that by banning liquor, the government had, since 1920, cut itself off from extremely valuable tax revenue. In the affluent 1920s, this had not been of over-riding importance. But as one depression year followed the next, with no sign of an upturn, with rival government departments scrambling for shrinking federal funds, and with states cutting back on essential expenditures because widespread unemployment was leading to huge shortfalls in tax revenues, the folly of it all struck home.

The irony was that some of the new sponsors of repeal had been, in the past, the staunchest advocates of a totally dry America. The Du Ponts, one of America's most powerful families, had been as uncom-promising as Henry Ford in enforcing a "no drink, no saloon" rule wherever there were Du Pont munitions factories. New converts in their wake included Elihu Root, a prominent corporation lawyer, the CEOs of Standard Oil and Macy's, and influential bankers such as Paul-ine Sabin's husband. Their membership in the AAPA — the American Anti-Prohibition Association — was not simply another nail in what was fast becoming an ASL coffin: it signified that the pendulum was in motion, and that the "establishment" was preparing to burn what it had worshipped for so long.

The Depression accelerated the swing away from Prohibition — it did not initiate it. The change of mood among the Du Ponts, and other like-minded ex-Prohibitionists, had been gradual. Moral and religious considerations were conspicuously absent, and an altruistic concern for the new unemployed was farthest from their minds. What motivated them was exclusively self-interest. Taxes had increased dramatically be-tween 1916 and 1921, and had continued to rise since. Canvassing heavily taxed fellow millionaires, Pierre Du Pont now spoke for many disgruntled CEOs when he claimed that if Britain's liquor tax system were applied to America, this would "permit the total abolition of income tax, both personal and corporate."

A number of millionaires fell for this unlikely, simplistic the-sis — and their new anti-Prohibition zeal got a new boost when Prohi-bition Commissioner James M. Moran told Congress that any attempt to enforce the Volstead Act would cost at least $300 million. Nor were the new zealots all wealthy: newspaper polls, from 1927 on, revealed a growing majority (from 75 to 81 percent) in favor of repeal.

If any single public statement sounded Prohibition's death-knell, it was John D. Rockefeller's open letter to Columbia University Presi-dent Nicholas Murray Butler, published in the *New York Times* on

June 6, 1932, announcing his endorsement of repeal in almost tearful terms. "I was born a teetotaler," he wrote. "All my life I have been a teetotaler on principle. . . . My mother and her mother were among the dauntless women of their day, often found with bands of women of like mind, praying on their knees in the saloons."

He described his enthusiastic support of the Volstead Act (he had been a major ASL contributor for many years before that, though he did not mention this). But "drinking has generally increased," as had crime. "The speakeasy has replaced the saloon; a vast army of law-breakers has been recruited and financed on a colossal scale." For all these reasons he now favored immediate, total repeal. His arguments were all moral ones. The tax issue was unmentioned. Hypocrisy takes many forms.

The 1932 presidential contest between Hoover and Roosevelt illustrated the American propensity to downgrade the importance of issues once regarded as of the utmost gravity when newer, more dramatic issues come to the fore. There had been several historical precedents, the most important swing of the pendulum occurring just before the outbreak of the Civil War. In the mid-1800s, as the debate on abolitionism became more critical, with the threat of a Southern breakaway increasingly dividing the nation, the seemingly unstoppable Prohibitionist movement had faltered, and then practically disappeared as a vocal force in politics. Prohibition would not become a serious issue again until long after the Civil War had ended.

What happened then was happening again in 1932. Jungians might argue that while history never repeats itself, archetypal behavior patterns do not go away, even if they may fade into the woodwork for a long, long time. There is a simpler explanation: leaving psychological jargon aside, let's say that in both centuries Americans had belatedly realized that there were more important things to worry about.

In 1932, the ongoing Depression was the major, perhaps the only, issue at stake, exacerbated by Hoover's repeated (and increasingly unconvincing) claims that there was light at the end of the tunnel. Unlike the 1924 and 1928 presidential contests, Prohibition was no longer part of the political debate. In fact, it was seldom mentioned as an issue, except by Roosevelt, who told a delighted St. Louis crowd that he would "increase the federal revenue by several hundred million dollars a year by placing a tax on beer," indicating his support of repeal.

Much was made of his exchange with Fiorello La Guardia, asking him whether there was a way of enforcing Prohibition in New York. La Guardia replied that not only would this compel disbanding the existing force and recruiting 250,000 men but the raising of a separate force of 250,000 inspectors to monitor police activities.

As La Guardia well knew, the question had been rhetorical: Roosevelt had already made up his mind. He knew he could promise repeal without losing more than a fraction of the popular vote.

The leading underworld bootleggers already knew what Roosevelt planned because an emissary had told them. "Lucky" Luciano, in his posthumous "Testament," even accused Roosevelt of welshing on a deal. New York's Mafia bosses initially intended to use their considerable clout to get the local politicians under their control to cast their votes for Roosevelt's rival, Al Smith, in the forthcoming presidential Democratic nomination contest. Luciano claimed that the Roosevelt emissary told them that if they switched their support, Roosevelt would soft-pedal investigations against them being conducted with exemplary honesty and zeal by Judge Samuel Seabury. After the Roosevelt nomination, Al Smith, according to Luciano, told "Lucky": "You fellas are crazy. I would've murdered Seabury for you. . . . He looked me square in the face and shook his head and said: Frank Roosevelt'll break his word to you. This is the biggest mistake you ever made in your entire life, by trustin' him. He'll kill you."

Luciano may have twisted some of the facts to suit himself, but Al Smith was right: Roosevelt, as soon as he became president, urged Seabury to get even tougher with the mob. In 1936, "Lucky" Luciano was sentenced to twenty-five years in jail.[7]

Even in that dry sanctuary of America, its rural heartland, farmers were beginning to respond favorably to pro-repeal arguments. Here too the reason was self-interest. They were among the hardest-hit Depression victims of all, aware of the grain and hops they could expect to sell to breweries and distilleries. Roosevelt was certainly under no illusion: he knew that for all their new anti-Prohibitionist zeal, the Du Ponts and other members of the AAPA would never vote for someone branded as a "dangerous socialist."

Repeal, after Roosevelt's election, turned out to be a surprisingly easy process. On December 6, 1932, a resolution was tabled to void the Eighteenth Amendment, and this took a mere three days, including a one-day filibuster by Texan Senator Morris Sheppard, whose lone voice only emphasized the impotence of the depleted dry lobby. Although it required, as the previous amendment had, a two-thirds ratification by the states, this would occur within a year. Utah, in December of 1933, became the thirty-sixth state to vote for the Twenty-first Amendment, which declared the Eighteenth Amendment null and void.

In the meantime Roosevelt had already taken steps to placate the AFL, and other advocates of real beer. One of his first decisions, as President, was to ask Congress to modify the Volstead Act to increase its alcoholic content to 3.2 percent, and Congress speedily complied. The protests of WCTU spokespersons and once-famous dry propagandists such as Billy Sunday now had a distinctly archaic flavor.

The two-step repeal — first legalizing real beer, then, a few months later, wine and hard liquor — meant that celebrations, the second time around, were less frenzied than expected. It was the return of real beer in the spring of 1933 that provoked hysteria. There were parades, floodlights, and torchlit processions in St. Louis, home of the Anheuser-Busch brewery, and in Milwaukee, and much ecstatic beer-tasting in packed former near-beer bars, now preparing for their new status, for they would no longer be "saloons" (the word remained anathema).

The evening of December 5, 1933 — marking the return of the legal consumption of hard liquor — began as a carnival but soon degenerated into frustration. Owing to the Depression, many of the former speakeasies had closed, and some had not yet obtained their legal licenses. In a sudden excess of legalism, they were unwilling to risk penalties by serving liquor without a permit. All over America, wines and reputable hard liquor were in short supply, and those establishments that had obtained stocks soon ran out of whiskey, gin, and champagne. New Jersey Governor Harry Moore solved the problem by announcing that "liquor has been sold illegally (in the state) for thirteen years and it will not hurt if this is done a few days more."

Prohibition had become a joke.

17

THE AFTERMATH

In Studs Terkel's *Hard Times,* a Depression survivor recalled the mood of the people on his street when Roosevelt's first Civil Works Administration paychecks arrived, shortly after his election.

> Everybody was out celebrating. It was like a festival in some old European city. . . . You'd walk from tavern to tavern and see people buying ponies of beer and sharing it. They had the whole family out. It was a warm night as I remember. Everybody was so happy. . . . I never saw such a change of attitude. Instead of walking around feeling dreary and looking sorrowful . . . it was like a feast day. They were toasting each other.

It could have been a description of Cincinnati's pre-Prohibition "Across the Rhine" neighborhood. It certainly proved the fallacy of the narrow-minded extremists who had claimed there was no such thing as moderate drinking. Even on the night of December 5, 1933, reporters noted there was very little actual drunkenness on the streets. Even if shortages of supplies — and of cash — were partially responsible, America appeared to have come of age.

Roosevelt's "New Deal" helped to dissipate memories of the previous thirteen years. In the new, more hopeful ambiance, there was less concern for the immediate past, and more interest in the immediate future. The Prohibition era had been a singularly unedifying, shameful thirteen-year-long hangover. It was as if most Americans were eager to forget it entirely, wiping its memories from their individual consciousness. It is significant that this period has attracted less attention, among professional historians, than almost any other epoch in American history.[1]

One of the most consistent critics of the Prohibition era had been H. L. Mencken, the prolific *Baltimore Sun* columnist and uncompromising scourge of other people's prejudices (though he was blind to some of his own). Once a humorist as revered by the American public as Will Rogers or Art Buchwald, Mencken has largely gone out of fashion because his Swiftian irony is no longer appreciated, or even understood, by present-day critics. They fail to grasp that when Mencken proposed that defeated presidential candidates be hanged, on the grounds that they would otherwise remain an intolerable nuisance for the rest of their lives, or that the world would be a safer place if the human race remained in a perpetually drunken state, he did not mean this literally.

What infuriated him most was the mediocrity of all those concerned with Prohibition. William Jennings Bryan had been "a charlatan, a mountebank, a zany without any sense of dignity," Harding "a numbskull," Coolidge "a dreadful little cad," and Hoover "a pious old woman, a fat Coolidge." Mencken's distrust of all those involved in good works was total: to him any reformer was "a prehensile Methodist parson, bawling for Prohibition and its easy jobs."

On its repeal, he wrote: "Prohibition went into effect on January 16, 1920, and blew up at last on December 5, 1933 — an elapsed time of twelve years, ten months and nineteen days. It seemed almost a geologic epoch while it was going on, and the human suffering that it entailed must have been a fair match for that of the Black Death or the Thirty Years War."[2]

Was the Prohibition balance sheet *that* overwhelmingly negative? The answer must be yes. Mencken may have deliberately exaggerated the number of dead and physically maimed — but in all sorts of ways, there was a fatal impact. Walter Lippmann, the famous liberal columnist and critic, whose career began during the Prohibition years, denounced the "circle of impotence in which we outlaw intolerantly the satisfaction of certain persistent human desires, and then tolerate what we have prohibited."[3] His remarks could well apply to certain current by-products of "political correctness."

Like ex-President Taft, Lippmann also pointed out the dangerous consequences of attempting to stamp out later "tolerated vices," thereby "turning over their exploitation to the underworld." For Prohibition was not the end of organized crime in America but only its beginning.

Perhaps the most ominous consequence of Prohibition had to do with a change in American attitudes toward organized crime in general. Even today, awareness of its ravages goes hand in hand with a certain passivity. Americans admire the quixotic qualities of a Serpico, the New York cop who waged a one-man war on his corrupt colleagues, but are not surprised that he ended up a loser. In the fight between good and evil, in real life as in "films noirs," good now seldom prevails over evil, and this is unsurprising, for Americans have been conditioned to believe that criminal vested interests are so powerful that the fight against them is inevitably rigged. In other words, they have lost the capacity to react.

For all his caricatural exaggeration, Mencken was right when he first spotted this tendency. Writing while Prohibition was still in force, he noted that

> It no longer astonished anyone when policemen were taken in evildoing. . . . If, before that time, the corps of Prohibition enforcement officers — i.e. a corps of undisguised scoundrels with badges — had been launched against the populace, there would have been a great roar of wrath, and much anguished gnashing of teeth. People would have felt themselves put upon, injured, insulted. But with the old assumption about policemen removed from their minds, they met the new onslaught calmly and even smilingly. Today no one is indignant over the fact that the extortions of these new *Polizei* increase the cost of potable alcohol.

Mencken went on to argue that there was no such thing as an honest politician, cop, public relations person — or journalist, for that matter. Current American perceptions are not so very different, even if measures have since been taken to limit election campaign contributions. Organized crime no longer openly funds politicians — as it did in Chicago during the Prohibition years. But the log-rolling persists, as do the expectations of major contributors.

That Prohibition helped to shape such prejudices is not surprising. Those who failed to apply the Volstead Act provisions were not necessarily deeply corrupt: they simply did not regard breaking them to be a crime. But even benign neglect of these provisions had the effect of encouraging organized crime — the financial rewards simply being too huge.

The major bootleggers rapidly completed their reconversion into the legitimate liquor business. Joe Kennedy, Sr., father of JFK, became the official distributor of Haig and Haig and Pinchbottle whiskey and Gordon's gin even *before* Prohibition's repeal; Samuel Bronfman, Canada's biggest bootlegger (and "Lucky" Luciano's biggest supplier) founded Seagram's; Frank Costello and his underworld partners set up Alliance Distributors, selling the same brands of Scotch (King's Ransom, House of Lords whiskey) they had smuggled into the United States during Prohibition. They also acquired a controlling interest in J. Turnley and Sons, another Scotch distributor. Meyer Lansky — with Luciano, "Bugsy" Siegel, and others — set up the Capitol Wine and Spirits firm, and became leading importers of vintage French wines, Scotch, and Canadian whiskey. Even in jail — and after (he was deported to Italy in 1946) — Luciano continued to receive a large share of the profits.

As students of organized crime well know, racketeers simply found new targets. After December of 1933, New York's underworld bosses began extending their protection activities to bakeries, restaurants, laundries, limousine services, the garment industry, and New York's Fulton Fish Market. Today, underworld bosses in New York's Chinatown display a businesslike ruthlessness that Al Capone could well have envied. More ominously, from time to time evidence surfaces of a form of gangland-police collusion (at least in Chinatown) that was so prevalent during Prohibition.

The relationships forged during those years did not vanish overnight. When Mafia leaders staged their much-publicized conference in the Appalachians in 1957, it was discovered that many of their pistol permits had been signed by New York and New Jersey police officials. In 1958, Paul W. Williams, a U.S. district attorney for the southern district of New York, was the first to refer to "the Invisible Government," tracing its origins back to the Prohibition era. And just as corrupt law enforcement officials had been able to call a halt when overly zealous policemen and Prohibition agents threatened the livelihood of politically powerful underworld bosses, so a notorious post-Prohibition politician-entrepreneur like New York's James J. Hines was able to put a stop to the NYPD's attempt to crack down on gambling operations, using his clout to have honest cops transferred and gambling cases dealt with by "friendly" magistrates.

Even a hugely respected, influential anticrime crusader such as Mayor La Guardia could not prevent the election of William Copeland Dodge as Manhattan district attorney, whose links with organized crime were an open secret.[4] And his repeated attempts to rid the Fulton Fish Market of racketeering elements were only temporarily successful: in 1995, an investigative report in the *New York Times* revealed that the mob was still as active there as ever.

It would of course be overly simplistic to put the blame exclusively on Prohibition for the shifting patterns of post-1933 organized crime. But there can be no doubt that the laxity of the law enforcers during the Prohibition years encouraged underworld crime bosses in their belief that anyone could be bought. "I just couldn't understand that guy [La Guardia]," "Lucky" Luciano told his ghostwriters. "When we offered to make him rich he wouldn't even listen. . . . So I figured: what the hell, let him keep City Hall, we got all the rest, the D.A., the cops, everything."[5]

Prohibition may not have initiated, but it certainly underlined, the two-tier element in American justice so dramatically illustrated in 1995 by the O. J. Simpson case. As court records from 1920 to 1933 show, Prohibition agents concentrated their efforts on those they could *not* shake down; that is, the poor, the barely literate, the recent immigrants least able to defend themselves. With a few exceptions (George Remus was one of them), the wealthy were virtually immune from prosecution, as were bankers and wealthy entrepreneurs responsible for establishing lucrative contracts with bootlegging investors, often with the complicity of congressmen.

The methods used to enforce Prohibition anticipated those of the DEA in its war on drugs. Although it would be ridiculous to compare the DEA to the Prohibition Bureau — the former a highly professional, motivated organization staffed by high-caliber agents of the greatest integrity; the latter a motley crew of venal political appointees — the *results,* in both cases, are startlingly similar. At no time did Prohibition law enforcers seize more than 5 percent of the quantities of liquor illegally entering the United States. The DEA's record of drug seizures, though higher (around 10 percent), is comparable, inevitably raising all sorts of questions. Should drugs be legalized? Are not current antidrug laws responsible for perpetuating organized crime? With over half of America's current prison population in jail for drug-related offenses, a drastic overhaul of antidrug legislation is not just in order, it is badly overdue.

But perhaps the least-learned lesson of Prohibition is that legislation alone is no answer to America's problems. The moralists and evangelical pioneers without whom Prohibition would have remained a dead letter believed that enactment of the Eighteenth Amendment would be sufficient to change the habits of American society as a whole. They were quickly proved disastrously wrong.

The cart-before-the-horse mentality is the same, as is the strident vocabulary of the new "moral majority." The reason the evangelist Billy Sunday became the popular hero of the twenties, among so many millions of God-fearing households, was that he was the very incarnation of the belief in an endearing, yet hopelessly naive panacea. Today's new repressive penal measures (chain gangs, "three-strikes-you're-out" sentences for habitual offenders, and so on) are not so very different from the special prisons for alcoholics advocated in the early 1800s, or indeed the whole array of laws contained in the Volstead Act.

The thinking in both cases is that such measures (either federal in nature or passed by different state legislatures) can radically reform a sick society, or at least make it tolerable to its law-abiding majority. Only the handful of intellectuals left on the political scene (foremost among them Senator Daniel Patrick Moynihan) are aware of this fallacy, and campaign against it: they know from experience that repression is like morphine — it masks the pain, but in no way cures the sickness.

The Prohibition disaster should have made this clear, but most

American decision-makers are singularly indifferent to the lessons of the past. The American educational system has become highly selective where the teaching of history is concerned. We tend to forget an important lesson: that those who know no history condemn themselves to repeat it, either as tragedy or as farce.

NOTES

INTRODUCTION

1. Andrew Sinclair, *Prohibition: The Era of Excess,* Atlantic, 1962.
2. John J. Rumberger, *Profits, Power, and Prohibition,* State U. of New York Press, 1989.
3. Norman H. Clark, *Deliver Us from Evil,* W. W. Norton, 1976.
4. "Drug War Two," January 30, 1995.

CHAPTER ONE: THE GOOD CREATURE OF GOD

1. Herbert Asbury, *The Great Illusion,* Doubleday, 1950.
2. This practice was known, from the seventeenth century on, as "eleven o'clock bitters." There was a similar break at four P.M.
3. Nine cents a gallon for liquor distilled from grain (whiskey), eleven cents for rum.
4. *The Great Illusion.*
5. The term originated from early smuggling habits, when contraband was hidden in the tops of then-capacious boots.
6. Norman H. Clark, *The Dry Years,* U. of Washington Press, 1965 and 1988.
7. Edwin M. Lemert, *Alcohol and the Northwest Indians,* U. of California Press, 1954.

CHAPTER TWO: FERVOR AND FANATICISM

1. For these and other quotes from nineteenth-century documents, diaries, and sermons I am indebted to the Rev. W. H. Samuels, *Temperance Reform and Its Great Reformers,* A. M. Cincinnati, 1879.
2. *The Great Illusion.*
3. Published by the American Tract Society, New York, in 1847.
4. My italics.

CHAPTER THREE: THE WOMEN'S WAR

1. John Kobler, *Ardent Spirits: The Rise and Fall of Prohibition,* Putnam, 1973.
2. It was part of Carry Nation's eccentricity to believe that Freemasons did the "devil's work."
3. She reproduced them, later, in her rambling autobiography. Her favorite:

This is a joint [as saloons were called]
Touch not, taste not, handle not!
Drink will make the dark, dark blot
Like an adder it will sting!
And at last to ruin bring
They who tarry at the drink!

CHAPTER FOUR: THE LINEUP

1. Norman H. Clark, *The Dry Years,* U. of Washington Press, 1965 and 1988.
2. *The Dry Years.*
3. Nov. 10, 1883, and Jan. 19, 1884.
4. *The Dry Years.*
5. Justin Stewart, *Wayne Wheeler: Dry Boss,* Fleming H. Revell Company, 1928.
6. *Wayne Wheeler: Dry Boss.*
7. *Wayne Wheeler: Dry Boss.*
8. *New York Times,* March 29, 1926.
9. *Wayne Wheeler: Dry Boss.*

CHAPTER FIVE: PROHIBITION'S FIRST VICTIMS

1. I am indebted to Dr. Don Heinrich Todzmann of the U. of Cincinnati for his help and expert advice in this chapter, and for allowing me to consult his Ph.D. thesis: "The Survival of an Ethnic Community: The Cincinnati Germans" (Ph.D. dissertation U. of Cincinnati, 1983).

CHAPTER SIX: AMERICA GOES DRY

1. Examples: The "Prohibition Battle Hymn"
We've played the Good Samaritan
But now we'll take a hand
And clear the road to Jericho
Of the robbing, thieving band;
Distillers and Saloonists
Shall be driven from the land
As we go marching on.

And "The Anti-Saloon War Song"
Tramp, tramp, tramp the States are marching
One by one to victory;
But we cannot win the fight
Until thirty six are white
So we'll press the battle on from sea to sea.
2. *The Great Illusion.*
3. *Ardent Spirits.*

CHAPTER SEVEN: THE PROVIDERS

1. Although his byline does not appear, the series was also researched by a Pulitzer Prize–winning reporter, John T. Rogers, who also spent considerable time with Remus after his release from jail.
2. The land on which it stood is now part of densely populated Cincinnati suburbia.
3. St. Louis *Post-Dispatch,* Jan. 4, 1926.

CHAPTER EIGHT: HARDING AND THE RACKETEERS

1. F. L. Allen, *Only Yesterday: An Informal History of the 1920s in America,* Penguin, 1931.
2. Francis Russell, *The Shadow of Blooming Grove,* McGraw-Hill, 1968.
3. Samuel Hopkins Adams, *The Incredible Era: The Life and Times of Warren Harding,* Houghton Mifflin, 1930.
4. Nan Britton, *The President's Daughter,* Elizabeth Anne Guild, 1927.
5. Charles Mee, *The Ohio Gang,* Evans and Co., 1981.
6. Alice Roosevelt Longworth, *The Crowded Hours,* Scribners, 1933.
7. Among the more absurd changes, Judges ix, 13 became: "Shall I leave my juice that gladdens gods and men," and "He distributed to the whole assembled multitude a roll of bread, a portion of meat, and a cake of raisins."

CHAPTER TEN: THE ADVENTURERS

1. Everett S. Allen, *The Black Ships,* Little, Brown, 1965.
2. Moet et Chandon exports to Canada:

$$
\begin{array}{ll}
1923 & -\ 22,400 \text{ cases} \\
1924 & -\ 20,600 \text{ cases} \\
1925 & -\ \ \ 6,900 \text{ cases} \\
1926 & -\ 11,700 \text{ cases} \\
1927 & -\ 11,600 \text{ cases} \\
1928 & -\ \ \ 1,200 \text{ cases} \\
1929 & -\ 13,100 \text{ cases}
\end{array}
$$

Amounts fell markedly after the 1929 crash. After Prohibition ended, they only exceeded 1,000 cases for the year 1938.
3. Roy A. Haynes, *Prohibition Inside Out,* Doubleday, 1926.
4. Studs Terkel, *Hard Times,* Pantheon Books, 1970.
5. *The Great Illusion.*
6. *The Black Ships.*
7. Ibid.
8. New Bedford *Evening Standard* series on McCoy, August 9–12, 1921.
9. David Kahn, *The Code Breakers,* Macmillan, 1967.
10. *The Black Ships.*
11. Aug. 13, 1927, issue.

12. *The Black Ships.*
13. Interview with author.

CHAPTER ELEVEN: "PROHIBITIONS WORKS!"

1. *Cincinnati Enquirer,* Sept. 8, 1921.
2. "Booze" owed its name to an enterprising manufacturer called Edmund C. Booze, who for the 1840 presidential campaign marketed whisky in bottles shaped like log cabins.
3. *Prohibition Inside Out.*
4. Mabel Willebrandt, *The Inside of Prohibition,* Current News Features, 1929.
5. Izzy Einstein, *Prohibition Agent Number 1,* Frederick Stokes Co. 1932.
6. Slang term for French World War I soldier.

CHAPTER TWELVE: "PROHIBITION DOESN'T WORK!"

1. Current News Features, 1929.
2. My italics.
3. My italics.
4. My italics.
5. Although sometimes the "little people" got their own back. In Studs Terkel's *Hard Times,* a working-class woman's son reminisced: "A cop started coming around and gettin' friendly. She knew he was workin' up to a pinch. So, she prepares a bottle for him. He talked her into sellin' it to him. He pinches her, takes her to court. He said: 'I bought this half a dog of a booze. Half a pint.' The woman said: 'How do you know it's booze?' The cop takes a swig of it and spits it out. It was urine. Case dismissed."
6. *Collier's,* Sept. 10, 1949.
7. *Wayne Wheeler: Dry Boss.*
8. Thomas Kessner, *Fiorello La Guardia,* Penguin, 1989.
9. Kenneth Allsop, *The Bootleggers,* Arlington House, 1968.

CHAPTER THIRTEEN: CHICAGO

1. Fletcher Dobyns, *The Underworld of American Politics,* Fletcher Dobyns Publishing, 1932.
2. He owed this nickname to his diminutive size.
3. Lloyd Wendt and Herman Kogan, *Lords of the Levee,* Garden City Publishing, 1943.
4. In Chicago, Prohibition became effective in 1919.
5. Martin A. Gosch and Richard Hammer, *The Last Testament of Lucky Luciano,* Little, Brown, 1974.
6. Lloyd Wendt and Herbert Kogan, *Big Bill of Chicago,* Bobbs-Merrill, 1953.
7. Ibid.

CHAPTER FOURTEEN: REMUS ON TRIAL

1. *Cincinnati Enquirer,* Dec. 1–17, 1927.
2. *Cincinnati Enquirer,* Dec. 1927.
3. *Cincinnati Enquirer,* Dec. 1927.

CHAPTER FIFTEEN: REMUS REDUX

1. *Cincinnati Enquirer,* Dec. 1927.
2. Years later, a *Cincinnati Times-Star* columnist, Jame L. Kilgallen, who had covered the trial for the International News Service agency, claimed that he had suggested this dramatic opening to Remus. He also recalled that there was, in fact, no empty chair: Conners's wife was sitting in it.

CHAPTER SIXTEEN: A FATAL TRIUMPH

1. *Wayne Wheeler: Dry Boss.*
2. Oswald Garrison Willard in *Nation,* Nov. 30, 1927.
3. Virginius Dabney, *The Dry Messiah: The Life of Bishop Cannon,* Knopf, 1949. The speech, and an interview, appeared in the *Baltimore Sun.*
4. In later life, she became a Catholic convert.
5. Willebrandt herself had confirmed that on the night of Al Smith's nomination, she had ordered extensive raids on New York's major nightclubs and speakeasies.
6. *The Dry Messiah.*
7. *The Last Testament of Lucky Luciano.*

CHAPTER SEVENTEEN: THE AFTERMATH

1. The swing against Prohibition was not total. Pockets of resistance, the dry counties in what was once rural America, still exist; so does a tiny "Prohibition Party," and drivers caught on certain Alabama or Georgia highways with liquor in their cars face huge fines unless the liquor is stored in the trunk, with the cap or seal intact.
2. H. L. Mencken, *A Choice of Days,* Knopf, 1980.
3. Quoted in Francis Ianni and Elizabeth Reuss-Ianni's *Crime Society,* New American Library, 1976.
4. *Fiorello La Guardia.*
5. *The Last Testament of Lucky Luciano.*

BIBLIOGRAPHY

Adams, Samuel Hopkins. *The Incredible Era: The Life and Times of Warren Harding*. New York: Houghton Mifflin, 1930.

Allen, Everett S. *The Black Ships*. New York: Little, Brown, 1965.

Allen, F. L. *Only Yesterday: An Informal History of the 1920s in America*. New York: Penguin, 1931.

Allsop, Kenneth. *The Bootleggers*. London: Arlington House, 1968.

Asbury, Herbert. *The Great Illusion*. New York: Doubleday, 1950.

Britton, Nan. *The President's Daugter*. New York: Elizabeth Anne Guild, 1927.

Clark, Norman H. *Deliver Us from Evil*. New York: W. W. Norton, 1976.

————. *The Dry Years*. Seattle: University of Washington Press, 1965, revised ed. 1988.

Dabney, Virginius. *The Dry Messiah: The Life of Bishop Cannon*. New York: Knopf, 1949.

Dobyns, Fletcher. *The Underworld of American Politics*. New York: Fletcher Dobyns Publishing, 1932.

Edwards, Rev. Justin. *Temperance Manual*. New York: American Tract Society, 1847.

Einstein, Izzy. *Prohibition Agent Number 1*. New York: Frederick Stokes Co., 1932.

Gosch, Martin A., and Richard Hammer. *The Last Testament of Lucky Luciano*. Boston: Little, Brown, 1974.

Haynes, Roy A. *Prohibition Inside Out*. New York: Doubleday, 1926.

Ianni, Francis, and Elizabeth Reuss-Ianni. *Crime Society*. New York: New American Library, 1976.

Kahn, David. *The Code Breakers*. New York: Macmillan, 1967.

Kessner, Thomas. *Fiorello La Guardia*. New York: Penguin, 1989.

Kobler, John. *Ardent Spirits: The Rise and Fall of Prohibition*. New York: Putnam, 1973.

Lemert, Edwin M. *Alcohol and the Northwest Indians*. Los Angeles: University of California Press, 1954.

Longworth, Alice Roosevelt. *The Crowded Hours*. New York: Scribners, 1933.

Mee, Charles. *The Ohio Gang*. New York: Evans and Co., 1981.

Mencken, H. L. *A Choice of Days*. New York: Knopf, 1980.

Rumberger, John J. *Profits, Power, and Prohibition*. New York: State University of New York Press, 1989.

Russell, Francis. *The Shadow of Blooming Grove*. New York: McGraw-Hill, 1968.

Samuels, Rev. W. H. *Temperance Reform and Its Great Reformers*. Cincinnati: A. M. Cincinnati, 1879.

Sinclair, Andrew. *Prohibition: The Era of Excess*. Boston: Atlantic, 1962.

Stewart, Justin. *Wayne Wheeler: Dry Boss*. New York: Fleming H. Revell Co., 1928.

Terkel, Studs. *Hard Times*. New York: Pantheon Books, 1970.

Todzmann, Dr. Don Heinrich. "The Survival of an Ethnic Community: The Cincinnati Germans." Ph.D. diss., Cincinnati University, 1983.

Wendt, Lloyd, and Herman Kogan. *Big Bill of Chicago*. New York: Bobbs-Merrill, 1953.

———. *Lords of the Levee*. New York: Garden City Publishing, 1943.

Willebrandt, Mabel. *The Inside of Prohibition*. New York: Current News Features, 1929.

INDEX

SMALL PLEASURES

A NOVEL

CLARE CHAMBERS

CUSTOM
HOUSE

SMALL PLEASURES. Copyright © 2021 by Clare Chambers. All rights reserved. Printed in Italy. No part of this book may be used or reproduced in any manner whatsoever without written permission except in the case of brief quotations embodied in critical articles and reviews. For information, address HarperCollins Publishers, 195 Broadway, New York, NY 10007.

HarperCollins books may be purchased for educational, business, or sales promotional use. For information, please email the Special Markets Department at SPsales@harpercollins.com.

Originally published in the United Kingdom in 2020 by Weidenfeld & Nicolson.

FIRST U.S. EDITION

Library of Congress Cataloging-in-Publication Data has been applied for.

ISBN 978-0-06-309472-7

21 22 23 24 25   GV   10 9 8 7 6 5 4 3 2 1

To Peter

RAIL DISASTER

Rush hour trains collide in thick fog— many dead.

Tragedy struck office workers and Christmas shoppers on the evening of December 4 when two trains collided in thick fog under the Nunhead flyover. The 5:18 from Charing Cross to Hayes and the 4:56 steam train from Cannon Street to Ramsgate had been delayed by the poor weather. Coaches on both trains were packed, with passengers standing as well as sitting.

The Hayes train had stopped at a signal outside St. John's at 6:20 p.m. when the steam train plowed into the rear coach. This was just the beginning of an unfolding disaster, which left more than 80 dead and 200 wounded.

The steam train swung to the side and struck a steel column of the Nunhead flyover, causing the bridge to collapse, crushing two coaches below. A third train, from Holborn Viaduct, was just approaching the fallen flyover, when quick action by the driver brought it to a halt, preventing further catastrophe. The coaches were derailed but no one on board was injured.

The rescue efforts of firemen, police, railway staff, doctors and nurses were hampered by fog and darkness. Worse still, the ruined bridge was in danger of falling further, crushing rescuers and trapped victims alike.

But through the long night of toil the army of volunteers continued to grow, with many local residents throwing open their doors to assist the injured. Eleven ambulances attended the scene, driving casualties farther and farther afield as nearby hospitals struggled to cope.

Local telephone lines became jammed by worried relatives as news of the accident spread. Hundreds of passengers were marooned in London for the night with the mid-Kent line completely blocked.

Many of the dead and injured were from Clock House and Beckenham. Passengers alighting at those stations were more likely to choose rear coaches because of their proximity to the station exits. It was these that took the brunt of the collision.

Southern Region authorities have launched an immediate inquiry.

The *North Kent Echo*, Friday, December 6, 1957

I

June 1957

The article that started it all was not even on the front page, but was just a filler on page 5, between an advertisement for the Patricia Brixie Dancing School and a report on the AGM of the Crofton North Liberals. It concerned the finding of a recent study into parthenogenesis in sea urchins, frogs and rabbits, which concluded that there was no reason it should not be possible in humans. This dusty paragraph might have been overlooked by most readers of the *North Kent Echo* were it not for the melodramatic headline "Men No Longer Needed for Reproduction!"

The result was an unusually large postbag of mostly indignant letters, not just from men. One wounded correspondent, Mrs. Beryl Diplock of St. Paul's Cray, deplored the article's sentiments as dangerous and unchristian. More than one female reader pointed out that such a proposition was liable to give slippery men an excuse to wriggle out of their responsibilities.

There was one letter, however, that stood out from all the rest. It was from a Mrs. Gretchen Tilbury of 7 Burdett Road, Sidcup, and read simply:

Dear Editor,
    I was interested to read your article "Men No Longer Needed

for Reproduction" in last week's paper. I have always believed my own daughter (now ten) to have been born without the involvement of any man. If you would like to know more information you may write to me at the above address.

The next editorial meeting—usually a dull affair involving the planning and distribution of duties for the week and a postmortem of the errors and oversights in the previous issue—was livelier than it had been for some time.

Jean Swinney, features editor, columnist, dogsbody and the only woman at the table, glanced at the letter as it was passed around. The slanted handwriting, with its strange continental loops, reminded her of a French teacher from school. She, too, had written the number seven with a line through it, which the thirteen-year-old Jean had thought the height of sophistication and decided to imitate. Her mother had put a stop to that; she could hardly have been more affronted if Jean had taken to writing in blood. To Mrs. Swinney, all foreigners were Germans and beyond the pale.

Thoughts of her mother prompted Jean to remember that she needed to pick up her shoes from the repair shop on the way home. It mystified her why someone who seldom left the house should need so many pairs of outdoor shoes. Also required were cigarettes, peppermint oil from Rumsey's and kidneys and lard if she could be bothered to make a pie for dinner. Otherwise it would just be "eggs any which way," that old standby.

"Does anyone want to go and interview Our Lady of Sidcup?" asked Larry, the news editor.

There was a general creaking backward in chairs, indicative of dissent.

"Not really my thing," said Bill, sports and entertainment editor.

Jean slowly extended her hand to take the letter. She knew it was coming her way sooner or later.

"Good idea," said Larry, huffing smoke across the table. "It's women's interest, after all."

"Do we really want to encourage these cranks?" said Bill.

"She may not be a crank," said Roy Drake, the editor, mildly.

It made Jean smile to remember how intimidating she used to find him when she had joined the paper as a young woman, and how she would quake if summoned to his office. She had soon discovered he was not the sort of man who took pleasure in terrorizing his juniors. He had four daughters and treated all women kindly. Besides, it was hard to be in awe of someone whose suits were so very crumpled.

"How can she not be?" Bill wanted to know. "You're not saying you believe in virgin births?"

"No, but I'd be interested to know why this Mrs. Tilbury does."

"She writes a good letter," said Larry. "Concise."

"It's concise because she's foreign," said Jean.

They all looked at her.

"No Englishwoman is taught handwriting like that. And 'Gretchen'?"

"Well, clearly this is the sort of interview that is going to require some tact," said Roy. "So obviously it's going to have to be you, Jean."

Around the table heads nodded. No one was going to fight her for this story.

"Anyway, the first thing is to go and check her out. I'm sure you'll be able to tell pretty quickly if she's a charlatan."

"Give me five minutes alone with her—I'll tell you if she's a virgin," said Larry, to general laughter. He leaned back in his chair, elbows out, hands behind his head, so that the gridlines of his vest were clearly visible against his shirt.

"She doesn't say she's *still* a virgin," Bill pointed out. "This happened ten years ago. She may have seen some action since then."

"I'm sure Jean can manage without your expertise," said Roy, who didn't like that sort of talk.

Jean had the feeling that if he wasn't there, the conversation would rapidly turn coarse. It was curious the way the others moderated their language to suit Roy's prudishness, while Jean herself was treated as "one of the boys." She took this as a compliment, mostly. In darker moments, when she noticed the way they behaved around younger, prettier women—the secretaries, for example—with a heavy-handed mixture of flirtation and gallantry, she wasn't so sure.

Jean divided the rest of the afternoon between her Household Hints column and Marriage Lines—a write-up of the previous week's weddings.

> After a reception at St. Paul's Cray Community Center, Mr. and Mrs. Plornish left for their honeymoon at St. Leonard's, the bride wearing a turquoise coat and black accessories . . .

Household Hints was a cinch because these were all supplied by loyal readers. In the early days Jean used to put some of these to the test *before* publication. Now, she took a certain pleasure in selecting the most outlandish.

That done, she wrote a brief note to Gretchen Tilbury, asking if she could come and meet her and her daughter. Since she had provided no telephone number, the arrangements would have to be conducted by letter. At five o'clock she covered her typewriter with its hood and left the building, dropping the letter off at the mailroom on her way out.

Jean's bicycle, a solid, heavy-framed contraption that had come down, like most of her possessions, through generations of the Swinney family, was leaning against the railing. Standing in front of it, too much in the way to be ignored, was one of the typists locked in a deep embrace with a young man from the print room. Jean recognized the girl but didn't know her name; there wasn't much interplay between the reporters and the other departments on the paper.

She had to step around them, feeling rather foolish, to retrieve her bicycle, until they finally acknowledged her and pulled away, giggling their apologies. There was something almost cruel in their self-absorption and Jean had to remind herself that it was nothing personal, just a universal symptom of the disease of love. Those afflicted could not be blamed, only pitied.

Jean took a silk headscarf from her pocket and knotted it tightly under her chin to stop her hair from blowing in her face as she cycled. Then, squashing her bag into the basket on the handlebars, she wheeled the bicycle to the curb and swung herself onto the seat, smoothing her skirt beneath her in one practiced movement.

It was only a ten-minute ride from the offices of the *Echo* in Petts Wood to Jean's home in Hayes and even at this time of day there was little traffic. The sun was still high in the sky; there were hours of daylight left. Once she had seen to her mother there might be time for some gardening: ground elder was coming in under the next-door fence and menacing the bean rows; it required constant vigilance.

The thought of puttering in the vegetable patch on a summer evening was infinitely soothing. The lawns, front and back, would have to wait until the weekend, because that was a heavy job, made heavier by an obligation to do her elderly neighbor's grass at the same time. It was one of those generous impulses that had begun as a favor and had now become a duty, performed with dwindling enthusiasm on one side and fading gratitude on the other.

Jean stopped off at the parade of shops that curved down the hill from the station to complete her errands. Steak and kidney would take too long but the thought of eggs for supper again had a dampening effect on her spirits, so she bought some lamb's liver from the butcher. They could have it with new potatoes and broad beans from the garden. She didn't dawdle over the rest of her list—the shops shut promptly at five-thirty and there would be disappointment indoors if she returned home without the shoes or the medicine, and utter frustration for herself if she ran out of cigarettes.

By the time she reached home, a modest 1930s row house backing on to the park, her cheerful mood had evaporated. Somehow, in transferring the waxed paper package of liver to her tartan shopping bag she managed to drip two spots of blood on the front of her dust-colored wool skirt. She was furious with herself. The skirt had not long ago been cleaned and she knew from experience that blood was one of the most tenacious stains to treat.

"Is that you, Jean?" Her mother's voice—anxious, reproachful—floated down the stairs in response to the scrape of her door key, as it always did.

"Yes, Mother, only me," Jean replied, as she always did, with a degree more or less of impatience in her tone, depending on how her day had gone.

Her mother appeared on the landing, fluttering a blue air-mailed letter over the banisters. "There's a letter from Dorrie," she said. "Do you want to read it?"

"Maybe later," said Jean, who was still taking off her headscarf and divesting herself of her various packages.

Her younger sister, Dorrie, was married to a coffee farmer and lived in Kenya, which might as well have been Venus as far as Jean was concerned, so remote and unimaginable was her new life. She had a houseboy and a cook and a gardener, and a nightwatchman to protect them from intruders, and a gun under the bed to protect them from the nightwatchman. The sisters had been close as children and Jean had missed her terribly at first, but after so many years she had grown accustomed to not seeing her or her children in a way that their mother never would.

"Is there something nice for supper?" Having noticed the paper bag containing her mended shoes, her mother began a slow and wincing descent of the stairs.

"Liver," said Jean.

"Oh good. I'm ravenous. I haven't eaten anything all day."

"Well whyever not? There's plenty of food in the larder."

Sensing resistance, Jean's mother backtracked a little. "I slept rather late. So I had my oatmeal instead of lunch."

"So you *have* eaten something, then?"

"Oh, I don't call that *eating*."

Jean didn't reply to this but took her purchases into the kitchen and deposited them on the table. The room faced west and was warm and bright in the early evening sun. A fly fizzed and bumped against the windowpane until Jean let it out, noticing as she did so the specks and smears on the glass. Another job for the weekend. They had a woman who came in to clean on a Thursday morning, but she seemed to Jean to achieve very little in her allotted hour, apart from gossiping to her mother. But this was a chore of sorts, Jean supposed, and she didn't begrudge her the five shillings. Not really.

While her mother tried on the newly mended shoes, Jean took off her skirt and stood at the sink in her blouse and slip, inspecting the spots of dried blood. In the curtained dresser she located a box of rags—the earthly remains of other ruined garments—and, using the severed sleeve of a once-favorite cotton nightgown, began to dab at the stain with cleaning spirit.

"What are you doing?" said her mother, peering over her shoulder.

"I got blood on it," said Jean, frowning as the rust-colored patch began to dissolve and spread. "Not mine. The liver, I mean."

9

"You messy girl," said her mother, extending a twiggy ankle to admire her shoe, a beige kidskin pump with a Cuban heel. "I don't suppose I'll ever wear these again," she sighed. "But still."

The mark was slightly fainter now, but larger, and still quite visible against the gray fabric.

"What a pity," said Jean. "It was such a good skirt for cycling."

She took it upstairs with her to change. She couldn't wear it, but neither could she quite bring herself to consign it to the rag box yet. Instead, she folded it up and stowed it in the bottom of her closet, as if an alternative use for unwearable skirts might one day present itself.

After tea—liver and onions cooked by Jean and a pudding of canned pears with evaporated milk—Jean weeded and watered the vegetable patch while her mother sat in a deck chair, holding but not quite reading her library book. She would never sit outside alone, Jean noticed, however pleasant the weather, but only if there was company. From the park came the high, bright shouts of children playing, an occasional sequence of barks from the dogs in the street as a pedestrian passed along and the even less frequent rumble of a passing car. By the time dusk fell, all would be silent.

Jean and her mother moved into the sitting room at the front of the house, drew the curtains and switched on the lamps, which gave out a grudging yellowish light behind their brown shades. They played two hands of gin rummy at the small card table and then Jean picked listlessly through a basket of mending, which she had been adding to but otherwise ignoring for some weeks. Her mother, meanwhile, took out her leather writing case to reply to Dorrie's letter. By way of preparation for this task, she reread it aloud, which Jean could only presume was for her benefit, since her mother was already well acquainted with the contents. She did the same thing with newspaper and magazine articles when she was finding the silence of a Sunday afternoon irksome.

Dear Mother,

Thank you for your letter. It sounds lovely and peaceful in Hayes. I wish I could say the same—it's been non-stop here. Kenneth has been staying on the farm—he's got a new manager at last who needs to be "broken in." Let's hope he lasts a bit longer than the previous one—now referred to in private as "Villainous Vernon."

[Mrs. Swinney tittered at this.]

I have joined the Kitale Club and it's become my second home while Kenneth's away. There are some real "types" there as you can imagine. I went to see the Kitale Dramatic Society's production of Present Laughter *on Friday night. Pru Calderwell—the absolute queen of the social scene here—was ever so good as Liz Essendine. The rest of the cast were pretty wooden. I thought I might as well audition for the next one myself if that's the standard!*

We've got ourselves a new black Alsatian pup called Ndofu. We're completely besotted with him. I'm supposed to be training him up as a guard dog for when I'm here by myself but he's such a mushy creature, he'll just roll over for anyone who tickles him.

The children will be home for the holiday in a few weeks' time so I must take advantage of my last few weeks of freedom and get some more tennis in. I've been having some lessons and I'm playing in a mixed doubles tournament tomorrow with a chap called Stanley Harris who is about 60 but madly competitive and throws himself all over my half of the court shouting, "Mine! Mine!" so I shan't have much to do.

Must dash for the post office now. Keep well. Much love to you and Jean.

Dorrie

"She writes a super letter," Jean's mother said.

"Well that's because she has a super life to write about," Jean retorted.

These breezy bulletins always left her feeling a trifle sour. Fond memories of their shared childhood closeness were now clouded by resentment at their contrasting fates.

At eight-thirty Jean's mother rose effortfully from her chair and said, as though the idea had just that moment occurred to her, "I think I'll have my bath."

Although Jean had occasional misgivings about their domestic routines, and intimations sometimes reached her that other people had a different, freer way of doing things, her mother's bath-night ritual was one she was keen to uphold. Twice a week, on Tuesdays and Fridays between eight-thirty and nine, Jean was mistress of the house, free to do as she liked. She could listen to the wireless without her mother's commentary, eat standing up in the kitchen, read in perfect silence or run naked through the rooms if she chose.

Of all the various liberties available, her favorite was to unfasten her girdle and lie at full stretch on the couch with an ashtray on her stomach and smoke two cigarettes back to back. There was no reason why she couldn't do this in her mother's presence—lying down in the day might prompt an inquiry about her health, no more—but it wasn't nearly so enjoyable in company. The summer variant of this practice was to walk barefoot down the garden and smoke her cigarettes lying on the cool grass.

On this particular evening, she had just peeled off her musty stockings and stuffed them into the toes of her shoes when there was a tremendous clattering from the back parlor, as if all the tiles had fallen off the fireplace at once. Upon investigation she found that a blackbird had come down the chimney, bringing with it an avalanche of soot and debris. It lay stunned in the empty grate for a few seconds and then, at Jean's approach, began to thrash and struggle, battering itself against the bars.

Jean recoiled, her heart heaving in horror. She was quite unequal to the task of either rescuing or finishing off a wounded bird. She could see now that it was a young pigeon, blackened with soot, and that it was perhaps more terrified than injured. It had flopped out of the grate and was beginning to flap unsteadily around the room, imperiling the ornaments and leaving dark streaks on the wallpaper.

Throwing open the door to the garden, Jean tried to wave it toward the doorway, with stiff-armed gestures more suited to directing traffic, until it finally sensed freedom and took off, low across the lawn, coming to rest on the branch of the cherry tree. As Jean stood watching, next door's ginger cat came stalking out of the shrubbery with murder in its eyes.

By the time she had swept up the gritty mess from the hearth, wiped the worst of the marks from the walls and closed the door on the damp, subterranean smell of soot, she could hear the bath-water thundering in the drain outside. She smoked her cigarette standing up at the cooker waiting for the milk to boil for her mother's Allenburys.

Now that her heart rate had returned to normal she felt quite a sense of accomplishment at having seen off another domestic crisis without having to call on anyone else for help—even supposing there had been anyone to call.

Sawdust is excellent for cleaning carpets. Damp the sawdust, sprinkle lightly over the carpet to be cleaned and then brush off with a stiff brush. It leaves no stain on the most delicate-colored carpet.

2

Number 7, Burdett Road, Sidcup was a 1930s row house in slightly
better condition than Jean's own. In the front garden a symmetri-
cal arrangement of marigolds and begonias bloomed in weedless
borders on three sides of a neat rectangle of lawn. A matching pair
of tame hydrangeas flowered at either end of the low front wall.
The brass letterbox and door knocker had been polished to a high
shine. Jean, standing on the doorstep, taking a moment to collect
herself before ringing the bell, resolved to pick up some Brasso
on the way home. It was all too easy to overlook the chores that
related to those parts of the house her mother didn't see.

After a few moments a shape loomed behind the stained-glass
panel and the front door was opened by a slender woman of about
thirty with dark brown curly hair pinned off her face by a tortoiseshell clip. She was holding a balled-up duster and a pair of
rubber gloves, which she passed uncertainly from hand to hand
before depositing them on the hallstand beside her.

"Mrs. Tilbury? I'm Jean Swinney from the *North Kent Echo*."

"Yes, come in, come in," said the woman, simultaneously holding out a hand to shake and standing back to let Jean in so it was
now out of reach.

After they had negotiated this rather bungled introduction,

Jean found herself ushered into the front parlor, which smelled of wax polish and had the pristine, dead feel of a room that was saved for best.

Mrs. Tilbury offered Jean the more comfortable of the two chairs by the window, angled toward each other across a small table.

"I thought you might need to make some notes," she said. It wasn't so much her accent as the faintly staccato delivery that marked her out as foreign.

"Thank you—I usually do," said Jean, taking out her spiral notebook and pencil from her bag and laying them on the table.

"I've made some tea. I'll just get it."

Mrs. Tilbury whisked out of the room and Jean could hear her clattering in the kitchen. She took advantage of this momentary absence to glance at her surroundings, evaluating them with a practiced eye. Bare floorboards, a tired-looking rug, tiled fireplace, the grate empty and swept. On the piano in the alcove were half a dozen photographs in silver frames. One was a family group, posed with unsmiling Edwardian rigidity, the patriarch standing, his wife seated with a baby in christening robes on her lap, a girl in a pinafore staring glassily into the camera. Another was a studio portrait of a girl of nine or ten with a cloud of dark curls—Mrs. Tilbury herself, perhaps—gazing up as if in wonder at something just out of shot. African violets and a Christmas cactus on the windowsill; a tapestry on the wall depicting an Alpine scene with snow-capped mountains and a wooden hut surrounded by fields of wild flowers; an embroidered sampler, reading "Home Sweet Home."

Mrs. Tilbury came back in carrying a tray on which were two delicate china cups, milk jug, sugar bowl and a teapot wearing a crocheted cozy. As she poured the tea her hand shook a little, jangling the spout against the edge of the cup. Nervous, perhaps, thought Jean. Or just butterfingered with the best china.

Now that she had a proper look at her, Jean could see that Mrs. Tilbury was one of those women blessed by nature. She had a clear creamy complexion, a tiny straight nose and slanting blue eyes, which gave her face an un-English kind of beauty. She wore a round-collared top tucked into a fitted skirt.

Jean found herself caught between admiration and envy. She would have liked to wear that style of nipped-in waist herself, but she had no waist to nip. Even as a young girl she had been solidly built. Not fat exactly—portions had never been generous enough for that—but with a straight up-and-down figure, much more like a grandfather clock than an hourglass.

"You're not English?" Jean tried not to make this sound like an accusation.

"No. I'm Swiss. From the German-speaking part, actually. But I've lived here since I was nine."

They smiled at each other across their teacups and a silence descended while Jean deliberated whether to make more general conversation about Mrs. Tilbury's background or to cut straight to the matter at issue.

"We were all very interested in your letter," she said at last. "You didn't give much away but it was most intriguing."

"I expect you have a lot of questions. You can ask me anything. I don't mind."

"Well, perhaps you could start by telling me about the birth of your daughter."

Mrs. Tilbury clasped her hands in her lap and fiddled with her wedding ring. "Perhaps first of all I should say that although I was a very innocent girl growing up, I did know where babies came from. My mother was quite strict—she was a very religious woman—and of course there were no boyfriends or anything of that sort; but I was not kept in ignorance. So when I went to the doctor, not long before my nineteenth birthday, feeling tired and my breasts aching, I couldn't believe it when he said I was going to have a baby. Because I knew it wasn't possible—I had never even so much as kissed a man."

"It must have been a terrible shock."

"Yes, it was," said Mrs. Tilbury. "But I really thought, it can't be right. They'll realize they've made a mistake soon."

"Presumably you explained all this to the doctor who had examined you?"

"Yes, of course. He said the manner of conception wasn't his concern and my surprise did not alter the fact that I was most definitely expecting a baby."

"In other words, he didn't believe you."

"I suppose not. He said he had met many girls in my condition who were equally confounded to learn that they were pregnant. But they soon came round to the idea when they realized that their denials would make no difference to the outcome, and he hoped I would, too."

"What a horrible man," said Jean with more force than she had intended. "I despise doctors."

If Mrs. Tilbury was taken aback, she was too polite to show it.

"But of course he was quite right. And he looked after me very well in the end," she conceded.

"So, when it became clear to you that there was no mistake, how did you account for it to yourself? I mean, what do you think *happened*? Did you think it was a visitation from the Holy Spirit—or some kind of medical phenomenon that science can't explain? Or what?"

Mrs. Tilbury spread her hands out in a gesture of helplessness. "I don't know. I'm not a scientist. I'm not religious like my mother. I only know what *didn't* happen."

"And how did your parents react to the news? Presumably you had to tell them."

"My father was dead by this time, so there was just my mother."

"And she believed you?"

"Of course."

"Not all mothers would be so amenable." Jean thought of her own mother and had to subdue a sudden surge of hatred.

"But she knew I couldn't have had relations with any man. You see, at the time of the supposed conception I was in a private clinic being treated for severe rheumatoid arthritis. I was bedridden for four months, in a ward with three other young women."

"Oh."

Jean was unable to hide her surprise at this revelation. It seemed to provide an unexpected level of corroboration to Mrs. Tilbury's account. Her claim had suddenly become much harder to dismiss and to Jean's surprise, she was glad. For reasons that were not just to do with journalistic hunger for a good story, she wanted it to be true.

"I suppose you'd be happy for me to check out all the dates and so forth," she said.

"Oh yes. I was in St. Cecilia's Nursing and Convalescent Home from the beginning of June 1946 to the end of September. It was November first when I found out I was pregnant and Margaret was born on the thirtieth of April, 1947."

"She wasn't premature or anything like that?"

"No. Late in fact. They had to bring her on because my blood pressure was too high."

"Mrs. Tilbury, do you mind if I ask you a personal question? I'm afraid if we go ahead with this you are going to be asked many personal questions."

"I understand," Mrs. Tilbury replied, a faint blush rising to her cheeks.

"At the time you went to the doctor, had you not noticed that you weren't menstruating? Wouldn't that have rung alarm bells?"

"Well, it wasn't the first time that there had been a gap. I was never very regular in that department. Sometimes months would go by."

The two women exchanged a smile of complicity at the trials of womanhood. Jean was struck by the strangeness of discussing these intimate details over the best china with someone she had only just met. Now that the ice had been broken she decided to press on with other delicate questions.

"It was a brave decision to keep the baby," she said, although the alternatives were surely braver, involving as they did more suffering for the mother. "Did you ever consider giving her up for adoption . . . or . . ." She couldn't say the other word aloud.

"Oh no," said Mrs. Tilbury. "Never that. My mother was a devout Catholic. And she believed the baby was a gift from God."

"She wasn't worried what the neighbors would think of an unmarried mother? People can be very quick to judge."

"We were already outsiders anyway." She stopped suddenly. "That's Margaret," she said, her vigilant maternal ear picking up some signal inaudible to Jean.

Only now could she hear the clang of the gate and the scuff of shoes on the path. A moment later the back door creaked open.

"We're in here," Mrs. Tilbury called. "Come and say hello."

A girl in a green gingham school dress and straw hat came into the room, flushed and panting from the heat.

"May I go to Lizzie's?" she asked. "They've got kittens." She pulled up as she noticed Jean.

"This is Margaret," said Mrs. Tilbury, her face glowing with pride at her own creation. "This lady is Miss Swinney." Her Swiss accent rendered it "Miss Svinny." "She works for a newspaper."

"Hello," said Margaret, taking off her hat and shaking out her hair. She eyed Jean suspiciously. "Have you ever met Queen Elizabeth?"

"No," admitted Jean. "But I did meet Harold Macmillan, when he was elected MP for Bromley."

Margaret looked unimpressed. She has probably never heard of Harold Macmillan, Jean thought. And why should she, at ten years

old? Jean couldn't help smiling at the delightful resemblance between mother and daughter. She had never seen so disconcerting
a likeness between two people who were not twins. In Margaret's
cloudy curls and delicate features she could see a faithful reproduction of the pretty child Mrs. Tilbury had been twenty years
ago. It was no struggle to believe they belonged entirely to each
other. If someone else had played a part in Margaret's conception,
he had left no visible trace.

"Well, there's no doubting she's yours," said Jean. "She's the
image of you."

Margaret and her mother looked at each other and laughed,
pleased. The little girl was still young enough to be flattered by
the comparison. In a few years, thought Jean, it will be odious
to her.

Mrs. Tilbury went to the piano and picked up the photograph
Jean had noticed earlier.

"This is me when I was just a little older than Margaret is now,"
she said, holding it up.

Margaret obliged by assuming the same wistful expression, eyes
raised heavenward. There was nothing to tell them apart, except
perhaps that melancholy aura that always seemed to surround the
subjects of old photographs.

"Would you mind lending me this?" Jean asked, imagining
how the two images might look side by side in the paper. "We
could take one of Margaret in the same pose, if you're agreeable."

"Yes, of course, do take it," Mrs. Tilbury said.

Really, thought Jean, the woman is so straightforward, it's impossible to believe she is anything other than completely genuine.

"May I go to Lizzie's now?" Margaret wheedled.

Her mother ruffled her hair. "Yes, all right. For half an hour.
But you must do your piano practice as soon as you come back."

Margaret nodded eagerly, said a polite goodbye to Jean and
scurried out of the room.

What a dear little girl, thought Jean with an uprush of longing. Aloud she said, "You are very fortunate."

"I know," said Mrs. Tilbury. "She's an angel."

The tea had gone cold now but Jean refused the offer of a fresh pot. Now that Margaret was out of earshot they could talk freely again and there was so much more to be said.

"Did they cure you?"

"Who?"

"St. Cecilia's. You said you were bedbound for four months."

"I wouldn't say it was the doctors who cured me. But toward the end I was certainly much better and although I have had occasional flare-ups since, nothing like I had as a child. Since I had Margaret, in fact, my symptoms seem to have almost disappeared." She waggled her hands. "If I have been doing a lot of hand-sewing I sometimes feel the old stiffness in my wrists and then I just wear my funny bandages until it goes away again."

"You're a dressmaker?"

"Yes—I do alterations and repairs and make clothes to order. Wedding dresses and things like that."

"Goodness. You must be very accomplished." Jean's own needlework skills were rudimentary and confined to essential mending. Falling hems, dangling buttons. Darning was a particular horror, performed so untidily that her mother had been forced to reclaim the task for herself. "I could never make a dress."

"It's terribly simple," said Mrs. Tilbury. "I could teach you."

"I'm unteachable," said Jean. "I have the school reports to prove it."

They smiled at each other.

"Does Margaret know about her . . . origins?" Jean asked, struggling for the appropriate word. "Parentage" seemed to imply skepticism on her part.

"She knows that her birth was special. She calls my husband

Daddy, but she knows he's not her real father. I mean he *is* her real father, in the important sense, that he has brought her up and loves her as his own."

"May I ask what it is you are hoping to achieve by pursuing this investigation? You don't strike me as someone who craves notoriety."

This was it—the question that had troubled her more than any other. What did Gretchen Tilbury possibly have to gain from exposing her family to public scrutiny? If her case was proven she would become a phenomenon, an object of ravenous and intrusive curiosity to medical science. If she was found to be a fake, her reputation and possibly her marriage would be in shreds.

"I suppose I just read that article in your paper and I thought, Yes! That's me! And I wanted someone to prove what I had always known."

"But you must understand that our position—mine, the paper's, the scientists', the public's—will be one of extreme skepticism. It's not like a court of law—your word will be doubted until it can be proved true. And I won't leave any stone unturned."

"I understand that. But I don't have anything to hide so I have nothing to worry about."

"What about your husband? Is he in agreement?"

"Yes, of course."

"And he's not putting you under any pressure to . . . prove yourself?"

"No, no. He already believes me absolutely."

"All the same, I think I'd like to speak to him, if that's all right with you. And even if it isn't," Jean added, remembering the stones unturned.

Mrs. Tilbury glanced at her watch. "He doesn't get home until six-thirty. He has a jeweler's shop near Covent Garden—Bedford Street. There is a telephone at the shop. We don't have one here."

Jean turned her notepad to face her and Mrs. Tilbury wrote down his name and number in her strange continental script; those crossed sevens and the nines like little *g*s.

"Thank you," said Jean, though she had no intention of calling him. She planned to turn up at his shop unannounced. She closed her notebook to signal that the interview was over.

"What happens now?" asked Mrs. Tilbury.

"I'm going to contact the geneticist who wrote the original article and ask if there are some tests that can be run on you and Margaret to establish whether or not parthenogenesis took place. You'd need to be able to get up to London. I assume that's not going to be a problem?"

"Will you come with us?"

Jean hadn't considered this far ahead, but she only hesitated for a second before saying, "Yes, of course."

The paper would have to live with it. It was her story now and she'd do it her way. Someone else could take over The Garden Week by Week if it got too much. She surely couldn't be the only person on the paper who knew how to prune roses.

"Oh good."

Mrs. Tilbury seemed relieved, as though she was depending on Jean to be some kind of advocate and protector throughout the whole process.

Jean felt the tug of friendship, but it would have to be resisted. If it came to delivering unwelcome news in due course then it was essential to maintain a sensible, professional distance.

3

"So you're saying you believe her?"

"I'm saying I haven't found any reason to disbelieve her. Yet."

Jean sat in Roy Drake's office, watching him water the desiccated plants on the window ledge. A column of smoke rose straight from his parked cigarette and then rippled into the already dense cloud below the ceiling. While he had his back to her Jean took a sly puff and replaced the cigarette on the ashtray.

"Oh, sorry, have one of mine," he said without turning round.

Jean gave a start and looked up, their eyes meeting in the reflection in the window.

"Nothing gets past you, does it?" sighed Jean, helping herself to a cigarette from the packet on his desk.

He shook his head complacently. Years ago, during the very worst time of Jean's life, he had come across her weeping in the mailroom at the end of the day. He had put his arms around her in a fatherly way (though he was not quite old enough to be her father) and without showing any curiosity or distaste, said, "Come on, old girl." In the absence of any other comforter she had found his kindness deeply touching. They had never mentioned it again, but it was always there as a thread between them.

"But it can't really be true, can it?" Roy said.

"There have been instances of spontaneous parthenogenesis in fish and invertebrates, not mammals. But experiments on rabbits have proved that it's possible to induce it artificially in a laboratory."

Roy raised his eyebrows. "Rabbits? If one mammal why not another?" He had finished with the plants now and spun back to face her in his leather chair.

"It involved quite a high degree of interference—freezing the fallopian tubes—and the failure rate was very high."

"Poor creatures." Roy pulled a face. "How do you know all this?"

"I've contacted the doctor whose article started all this—Hilary Endicott—and she sent me some of her research papers. They weren't an easy read, so I asked her whether or not in her opinion a virgin birth was scientifically possible, yes or no. She got on her high horse and said science wasn't in the business of declaring what was or wasn't possible. All that could be said was that there had been no verifiable instances of spontaneous parthenogenesis in mammals so far."

"That sounds like no to me."

"Well, she conceded that she thought the chances vanishingly small, but many new scientific discoveries were once thought impossible and she was interested in seeing what the tests showed."

"And yet you find her less persuasive than Mrs. Tilbury?"

"Yes. No. I don't know. Do you think it's possible to hold two contradictory views at the same time?"

"Perfectly. Religious folk do it all the time."

"So let's say I think Mrs. Tilbury is telling the truth, but I still don't believe in virgin birth, and I see it as my job to close that gap."

"How do we want to proceed then?"

"Cautiously. I don't want anything to go in the paper until we've got all the test results. If it turns out to be true, it'll be massive, and it's *ours*. I don't want one of the nationals to steal it before we even know whether there's a story. There's no rush, is there?"

"None at all."

"I wish you could meet her. She looks a bit like Deanna Durbin."

Roy clutched his heart. "Now I really am interested."

"And the little girl is a treasure." Jean took the silver-framed photograph from her bag and propped it on the desk.

"Is this the daughter?"

"No—it's the mother, but it could be either."

"And this Endicott woman is keen to get involved?"

"She's keener than keen. She's got a whole team at Charing Cross Hospital who can't wait to get their surgical gloves on them."

"Splendid."

"And while they're running the medical tests, I'm going to do a bit more background research to see if the story holds water."

"Are you going to be able to fit all this in around your regular duties, or are you looking to drop something?"

Roy's tone was neutral, but she knew the answer that was expected.

"No. I'm aiming to fit it all in."

"Good chap. Everything else all right *chez* Swinney? How's Mother?"

He often asked after her, though they'd never met. Jean had told him some stories of her foibles over the years and he now had her fixed in his mind as a "character." If they ever did meet he would be disappointed. She was able to quell any stirrings of disloyalty by reasoning that the "Mother" described was almost a work of fiction, not unlike the imaginary friends of early childhood.

"Mother is finding the warm weather a trial."

"But I thought it was cold weather she didn't like?"

"Yes it is. Also windy weather. For someone confined to the house, she has quite particular views on the subject."

Roy laughed, delighted. "I imagine her as an orchid."

"But she will be in a good temper tonight because there are strawberries for tea."

"Well, give her my best," said Roy.

4

H. R. Tilbury Jeweler (Secondhand and Antique—Repairs—Best Prices Paid) was in one of those narrow streets north of the Strand, between a tobacconist and a shop selling antiquarian books and sheet music. The name was picked out in elegant gold lettering against the bottle-green paintwork.

Through the leaded panes of the door Jean could see that there was just one customer, in conversation with the man behind the counter. She was evidently buying a watch or having a new strap fitted, as she emerged a few moments later, turning her wrist this way and that to see how it looked. Jean waited for her to head up the street before entering the shop, setting the bell above the door jangling.

The proprietor had retreated into his workroom, leaving the adjoining door open, and Jean could see him sitting at a bench above which racks of tools were neatly arranged. At the sound of the bell he looked up and laid aside the file he had been holding.

The interior of the shop was tiny. Surrounded on three sides by glass display cabinets, Jean felt as though she filled all the remaining space and was liable to smash something if she made any sudden movement.

"I'm looking for Howard Tilbury," she said, not quite convinced that the man who now stood before her could be the husband of the pretty young woman with the nipped-in waist and the Deanna Durbin hair.

He was thin and stooped and balding; what remained of his hair was gray. He was dressed on the hottest day of the year so far in a tweed jacket, flannel trousers, hand-knitted pullover, shirt and tie and, in all probability, full-length combinations underneath. But when Jean introduced herself he stood a little straighter and smiled and for a moment didn't look quite so old.

"Oh, yes, you're the lady my wife was telling me about." They shook hands across the counter and he added with a worried frown, "Was I supposed to be expecting you today?"

"Not at all. I was just passing, so I thought I'd call in. Could you spare me a moment or two between customers?"

He looked wary but she had intended no irony.

"Tuesday is a slow day for customers. I don't know why. So I mostly do repairs. We could sit in the workshop." He unlatched the countertop between two cabinets to allow her through.

"If you're sure," Jean said, glancing back at the unattended valuables in the window as he showed her into the workshop, which was hardly more spacious.

"The bell will ring if anyone comes in and I'll leave the door open."

Full of apologies for the lack of comforts, he offered her a sagging green armchair in one corner. When she sat in it the arms were level with the tops of her ears, the seat inches from the ground. Her long legs sprawled across the floor between them, as ungainly as a fallen horse. The only other seat, which Mr. Tilbury now took, was the revolving stool at the bench where he had just been working. Beside her on a low table was an electric hotplate, kettle, cup, the remains of a sandwich in a greaseproof paper wrapping and a skinny apple core. He whisked the debris away and threw it into a wastebasket under the bench.

"May I offer you a cup of tea, Miss Swinney?" he asked.

His relief when she declined confirmed her sudden flash of intuition that the used cup beside her was the only one he had and that she was the only visitor he had ever entertained here.

"You and your wife have obviously discussed the *North Kent Echo*'s interest in her story," Jean began, looking up at him from her disadvantaged position near the ground. "I wanted to reassure myself that you were comfortable with the idea."

"That's thoughtful of you," he replied. "But this matter is so very much my wife's concern that I take my lead from her. As long as it has no ill effect on Margaret."

"Yes. Margaret." Jean shuffled forward onto the rigid seat edge to gain a few precious inches of height. It was hard to assume any kind of authority with her knees higher than her hips.

"You've met her?" At the mention of her name his worried expression lightened.

"Briefly. I thought her delightful."

"Yes," he beamed. "She is. Quite the best thing that has ever happened to me."

Jean flipped through her notebook to the pages of scribbled shorthand she had written during her visit to the Tilburys' house in Sidcup the previous week.

"How old was Margaret when you first met your wife?"

"About six months. I came as a lodger to their house in Wimbledon. Gretchen's mother, Frau Edel, let out rooms to bring in money. One of the other tenants had moved out because she didn't like the idea of living with an unmarried mother. It didn't worry me, of course. And then when I got to know the Edels better, they told me Gretchen's story." He recounted it, at Jean's prompting, all just as Mrs. Tilbury herself had described.

"And you never doubted this version of events?"

"No. I know to an outsider it sounds far-fetched. But not if you knew the Edels. I've never had any reason to doubt my wife's honesty. I don't think she's capable of telling an untruth."

"But unmarried women have very good reason to lie about the circumstances of a pregnancy. Society is so unforgiving."

"People are quick to judge, that is true. All I can say is she had no reason to lie to me. I made it quite clear that it made no difference to me how Margaret came into being."

"But she never wavered from her story?"

"Never. And I have to believe her."

"Presumably you would be happy to see science prove her right?"

"I have never felt the need for any 'proof.' But if you are asking whether I would be glad, on balance, to know that no other man than me has any stake in Margaret, then yes."

"And perhaps glad to see any doubters silenced once and for all?"

"I don't know about that," Mr. Tilbury said, flattening the hair on the back of his head with one hand. It was a nervous habit; every few minutes his elbow would shoot out again as he clasped the back of his neck. "I'm not sure there are any doubters to bother us. Frau Edel died soon after Gretchen and I married, and we moved away from Wimbledon to Sidcup and started afresh as just another couple with a baby. None of our new neighbors knows anything about our past."

Exactly, thought Jean. So why on earth would you want to risk your privacy now? Instead, she said, "Are you a religious man, Mr. Tilbury?"

"No more, nor less, than most people, I suppose. I don't go to church much, except for weddings and funerals, but I'm glad it's there."

"Did you marry in church?"

"No. It was easier not to, in the circumstances. Frau Edel's priest wasn't very accommodating."

"You would think a priest of all people would be open to the idea of a virgin birth," Jean said.

Mr. Tilbury met her glance for the first time. "They can be rather possessive about miracles, I've found."

"Was it a long courtship?"

"Four months or so. We were living in the same house, of course, which accelerated things. And Frau Edel was already ill by then so there was a certain urgency for her to see Gretchen safely married, as it were." There was a pause. "I know what you're thinking," he said quietly.

Jean blushed. "Oh, I'm sure you don't," she replied.

She had in fact been wondering if she could have a cigarette, or whether the workshop contained material and equipment sensitive to smoke. There was no sign of an ashtray.

"You're thinking a woman like Gretchen would never have looked twice at a man like me if it wasn't for the baby."

"I wasn't. Really."

"Well, you're right. She wouldn't. I know that. A woman like her could have had anybody, and I'm certainly nothing special."

"I'm sure she feels very fortunate to have you," said Jean, finding this display of self-abasement embarrassing and unwarranted.

To her mind, Gretchen had nothing to complain of. With a mother and a doting husband convinced of her virtue, the woman had already been doubly blessed. And she had Margaret. What more could she possibly want?

The shop bell tinkled and Mr. Tilbury stood up. "Do you mind?" he said. "Please make yourself comfortable."

Easier said than done in such a chair, Jean thought, levering herself up to standing and feeling the blood tingle in her numb legs and feet. From the other side of the door came the murmur of voices, male and female. She began to inspect her surroundings, as she always did when unobserved. A lifetime of quiet watchfulness had convinced her that the truth about people was seldom to be found in the things they freely admitted. There was always more below the surface than above.

She opened the topmost of a chest of wide, shallow drawers. It was subdivided into dozens of tiny wooden compartments, each containing a piece of jewelry awaiting repair. There were cameo brooches, engagement rings, bracelets, lockets, all with broken clasps or missing gems, and each bearing a brown paper label, numbered and dated in minute handwriting. In the drawer below were the corpses of numerous wristwatches, their body parts cannibalized for repairs.

Jean picked up a dainty coping saw and touched the pad of her finger against its hair-thin blade. She flinched as the skin peeled apart and blood welled up in the cut. She was still blotting it with her handkerchief when Mr. Tilbury returned, holding a sapphire brooch, which he labeled and consigned to the shallow drawer.

Since he had politely declined to notice her snooping, Jean felt a perverse urge to confess.

"I'm afraid I was fiddling with that little saw," she said, holding out her hand for his inspection and feeling rather foolish. "I wanted to see how sharp it was."

He seemed to find this highly amusing.

"Well, Miss Swinney, it's lucky I came back before you decided to test the soldering iron to see how hot it is."

"I'm very inquisitive, I'm afraid," said Jean. "It comes with the job."

He took down a battered first aid kit from a shelf and from it took a Band-aid with which he proceeded to dress her finger.

"Such tiny hands you have," he said when he had finished. From any other man it might have struck her as a paltry kind of compliment, as if this was the one physical attribute that he could find to praise. But he went on to say, "You'd make a good jeweler with those delicate fingers," holding up his own chunky hand in comparison. "Some days I feel like a bear in boxing gloves."

"I was just thinking what a satisfying job it must be," Jean replied, taking her seat again. "Making and mending people's treasures. I'm far too clumsy to do anything like that."

"There's nothing very exalted about sizing wedding bands or altering watch straps," he said. "But it's my bread and butter, so I can't complain."

"When you spend all day at a typewriter, the idea of making something real with your hands is very appealing."

"I'm sure most people would think your world the more exciting," he replied.

Jean shook her head. "Fleet Street, maybe. But the *North Kent Echo* is very staid. It makes the front page if somebody breaks into the British Legion and pinches a bottle of gin."

She thought of the piece she had dashed off that morning to mark National Salad Week:

....

The humble lettuce, if properly dressed, can be the foundation of many nutritious family meals. Try serving with baked
or fried forcemeat balls for a crisp new touch . . .

....

"You don't wear jewelry yourself, I notice," he said.

Jean's hands, wrists and neck were, as always, unadorned.

"No, but not as a matter of principle. I just don't own any. It's not the sort of thing one buys for oneself." She stopped, conscious that she was straying into territory that was more personal than professional.

"I suppose not. Though there's no reason why."

"And if I did, I would probably never wear it, just keep it in a box and look at it from time to time." She knew this much about herself.

"That would be a waste. It needs to breathe."

Jean felt her own breath tighten. This was the most intimate conversation she had had with a man for years.

The shop bell rang again. Jean took this as a signal to leave. She had satisfied herself that husband and wife were in perfect accord over Mrs. Tilbury's approach to the *Echo*, and that he had not brought any pressure to bear on her. Of course, it was impossible to know what went on in a marriage behind those neat bay windows, but she had met bullying men before, at work and elsewhere, and Mr. Tilbury was quite unlike them.

"I must let you get on," she said.

He sprang forward to help her out of the chair. There was a dangerous moment as she took his hand and pulled herself up rather heavily, when their balance faltered and it seemed as though she might topple back and drag him down on top of her. A look of panic passed between them and then he planted his feet more firmly and gripped her hand until she was steady again.

"Goodness, we made heavy weather of that," Jean laughed. "I told you I was clumsy."

"I don't feel I've been much use at all," Mr. Tilbury said. "But I've enjoyed talking to you anyway."

"There is one other question," Jean remembered. "Your wife said she was in a clinic or sanatorium before Margaret was born. I wondered if she was still in touch with any friends from that period of her life. Or anyone who knew her as a young girl."

Mr. Tilbury considered, his head on one side, but seemed to draw a blank.

"Do you know, I can't think of anyone who comes to mind. The clinic was down near the coast—Broadstairs, I believe. Before that she was at school in Folkestone. I suppose any friends would have lived down that way. By the time I met the Edels they were living in Wimbledon, and the few people they knew there were recent acquaintances, so I don't know. My wife has friends now in

Sidcup, of course. Mothers of Margaret's little chums and so on. But you'd have to ask her about anything further back."

Jean followed him into the shop where the customers, a young couple, were waiting. Newlyweds, Jean decided, from the way the girl clung to his arm and gazed at him so adoringly. Or perhaps newly engaged and wanting a large and costly ring. Jean hoped so, for Mr. Tilbury's sake. As she squeezed past in the cramped space she could feel the happiness streaming from them.

Later, when Jean had cooked meat and potatoes for dinner, and washed up, and watered the garden, she wrote up her shorthand notes of the meeting and underlined the word Broadstairs. Then flicking back to her interview with Gretchen Tilbury she found a reference to St. Cecilia's and circled that also. This would be her next focus of enquiry.

There was no urgency, of course. Mrs. Tilbury and Margaret were due at Charing Cross Hospital for their first set of tests and observations soon; the results might preclude any further investigations on her part. But she was already looking forward to it. It was quite a few years since she had been to the coast. There was Worthing, of course, in '46, but she didn't count that because of what came afterward.

Perhaps, she thought, turning her mind firmly to Broadstairs, she might even stay the night and drive home the following day. It took no more than a moment's consideration to dismiss the idea, appealing though it was to imagine waking to the high call of gulls and the shush of waves on sand. It was quite impossible; her mother wouldn't be left, even for one night. The mere suggestion would aggravate her already highly developed sense of helplessness.

Because they depended on Jean's salary to live, Mr. Swinney having left neither pension nor savings, she was able to accommodate Jean's absence for the length of a working day, no more.

Crises that could be held off between nine and five-thirty were likely to rear up outside of those hours and overwhelm her. Jean, as a rational woman, had always intended to challenge this principle, but time had passed and she never had, and now the habit was fixed.

There had been occasions in the past when she had regretted this. On Friday evenings Bill, Larry, Duncan the picture editor and some of the subs would go over to the Black Horse in Petts Wood for a drink after work. Once or twice they had invited her along, because she was, after all, one of the guys, but she had declined because she hadn't cleared it with her mother in advance, and now they didn't ask anymore.

Now, Mrs. Swinney was installed in her wing-backed armchair in the front room, waiting for Jean to help her to wind some wool. She had knitted a pullover to send to Dorrie for Christmas, but it had kept growing and stretching as she worked at it and the end result would have fitted two Dorries standing side by side. Privately, Jean doubted that it ever got cold enough in Kitale to warrant such an abundance of wool, but her mother was adamant. There was nothing for it but to unravel the whole thing, wash and dry the skeins and start again.

But Jean couldn't seem to settle. Every time she sat down she would jump up again, needing her glasses or remembering some urgent unfinished chore elsewhere. She prowled from room to room, bored and restless, and finally found what she was looking for—an old leather manicure set of pearl-handled implements, with which she began to trim and neaten nails coarsened by housework. This task done, she leapt up again and hurried from the room.

"Where are you off to now?" Her mother's plaintive voice followed her up the stairs.

In Jean's bedroom was a dressing-table drawer filled with things too precious ever to be used. Soaps, cosmetics, perfume, stationery—mostly gifts, or the occasional rash purchase—they had been accumulated and hoarded over many years. The contemplation of these treasures, still pristine in their packaging, gave Jean far more satisfaction than using them ever could. A leather notebook with marbled endpapers and gold-tipped pages was a thing of beauty only so long as its pages remained blank. A lipstick was spoiled the moment it touched her lips—unused, its potential was infinite.

Tonight, though, Jean opened a pot of rich hand cream, releasing a gust of rose-scented air, and drew her finger across the surface with only a faint tremor of regret. As she rubbed her hands together her crumpled skin seemed to soften and uncrease. She knew the transformation was only illusory and fleeting, but for a moment she felt a rare kinship with those legions of women who bother with such things and take pleasure in them.

"What's that smell?" her mother asked on Jean's return. Her nose had become keener lately, perhaps acquiring territory from her hearing, which was in brisk retreat.

"Pink roses."

"I thought so. You usually smell of the office." Her mother's face puckered. "Cigarettes and newsprint and work. I prefer the roses."

"Well, I haven't been in the office this afternoon. I've been to visit a jeweler's near Covent Garden."

"Jewish?"

"I've no idea. I didn't ask."

"I expect so. They usually are."

"His name was Tilbury. He showed me his workshop where he does all the repairs. It was rather interesting."

"I should think it was. I wonder if he'd be able to mend this." She began to drag at the garnet-and-pearl cluster ring on her middle finger, forcing it over her knotted knuckle. "There's a stone missing."

"It would be expensive to replace a stone."

"Well. It's valuable. And it will be yours one day."

All her geese are swans, thought Jean.

"Don't take it off now—it'll only get lost. I might not be seeing him again for some time, if ever." But as she said this she felt sure that she would, and soon.

"Shall we wind this wool, then?" she said, drawing up her chair so that they sat opposite each other, knees nearly touching.

From her knitting bag her mother produced the front panel of Dorrie's jumper and unhitched it from its holding pin. It took no more than a gentle tweak to begin the process of unraveling months of painstaking work. Jean held out her arms and watched with secret satisfaction the scribbled wool turning and turning around her tiny, delicate hands.

To keep your fingers white and soft, dig your nails into the pith of an old lemon skin after completing any dirty jobs at the kitchen sink.

5

The former matron of St. Cecilia's clinic in Broadstairs was called Alice Halfyard, for which curious and memorable name Jean was very grateful, as it made the job of tracing her considerably easier. Jean had made inquiries ahead of her visit and discovered that St. Cecilia's itself was no longer a convalescent home of any kind but a boy's prep school on the south side of the town, on Ramsgate Road.

Less than a year after Gretchen Edel's residency, the boys' school around the corner had looked to expand into new premises and made an offer for the large Edwardian villa. The patients were sent home or dispatched to other sanatoriums along the coast, and what were once wards and treatment rooms for the sick now held desks and chairs, blackboards and coat hooks.

The headmaster of this establishment, now Anselm House, had a wooden leg and walked with an ebony cane. He offered to take Jean on a tour of the building before showing her the St. Cecilia's archive. It was lesson time and the school was quiet; the classroom doors were open because of the heat and as they passed along the corridor the murmured voices within fell silent at the tap and shuffle of his approaching footsteps.

He halted at the last class. The boys rose, as one, with a solemn scraping of chairs. The teacher, evidently accustomed to this kind of unheralded interruption, paused at the blackboard, on which he was drawing what looked to Jean like some terrible monster but was in fact just a flea, greatly magnified.

"This is Miss Swinney, an important newspaper reporter from London," he said in a rather free interpretation of the facts. Perhaps to the people of Broadstairs, London was a concept that stretched as far as the Medway River. "So we must hope she takes away a good impression of the place."

Jean gave the room her warmest, most reassuring smile. She would have liked to see how the lesson proceeded.

"That looked rather interesting," she said, in a half whisper, when they had walked on. "I wondered if it was an introduction to the poetry of John Donne."

"I sincerely hope not," said the headmaster with a frown.

Jean decided it was pain that made him humorless and chose to pity him.

She had taken an early train from Bromley South. The platform was crowded with children in uniform going on a school journey. Two teachers with clipboards were trying to marshal them into lines, while groups of boys kept drifting off to look at a steam engine on the opposite platform.

Jean put her bicycle in the guard's van and chose a compartment near the front of the train. The only other occupant, a woman, glanced up from her book as the door opened and gave her a smile of relief, which Jean understood and returned. She chose a seat in the corner, diagonally opposite, to allow them both the maximum possible space. In her bag was her lunch, an Agatha Christie for the journey, her notebook, of course, and a swimsuit and towel in case there was time to go to the beach.

It was the part of the day she was most looking forward to; she was a good swimmer and in the sea she felt both strong and graceful, a sensation not replicated in the public baths at Beckenham with its chilly tiles and chlorine smell, or indeed on dry land. She had intended to read, but she hadn't opened her book once, preferring instead to gaze out of the window as the dwindling suburbs gave way to the sun-baked fields of north Kent.

After a brief tour of the classrooms, the headmaster took Jean to his office to view St. Cecilia's archive, which had lain undisturbed for nearly a decade. He unlocked a wooden cabinet and laid out various ledgers and a photograph album on his desk for her inspection. There were also some artifacts left behind in the move, which no one had ever bothered to reclaim—a kidney bowl, a bedpan, a selection of prayer cards, some leather finger cots and a set of calipers.

Jean picked up one of the prayer cards and read:

Let nothing disturb thee; nothing affright thee
All things are passing
God never changeth;
Patient endurance attaineth to all things;
Who God possesseth in nothing is wanting.
Alone God sufficeth.

ST. TERESA OF ÁVILA

"May I keep this?" she asked.

"You may take the lot," the headmaster replied. "I've no use for them."

"I suppose the nuns used to give them to the patients," Jean said, turning the pages of the photograph album and stopping at a staff picture of a group of women standing on the gravel drive in front of the house.

Some were in nurses' uniforms; some in nuns' habits. They were smiling and squinting into the sun; some were even shielding their eyes with one hand, as though unused to posing for photographs.

"I don't doubt it," said the headmaster.

She wondered whether his distaste was for religion or just the Roman Catholic arm of it.

"Would it surprise you to discover that a miracle had taken place within these walls?" Jean asked him.

"I think my staff feel they perform miracles here daily," he said with the ghost of a smile.

He does have a sense of humor then, Jean thought. She hadn't intended to give out any more details of the reason for her interest in St. Cecilia's than was absolutely necessary, but his lack of curiosity made her talkative.

"A female patient claims to have conceived a child here. Spontaneously, as it were."

She had his attention at last.

"I should think that unlikely. Other explanations come to mind."

"Such as?"

"The woman is either deluded or dishonest."

How ready people are to think a woman they have never met is a liar, thought Jean.

"And yet she seems genuine."

"Dishonest people often do. Are you looking for evidence to discredit her?"

"If it exists, certainly."

"Well, I hope you find it. I don't like the thought of this place becoming a shrine."

Jean laughed. "I must admit, I hadn't considered that as a by-product."

"We will be besieged by virgins," he said with a shudder.

You probably think I am one, Jean thought.

"This person here," she said, pointing to a photograph in which a middle-aged woman in a dark dress and white bonnet was seated in the center of a row of nurses in pale uniforms and starched aprons, "must be the head nurse." She appeared, similarly attired, in several other pictures. "Do you mind?"

Jean lifted the print carefully from its fragile, tissue-thin corners and turned it over. As she had hoped, some dutiful record keeper had written on the back in brownish ink: L to R: J. Soames, R. Forbes, M. Cox, A. Halfyard, M. Smith, D. Baker, V. (Pegs) Austin, 1946.

"A. Halfyard," said Jean. "That must be her."

"That's a blessing," said the headmaster, taking the picture from her and replacing it in the album. "There can't be many of those in the telephone directory. Miss Trevor will have one in her office."

The secretary was talking on the telephone and simultaneously cranking the handle of a mimeograph in full cry when Jean knocked on the open door. She summoned Jean in with a jerk of her chin, without pausing.

"I suppose we could manage modest expenses," she was saying. "Though the other candidates are coming from farther afield and they haven't asked."

The air was heavy with the smell of spirit; Jean could feel it stinging her eyes. Miss Trevor continued to belabor the mimeograph until the last sheet of blurry violet type had flopped out into the tray. Her desk was buried under cliffs of clutter—books, ledgers, manila folders, box files. And yet in spite of this, at the words, "Yes, all right, let me take your details," she flailed helplessly for want of something to write with or on until Jean felt obliged to offer her own notebook and pen.

Having dispatched the caller and straightened her skirt, which had become rather twisted during her exertions, she gave Jean her full attention.

"Do you have a local telephone directory?" Jean asked.

"Somewhere," Miss Trevor replied, giving the overflowing desk a baleful glance. "It's not usually like this," she confided in a lowered voice. "We've got a bunch of interviewees coming tomorrow and I've just changed offices. Everything's at sixes and sevens."

"I won't get in your way," Jean promised. "I'm trying to track down someone who used to work here when it was a private clinic. I'm hoping she's still in the area."

The secretary had ducked under the desk and bobbed up again holding a slim yellow booklet with an air of triumph.

"I knew I had it somewhere. What name are you after? Goodness, this type's small."

Jean began to find her lack of confidence in even the simplest administrative task rather disarming.

"Halfyard," said Jean. "There surely can't be many."

Miss Trevor stopped peeling through the pages. "Alice Halfyard? Well, I can tell you where *she* lives."

"You know her?"

"She's a friend of my mother's. She lives on Wickfield Drive—the corner house. You can walk from here—it's only a mile or so."

"She used to be the head nurse at St. Cecilia's?"

"Yes, that's right. She worked here right through the war up until it closed."

"I don't suppose you know any of the other people who would have been working here just after the war?"

Miss Trevor shook her head. "No. I didn't have any connection with the place until the school took over the buildings. I only know Alice because she was a friend of Mother's. I used to call in myself once in a while after Mother died, but I've got out of the habit. I expect she'll be glad of a visit. She's had a rotten life really, but she was always happy to see me."

The telephone started to ring again and so Jean was able to escape without hearing the detail of Alice Halfyard's rotten life, which Miss Trevor looked all too eager to relay.

★

47

It was now midday, so Jean decided to postpone her trip to Wick-field Drive until the afternoon, on the basis that a former head nurse would surely have strict views on visiting times. She cycled back into town and sat on a bench overlooking the beach to eat her sandwich—Cheddar cheese and the last of the green tomato chutney from the previous year. It had to be made, and once made it had to be eaten, but it gave her no pleasure. I have measured out my life with preserving pans rather than coffee spoons, she sometimes thought.

Down below on the sand were encampments of deck chairs and windbreaks, tiny children toddling in the waves, parents sunbath-ing, old men with trousers rolled to the knee, a few brave souls jumping over waves. Jean longed to join them, but it would have to wait.

There was hardly a cloud in the sky, which was the deep blue of midsummer, and just the right amount of cooling breeze. Jean had thrown off her cardigan, exposing her winter-white arms to the sun. By evening they would be pink and prickling, and the V of skin revealed by her open-necked blouse would be a fiery red, but for the moment the heat was delicious and comforting.

Her sandwich finished, Jean bought an ice cream from a café on the hill. She was a messy eater at the best of times and this particular treat, a rectangular slab of vanilla ice cream between two wafers, rapidly melting and vulnerable on all sides, presented a challenge too far. Her blouse took a direct hit and she had to eat the rest of the slippery mess leaning over a rubbish bin to catch the drips. Eating in public, something her mother would never do, even assuming she were to go out in public, still struck her as bold and rebellious, adding greatly to her enjoyment.

Number 1, Wickfield Drive was a single-story cottage on a large corner plot, shielded from the street by overgrown laurels and tall trees, an arrangement at odds with the rest of the houses in the street, which had neat, unfenced lawns running down to the pavement. In Jean's experience, this kind of foliage barrier usually heralded a certain level of dilapidation beyond, but she was surprised to find it concealing a well-tended garden and a pristine cottage. The red tiled doorstep was polished and dustless; the windows, dressed with white nets, were clean to the corners, their paintwork bright and new.

Having buttoned her cardigan to cover the ice-cream spill, untied her headscarf and raked a hand through her flattened hair, Jean pressed the bell. Somewhere inside the house it chimed faintly and a moment later the door was opened by a white-haired woman, dressed as if for midwinter in a woolen dress, housecoat, thick stockings and sheepskin slippers. She was instantly recognizable from the photographs in the St. Cecilia's archive, and there was in any case something both authoritative and soothing in the steady gaze now fixed on Jean that was decidedly matronly.

"Come in, I've been expecting you," she said, then seeing Jean's look of surprise, added, "I'm not a clairvoyant. Susan Trevor called from the school and told me you were coming."

Introductions now superfluous, Jean was shown into the back room, which was dominated by an open display cabinet of china dolls. There were perhaps thirty or forty staring down at her with their glassy eyes and still more laid out on the table, amid various rags and sponges, in the process of being cleaned. A fat tabby cat, taking advantage of its mistress's temporary absence, had jumped up on the table and was trampling on the delicate lace dresses as though flattening grass.

"Get down, Ferdie, you tinker," said Alice, swatting him away. "You've caught me giving my girls a spring clean," she said. "They are a devil for trapping dust."

"I can imagine," said Jean, who found the china faces, limp bodies and dead hair, in such quantities, faintly disturbing, and thought collecting them a pitiable hobby for a grown woman. But out of politeness and perhaps overcompensating for her instinctive aversion, she bent over the specimens on the table, murmuring her admiration, and pointed out one in a shepherdess costume, less ghoulish than the others, saying, "She's rather pretty. What a sweet face." Was it the dark curls and blue eyes, the faint resemblance to Margaret Tilbury, perhaps, that had directed her hand? she wondered later.

Alice Halfyard was delighted. "Oh, do you like her? She's my absolute favorite. Such an intelligent expression—for a shepherdess."

"And the detail," Jean added, peering at the miniature smocking on the bodice and the tiny covered buttons, marveling that so much industry should have been expended in dressing a mere toy. Her own clothes were never this well made.

"I dare say you think I'm a silly old woman, playing with her dolls," Alice said.

"Not at all," Jean replied, though this was more or less what she did think. "It's quite a collection—you could open a museum."

"I keep saying I'm not going to buy any more, but then I pass a secondhand shop and see one looking neglected and I can't help myself. Do you collect anything yourself?"

"Not really," Jean replied, remembering with sudden disquiet her drawer of unused "treasures."

"Well, if you're a newspaper reporter you collect stories, I suppose," said Alice.

"That's a nice way of looking at it," Jean said.

Next time she wrote up the Magistrates' Court Reports she would think of herself as a curator of people's stories. Beatrice Casemore of Frant Avenue, Sidcup, who pleaded guilty to stealing a pair of gloves worth two shillings, eleven pence from Dawson & Co., Drapers. Roland Crabb who was fined ten shillings for keeping a dog without a license. These were her dolls.

"The story I'm collecting at the moment," she added, feeling that the conversation had neatly arrived at its proper destination, "is about a patient who was at St. Cecilia's while you were head nurse there. If true, it's rather remarkable."

Alice put down the doll she had been holding and gave Jean the benefit of her attentive, probing gaze. The blue of her eyes was made brighter by a yellowish tinge to the white, not unlike the color of the doll's porcelain face.

"Go on."

"I wonder if you remember a girl called Gretchen Tilbury, I mean Edel, as she was then."

"I remember all my patients," Alice said, "so yes, I do remember Gretchen very well. A lovely girl. She suffered dreadfully from rheumatoid arthritis; she was in constant pain, poor thing."

"Would you call her a truthful kind of person?"

Alice needed no time to reflect. "Yes, I would. I wouldn't necessarily say that about all the girls at St. Cecilia's during my time, but Gretchen was what you'd call a good girl."

"Did she ever leave the clinic for any reason during her stay?"

"Oh good heavens no. She barely left the bed. It took two nurses to get her up and onto the commode. She really could hardly move."

"I suppose if I told you the dates she was a patient you'd be able to confirm them?"

"Not from memory," Alice replied. "But I have my diaries of the years I worked there."

This was promising—better than Jean had expected.

"You kept a diary the whole time?"

"Not a *personal* diary. Just a record of the working day—who was admitted or discharged, who had what treatment. If the boiler broke down. That kind of thing."

"That would be tremendously helpful—if I could read it," said Jean.

She was already wondering how feasible it would have been for Gretchen to have been impregnated by a visiting boiler repairman.

"You're being very mysterious," said Alice. "I hope you aren't going to tell me something has happened to Gretchen."

"Oh no, Gretchen is alive and well."

"I'm very pleased to hear it."

"And the mother of a little girl, who was apparently conceived during her stay at St. Cecilia's."

Alice Halfyard's hands flew up to her throat, coming to rest on her gold crucifix. "No! That's impossible. Who on earth would have told you such a story?"

"Well, Gretchen herself, and she was as dumbstruck as you. She is adamant that the child was a virgin birth."

In Alice's pale face Jean thought she could identify the transit of emotions—shock, disbelief, dismay. It was a moment or two before she was able to find her voice again.

"I don't know what to say. It can't be." She shook her head. "That child was as innocent as a lamb. She wouldn't have known one end of a man from another. Not that there were any men around the place. The nuns would never have allowed it. *I* would never have allowed it."

"What about doctors? Surely some of them must have been men?"

"Doctor Reardon was a lady doctor, and a very good one. And Gretchen was on a ward with three other girls—one with the rheumatoid, what was her name? Martha. And Brenda—they didn't like her so much—and poor Kitty in the iron lung. The girls were never alone for one minute. They couldn't sneeze without one of the nuns knowing about it."

"What about visitors? Fathers, brothers, odd-job men?"

"We didn't have an odd-job man. We had nuns, and very practical they were, too. The families used to visit on Saturday afternoons. Most of the patients lived some distance away, so the parents only came once a week. There was no opportunity for the girls to be alone with a visitor—they were all in the ward together. And the sister was in there too, making sure things were kept calm and quiet for the patients."

"Did Gretchen have any male visitors?"

"No—just her mother. They were very close."

"So in your professional opinion, it would have been impossible for this child of Gretchen's to be conceived in the ordinary way?"

"Quite impossible," said Alice firmly.

Of course you would say that, thought Jean, who had still to decide how she rated Alice as a witness. She seemed an intelligent woman, but those dolls weighed heavily in the balance. She was never going to admit that it was perfectly feasible for a sick and vulnerable young girl to have gotten pregnant while under her care, but a really unscrupulous person would be looking for an alternative version that deflected blame elsewhere. Jean decided to test her.

"The obvious explanation is that Gretchen is lying and was already pregnant when she was admitted and has somehow falsified the dates."

Alice shook her head. "I don't accept that for one minute. She wasn't that kind of girl."

"But it's the only logical solution."

"Then you must start to consider illogical ones."

"You are medically trained. You surely don't believe in virgin birth?"

"It's hard to imagine it here in Broadstairs." She gave Jean a faint smile. "But I have seen so many strange things in my career— things that if not miraculous are certainly unexplained—that I have had to accept that there are limits to human understanding. My understanding, at least."

"I prefer to think that the answers are out there to be discovered, if we try," said Jean, realizing this about herself for the first time.

"Ah, but that's because you're still young," said Alice. "You've got time."

Jean laughed. At thirty-nine, it was quite some years since anyone had called her young. There were advantages to spending
one's time in the company of pensioners after all.

"I must get you that diary." Alice rose to her feet with some
effort. "I might need you to help me."

Jean followed her along the hallway into a sparsely furnished
bedroom overlooking the garden. It contained a single bed, desk
and wooden chair with a tapestry seat, and a huge Victorian wardrobe that darkened one entire wall. Though tidy, it had the stale,
neglected smell of a room seldom entered. Above the fireplace was
a framed photograph of what appeared to be four generations of
female Halfyards—ranging from a chubby toddler with flowing
curls to a white-haired woman in an armchair. Jean thought she
recognized Alice among them.

"My family," said Alice, noticing the direction of Jean's glance.
"Before the war."

Jean smiled. The last picture of her own family all together
would have been taken at about the same time. But it wasn't out
on display, naturally.

"The diaries are in there," said Alice, pointing to a green suitcase with a rope handle and metal hasps, wedged into the gap on
top of the wardrobe between the carved cornice and the ceiling.
"If you wouldn't mind hopping up on the chair."

Jean did as she was told, feeling a moment's anxiety as the slender chair swayed and creaked under her weight. She pulled the
suitcase down, steadying its bulk against her chest before lowering
it gently onto the bed, toward Alice's fluttering hands.

Nested inside was a smaller case; inside this yet another. This
kernel seemed to be the receptacle for all manner of curious
keepsakes—a shabbier, dustier version of Jean's drawer of treasures. As Alice rummaged through the contents, Jean noticed an
ear trumpet, a pair of lace gloves, a baby's bonnet, a harmonica, a
coil of brown hair tied up with ribbon, a cricket ball, a music box,

snarled-up strings of pearls and chains. Once she had extracted from the core a cardboard box and from this a diary, one of many identical volumes, it took Alice no time to locate a reference to Gretchen Edel.

"Admitted June second, 1946. Discharged on September twenty-eighth of that year."

Jean nodded. It was no surprise to her that the dates confirmed what Mrs. Tilbury had told her. Only a fool would lie about something so easily verified.

"What about the nuns that were here at the same time as Gretchen? Are they still in this area?"

"They went back to Ireland when St. Cecilia's was sold. To Galway, I believe."

"That's a pity," said Jean, dismissing this line of inquiry.

"Campkin!" exclaimed Alice, still browsing through the entries. "That was the name. Martha Campkin. They were tremendous chums. They'd have chattered all through the night if we'd let them. It often happens with patients stuck on a ward together—especially when they're suffering from the same complaint."

Jean had only spent one week in her entire life in a hospital. She would have given all of her possessions for a friendly soul in the next bed.

"Gretchen never mentioned her," she said. "And when I asked her husband if she kept in contact with any friends from that time, he said no."

"Well, those friendships don't always last on the outside," said Alice. "Martha's people came from Chatham, I believe. Whereas I think the Edels lived somewhere in London."

"Wimbledon," said Jean.

"People make such promises to keep in touch," said Alice. "But they seldom do." She sounded suddenly wistful. "The only one who still sends me a Christmas card is Brenda, but she lives in South Africa now."

"Do you have her address?"

"I do. If you wanted to write to her care of me, I would be happy to post it on."

"It sounds as though Martha Campkin might be worth talking to as well," said Jean. "If I can find her."

"Her father was a vicar, if that helps."

"It might."

"She wasn't as compliant as Gretchen. A bit more spiky, if you know what I mean. But a nice enough girl," she added loyally. "And very brave. Nothing we tried ever seemed to work for her." She held out the little diary. "You can borrow it for as long as you need. But I'd be glad to have it back eventually. I don't know why."

"Of course." Jean realized this was a cue to leave, only now noticing that Alice was looking weary. "I must let you get on. You've been so helpful."

"I've enjoyed talking to you, Miss . . ."

"Swinney. Jean."

"Perhaps you'll come back sometime and tell me the outcome of your investigation. I don't think we get the *North Kent Echo* out here."

"I'd be glad to."

"And do remember me to Gretchen," Alice said as they reached the front door. "I was so fond of her. And Martha too, if you find her."

After picking up her bicycle, which had fallen into the laurel hedge, and retying her headscarf, Jean turned for a last look up the path. In the front room, between the parted net curtains, Alice stood holding the shepherdess doll up to the window. Jean had a horrible feeling that if she waved goodbye Alice would make the doll wave back, and she couldn't bear that, so she just smiled and quickly turned her back.

6

Mrs. Tilbury and Margaret were waiting at Charing Cross Station by the ticket office at ten o'clock as arranged. All communications concerning this meeting had been made through Mr. Tilbury at the jeweler's shop. Margaret was dressed in her school uniform with satchel and hat, as Jean had promised she would be back in time for afternoon lessons. Mrs. Tilbury was wearing a green cotton dress embroidered with daisies and a little white jacket, as though she were going to a summer wedding rather than a pathology lab in a dingy hospital annex.

Heads turned as she clipped across the concourse in her strappy sandals, perhaps in admiration or just charmed by the likeness between mother and daughter. Jean smiled to herself. Who on earth would choose to wear white for such a trip?

"That's a pretty dress," she said, almost having to shout over the sound of whistles, the shriek and hiss of shunting trains and the unstoppable flow of announcements from the PA system. "I suppose you are going to tell me you made it yourself."

"Of course," Mrs. Tilbury replied. "I make all my clothes."

They hurried toward the exit, buffeted by the tremendous symphony of noise.

"It fits you far too well to have come from a shop."

Jean plucked at her own formless garment in brown paisley, gathering a fistful of surplus fabric at the waist. It had been chosen to withstand the inevitable dust and grime of the city and fitted her across the shoulders but nowhere else.

"I could make one for you, if you like," Mrs. Tilbury said as they halted at the curb to allow a black taxi to sweep past. "You could look through my pattern book and choose some material. It wouldn't take me two minutes."

"I'm sure you have quite enough to do," said Jean.

"Oh, but I'd like to. It would be my way of thanking you."

"For what? I haven't done anything yet. And I may still not."

"You have. You read my letter and took me seriously."

Let's just see what the scientists turn up, thought Jean as they waited on the Strand for the lights to change. Then we'll see how grateful you are. She had been in correspondence with Hilary Endicott, the author of the original paper on parthenogenesis, and there was now a team of learned physicians at the Charing Cross Hospital eager to meet and measure and test and analyze mother and daughter.

It was clear from some remarks made by Dr. Endicott that her colleagues were nothing if not thorough and that six months was but the blink of an eye in the life of a research project. They would be fortunate indeed to have any results before the end of the year. Jean had not yet broken this news to Mrs. Tilbury, who seemed to be under the impression that enlightenment was only hours away.

"I'll tell you what," Jean said. "If you let me pay your usual rate, I'll accept. But you'll have to choose the style and fabric. I haven't got a clue."

"That's settled then. You must come round and be measured up, and we'll choose a pattern together. Something fitted. Not too fussy, I think," she said, squinting at Jean as though already sizing her up.

"Oh dear," said Jean, sensing mortification ahead.

"Am I going to have an *injection* today?" asked Margaret as they crossed the road, almost borne along by the surge of pedestrians.

The smell of diesel exhaust from idling buses was overpowering here on the Strand. Jean could taste the fumes on her tongue.

"I already told her there may be needles involved," Mrs. Tilbury said.

"No—the opposite of an injection," Jean replied to Margaret. "An injection is where they put something into you and a blood test is where they take something out. It won't hurt."

"I'm not scared," Margaret insisted. "I didn't even cry when I trod on a wasp. I haven't cried since I was seven."

"What happened when you were seven?" Jean asked, feeling that this was expected.

"I was going to be Mary in the nativity, but I got chicken pox so I had to miss it and I cried."

"That's right," said Gretchen. "I made you a little blue costume and then that other girl had to wear it."

Margaret's face clouded for a moment and then just as suddenly brightened. "You bought me my Belinda doll to cheer me up," she said.

Her emotions were so delightfully close to the surface, Jean thought.

"By the way," Jean said to Gretchen, this mention of dolls stirring a memory of her own. "I met someone the other day who wanted to be remembered to you. I wonder if you can guess who."

A flicker of uncertainty passed across Mrs. Tilbury's face and a faint blush rose to her cheeks. It took no more than a second for her to master herself and say, "No, I can't. You'll have to tell me."

Jean hadn't intended to mention the visit to Broadstairs at all. It seemed somehow indelicate to remind Mrs. Tilbury that she was still under investigation. But Jean had noticed her momentary loss of composure with interest. She had someone in mind, then.

"Alice Halfyard. From St. Cecilia's. She sent you her good wishes."

"Oh!" Mrs. Tilbury gave a laugh and a little shake of her curls.

Was she disappointed or relieved? Jean couldn't tell; her face was a mask again.

"*Matron.* I never knew her name was Alice. She doesn't look a bit like an Alice. She was always just Matron to us."

"She remembered you very affectionately."

"Did she? I was a tiny bit afraid of her."

"Really? She didn't strike me as very fearsome. She seemed quite . . . motherly."

"I suppose I was afraid of almost everyone in those days. I was such a timid child. She wasn't unkind but, you know, she was Matron and she didn't stand any nonsense. She once scolded me for talking when we were supposed to be having quiet time and after that I was a bit in awe of her."

"She said you were good friends with another girl called Martha."

"Oh yes, Martha. I wonder whatever happened to her. And Brenda."

"You didn't keep in contact with them when you left?"

"Not really. I always meant to. I did go and see Martha once, at her home in Chatham, but it was a long way and when you are back in the outside world other things come along to take up your time."

"Margaret, for instance."

"Yes. Everything changes when you have a baby."

Hearing her name, Margaret perked up. "Is this the Strand?"

"Yes, darling."

"If there's time can we go to Simpson's for lunch?"

Mrs. Tilbury laughed and squeezed the back of her daughter's neck. "Of course we can't. I've made you sandwiches and we have to get you back to school." She turned to Jean. "Last year

60

we came up to London for Margaret's piano exam, and afterward we went to my husband's shop and he took us out to Simpson's for lunch as a special treat. Now Margaret thinks we should go there all the time."

"Have you ever been to Simpson's on the Strand?" Margaret asked.

"No, I never have," Jean admitted. Eating out was something other people did. Over the years she had trained herself not to mind.

"I had roast beef and sherry trifle. I didn't get drunk, though."

"When all this is over I'll take you there to celebrate," said Jean impulsively and then regretted it.

Who knew how soon and in what way "all this" would be over, or whether there would be anything in the end to celebrate. And it was reckless to make promises to a child that might have to be broken. They never forgot.

"We're not far from Daddy's shop now," said Mrs. Tilbury, coming to her rescue. She gestured vaguely off to their left. "Perhaps we can pop in and surprise him afterward if there's time."

"Can we?" pleaded Margaret. "Have you seen my daddy's shop?" she asked Jean.

"Yes, I have, actually."

"There's a ring in the window that costs *four hundred pounds*."

"Goodness. I hope he keeps it locked away."

They had reached Agar Street now and Jean steered them toward a short flight of stone steps leading up to an anonymous wooden door. From the outside, the building looked more like a foreign embassy or a publishing house, but inside the marble lobby was that unmistakable smell, pungent and antiseptic, common to every hospital Jean had ever visited.

A signboard directed visitors to phlebotomy, pathology, X-rays, waiting rooms. A cleaner was working her way slowly down the wide staircase, plunging her string mop into a tin pail of disinfectant and twirling it into the corners before giving each tread a double sweep. There was something almost hypnotic in her rhythmical movements and the clang, slap, swish of mop and bucket. On either side of the corridor swing doors opened and shut with a faint "whump" of compressed air as nurses and orderlies came and went, moving silently on soft-soled shoes but with a tremendous sense of purpose and urgency. The patients, Jean's party included, tended to walk with less certainty.

At the reception desk two women sat, chatting in low tones and filing a stack of index cards. They continued their conversation until it reached a natural break—a perfectly judged interval designed to signal that they served the public on their own terms—before acknowledging the visitors.

"We're here to see Dr. Sidney Lloyd-Jones," Jean said, bridling.

At the mention of his name the two gatekeepers became instantly deferential.

"Oh yes, Miss Swinney, is it? He said you were to go straight through to his consulting room at the end of the corridor."

"We're expected," Jean whispered to Mrs. Tilbury. "That's a good start."

Dr. Lloyd-Jones was a tall, donnish man in his late fifties, with wild hair and smudged glasses over which he peered, blinking, as though dazzled by the manifestation of parthenogenesis-in-the-human-female before him. He shook hands with them all, even Margaret, before summoning his colleague from next door to appraise the resemblance between mother and daughter.

"This is Dr. Bamber from the department of pathology," said Dr. Lloyd-Jones as the five of them stood awkwardly in his consulting room like guests at a sherry party. "He will be doing the analysis of the blood tests. He is a great authority on blood types, so you can have absolute confidence in his findings." He turned to Dr. Bamber. "A good start, wouldn't you say?"

"It could hardly be better."

They beamed at each other and then at Mrs. Tilbury. Jean had the feeling that they were already sharpening their scalpels, ready to slice her up for microscope slides.

"I suppose it must be a nice change not to have to go to the trouble of curing someone," she observed.

"This is much more fun," Dr. Bamber agreed. He was the younger, shorter and more personable of the two men. "Obviously we're very excited. An opportunity like this doesn't come along very often in one's career. It's very good of you to place yourselves in our hands."

Jean glanced at his hands, which were unblemished by physical labor and almost unmanly in their smoothness.

"Perhaps," Dr. Lloyd-Jones said, "you might take mother and daughter over to phlebotomy for the blood tests and you can answer any questions they may have, while I talk to Miss Swinney."

As soon as the door had closed on them, Jean said, "How many other people are going to be involved in these tests? I'm only thinking of the story leaking out."

"Oh, don't worry about that," came the reply. "It's all absolutely confidential. I mean, patients' medical notes are always confidential, but in this case I'm keeping them under lock and key. They will be referred to only as Mother A and Daughter. The nurses will just take the blood—they have no idea what we are testing for. Dr. Bamber will be doing all the analysis himself."

"I didn't mean to sound distrustful," said Jean. "But this is a big story for us."

"For us too, possibly."

"I couldn't bear it for one of the dailies to get wind of it prematurely."

"No indeed. I must admit, I had some concerns when we first spoke about this. But Mrs. Tilbury seems a sensible woman and her case is very persuasive."

"I'm still investigating," said Jean. "My first instinct was to believe her. But my second was not to trust my instincts."

"It will be a blow to you if the blood test results tell a different story."

"Yes. I've probably overinvested in the whole idea. But it will be worse for Gretchen. Mrs. Tilbury, I mean."

"One has to wonder at her motive. You haven't offered money?"

"Not a penny."

"A quester after truth, perhaps. Like ourselves. I hope she is not too disappointed."

"You don't expect her to be proved right?"

"On balance of probabilities, no. But let's not prejudge the results."

The phone rang on Dr. Lloyd-Jones's desk. He answered it and listened for a moment without speaking. Jean could hear the distant bubbling of a male voice on the other end.

"Yes, will do," he said before hanging up.

"That was Dr. Bamber. He wants to talk to the mother without the little girl there for a minute or two. Perhaps you could wander along and entertain her."

"Gladly," said Jean.

"It was good to meet you at last, Miss Swinney. Here's to a—I hesitate to say *positive,* so let's just say *interesting* outcome for all concerned." He thrust an arm across the desk and she allowed her hand to be tugged.

She found Margaret sitting on one of the hard wooden chairs in the phlebotomy waiting room, swinging her legs and reading a health education leaflet about smoking, titled *The Adventures of the Wisdom Family.* A wad of cotton wool was stuck to the inside of her elbow with surgical tape. The sight of her white ankle socks, smudged with blue where they rubbed the edge of her T-bar sandals, made Jean's heart ache. She remembered her own mother taking out the box of brushes and cans of polish to clean her and Dorrie's school shoes every Sunday evening, and felt a momentary regret that she would never be called upon to perform that solemn ritual.

"I thought it was going to be a comic book," Margaret said, laying aside the leaflet, "but it's not."

"We could go and find a newsstand if you want a comic book," Jean suggested. They had passed one on the Strand earlier.

"Why do people smoke?" Margaret asked as they walked back down Agar Street. "What does it taste like?"

"Strange to say, it tastes exactly how it smells. Of burning leaves. It's unpleasant at first, a bit like drinking tea without sugar, but you persevere and after a while it tastes just fine. And then after another while you can't stop."

"I'm never going to smoke. Have you ever sleepwalked? I have."

"No, I don't think so. Where did you walk to?"

"Just into Mummy's room. You're not supposed to wake people up when they're sleepwalking."

"I'd heard that."

"They can die. Have you got any pets?"

"No. Have you?"

"I really, really want a rabbit. Or maybe a kitten. But kittens grow up and get run over."

Jean couldn't help laughing. She was finding Margaret's scatter-gun approach to conversation and morbid imagination thoroughly entertaining. She felt more than a hint of envy for Gretchen; to have the unthinking love of a daughter like this, to watch her grow every day and know that she was completely yours.

They had reached the newsstand by now and after some prompting, Margaret shyly pointed out a copy of *Girl*. Her gratitude when she at last had the magazine in her hands was out of all proportion to its value; she was almost vibrating with excitement.

Spontaneous generosity was a new experience for Jean—until today such opportunities had seldom come her way and would probably have gone unnoticed. She and her mother exchanged small, practical gifts at Christmas, of course, but she was a stranger to more ambitious forms of giving. Dorrie had long ago forbidden her from sending anything to Kitale for her or the children. The postage was exorbitant and things were too likely to be impounded at customs or go astray.

It used to give Jean a pang when she passed a shop window and saw some toy or trinket that would have delighted her nephew or niece, and for a while she had ignored Dorrie's injunction and sent gifts anyway. But no word ever came back to say that they had been received and Jean couldn't bring herself to ask, so she had let the habit lapse. Recalling all this now, she felt ashamed of herself.

Beside her Margaret was jabbering away. Jean caught up as she said, "Have you ever seen one?"

"One what?"

"*Angel.*"

"No," Jean replied, firmly, and then relented a little. "But then I've never seen gravity either, but it's there all the same."

Margaret seemed quietly impressed by this. "I've never seen one," she said. "But I've heard them."

This was such an unexpected remark, delivered in such a matter-of-fact way that Jean felt her scalp prickle. "What do they say?" she asked with a sense of unease.

"They don't *say*. They *sing*. That's how I know they are angel voices."

"Oh. Do they sing hymns?"

"No. Just funny words, over and over. Like gabardine."

Jean gave a burst of laughter. What sort of practical-minded angel concerned itself with raincoat fabric? An angel whose mother was a dressmaker, perhaps?

Margaret laughed too, revealing a half-built smile of milk teeth, gaps and new serrated incisors. "Don't you ever hear voices?" she asked.

"Sort of," said Jean, treading carefully. She had no intention of encouraging any supernatural claptrap, but there was no need to lay about her with common sense like a great fly whisk. "But my voices tend to say things like, 'That's probably enough cake for you,' or 'Isn't it about time you wrote to your sister?'"

Margaret was not to be so easily fobbed off. "Oh, I have those too, but that's not the same. That's just me thinking things. Angel voices are different."

"I'm sure they're nothing to worry about," said Jean, though Margaret herself already seemed quite untroubled.

"I'm not worried," came the reply. "I like them. Except when they say a word I don't know—then it's annoying."

"When you say 'a word you don't know,' do you mean a word you have heard before but don't know the meaning of?"

"No. I mean a word I've never ever heard. Like Lindenbaum. Or phalanx."

With this conversation, Jean felt herself being tugged, as if by a muddy tide, far out of her depth. How was it possible to hear a voice in your head saying a word that didn't already exist in your head?

"You are much too clever for me," she said, finding herself repeating, to her horror, a phrase her mother used to say to her and Dorrie to terminate any discussion that threatened to take an unconventional path. It had seemed like a compliment at the time, but it was a door flung shut in their faces, and now she was doing it herself. "I do like talking to you, Margaret," she said. "You are much more interesting than most of the adults I know."

"Mummy says I ask too many questions."

"Asking questions is all right. It's a sign of intelligence. How else can you find things out?"

Perhaps it's just loneliness, Jean thought. She needs that rabbit or kitten. She considered other only children she had known; too much in the company of adults and sheltered from the weathering effects of siblings, they often seemed precocious or strange.

Margaret squinted up at her through sweeping eyelashes. "You're nice," she said with an air of finality, and Jean, unpracticed at receiving compliments, felt herself blushing with pleasure and surprise.

They had reached the foyer of the clinic now and there was Mrs. Tilbury emerging from the ladies' cloakroom looking flustered and a little red around the eyes. She had reapplied powder to her nose but the skin beneath was taut and shiny. For an awful moment it occurred to Jean that she may have been worrying where Margaret had gone and fretting herself into a state of anxiety.

"I'm sorry—you must have been wondering where we'd got to."

"No—I've only just come out."

"Look, Miss Svinny bought me a magazine." Margaret held up her copy of *Girl* for inspection.

"That was very kind of her."

"Has something upset you?" Jean said, lowering her voice. "Are you all right?"

"Yes, it's nothing." Mrs. Tilbury's voice was bright with self-control. "I'm fine."

"Are you sure? They didn't do anything to hurt you, did they?"

"No, not at all. It was all very painless. I was just . . ." She blinked a few times and shook her head. "So silly of me. I thought it would all be done and decided now."

"Oh dear," said Jean.

"But Dr. Bamber said this is just the beginning of many tests. It could be weeks or months."

"I should have explained better," said Jean, steering her toward a row of chairs. "I didn't realize there was any great urgency."

"I just thought it would be settled and that would be that."

"No, I'm afraid it's a bit more complicated than that. I'm sorry you're disappointed."

Mrs. Tilbury dabbed at her eyes with a dainty handkerchief.

"Is it the traveling up to London that bothers you? Of course we'll reimburse your fares."

Jean would have to grovel to the waspish Muriel in Accounts. She never surrendered a penny of petty cash without a struggle.

"Oh, it's not that," Mrs. Tilbury gulped. "I don't mind the journey."

"I like coming up to London with you, Mummy," said Margaret, squeezing her mother's hand. "I don't mind missing school."

"Dr. Bamber said even if the blood tests are a match, it doesn't prove anything. So what's the point in doing them?"

"Well, the blood test on its own can't prove the case *for* a virgin birth. But a negative result—a mismatch—would certainly *dis*prove it. It's just the first step."

"It makes me feel as though you don't believe me."

"Whether I believe you or not is not important," said Jean, who had an uncomfortable feeling that Mrs. Tilbury was having second thoughts about the whole business—was in fact looking for excuses to back out.

"It is to me," came the reproachful reply.

"I don't disbelieve you." This double negative didn't quite add up to a positive, but it was already further than she had intended to go.

Mrs. Tilbury nodded and seemed to gather herself together. "I'm sorry. You're quite right. I shall just have to let the doctors do their job. I think it's hospitals that make me emotional. Please ignore me."

"It's quite understandable," said Jean, and they made their way back toward the Strand, parting company so that mother and daughter could go to Bedford Street to call on Mr. Tilbury, while Jean headed to Charing Cross.

The general mood had quite recovered from this hiccup by the time they said goodbye, but Jean found herself turning over the conversation on the way home, puzzled and unconvinced that she had really got to the bottom of Mrs. Tilbury's curious impatience.

7

Dear Mrs. Van Lingen,

I hope you don't mind me contacting you in this roundabout way.

Our mutual acquaintance, Mrs. Halfyard, has kindly offered to forward this letter to you, because I am interested in your recollections of the time you spent in St. Cecilia's Nursing and Convalescent Home between June and September 1946. I am particularly interested in your memories of a fellow patient, Gretchen Edel, who conceived a child while a patient on the ward during that period—an extraordinary occurrence, you will agree, to have taken place under your noses, as it were.

If you can throw any light on this or recall anything that may be significant, I would be most grateful to hear from you at the above address, or you may telephone me during office hours, reversing the charges.

[Jean blanched as she typed those words, wondering how she would ever justify this expense to Muriel in Accounts.]

I should add that it is with Gretchen Edel's full consent that I am conducting this research.

Yours sincerely,
Jean Swinney
Staff Reporter
The North Kent Echo

8

"Relax. Don't hold yourself in so much or I won't get a true measurement."

Jean was standing with her arms straight out from her sides as though crucified while Gretchen whisked around her with a tape measure, jotting down figures on a diagram of the female form crisscrossed by many lines. As well as bust, waist and hips, there were apparently other statistics just as vital to be recorded in pursuit of a well-fitting dress. Nape to knee (back); underarm to elbow; waist to knee (front); shoulder to shoulder (back); armpit to waist (side); upper arm (circumference).

Jean was glad she had taken the precaution of wearing her least ancient slip—the best of a bad lot—and some sturdy underwear, which was now corseting the cushion of soft flesh at her belly while cutting into the tops of her legs.

"It's hard to relax when it's so ticklish," she said, twitching as the tape measure slithered over the silky nylon fabric.

"All done. I think you are a size fourteen in need of some adjustments."

"That's one way of putting it," said Jean, reaching for her skirt and blouse. Tact was often the first casualty of Gretchen's imperfect fluency.

They had come upstairs to the room Gretchen used for her needlework. In one corner stood a dressmaker's mannequin wearing a gray satin evening gown, inside out and held together with tacking stitches and pins. A Singer sewing machine sat at one end of a large cutting table on which an expanse of printed cotton was spread out; tissue-thin pieces of pattern for some unidentifiable garment were pinned in place—strange abstract shapes that seemed to bear no relation to the human form. Jean looked at Gretchen with new respect; there was more artistry and skill than drudgery in this work.

Somehow, without discussion, they had progressed to Christian names now. It was too bizarre to be calling each other Miss This and Mrs. That when in this state of undress and intimacy. Jean wasn't sorry to see the back of "Miss Svinny."

The invitation had come while she was at work. Howard, at Gretchen's urging, had called her at the paper. His voice sounded faraway and hesitant, and Jean could imagine his reluctance in undertaking this particular errand.

"My wife wondered if you would like to join us for tea on Sunday. She said something about dressmaking. It'll be just us and Margaret—nothing formal."

Since her last meeting with Gretchen at the hospital she had told herself to maintain a strictly professional distance, avoiding any overtures of friendship in case it clouded her judgment and made a potentially tricky conversation in the future even trickier. But in the face of this stammered invitation, she had caved in and accepted immediately.

The truth was that congenial new acquaintances were too rare a phenomenon to be dismissed. Her colleagues at the paper were pleasant enough company, but only during office hours. They didn't socialize outside work, apart from those Friday pub nights, from which Jean had already excluded herself. Old school friends were married now and scattered, their weekends taken up with family life. A single woman was an awkward fit. But the Tilburys seemed to like her, to look up to her, even, as someone of influence and importance.

It was impossible not to be flattered and charmed by their interest, to blossom and expand in their company and become the interesting woman they thought she was. And besides, there was Margaret, who was either a perfectly ordinary child, or uniquely, miraculously special. Whichever she was, she had stirred in Jean a longing she had thought safely buried.

Having accepted, Jean had now acquired two new problems: how to manage the abandonment of her mother for the best part of Sunday, and how to reciprocate in due course. The solution to the first came providentially one evening as she cycled home from a doctor's appointment. Ahead of her, toiling up the hill carrying several distended string bags of shopping, was Winnie Melsom, an acquaintance of her mother's from the days when she used to attend church.

There had been a disagreement about the annual collection of Christmas gifts for the poor children of the parish. Someone had suggested that hand-knitted toys, stuffed with chopped-up nylon stockings, were not hygienic. Mrs. Swinney, who had enjoyed making these little dolls, had taken umbrage and stopped attending. She was not a religious woman and had never much liked the services anyway, so it was no great hardship.

Jean pedalled faster and drew alongside Mrs. Melsom, who looked up fearfully at this interruption.

"Hello. Why don't I help you with those?" Jean said, slipping down from her bicycle and relieving the struggling woman of her bags, putting one in her pannier and hanging the other two from the handlebars.

"Oh, you are kind," said Mrs. Melsom, who had taken a

moment or two to recognize Jean and recover from the idea that she was being robbed in broad daylight. "I made the mistake of buying rather more than I could carry. I'm glad you came past."

They continued to walk up the hill together, Jean pushing the bicycle. Mrs. Melsom lived in one of the Victorian cottages on Keston Road, some way farther than Jean needed to go. She remembered that there was a daughter, Ann, who lived overseas, like Dorrie. The pain of separation had once been a bond between the two mothers—up to a point. Unlike Dorrie, Ann made regular trips home.

"How is Ann?" Jean asked.

"Oh, very well. I had a letter from her just yesterday. She writes every fortnight."

"So does Dorrie," Jean replied, determined to keep their end up, for her mother's sake rather than Dorrie's.

It had been true once, but now even that meager sacrifice was apparently too much to ask. The Kitale social scene—tennis, cocktails, play-reading—had crowded out even that small act of filial observance. Jean felt the familiar churning resentment and tried to suppress it. It would only give her dyspepsia.

"I've been meaning to call on your mother. I heard from someone, I can't remember who, that she doesn't get out much anymore."

"No. She's not terribly steady on her feet. She's lost confidence, I'm afraid."

This was not the whole story, but a portion of it that could be offered up to outsiders without embarrassment.

"I wonder if she would like a visit?"

"Yes, she would." Jean had to stop a note of desperation from creeping into her tone. "I think she gets a little lonely with just me for company."

"Perhaps I could pop in at the weekend?"

It had taken very little maneuvering to get Mrs. Melsom to settle on Sunday afternoon as the ideal time. It only remained for

Jean to promote the idea to her mother, who might resent the suggestion that she was being babysat. She decided not to mention her own plans until the Melsom visit had been accepted as fact.

Thursday, hair-wash night, was the most auspicious time for such a conversation. Jean's mother was at her most compliant and grateful while having her hair set. She leaned over the sink while Jean rubbed in Sunsilk shampoo and rinsed off the lather with a jug of water, and then sat at the kitchen table with a towel round her shoulders and a bag of curlers in her lap. She looked ancient and vulnerable with wet hair, and barely recognizable as female at all. Jean felt her eyes brimming with tenderness as she ran a comb over her mother's nearly naked scalp and resolved to be kinder.

"I met Mrs. Melsom the other day," she said, drawing up a section of hair and teasing it around a pink nylon curler. "*Pin*."

Her mother passed up a hairpin, wincing slightly as Jean over-tightened it.

"She said she's going to call in and see you on Sunday."

"Did she? I wonder what she wants."

"She doesn't want anything. *Curler*. She's just coming to see how you are."

"Well, you'll have to do the talking. I've got nothing to say."

This wasn't going as Jean had hoped.

"You've got plenty to say. *Pin*. It isn't me she's coming to see."

"Well, I don't know why. I haven't seen her for years. Ouch."

"Sorry. I'll have a yellow one now."

Jean's mother rooted in the bag and passed up a yellow curler. These were fatter with longer bristles and gripped like a dream.

"We used to be quite friendly."

"Exactly. It will do you good to have some company. *Pin*."

"I don't suppose she'll come."

"Of course she will. It's all arranged. I'll make you a nice sponge." She winced. The pronoun was a giveaway and Jean's mother pounced.

"Where will you be, then?"

"I'm . . . having tea with the Tilburys. *Yellow, please.*"

"Never heard of them."

"I told you. The Swiss woman. I'm doing a story about her."

"On a Sunday? They're never making you work weekends?"

"No. It's a social visit."

"Oh. Well, I suppose I'll have to entertain Mrs. Melsom by myself, then."

They lapsed into silence, Jean privately jubilant that she had prevailed, her mother suspicious that she had been outmaneuvered. She cheered up later when her hair was dry and brushed into a neat white cloud and her looks were restored.

"Very nice, thank you," she said, turning her head one way and then the other to check her appearance in the two hand mirrors that Jean held up fore and aft for her appraisal.

Having completed her chart of measurements, Gretchen produced a heavy catalogue of Simplicity patterns and flipped it open to the section on dresses, inviting Jean to browse. The watercolor illustrations depicted a freakish race of women, impossibly tall and slender, with strangulated waists, foreshortened bodies and elongated legs culminating in archly pointed toes. It was hard to feel anything other than dispirited confronted by this cartoon glamour and Jean turned the pages listlessly.

"I don't know much about fashion," she said at last. "You choose—something not too difficult."

"I don't mind if it's difficult. It's more interesting to make. But I think a simple style is better for you." Gretchen turned to a page marked with a turned-down corner. "I think this would look elegant on you."

It was a fitted shift with a round collar and white piping, and three-quarter length sleeves. It certainly looked very elegant as depicted by the artist, but would surely be less so on Jean's size-fourteen-in-need-of-adjustments frame. However, she was impressed that Gretchen had, without any discussion or prior knowledge of her tastes, singled out from this vast selection something that she herself might have chosen and could imagine wearing with pleasure.

"Yes, it's lovely."

"Not black, though. Too severe. I think navy blue or green."

"Yes. Blue."

"It will be just right," said Gretchen, closing the heavy book with a sound like gunshot.

But when will I have any call to wear it? thought Jean.

On their way downstairs she couldn't help glancing in at the open bedroom door and was surprised to see two single beds, side by side, neatly made with matching pink-and-green eiderdowns and a narrow channel between, not wide enough to stand in but a chasm nevertheless. She had never come across this arrangement before between married people, except as an alternative to (unthinkable) divorce. Her grandparents had cohabited joylessly in this fashion for decades until released by death, but the Tilbury marriage bore no resemblance to their frosty stand-off.

Outside in the garden, Margaret and her friend Lizzie were playing badminton across a chewed piece of net strung between the fence and a plum tree. The court area was delineated by the flower beds to each side, the rockery at one end and the vegetable patch at the other.

Howard was in among the bean rows, taking on the blackfly with a pail of soapy water and a spray pump. His jacket hung over a spade planted in the soil. He was dressed in shirt and tie as if for a day at the office. He gave the two women a wave as they came out onto the little patio, where a table and three canvas chairs had been set out for tea.

"Your garden is immaculate," said Jean. "You put me to shame."

This was not mere politeness; the flower beds were parallel strips of crumbly soil playing host to tame shrubs of varying colors, textures and heights, and neat clumps of annuals in full bloom. The edges of the lawn were fiercely clipped; the leeks and cabbages in the vegetable patch grew in straight lines at perfect intervals.

There was a kind of beauty in this imposition of order, Jean thought. She was a conscientious gardener herself but had never managed to achieve results like these in the few hours a week she could spare for the job. All her time seemed to be spent holding back chaos rather than on these refinements.

"It's all Howard," said Gretchen. "We are dividing the chores very rigidly. I'm housework, he's garden."

"Well I'm both," said Jean. "Neither to a very high standard, I'm afraid."

She couldn't now recall what, if anything, she had previously revealed about her domestic situation, so she mentioned now the fortuitous intervention of Mrs. Melsom in making her visit possible.

Gretchen was mortified. "I had no idea this would be difficult," she said. "Your mother would have been very welcome to come too, naturally."

"That's kind of you, but sometimes it's nice to get away by myself."

"Of course. Is your mother so very infirm that she can't be left?"

"Not exactly infirm, but she hardly ever leaves the house. She's fine when I'm out at work because she understands that it's a necessity. But outside of that . . . She's never said in so many words, 'You mustn't go out and leave me.' It's more subtle than that. I feel guilty if I'm out enjoying myself when she isn't."

"She wouldn't want to stop you having fun, surely?"

"I don't think she really believes in 'fun.' Not since my father died." She had said too much. This was not teatime talk. She plowed on: "She's too old for change. Now, it's all about comfort and routine and taking pleasure in tiny treats." For a moment Jean had a ghastly sense that she was describing herself.

"Routines can be very useful," said Gretchen. "Especially if you are trying to run a household. But they have to be"—she drew her hands apart—"*elastisch*."

Jean laughed. "A dressmaker's metaphor." Something about this conversation stirred her memory. Gabardine, that was it. She lowered her voice. "Margaret was telling me about her angel voices the other day. I didn't know quite what to make of it."

Gretchen smiled. "Perhaps it's not so unusual. Children have such imagination."

"I didn't," said Jean.

"But to me, Margaret is already a miracle, so this is far from the most extraordinary thing about her."

"I suppose. I just wanted to check that it was something she had discussed with you."

"Oh yes. I didn't think it was anything to worry about. They seem very harmless voices."

"Did the idea of angels come from Margaret herself, or was that something you suggested?"

"That was me," Gretchen admitted. "I thought it was more reassuring to imagine that the voices were coming from heaven."

"The idea of a guardian angel is rather appealing," Jean agreed. She felt something approaching envy for those who could believe such comforting nonsense.

"It's not so very different from an imaginary friend. And we have all had those. As long as Margaret isn't troubled by it, I choose not to worry." A wasp landed on her arm and she flicked it away with a polished pink fingernail.

"You are very level-headed," said Jean.

"I'm sure she'll grow out of it, but thank you for mentioning it. I wouldn't want her to have any secrets from me."

"Parenthood is quite a minefield."

"I haven't found it to be yet," Gretchen said. "They say the difficult years are ahead."

They glanced down the garden to where Margaret and Lizzie were chasing the swooping shuttlecock as it caught the breeze. Their high cries of laughter chimed like bells. Presently the two girls gave up, exhausted, and flung themselves down on the grass, panting. It was hard to imagine any turbulent emotions ever clouding their innocent faces.

Gretchen excused herself and went indoors to fetch the tea. Seeing Jean momentarily abandoned, Howard left off his toiling in the vegetable patch and came to join her, carrying a basket of freshly harvested rhubarb, beetroot and lettuce. As a concession to casual wear he had undone his top button and loosened his tie. Now he hastily redid it, leaving a muddy smudge on his collar.

"Would you like to take some of these home with you?" he asked, laying the basket at her feet for inspection. "We have a glut in some areas."

"I'd love to," said Jean. "I'm very partial to rhubarb." The crop looked indecently healthy; some of the stems were dark pink and as thick as her wrist. A spirit of mischief entered her and she said, "I've never seen anyone wear a shirt and tie to weed a vegetable patch before."

He looked nonplussed for a moment and then smiled. "Oh, well, I think formal dress shows the slugs and blackfly who's boss."

Gretchen had appeared in the doorway carrying a laden tea tray in time to hear this exchange.

"Howard is the only man I know who wears a jacket and tie to the beach," she said as he sprang forward to relieve her of the teapot, which was slipping dangerously.

He endured the women's laughter with a gracious shrug.

"It's a matter of eliminating unnecessary decisions," he said.

Having put down the tray, Gretchen snapped open a dish towel and held it under her chin, concealing her upper body. "Now, what color blouse am I wearing today?"

Howard looked stricken. "Pink? White? I'm sure it's very pretty whatever color it is."

Gretchen whisked aside the dish towel to reveal her primrose-yellow blouse.

"I remember now," Howard said, shamefaced. "Miss Swinney will think I'm a monster."

"It's Jean now," said Gretchen. "We are not being formal anymore."

Margaret and Lizzie had joined the table. There were only three chairs, so they sat on cushions on the back steps with plates on their knees.

"Is that a new teapot?" asked Margaret.

"No, it's not new. It's rather old—older than you, in fact," said her mother, beginning to pour.

"Well, I've never seen it before."

"It's the one we use when we have visitors," said Gretchen.

Not completely done with formality then, thought Jean.

"But we never have visitors, apart from Great Aunt Edie, and she gets the brown teapot."

"How do you know whether or not I have visitors when you are out at school all day?"

This stopped Margaret in her tracks. It was clear that she had never considered the possibility that anything interesting could ever happen to her mother if she was not there to witness it.

"Your mother has all sorts of fun while you are out of the way," said Howard. "As soon as she has waved you off to school, she kicks up her heels and out come the best teapots."

"You're just being silly," said Margaret. "Mummy doesn't do anything while I'm at school."

This remark was greeted with splutters of outrage by the two women and guffaws from Howard.

"Well, if I do nothing all day I can't have made this *Sachertorte*, so you won't be wanting a piece of it." Gretchen cut large slices for Jean and Lizzie and then laid aside the cake slice with a sigh. "Such a pity."

"I meant you don't do anything *fun*," said Margaret, batting her long eyelashes. "Because you are too busy making the best *Sachertorte* in the whole of England."

"That's more like it," said Howard, cutting three more pieces. There was an appreciative silence as they ate.

At last Jean said, "I've never tasted anything so delicious."

She had no time or talent for elaborate baking herself and had to satisfy her sweet tooth with toffees that she hoarded in her room or a spoonful of golden syrup on her morning oatmeal. But this was something special—closer and denser than a sponge, more grainy than a cake, with a delicious nutty sweetness and the bitterness of dark chocolate. As well as the torte there were little meringues filled with coffee cream and crushed hazelnuts, and some slices of dark, dry bread with a thin scraping of butter. The bread was much less to Jean's taste but she ate it dutifully.

After tea was over, the girls returned to their game of badminton, pleading with the adults to make up a four. The breeze had dropped now and barely a leaf stirred. The garden shimmered in the afternoon heat.

"I'm happy to play," said Jean, who had a former tomboy's love of all sports.

She kicked off her shoes to spare the grass, which had already taken some punishment over the course of the season, with worn patches either side of the net.

"Howard, why don't you and Lizzie take on Jean and Margaret?" Gretchen suggested. "You know how hopeless I am. Nobody ever wants me on their side."

"Come along then, Lizzie," Howard said, picking up one of the spare rackets and bouncing the heel of his hand against the strings.

"We won't spare you just because you're a guest, you know," he said to Jean before ducking under the net. "In this house winning is everything."

"We don't need any favors, do we, Margaret?" Jean replied, and the little girl shook her head gravely.

She felt inexplicably light-hearted. It was years since she had played, but people who are good at racket sports never lose the skill, and it only took her a few rallies to remember the rhythm of the strokes, and the delicate touch needed to tip the shuttlecock just over the net and no farther.

Howard, still in shirt and tie, and looking like no kind of sportsman, was surprisingly deft and agile, retrieving Jean's best shots effortlessly from the back of the court while Lizzie guarded the net. He played a gentleman's game, Jean noticed, never crowding his partner or poaching her shots, or winning an easy point by belting the shuttlecock at Margaret, who was the weakest player. But at the same time, he didn't patronize her by underplaying, making them work instead for every point.

Gretchen had put her feet up on one of the empty chairs and was reading a magazine, occasionally looking up to throw out an encouraging comment, or to adjudicate a disputed line call.

"The vegetable patch is *out!*"

"What if it lands on a rhubarb leaf that is projecting slightly over the grass?"

"That's still out."

"Not fair!"

Every so often Jean would look up, through a mist of sweat, to see Howard laughing at her exertions as he drove her from corner to corner, and she would redouble her determination to win. They took a game each, but before they could play the decider, Lizzie remembered that she was supposed to be home by five, some ten minutes ago, to go and visit her grandparents in Bexleyheath.

"Just one more," Margaret pleaded with a child's infinite stamina for pleasure.

"We'll have to save it for another time," said Howard as all four shook hands across the net. "But I think a draw the only fair result." His handshake was brief and businesslike but it sent a jolt through Jean all the same. "You play well," he said to her. "You must have been practicing."

"Not since my school days," she replied. "I'd forgotten how much fun it is. And how exhausting."

She was aware of her fiery-red face and the sheen of perspiration on her forehead. Her cotton blouse clung damply to her back. She pushed her sticky hair off her face impatiently with the back of her arm. Up on the patio she could see Gretchen, cool and elegant in primrose yellow, pouring glasses of water for the thirsty players from a crystal jug—another item brought out for guests, no doubt.

"We must have a rematch sometime," Howard was saying.

She recognized this for a piece of conventional politeness, but Margaret was immediately eager.

"Yes. Tomorrow. After school."

The two adults laughed, acknowledging the impossibility of a life governed by reckless spontaneity.

"Miss Swinney doesn't want to come over here again tomorrow just to entertain you!" said Howard, ruffling Margaret's hair.

"How do you know? You haven't asked her!"

"Because she has a life of her own to live."

In fact, Jean could hardly think of anything she would rather do than play badminton with Howard and Margaret.

"But you're *grown-ups*. You can do anything you want to."

"Where on earth did you get the idea that grown-ups can do what they like?" asked her father with an expression of incredulity. "Not from me or your mother, that's for certain."

"They don't have anyone bossing them about all the time," she said. "They just do all the bossing."

In perfect illustration of Margaret's theory, there was a rattling at the side gate and Lizzie's mother appeared, bristling with impatience, to chase up her errant daughter.

"We agreed five o'clock, young lady," she said, tapping her watch face as Lizzie slouched up the garden to join her.

"See what I mean?" hissed Margaret after the visitors had been waved off.

"That was unfortunate timing," Jean laughed. "But adults don't get to do what they want all the time, or even most of it."

"There's this thing called Duty," Howard explained.

Whenever Jean pictured Duty it was as a woman, tall and gaunt, with long hair scraped back into a bun, and gray, drooping clothes. For some reason she wore a pair of men's lace-up shoes, the better to kick you with, perhaps.

"It usually means doing the thing you don't want to but know you must," she said.

"Like piano practice?"

"Yes. Or in my case, mowing Mrs. Bowland's lawn," said Jean, feeling a twinge of disloyalty to poor Mrs. Bowland, who would probably be mortified to think her patch of grass had become such a symbol of servitude.

"Or fixing the Wolseley," said Howard with a grimace.

"What about you, Mummy?"

They turned to look at Gretchen expectantly. She beamed back at them.

"I must be very selfish, or very clever, because I have everything arranged so I never have to do anything I don't want to."

Jean experienced the same stirring of unease that had first troubled her at the hospital. While the three of them had been talking she had glanced up the garden and been shocked to see a look of utter desolation come over Gretchen's face when she believed herself unobserved. The fit of melancholy, or whatever it was, had lasted a few seconds; as soon as Margaret called her name, she had snapped to attention, rearranging her features into the brightest of smiles.

Jean took the pause created by Lizzie's departure as the signal that it was time to make her own farewells. Although the Tilburys pressed her to stay a little longer, and Jean was in no hurry to get home, it was deeply ingrained in her that to overstay an invitation to tea beyond 6 p.m. was an affront to all that was civilized and she declined.

She couldn't decide whether the Tilburys were conventional people who set much store by these rules; it was hard to tell with Gretchen being foreign and she struggled to picture how they would spend their evening when she was gone. Listening to the radio perhaps, or quietly reading the Sunday paper while Margaret played the piano in the next room. Howard's time was possibly claimed by paperwork from Bedford Street, and Gretchen might withdraw to her workroom and proceed with her pattern cutting. None of these potential narratives quite convinced her; she would have to get to know them better.

"Did you come by bicycle?" Gretchen asked as Jean gathered together handbag, shoes, cardigan and began to reassemble herself.

"No. Bus."

It had been two buses, in fact, taking the best part of fifty minutes including the wait in between.

"Well, Howard will give you a lift home. The service on Sundays is terrible."

"I wouldn't dream of it," said Jean as Howard reappeared from the kitchen with a carrier bag into which he proceeded to transfer the contents of the basket—rhubarb, lettuce and beetroot. "The bus will be fine."

"We insist, don't we, Howard?"

"Yes, you can't carry all this like a market porter."

Their joint determination swept away all her objections.

"And you must come again soon for a fitting," Gretchen said as she and Margaret stood at the gate to wave her off.

"And to finish our badminton tournament," Margaret reminded her.

She was clutching this week's copy of *Girl* that Jean had brought her but been too tactful to hand over until Lizzie had left. By way of thanks she had given Jean a shy hug.

Unable quite to bring herself to return the invitation to tea until she had reflected on how her mother was to be accommodated in such an event, Jean said, "I'll be in touch the moment I hear from Dr. Lloyd-Jones."

It struck her as soon as the words were spoken that this introduction of a business—and, moreover, medical—matter into what was purely a social occasion had sounded a wrong note, but Gretchen didn't seem to notice.

The interior of the Wolseley smelled of gas and leather and the memory of every car Jean had ever ridden in. She sensed from its pristine condition, polished chrome trims, glossy walnut dashboard and dustless floor, and the way that Howard opened and gently closed the passenger door on her, that he was as proud of his car as Gretchen was of her orderly house.

"Do you drive?" he asked Jean as they set off along empty suburban streets.

"I do, as a matter of fact," she replied. "Although I don't have a car. I used to be a driver with the ATS in the war. I was even a driving instructor for a while."

"Were you?" He gave her a quick sideways glance as if he was seeing her in a new light. "I've tried to teach Gretchen but she's terribly nervous behind the wheel. She's happier being the passenger."

"Most husbands prefer it that way," Jean said.

"I did try to encourage her. But perhaps not enough," he conceded.

He took the corner with his foot on the clutch, something she had always told her students not to do, as it meant you were not fully in control of the vehicle.

"I think men like to keep their cars to themselves, so they put it about that driving is harder than it really is. There's nothing to it once you've learned."

"There might be something in that," he admitted.

His hand on the gear stick, brushed against the side of her knee as he changed down coming out of the turn, but he didn't seem to notice, so Jean decided she wouldn't notice either.

"The car is such an incredible thing, don't you think?" he was saying. "Not just the engineering. I mean the freedom it represents."

"Privacy too."

She was thinking that the whole history of human courtship might have been very different without the opportunities it provided for a man and woman to be alone in a confined space. But this was not perhaps an appropriate matter to discuss in just such a setting.

"You work somewhere around here, don't you?" he asked as they approached the Orpington War Memorial.

"Not far," Jean replied. "Petts Wood. It's very decent of you to run me home when you could be relaxing in the garden."

"I never relax in the garden," said Howard. "All I see when I look around are jobs that need doing. Anyway, it's a pleasure. I hope you'll come again. It's so nice for Gretchen to have a friend."

Jean was surprised and a little embarrassed by this compliment. She had considered herself to be transparently the lonely one among them.

"Gretchen doesn't strike me as someone who'd be short of friends," she said.

"Neither of us is what you'd call sociable," he replied. "You're the first person, apart from Aunt Edie, who's been round to tea in ages."

"We don't entertain much ourselves. In fact, never. So today has been a lovely treat."

"For us all."

This conversation, which Jean imagined as a stately dance, proceeding forward and backward, toward and then away from real frankness, brought them to her turning. Just as she pointed out the house as the one with the red door, it opened and Mrs. Melsom appeared, saying her goodbyes to Mrs. Swinney on the threshold. They both peered at the Wolseley with undisguised curiosity as Howard sprang out to help Jean with her bags.

Damn, thought Jean with a sense of annoyance that she couldn't quite account for.

"Well, goodbye then . . . Howard," she said, testing out the sound of his name for the first time.

"Goodbye . . . Jean."

This week in the garden:
Harvest radishes and beets. Sow lettuce seed.
Spray cabbage with salt water to keep cater-
pillars down. Plant out winter greens, kale,
cabbages and broccoli. Hill soil around main
crop potatoes. Feed berries with liquid manure.
Check fruit trees for woolly aphids; paint any
patches with derris.

9

Jean had always assumed Chelsea to be a fashionable district of expensive boutiques and cafés and was therefore surprised to discover among its elegant squares pockets of shabbiness and neglect not much better than slums.

Once, when she was a teenager, she had been invited to lunch by her elderly godmother who lived in a mansion flat in Cadogan Square. Given the courtesy title "Aunt Rosa," though she was no relative but the descendant of a dynasty of Belgian industrialists, she had taken the young Jean by taxi to lunch at the Anglo-Belgian Club in Knightsbridge. They had vichyssoise and rabbit fricassée—terrible, alien food that Jean had forced down with watering eyes and a bulging throat, all the while conscious that this was a huge treat, and of the envy of Dorrie, who had not been included. Not long after this Rosa had died of an aggressive type of cancer and that was the end of fine dining and rides in taxis.

It was possibly the memory of this outing that had informed her decision, now regretted, to dress smartly in her gray wool suit with the fur collar and court shoes. It had not seemed inappropriate in Sloane Square, where she had ducked into Peter Jones to buy a new nightgown for her mother and some florentines, but looked decidedly out of place in Luna Street.

On the corner an abandoned and crippled Ford Popular, sunk onto four punctured tires, its windows smashed, was being used as a drum kit by three shirtless boys wielding pieces of metal tubing. Farther along a soccer game was in progress in the empty road, a wire-haired terrier yapping and chasing after the ball and dancing around the children's legs. Jean was half inclined to ask why none of them were at school on a Thursday afternoon, but they were a feral-looking bunch, quite likely to swear at her for interfering, and she felt at a disadvantage in her Sunday best.

She had assumed that Martha Campkin was a respectable, affluent Chelsea-dweller, in the mold of Aunt Rosa, but the tall, soot-streaked villa in Luna Street, where she occupied the ground floor, seemed to tell quite another story. As Jean hesitated on the pavement, checking the address in her pocket diary, a shape moved in the basement shadows and a rat slunk out from behind an overflowing metal dustbin. It seemed to be in no great fear or hurry—swaggering rather, Jean thought as she scuttled, mouse-like herself, up the steps to the front door and rang the bell.

Having learned from Alice Halfyard the useful fact that Martha's father was a vicar, it had taken no more than a minute to find his entry in *Crockford's*: Campkin, William Sefton, St. John's Rectory, Chatham, b.1903; Keb. Coll. Oxf.; BA, MA Wells Th. Coll.

She had telephoned the rectory on a Sunday afternoon at a time she judged to be safely between the end of lunch and evensong. The voice that answered was soft and tentative, not one that could be imagined carrying from the pulpit, and Jean was surprised when the speaker identified himself as Reverend Campkin. In response to her request for Martha's whereabouts he said with some apology that he was no longer in contact with his daughter, which seemed an astonishing admission for a clergyman.

"I'm afraid I only have an old address for her, but someone there may be aware of her more recent movements. We, unfortunately, are not. She's not in any trouble, I hope?"

Jean was momentarily thrown by this. "Oh no," she said. "Well, not as far as I know. I'm just doing some research into residents of St. Cecilia's Nursing Home after the war."

"Oh, I see. Well, Martha was certainly there. Perhaps you'll remember us to her if you find her. Her mother is not in the best of health."

Having agreed to this bizarre commission from a complete stranger, she noted down Martha's last known number in Forest Hill.

It had taken her precisely two further calls to track Martha down to her current habitat in Luna Street. The chain of addresses was remarkably short, causing Jean to wonder what, if any, effort her father had made to find her, and what could have caused their estrangement.

When at last she found herself speaking to Martha, whose confident, cultured voice was perhaps another factor in her decision to overdress for the occasion, she didn't mention Gretchen but stuck to her story of interest in St. Cecilia's. It was still true, but not the whole truth.

"Yes, St. Cecilia's. I was there. I remember it well, particularly the ceiling."

"What was special about the ceiling?"

"Absolutely nothing, unfortunately. I just spent an awful lot of time on my back staring at it."

"Oh. I see. Sorry, I'm a bit slow today."

"How did you find me, anyway?"

"Dogged, journalistic spadework. May I come and talk to you sometime? This is a party line so I can't monopolize it."

"All right. Any day except Wednesday or Friday. I teach on those days."

"Thursday, then?"

"Afternoons are better for me. Three o'clock?"

"Three o'clock."

★

The door to 16 Luna Street was opened by a tall, striking woman with scarlet lipstick, a paint-smeared smock and a wide floppy skirt. Her dark hair was tied up in a headscarf, not under her chin the way Jean and all normal people wore it but around her forehead with the knot at the front. She peered at Jean's jacket with an appraising eye and asked, "Is that collar fur?"

"Yes," Jean admitted, taken aback by this curious welcome. "Probably fox, but I don't know—it's secondhand."

"Well, I'm afraid you'll have to leave it out here—I've got a hideous allergy. Sorry to be a bore."

She was wearing a pair of red backless leather slippers that made a slapping sound on the tiled floor as she led Jean down the shared hallway toward a row of coat pegs. The most noticeable thing about her, however, which Jean was doing her best not to notice as she struggled out of the offending jacket and hung it up, was that she walked with a stick. And her hands and wrists were bound with curious leather splints, leaving just her fingers and thumbs free.

"Would you like tea? It'll have to be black. The milk's spoiled," Martha said, opening the door to her apartment, which occupied the ground floor at the back of the building, and showing Jean into a large, high-ceilinged room.

It was done out as an artist's studio but with a divan against one wall and a couch and coffee table by the window. The space was dominated by an easel, on which was a prepared canvas marked with ghostly lines. A trestle table was covered with buck-led tubes of paint, jam jars of brushes, stained rags and crusted palettes. Canvases were stacked in one corner like giant slices of toast. There was a mixture of competing smells, none of them pleasant—turpentine, laundry, a full ashtray and the remains of lunch.

Recognizing poverty, Jean produced the florentines from

her Peter Jones bag and handed them to Martha, a trifle self-consciously. "I brought you these."

A slow, wide smile transformed Martha's pinched face and while it lasted she looked quite beautiful.

"Did you actually? Thank God for you. I haven't had a treat like this for ages. Let's eat them now." She began to tear at the cardboard packaging before Jean had even had a chance to sit down. "I'll make some coffee to go with them. I hate tea without milk. Come into the kitchen."

She waved Jean ahead of her with her walking stick into a long, narrow room in a state of considerable disorder. The sink and draining board were piled with unwashed dishes, while the small table, covered with yellow oilcloth, scorched and melted in places by contact with hot pans, held a pair of leather boots and a can of dubbin. The tiled walls were streaked with greasy condensation and spatters of oil, these markings increasing in concentration in the vicinity of the stove. On the bowed shelves chipped crockery, dusty jars of utensils and various unappetizing packages and cans jostled for space.

Jean proceeded gingerly across the sticky floor, which crunched underfoot from a coating of spilled salt or sugar, past a wooden frame hung with items of female underwear not normally on public display—stout black knickers, ribbed vests and flesh-colored stockings like withered legs. Even Jean, whose housekeeping efforts never went much beyond the surface of things, was dismayed. Martha herself appeared unembarrassed by or perhaps oblivious to the disarray, humming cheerfully as she hunted for two clean mugs among the debris, giving them a quick wipe on the hem of her smock.

When they were installed once more in the studio with their coffee and the ripped box of florentines between them, Jean said, "Do you remember much about your time at St. Cecilia's?"

"Yes," said Martha through a mouthful of cookie shards. "I

remember it all, apart from those times when I was dosed to the gills with opiates, of course. They couldn't do a thing for me. I was no better when I went out than when I went in. But perhaps the aim never was to cure me—perhaps it was just to provide respite for my parents. I didn't think of that at the time; it only occurred to me later."

"You don't see your parents anymore, I gather," said Jean, trying to feel her way around this delicate subject.

"How do you know that? Have you spoken to them?" Martha reached for another florentine.

"Only to try and get an address for you. Your father asked me to send you his good wishes." Something like that. Jean couldn't now recall his exact form of words, only an impression of aloofness that was both unparental and unchristian.

Martha raised her eyebrows. "Well," she said. "That's a surprise."

"He said your mother's not in the best of health. That was the gist."

"Oh hell. I suppose I'll have to get in contact."

"You might regret it if you don't," said Jean, now bizarrely cast as an agent of reconciliation between people who were strangers to her.

She couldn't help feeling that this unsought burden of responsibility entitled her to a measure of curiosity.

"Did you have a falling-out?"

"I got tired of their disapproval." She picked absently at a scab of blue paint on her smock.

"You don't share their beliefs?"

Beneath the crust the paint was still soft and in the space of a few seconds Martha had managed to transfer blue smudges to her coffee cup, skirt and face.

"That's a mild way of putting it. We disagree about everything. Religion, politics, art, life. My life, anyway. They're Edwardians essentially, absolutely at sea in the modern world. They can't help it."

"The world has changed so much since they were young," said Jean, somewhat distracted by the mess Martha was making and wondering if she should point it out.

"Not nearly enough in my view," said Martha, wiping her finger on her sleeve. "Anyway, what's your interest in St. Cecilia's?"

Jean took out her pen and notebook and flipped it to a clean page.

"Do you remember the girls on your ward?"

"Yes. Gretchen, Brenda and poor Kitty."

"Everyone calls her 'poor Kitty,'" said Jean.

"Well, she spent about twenty-three hours a day in an iron lung. What a life. And she was still madly religious. You wonder how she could have any time for a God who saw fit to create polio."

"I'm sure your father could explain the Christian teaching on suffering if you asked him," Jean replied.

She was beginning to resent having to do without her jacket. Although it was a warm day outside, in here it was mysteriously chilly and behind her back the couch felt damp.

"No, thanks. I wonder if Kitty's still there."

"Not at St. Cecilia's. It's been turned into a boys' school."

"That's quite a reversal. I don't think I so much as glimpsed a boy all the time I was there."

"Interesting you say that," Jean remarked. "It's Gretchen I'm here about. You were friends, I understand?"

"Yes, briefly. It was a choice between her on one side or ghastly Brenda on the other. Kitty was out of the frame, really."

"Poor Kitty."

Without breaking eye contact, Jean began to doodle on her notepad. It was always the same sketch—a single staring eye.

"Indeed. So what about Gretchen? Is she all right?"

"She's made a rather extraordinary claim, which I'm doing my best to verify, that she became pregnant while still a virgin during her time there."

Martha put down her coffee cup with a jolt and stared at Jean. "Seriously?" she said.

"She is deadly serious. And willing to be subjected to all sorts of medical tests to prove it."

"God. I can't believe she's still going on about that after all this time."

Jean's pen skated across the page. "You already knew?"

"Yes—she told me at the time. She came to visit me in Chatham not long after I left the place. She told me then that she was pregnant and that it was a 'miracle.'"

"What did you *think*? I mean, you were right there when it must have happened."

"I just assumed she was lying about the dates."

"Why would you think that? Why would she lie to you—her friend?"

"Why do women lie? To protect themselves, of course."

This exchange left Jean reeling.

"Do you know, you're the only person I've spoken to who knows Gretchen who has even hinted that she might be lying."

Martha gave a short rasp of laughter. "That's probably because you only talked to nice people. You should have come straight to the bitch."

They were interrupted by the sound of hammering on the front door and the simultaneous ringing of all the bells in the apartments.

"Oh, God. That'll be Dennis. His wife has kicked him out and he keeps coming back when she's at work hoping someone else will let him back in. Excuse me a moment." She unfolded herself from the chair and limped out to the hallway, pulling the door to behind her.

Jean didn't fancy Dennis's chances against Martha, with or without her walking stick. In the distance she could hear raised voices. She occupied herself during her hostess's absence by looking through the canvases propped against the wall. She was confident that Martha wouldn't mind her snooping and might even expect it.

The paintings, chiefly cityscapes of bomb-damaged buildings, derelict churches and patches of empty land, took Jean by surprise. She knew nothing of art, except what she had picked up from trips to the National Gallery, and had imagined Martha's style to be bold, abstract and incomprehensible. These were, to Jean's inexpert eye at least, old-fashioned, naturalistic and rather pleasing. In each of the scenes a tiny detail provided a note of beauty or optimism among the grayness—a delicate flower growing in a crack in a wall; a rainbow in an oily puddle; a bird nesting in a ruined chimney.

While she browsed, her thoughts kept straying back to Martha's curious assumption that Gretchen was lying to her. It didn't make sense. Why would Gretchen have needed to lie to Martha, her friend, and, moreover, someone who hardly seemed likely to disapprove or judge?

The commotion in the hallway reaching a crescendo, Jean felt moved to investigate. She found Martha and the would-be intruder engaged in a tug-of-war through the mail slot, with Martha's walking stick as the contested rope. Perhaps inspired by the arrival of reinforcements, Martha abruptly let go of the handle, which flew back, catching in the jaws of the mail slot and sending the assailant tumbling down the steps. She hastily snatched the stick back to her side of the door while he continued to shout abuse at her.

Several of the other residents of the house now began to descend to investigate the commotion, which was clearly a regular occurrence of no great moment. Having satisfied themselves that it was "just Dennis," they shrugged and returned to their apartments, leaving him raving outside on the pavement.

"Sorry about that," said Martha, cheerfully, adjusting her headscarf, which had become twisted in the scuffle. "It's par for the course."

She seemed quite invigorated by the altercation. Jean felt a rush of affection for her quiet, suburban street, where the only sound likely to disturb the peace might be the whir of a lawn mower or the jangle of a milk truck.

"I was looking at your paintings," she said. She was going to elaborate but lost courage when she saw Martha's expression darken. "I like them," she finished lamely.

"Please don't say any more," Martha said, holding up a hand as though to ward off blows. "I hate it when people praise my work."

"It's better than criticism, surely?" said Jean, feeling bound to defend herself. She had never met anyone quite so resistant to flattery.

"You can't accept compliments and then dismiss brickbats. You have to treat those two impostors just the same. For my own sanity, I choose to ignore them both." She fiddled nervously with her wrist bindings as she said this, unbuckling and tightening the straps.

"Do you exhibit? In galleries and things?" Jean sensed herself venturing across thin ice again but was unable to stop herself.

"I'm trying to build up a body of work that I feel completely comfortable with." Martha's tone was brittle. "It's a hard world to break into."

"I'm sure," murmured Jean, retreating to solid ground.

"Luckily, I have my two days a week teaching to bring in enough to live on."

"It must be difficult to do both."

"Teaching is a drain on my time and energy. But I'm good at it," she said, a trifle defensively. "And on the other days, I paint."

"Well, I won't keep you any longer," said Jean. "I don't want to take up precious painting time."

"It's all right. The light in here is lousy in the afternoons anyway. So . . . Gretchen." Martha sat back down and rummaged in the cookie box, looking puzzled to discover it was now empty. "I suppose she's married now."

"Yes, to a nice man called Howard. Not the father of the little girl, of course. Margaret."

"Margaret. Well, well. I feel guilty for disbelieving her now. But on the other hand, you can't really go along with all that virgin birth twaddle, can you?"

"I'm keeping an open mind," said Jean. "Or rather, I'm confident that the scientists will get to the bottom of it. But I'm interested to hear your view of Gretchen."

"I didn't mean to give the impression that I thought she was a regular liar. I didn't at all. But I don't believe in the supernatural, and she can't have got pregnant during her time at St. Cecilia's. We were never alone. You couldn't even unwrap a toffee without bloody Brenda hearing it."

"That's more or less Miss Halfyard's view. Although she wasn't so hard on Brenda."

"Matron," said Martha, shaking her head at the memory. "She didn't like me much. We had a few run-ins, as I recall."

"She sent you her good wishes, actually," said Jean, hoping to shame Martha into softening her outlook. She had observed before that when people said "so-and-so doesn't like me," the dislike was usually in the other direction.

"All these people wishing me well," exclaimed Martha. "I should be touched."

Jean recalled Alice's remark about Martha being "spiky." Certainly, it was hard to imagine her being good friends with the reserved and decorous Gretchen.

"I suppose you're not in touch with anyone else from those days?"

Martha snorted. "Hardly."

"Well, I'm afraid I can't pass on Gretchen's good wishes because she doesn't know I've come to see you," Jean said.

"Will you be in contact with her again?"

"Oh yes. The medical tests are ongoing."

"I wonder if you'd give her a little gift from me," Martha said, fetching a folder from a drawer in the workbench.

Inside was a selection of postcard-sized silk-screen prints of birds, fruit and flowers. Bold, graphic and colorful, they were quite different in style from the gray urban landscapes.

Her bandaged hand riffled through the collection for some time, selecting and discarding different possibilities before settling on a print of a bowl of tangerines.

"That's . . . er . . ." said Jean, remembering just in time the prohibition regarding compliments. "I'm sure Gretchen will be delighted."

Fortunately, Martha was preoccupied with trying to find an envelope to put it in and didn't notice or hear. She left the room for a moment, while Jean buttoned her jacket and gathered up her bags. She was wondering whether to replace the florentines on her way home or do without, when Martha returned with a stiff-backed envelope.

"Something for her to remember me by," she said.

"That's very kind of you," said Jean, trying to picture the tangerines on the Tilburys' wall between the Alpine scene and the embroidered sampler. "I wonder," she said as an idea struck her. "Do you remember the layout of St. Cecilia's well enough to draw me a floor plan?"

"Yes—at least the ground floor, where we were. I never made it upstairs."

Jean handed over her notebook, turned to a fresh page, and

watched as Martha, frowning with concentration, sketched a neat diagram with quick, confident strokes and added her signature with an ironic flourish.

"Thank you," said Jean, smiling her acknowledgment. "Now I must leave you in peace."

She wondered if it would be quite safe to depart, or whether Dennis might be skulking outside, ready to rush the door as soon as it opened, but all was quiet on Luna Street.

"Well, that was more interesting than I dared to hope," said Martha as they said goodbye. "You've certainly stirred up the past. St. Cecilia's and my parents—all in one day!"

Has the stiffening at the back of your house slippers worn down? I have successfully repaired several pairs by sewing a piece of old collar inside. The semi-stiff kind from a man's shirt is ideal and will prolong the life of your slippers.

10

There had been some kind of incident at Charing Cross and the station was in confusion. The rush-hour crowds gathered on the concourse, staring at the departure boards, which declined to display any platform numbers, and awaiting an explanation from the PA system, which had fallen mysteriously silent. Queues had formed at the taxi stand outside as people lost patience. Every few minutes a fresh load of travelers disgorged from the subway would join the throng. A rumor was going around that someone had fallen onto the tracks at London Bridge; incoming trains were delayed.

"If someone jumps in front of a train the driver gets a day off," the woman in front of Jean was saying to her companion in a tone of great self-importance.

"I never knew that," came the reply.

"They don't like to put it about," said the first woman, her words muffling those from the PA sysrtem, which had just crackled into life.

Idiot, Jean thought, clenching her teeth. This sort of complacent pronouncement of utter rubbish made her fume. And now she had missed the announcement. "What's that?" "What they say?" people were asking each other, appealing to left and right. There was a flutter from the departure board—Platform 4 for the Ramsgate train—and the crowd surged forward, the momentum sucking along even those with no intention of going to Ramsgate.

Jean fell back a few paces to escape the general drift, wondering whether her mother would think to reheat yesterday's half dish of leftover cauliflower cheese, or wait helpless and hungry for her arrival, when she noticed a familiar figure ahead. He was struggling to light a cigarette while holding his briefcase and a bunch of yellow roses.

"Howard," she called, threading through the crowds to join him.

"Hello," he said, attempting to tip his hat with the hand that still held the lighter and very nearly scorching the brim.

He parked the briefcase between his feet and the flowers under one arm before he could rescue the cigarette from between his teeth and bat the smoke from his streaming eyes.

Jean laughed. There was something reassuring, flattering almost, in his clumsiness.

"Here's a thing," he said, nodding to the departure board on which the word "delayed" was prominently displayed. "Do you know what it's about?"

"I haven't heard anything official. People have been saying someone's fallen on the tracks, but it's probably nonsense."

"They can't have fallen on all of the tracks," said Howard reasonably. "Some of the lines must be running. You need the Hayes train, I suppose?"

"Yes. Or I could take one to Orpington and get a bus, but that will make me very late. Mother will be frantic."

"Wait here, I'll go and find an employee," Howard said, heading toward the ticket office, which was already besieged by indignant commuters.

Jean's feet were beginning to hurt in her heeled shoes. She thought with some envy of Martha Campkin's red leather slippers and wondered if she would ever be able to carry off such a look. There had been something admirable in her solitary existence in that seedy apartment, laboring to produce some artwork of which she could feel proud. Martha hadn't said as much, but Jean was convinced that she hadn't sold or even exhibited a single painting.

At last the public address system coughed and a tinny voice announced the departure of the delayed Sidcup train from Platform 2. There was a corresponding stampede from the crowd on the concourse as the lucky ones hurried toward the train and a general slumping from those left behind. Jean looked around for Howard, wondering if he had heard the announcement, but there was no sign of him. She was debating whether to pursue him to the ticket office to warn him that his train was in and risk losing him altogether, when she saw him. He was weaving in her direction, against the flow, apologizing as people elbowed past or knocked into his bunch of flowers.

"Your train's in," Jean said as he reached her side, looking somewhat buffeted. "You'd better hurry."

"I can't leave you here," he protested. "You might be stranded for hours. Apparently there's someone on the track between London Bridge and Ladywell. It's caused a hold-up right down the Hayes line."

"I'll be fine," said Jean. "I'll wait for the Orpington train and then get a bus."

Her heart plunged at the thought of this detour, which would double her journey time. She would have to call ahead and warn her mother.

"Come and get the Sidcup train with me and then I'll drive you home. My car's at the station," Howard said.

"Oh no, really."

"Come on," he urged. "I can't abandon you here. Gretchen would never forgive me."

Gretchen's imprimatur, even if only assumed, seemed to give the plan an air of inevitability and Jean followed Howard, dodging and stumbling as fast as she could, through the waiting throng to Platform 2, where the guard was already walking the length of the train, slamming doors. Most of the rear carriages were full, with standing passengers crushed right up to the windows. At last a stationmaster took pity on them and held a door open for them, obliging those already inside to shuffle closer together, grumbling.

Howard handed Jean in first and then hopped in after her, the shriek of whistles reaching a crescendo as the train lurched forward in a series of starts as though tugged on elastic. Their eyes slid toward the bunch of roses, now limp and battered beyond redemption, and they began to laugh.

"Oh dear," said Jean, unable to stifle her giggles. "They don't look at all well. Were they for a special occasion?"

"No, nothing like that. I just picked them up at Covent Garden this morning on a whim. I'll have to have another whim tomorrow instead, because these have had it."

Lucky Gretchen, thought Jean, to have a husband who brought home flowers on a Thursday evening for no reason.

Around them the other passengers were stony-faced; either disgruntled at having to stand, or guilty and irritable at having a seat that could not be properly enjoyed because of those looming over them.

"If only I had a seat myself I'd offer it to you," Howard said a little too loudly, or perhaps just loudly enough, as a young man sitting in the middle of the row hauled himself to his feet with an air of resignation and nodded to Jean.

She would rather have stayed where she was, next to Howard, but didn't want to humiliate the young man, who was already looking flushed from his belated gallantry. And besides, now that he had stood up there really wasn't enough room, so there was nothing for it but to clamber past him, apologizing, over a tangle of feet, to take his seat.

The windows on both sides were opaque with grime and it was an unfamiliar line, so Jean had no idea where they were. The gray shapes of tall Victorian houses and narrow walled backyards slid past, one street indistinguishable from another. She looked in her bag for something to occupy her—the woman next to her was patiently crocheting, the ball of wool jumping in her lap—and noticed the envelope for Gretchen. She could give it to Howard to pass on and save herself a stamp. She took out her notebook and began to write, in her best Dutton's Longhand, an account of her meeting with Martha.

At Hither Green the compartment emptied a little and Howard moved to the seat opposite Jean. He took a copy of *The Times* from his briefcase and folded it into a small rectangle, to avoid overspreading himself, and seemed to be absorbed in the crossword. But every time Jean looked up he was watching her, unembarrassed, and would give her a smile or raise his eyebrows as if at the length and inconvenience of the journey.

Eventually they had the carriage to themselves and, having finished her note-writing, Jean moved to sit beside him to see what progress he was making with the crossword.

"You haven't done any!" she remonstrated. "It's completely blank."

"I don't have a pen," Howard replied with great dignity. "I've been doing it blind. When I get home, I'll fill it in just like that!" He snapped his fingers.

Jean handed him her ballpoint with a skeptical expression.

He gave her an unfriendly look and then began to write, at great speed and shielding the page from her inquisitive gaze. A moment later he cast the paper aside, with the word "Done!"

And when she retrieved it she saw he had filled in the grid with the words:

She gave a peal of laughter.

"Here we are," he said as the train drew into Sidcup station, stopping with a jolt that threw them backward in their seats. "I hope you won't be too late."

"Mother knows I'm up in town this afternoon, but she still gets anxious if I'm even slightly delayed."

"Is it just the two of you?" Howard inquired, directing her out of the station to the adjoining street where he had left the Wolseley.

"Yes. Just us two. My sister, Dorrie, lives in Kenya and my father died in the war. Like so many."

"No less a tragedy for you, though," said Howard.

Jean was usually adept at fielding personal questions and steering conversations onto safe, neutral territory. But there was something about the sanctuary and silence of a private car, where you could talk without having to make eye contact, that made her uncharacteristically open. She was aware that Howard was hardly an appropriate confidant, but he was so sensible and safe and unlikely to do anything at all except sympathize that she couldn't restrain herself.

"I've made him sound like a hero. He wasn't. He walked out on my mother just as the war started. I think he had some kind of breakdown. He'd fought in the first war and survived. And when it looked as though it was happening all over again it was too much for him."

"I don't think that was an uncommon reaction among veterans of the Great War," said Howard. "All that sacrifice for nothing."

"Yes, but he'd also met someone else. That was the real reason for leaving. He just took off. I don't think the marriage had been happy for some time; it was just duty holding them together."

Jean couldn't now recall ever witnessing any signs of physical affection between them—hand-holding or the welcoming kiss at the end of the working day—even before the rift. She had assumed this was normal and every marriage the same until she had noticed that her aunt and uncle in Harrogate did things differently: he called his wife Honeybun and never missed an opportunity to pull her onto his lap, or slide an arm around her waist; higher if he thought no one was looking.

"Perhaps he wouldn't have left if it hadn't been for the war. I think he just felt he'd already used up all his luck in the first war and needed to seize a last chance at happiness. And the thing is, he was *right*. It was his last chance."

"At least he got to choose," said Howard after a pause. "Your mother had no choice."

"Yes—that's it exactly," said Jean, all her reticence melting before the warmth of his compassionate good sense. "It was just imposed on her. And even so she felt this terrible shame and guilt, as though it was somehow her fault for not being able to keep her husband."

"Did she ever speak to you about this?"

"No, no, that would have been impossible. She couldn't talk about personal things. But I could tell—it was evident in every fiber of her being. The whole purpose of her life was to be a wife and mother."

They pulled up at the traffic lights on Croydon Road and were able now to exchange a quick smile of understanding on Howard's part and gratitude on Jean's.

"So she leaned on you instead?"

"Yes. Heavily. She doesn't have an independent bone in her body—she wasn't brought up that way. You read about these resilient women who raise five children single-handed and take in laundry and slaughter their own pigs and the rest of it. Well, she wasn't one of them. And then before she could even get used to the idea that he'd left her he was killed in an air raid. So it was as if he'd abandoned her twice over. She'd never had the chance to have it out with him and she couldn't even mourn him as his widow because everyone knew he'd already left her."

This was the hardest thing, Jean thought. On top of losing everything else—her husband, her future, her pension—she had even been cheated of the sympathy that was her due.

"And you've looked after her ever since?"

"More or less. It was clear that one of us girls would have to. Whoever married first would get away. And that was Dorrie."

The thought of her sister prompted, as always, a mixture of conflicting emotions, principally rancor and envy, but also powerful, protective love, and grief at the distance between them. She gave Howard a brief account of Dorrie's situation in Kitale, trying not to betray too much of her sense of injustice.

"Another abandonment," was his observation. "It must have hit your mother hard."

"Yes. Missing out on the grandchildren. A further blow."

"Did you ever see your father after he left?"

"Once. I went up to his office to ask for some money. He was a fruit wholesaler at Covent Garden, but he'd let the business get into debt. He was terribly apologetic and ashamed. It was horrible to see—we'd always got on so well before. He said he still loved Dorrie and me, but we were adults now, and he'd met someone else and that was that. He gave me all the cash in the office that he'd been about to bank. It wasn't very much. About twenty pounds."

"What an unhappy story," said Howard. "Men can be very selfish."

"And yet for the previous twenty years or so they seemed happy. To me, anyway. But who really knows what goes on in a marriage?"

"Who indeed?"

Jean glanced at him but he kept his eyes on the road and his face was expressionless.

"And most men aren't selfish. My uncle paid for Dorrie's wedding and helped us to get our house in Hayes. I thought Mother might be able to make a fresh start somewhere new where no one knew us. She was so ashamed of being deserted; she always felt the people in Gipsy Hill were gossiping and pitying her.

"But then about a month after we settled into our new house, we were at the movies and a woman in the line stopped us and said hello. It was one of our old neighbors who had moved around the corner. She was just trying to be friendly, but it was the worst thing that could have happened; Mother stopped going out almost entirely."

Howard shook his head. "Does your uncle still help out?"

"He lives in Harrogate, so he's a bit far away. We used to go on vacation there every year, but he's not in the best of health now. Anyway, we manage. My salary pays for the essentials. He still sends us a money order for birthdays and Christmas."

At this remark about money—one of the unmentionables—Jean

felt suddenly embarrassed. And yet it was nothing, really, compared to the revelations that had gone before. She was aware of the risk she had taken in unburdening herself so freely, but the relief was so powerful she couldn't regret it.

"I've never discussed this with anyone before. I'm sorry for rambling on."

"Please don't apologize. I'm honored that you felt you could talk to me."

They both stared straight ahead, making what seemed a solemn declaration of friendship without once exchanging a glance. That would have been too much.

"I've just remembered, I've got something for Gretchen," said Jean, taking Martha's envelope from her bag and laying it on the dashboard. This seemed to break the spell and draw the conversation back to its proper sphere—Gretchen, Margaret, the story, work. "I met a friend of hers from St. Cecilia's today. She wanted me to pass on a little gift."

"What a nice thought," said Howard. "She'll be so pleased."

Jean's mother was keeping watch at the window as the car drew up outside, a pale, ghostly figure in the unlit room.

"That man brought you home again," she remarked as the door shut. "I thought you were going to Chelsea."

"I did. Look what I brought you." Jean handed over the Peter Jones bag and smiled as her mother peered inside with a childlike delight in new things.

"A nightgown. Just what I need. Oh, clever you!" She held it against herself, extending one ankle and striking a pose as though modeling a ball gown.

"Very elegant," said Jean. "You'll easily be the best-dressed person in the house tonight."

"Did you get yourself anything nice?" her mother asked and

then a shadow of dismay clouded her face. There wouldn't have been enough money for two such treats.

"Oh, I don't need anything," said Jean, still feeling somewhat raw and exposed from her conversation with Howard, and yet strangely exhilarated. "Anyway, Gretchen is making me a new dress, so I'll soon be looking quite the thing."

The feeling of euphoria lasted right through the reheated cauliflower cheese, hair wash and beyond, to the point that Jean even offered to read aloud from her mother's library book, *My Cousin Rachel*. It was the most harmonious evening that either of them could remember.

Dear Dorrie,

I know we don't do gifts but I was passing an antique shop in Chelsea the other day and I saw this exquisite little cigarette box and thought of you. I'm going to parcel it up with tissue paper and hope it makes it through customs in one piece.

We're both well. No other news.

Love Jean

Alice's Diary

July 12, 1946

M caused a little scene today. She does love a drama. We were hopeful that the antimalarial drugs might work where the antibiotics, injections and diets have all failed. But she has been roaring with pain. Perhaps it would have been better if she had been in a room of her own, but we thought the companionship would be good for them all.

Her mother came to visit this afternoon, bringing a gift from one of their well-heeled parishioners—a bag of four tangerines. Nobody has seen a delicacy like this in years. Sister Maria Goretti said she hoped M was going to share them with the other girls. She meant well but she speaks bluntly sometimes. M said no, she damn well wasn't: B never shares a damn thing.

Sister MG tried (perhaps unwisely) to remove the bag, which split, sending the tangerines rolling onto the floor. M called her an awful name. Sister MG departed in high dudgeon, saying that M wouldn't be able to peel them herself with her bandaged hands, and surely no one else would help her when she was so selfish, ungrateful and foul-mouthed.

The tangerines were still on the floor when Sister Phil came on duty, so she returned them to M's bedside.

July 13

Overnight the tangerines have been eaten. G must have peeled them. I expect they shared them when the other two were asleep. Such an unlikely friendship.

M soiled herself—deliberately, no doubt—to punish Sister MG, who had to clean her up. Later, M complained that Sister MG had handled her roughly; the two are now sworn enemies. It is a bad business.

July 17

B has complained that she is kept awake at night by M and G whispering together. I suspect she feels excluded, poor thing. When I spoke to M and G separately about it, G immediately apologized. M denied it and accused B of making trouble. She would start a mutiny from her bed if she could.

B tried to enlist the support of K, but K, at the far end of the room, says she is not aware of any noise from the other beds. Perhaps the mechanical wheeze of the iron lung masks the noise, or perhaps she was just being diplomatic.

August 20

I have had to have stern words with Sister Phil. It has come to light that she has been less than vigilant in administering the evening doses of painkillers and sleeping tablets. M and G have apparently hoarded them for three days and then taken a triple dose.

When challenged, M explained that it was an attempt to guarantee a deep and painless sleep. On the pill-free nights they distracted each other by whispering through the night. It is a wretched story and my heart goes out to them in their pain, but M is a devil to take a risk like this. I don't believe G is the author of this reckless scheme—she is led along by M.

September 28

G was discharged today. You would hardly recognize her as the same girl who was brought in all those months ago in a wheelchair, so pale and pinched with pain. She left on foot, walking with two sticks, and made a point of thanking all the sisters individually. She is a sweet girl and a favorite with everyone. Her mother had tears in her eyes when she saw how improved she is.

September 30

M has been inconsolable without her friend. B tries to engage her in conversation, now that G is out of the way and she is not outnumbered. But M stubbornly feigns sleep or shouts across her to K. It is a curious thing—I have often observed that the arrival of someone new or the departure of someone established disturbs the equilibrium on a ward, even when that person is herself unassuming and compliant.

Charing Cross Hospital
Agar St.
London W1
July 1957

Dear Miss Swinney,

I am writing to inform you that the results of our preliminary blood tests of Mother A and Daughter have established that they share the blood type A1 rhesus phenotype c̄dēcde and the results of further, more detailed studies show a complete identity of blood groups—see the table enclosed.

We are therefore eager to proceed to the next stage of our investigation, and would be grateful if Mother A and Daughter could present themselves once more at the Charing Cross Hospital Annex at Agar Street on July 21 at 9:30 a.m. for further tests.

Yours sincerely,
Sidney Lloyd-Jones

Dear Jean,

I have made great progress with your dress and wonder if you would be able to come for a fitting this weekend whenever is convenient for you (and your mother). Perhaps you could ring Howard at the shop to confirm a time.

With good wishes,
Gretchen

12

"What on earth is that?" Jean's mother stood in the kitchen doorway, holding the fragments of a sugar bowl, which she had just
dropped on the tiled hearth.

Her mouth was slack with astonishment. As if she had seen a
unicorn, Jean thought.

"It's a rabbit," she replied. "Surely you can see that?"

The animal sat on the linoleum between them, nibbling at a
pile of outer cabbage leaves. Apart from a black smudge on its
nose, now twitching, and one black ear, it was completely white
and still small enough to fit in cupped hands.

"Yes, of course. But what is it doing *here*?"

"I bought it from a pet shop today, but I couldn't manage the
cage so the shopkeeper said he'd drop it round on his way home
this evening. I hope he remembers," Jean said.

At this disturbance the rabbit hopped in ungainly slow motion
toward a thumb of carrot that had rolled just out of reach and
Jean's mother flinched back against the doorframe.

"It won't eat you, Mother," Jean laughed. "They're herbivores."

"But why on earth did you buy it? We've never had pets before."

"It's a present for Margaret. She told me she wanted a rabbit or
a kitten. I think she's lonely."

Jean's mother seemed to take no comfort from the fact that the rabbit's occupancy of the kitchen was to be short-lived. If anything, this admission appeared to rattle her even more.

"You can't give someone a live rabbit as a gift," she spluttered.

"Well, I certainly wouldn't give her a dead one," said Jean. "That would be too macabre."

"Have you checked that her parents want her to have a rabbit? They may have strong objections."

"No," said Jean, experiencing a momentary loss of confidence in her brilliant scheme. "It's meant to be a surprise."

"It'll certainly be that," came the tart reply. "Whatever possessed you?"

"I thought it was a nice idea. It's not a python. It just sits in a hutch eating leftover cabbage leaves until Margaret wants to cuddle it. I can't see any objection."

"Well, I think you've been very rash," said her mother. "It will cause a huge rumpus if you turn up with it unannounced and the parents refuse to take it. The little girl will be terribly upset."

Jean felt stung by this remark; she had wanted only to make Margaret happy and in her enthusiasm for her own ingenuity she had allowed herself to get carried away. It occurred to her that her mother was describing exactly what would have happened years ago if they had been the unprepared recipients of a gift rabbit. For a moment she was that disappointed little girl; it was unbearable.

"Oh hell, I was only trying to be kind," she burst out, railing against criticism that she knew was just. "You had to spoil it."

Her mother went rigid, blinking in silent protest at this crossing of uncrossable lines. Whatever their divergence of views, raised voices or confrontation were as unthinkable as a knife at the throat.

"It's nothing to do with me," she said at last in a brittle voice. "You must do as you see fit."

Later, after dinner, they sat in the front room together listening to the *Light Programme* on the radio, friends again. Jean couldn't apologize for her outburst; to do that would only acknowledge the unpleasantness. Better to agree, without discussion, that it had never happened. There were other, established ways to show contrition: an unequal division of the shepherd's pie in her mother's favor; an offer to massage her sore feet; a suggestion that they look—again—through Dorrie's wedding album together.

The rabbit slumbered in Jean's lap on a folded towel and allowed itself to be stroked. Its weight and warmth were surprisingly comforting, and she found herself half hoping that the Tilburys might refuse to accept it after all.

The shopkeeper had called round with the hutch as promised. It looked larger in a domestic kitchen than it had in the shop, taking up most of the space by the back door. Jean lined it with newspaper and straw, and tied the glass water bottle onto the chicken-wire window with elastic.

For now it had the fresh, green smell of new wood; it would very quickly acquire a less appealing animal scent, which none of the ordinary kitchen smells—Ajax, Gumption, spent matches, cooking—could quite mask. Of course in the normal way it would have to go outside—basic hygiene demanded it—but there was no sense in carting it down to the shed if it was going to a new home in a few days anyway.

"Quite a placid little thing," Jean's mother conceded on her way to bed.

Not fully committed to touching the rabbit, her outstretched hand hovered just above its head as though giving it a blessing.

"Howard?"

"Yes. Speaking."

"Hello, Howard, it's Jean Swinney."

She had a cast-iron excuse for this call, which he was no doubt expecting and which gave her confidence, so her voice was quite steady. Whenever she thought back to their most recent conversation, she felt a mild panic at how much of herself she had revealed. Without the protective distance of the telephone between them she might have been less composed.

"Hello, Jean."

There was no trace of awkwardness in his greeting, only his usual warmth and politeness.

"Gretchen sent me a note about calling in this weekend for a dress fitting."

"Oh yes. She said."

"I'm sorry you've been cast as my social secretary, but she asked me to let you know a suitable time."

"Of course. I have my pen and paper ready to take dictation."

She could hear the smile in his voice.

"Shall we say 11 a.m. on Saturday?"

"Very good."

"And . . . Howard?"

"Yes."

"I think I've done something a bit rash."

"Oh?" His tone was suddenly serious. "Are you going to tell me what it is?"

"I want you to be completely honest."

"Go on."

"I've bought Margaret a rabbit. She said she was desperate for a pet, and I was passing the shop and went in and bought one on impulse. It was only when I stopped to think about it that I realized it might be a terrible imposition."

"Is that all? What a relief."

"Are you horrified by the idea? Please say. I won't be offended."

"A rabbit?" he mused. "What a thoughtful . . . thought. No, I can't say I feel any horror sweeping over me. Quite the opposite."

"What about Gretchen? Will she disapprove?"

"Do you know, I'm embarrassed to say I have no idea of my wife's views on rabbits. In nearly ten years of marriage it's not something we've ever discussed."

Jean felt herself beginning to relax.

"Perhaps I should write her a note."

"Why don't I ask her tonight and if she throws up her hands in horror I'll telephone you tomorrow. If you don't hear, you can assume she's in favor."

"The last thing I want is to cause any trouble."

In the months ahead she would remember this remark—so sincerely felt—and marvel at her own innocence.

13

Jean stood once more in Gretchen's workroom, hardly breathing, as the skeleton of a dress, inside out and bristling with pins, was lowered over her head and tweaked and tugged and tightened around her with still more pins until Gretchen was satisfied with the fit. The slightest movement on Jean's part and she was pierced by a dozen sharp points.

"You are losing weight since I last measured you?" Gretchen said with her curious foreign intonation that made questions of statements, pinching the fabric between finger and thumb.

"Not intentionally," said Jean, flinching. "I eat less when I'm busy, I suppose. And more when I'm miserable."

"And at the moment you are overworked but happy?" said Gretchen, lifting the dress carefully, inch by inch, over Jean's head and laying it on the cutting table.

"Yes, that would be about right."

She was busy because Gretchen's case took up so much of her time that every other moment at work was spent catching up with her regular duties. The reason for her happiness was something she chose not to examine.

The ordeal by piercing over, the two women made their way downstairs to the kitchen, where Margaret was sitting on the floor playing with the rabbit. Her outstretched legs formed the fourth side of an enclosure made up of the wall, the wooden dresser and a vegetable rack. She was in a state as close to ecstasy as could be imagined.

"I'm going to call her Jemimah," she said.

No follow-up call had come from Howard to discourage the gift of the rabbit, which had left Jean with the problem of how to transport the hutch to Sidcup. She had half hoped that Howard would foresee her difficulty and offer to come and fetch it, but this had not happened, and so she had been forced to order a taxi—almost doubling the cost of the gift. The driver had helped her to carry it to and from the car, earning every penny of his shilling tip. Between them they had threaded it down the narrow passage at the side of the Tilburys' row house and into the back garden, Jean skinning her knuckles on the brickwork as she stumbled.

All the expense and inconvenience proved worthwhile, however, when Margaret was summoned downstairs for the unveiling of the surprise. The expression on her face, as suspicion and curiosity gave way to rapture, made tears spring to Jean's eyes. The little girl was almost quivering with excitement as she flung herself at Jean and hugged her.

As Jean patted her heaving shoulders, she realized too late that this might well be the greatest, happiest moment of Margaret's childhood, the one that she would always remember. By rights it belonged to her parents, but she, Jean, an interloper, had appropriated it for herself.

She understood, now, her mother's misgivings and could hardly bring herself to look at Gretchen, expecting to see in her face some signs of resentment. Gretchen, however, seemed oblivious to these nuances, showing only a generous pleasure in her daughter's happiness and needing no credit for it.

"Wasn't that kind of Jean," was all she said.

There had been no sign of Howard in the house or garden, though the Wolseley had been there in the driveway. It was only when Margaret said something about Daddy building a run for Jemimah when he got back from work that Jean remembered that of course for jewelers and other shopkeepers Saturday was a working day like any other. She felt a jab of disappointment, which quite unsettled her.

It had not just been for the pleasure of seeing Margaret, then, that she had set off that morning with such a light heart. Ever since that conversation in the car, when she had poured out her disappointments and frustrations to Howard as though she had known him for years rather than weeks, she had found herself thinking about him in idle moments, more than was allowable or wise. She would have to watch herself.

As this visit had to be incorporated into her morning errands, which still had to be done, Jean couldn't linger once the dress fitting was completed, even though Gretchen invited her to stay and share their lunch of cheese on toast. She had promised her mother that this afternoon they would go through her winter wardrobe and sort out any items that needed spot cleaning or mending, and bag up anything especially threadbare for the church jumble sale.

As they said their goodbyes in the hallway, Gretchen became suddenly serious and confiding.

"You've been so thoughtful to Margaret and I know she likes you very much . . ."

"Oh, it was nothing, really," said Jean, wanting no reminders of the rabbit. "Buying a pet is easy. The hard work of caring for it will be all yours."

"Well, I'd like to think you would be a friend to Margaret. If anything happened to me. I'd be glad to think you would be someone she could turn to."

"Why should anything happen to you?" Jean asked, alarmed by the dark tone of this conversation. "You're not ill, are you?"

"No, no, of course not," Gretchen laughed. "Look at me!" She flapped her arms and made a little jump on the spot as if that somehow demonstrated rude health.

"Why do you say that, then?" Jean insisted. "Did something come up in the blood tests to make you concerned?"

"No, not at all. I promise. I was just thinking that it's a shame Margaret doesn't have any aunts or godmothers and that you seem to understand her so well. That's all."

"Of course, I've become very fond of Margaret and I'd be very happy to be a . . . special friend to her," said Jean, flattered but still uneasy.

"I think you'd be a good influence—someone she could look up to and respect. Girls don't always like to take advice from their mothers. And perhaps mothers don't always give the best advice."

Touched by this sudden acceleration in their friendship, Jean found herself tongue-tied. The idea of spending more time with Margaret, becoming perhaps a secular godparent, or unofficial "auntie," who might be permitted to take her on outings and spoil her, was everything she could have hoped for.

Mistaking her hesitation for reluctance, Gretchen said, "Perhaps I'm asking too much, too soon."

"Oh, not at all," Jean stammered. "I was just thinking, perhaps, with your permission, I could take her out now and then, to museums or concerts, if she was interested in that sort of thing."

She remembered her "aunt" Rosa, the rides in taxis and the alarming food and the sense of being singled out for special treatment.

"That would be lovely."

"I could even take her to the *Echo*, to see how a newspaper is made." She warmed to her theme, dismissing in her enthusiasm the looming obstacle of her mother, which lay like a boulder across her path. "Perhaps not the paper," she conceded, remembering the lively language of Bill and Larry and the subs. "But if you and Howard ever need a babysitter so that you could go out together sometime, then I could do that, too."

Gretchen smiled. "All of those things," she said. "I think it's a wonderful idea."

14

"You seem cheerful lately," said Roy Drake as Jean swept into the editorial meeting, early for once, and deposited her pile of papers on the desk. "Is anything the matter?"

"Very funny."

"You have a spring in your step. And a new dress, if I'm not mistaken."

They were the first to arrive and had the room to themselves; otherwise he would not have commented.

Jean gave a model's twirl. "Thank you for noticing. It's couture, you know. Not off the rack."

He raised his eyebrows.

"Mrs. Tilbury made it for me. She's an expert needlewoman as well as a Virgin Mother."

"Hmm. Accepting gifts from sources. That'll have to go before the board."

She laughed.

"Very smart, anyway."

"It's amazing the difference it makes when something actually fits."

Howard had dropped the dress off, wrapped in tissue paper, while Jean was still at work.

"That man came round with a parcel for you." Her mother had described the incident with a slight pursing of the lips, but she had relented when she saw the workmanship. It was so beautifully made—not a raw edge to be seen, French binding on every seam—you could have worn it inside out. "You'll be wanting to save it for best," she remarked.

"I don't have any *best* to save it for," Jean replied. "I'm going to wear it to work."

At the meeting, the main subject for discussion was the change in layout, moving the entertainments, listings, marriage lines, household hints, gardening, Pam's Piece, features and fashion to the middle pages (displacing "news from the estates" and motoring). This would then form an eight-page section, aimed chiefly at women, which could be detached from the main body of the paper. It was felt that this would enable couples to share and enjoy the *Echo* more harmoniously. The mailbag was split between those who viewed all change with hostility (the majority), those who approved of the principle of the supplement section but had alternative suggestions for its content based on their own preferences and those (few) who were in favor of the new layout.

After some debate it was decided to proceed as planned. Time, Roy's argument ran, would deal with the opponents of change. The new and threatening would become the old and familiar in due course. The second group's needs were too diverse and conflicting ever to be successfully addressed. That left the third and smallest group to carry the day.

The matter settled, it was Jean's turn to give an update on Our Lady of Sidcup, as Larry styled it. Her frequent absences from the office had been noted and Roy felt the rest of the team deserved a report on the progress of the medical investigations.

"You might remember, but we approached this story with some skepticism," Jean said, "imagining that it would be quite quickly dismissed."

Heads nodded. Most of those present had in truth imagined that this is exactly what had happened, weeks ago, and were surprised that the story was still live.

"I've investigated the woman's claims and interviewed various people connected with her during the crucial period, and I can't find anything that undermines her version of events. For what it's worth, I find myself inclined to believe her. What is more significant, though, is the results of various tests that she and her daughter have had at Charing Cross Hospital to try to prove beyond doubt that parthenogenesis—that's virgin birth to you—occurred. And, so far so good."

She was aware as she spoke that her colleagues had grown quiet and attentive. During the debate on the new layout there had been the usual distracted fidgeting, fiddling with pens and lighters, the grinding out of cigarettes, but they were all now focused on her.

"The blood tests were compatible, and," she looked down at her papers to the most recent letter from Dr. Lloyd-Jones, "I'm quoting the doctor here—in the 'taste test,' both mother and daughter could taste phenylthiocarbamide at exactly the same threshold value of 2:54 mg per liter. This is significant. In the saliva test, both mother and daughter were 'non-secretors' and produced identical titers after treating their saliva samples against an anti-A antiserum."

"Does this amount to proof?" asked Bill.

"Not 100 percent." She referred back to her notes. "The probability of this kind of agreement if there was a father involved is less than 0.01 percent. There is one more serum test and then if they pass that, the clincher is a skin graft, but obviously they wouldn't proceed with that if any of the previous tests failed."

"The really persuasive thing as I understand it," said Roy, entering the discussion for the first time, "is that Mrs. Tilbury presented herself as an example of a virgin mother before she was aware of the results of these tests and not the other way around."

"Yes, exactly," said Jean.

"Does the lady herself know the outcome of the tests now?" Larry wanted to know.

Jean nodded. "She's been kept informed at every stage. The doctor leading the project was adamant that results should not be withheld from her."

"What's to stop her, having proved her case at our expense, so to speak, running off to one of the nationals with her story? Has she signed any kind of exclusivity contract yet?"

"No," said Jean. "It's not necessary. She isn't the least bit interested in money or notoriety."

"She might be," said Larry. "If she knew how much was available."

"I've built up a relationship with her. She trusts me and I trust her. However," she turned to Roy, "if you think it's necessary, I'm prepared to ask her to sign something."

Roy looked at her over his glasses, considering.

"But," she went on, "I think it would bring the issue of money to the foreground and possibly damage our relationship, so I'd be against it on those grounds."

"I agree with Larry up to a point. It's not much to ask. But on this occasion, I'm going to trust Jean's judgment."

"Thank you," said Jean.

"What about the medics? Are they sound?" Larry asked.

"They are already operating under a code of patient confidentiality," Jean assured him. "They know that eventually the research will be theirs to publish and own if it has any scientific value. And unlike us, they don't expect everything to be done by yesterday."

"Suffice to say that in their cautious, academic way they are intrigued," said Roy.

"So they ought to be," said Bill. "It's a hell of a story."

"All credit to Jean," said Larry, and there was some appreciative thumping on the table, which she hushed with a raised hand.

"We're not there yet, folks."

"While we're showing appreciation," said Roy, "honorable mention also to the new tone of Pam's Piece."

"Why, what's happened to it?" Bill wanted to know.

"It's warmer, more reflective," said Roy.

"As you'd know if you ever actually read the paper," said Jean to general laughter.

He was lazy, she thought. Cut corners and did the absolute minimum, but he was always affable, quick to put his hand in his wallet, and for that reason you couldn't dislike him.

Later that afternoon he wandered over to her desk, where she was at work on a new Pam's Piece entitled "The Unofficial Aunt."

"Me and the lads are going over to the Black Horse for a quick one after work if you're interested. It's young Tony's birthday."

Young Tony was the new photographer. Jean had spoken to him only recently about taking some pictures of Gretchen and Margaret. He was only twenty-five or so and bounced as he walked as though in sprung shoes. (Old Tony was one of the subs. An alcoholic, he never went to the pub.)

"I know you generally like to get home, but I thought I'd ask."

"Sorry," said Jean. "It's my mother. But thanks for asking."

It was even less possible now: all opportunities for recreational absences had to be carefully preserved for the Tilburys.

15

Jean was up a stepladder in the front room, re-hanging the curtains, when she saw Mrs. Melsom approaching the house. It was
one of those jobs that should have been done in spring but was
somehow always neglected until late summer. The red damask
drapes, heavy with dust, had been hung over the washing line and
shaken and brushed before being left to convalesce in the fresh air
for a few hours to rid them of their stale smell.

"That tiresome woman," her mother said, looking up from her
letter writing. "What does she want?"

"Why do you say that?" Jean asked, hopping down from the
ladder. "She's perfectly nice."

Tiresome or not, she was Jean's best chance of achieving a
few hours of freedom at weekends, if only her mother would be
more agreeable. Since that first visit, Jean had tried to cultivate
Mrs. Melsom's acquaintance on her mother's behalf by calling
round with a bag of runner beans from the garden, on the pretext
that they had a glut.

"It was so kind of you to come and sit with her; Mother enjoyed it so much," she had said, hoping to prompt a repeat offer.

She didn't realize that her mother had already—so soon—taken
a dislike to the poor woman, but it was entirely predictable. Even

before she had made herself a recluse, she had a history of taking up new friends and then discarding them, usually over some imagined slight. Her fallings-out were swift and permanent; the casualties numerous. The rift with the church knitters was only one example.

Mrs. Melsom stood on the doorstep wearing a faded summer dress and a crushed straw hat, holding a Pyrex bowl of raspberries.

"I brought these for your mother," she said. "She mentioned how much she likes them and ours have done well. We've more than we can eat."

"That's very thoughtful of you," said Jean, accepting the bowl. "Won't you come in?"

"Who is it?" came her mother's fluting voice.

Jean glared at her mother over Mrs. Melsom's straw-hatted head as she showed the visitor into the front room.

"Look, Mother," she said, holding out the raspberries for her inspection as though they were an offering to pacify a peevish deity. "Isn't that kind?"

"They'll do nicely for tea," her mother conceded, screwing the cap back on her fountain pen.

She was a fussy eater and liked her little treats. Mrs. Melsom had, perhaps unwittingly, hit on the surest way to gain her approval.

"Hello, Mrs. Swinney," Mrs. Melsom said in that artificially high, bright voice used to address the hard of hearing or imbeciles. "I see you're doing your paperwork."

"I have a mountain of letters to write," the old lady replied, tapping her notepad.

Jean blinked in surprise. Apart from Dorrie, her mother's only other regular correspondent was an old friend in Toronto. The protective barrier of ocean between them had saved this from going the way of other relationships.

"The problem is thinking of things to say," she added, the mask slipping for a moment. "When you don't do much."

"Well, I was wondering if I could tempt you out of the house on Saturday," Mrs. Melsom said, casting a wary glance at Jean. "The Mothers' Union are doing a strawberry tea at the village hall. The handbell ringers are giving a little concert and there'll be a swap meet. It should be rather a nice afternoon." She put her head on one side.

Jean's mother looked momentarily panicked. "Oh, I think it might be too much for me," she said.

"Of course it won't," Jean exclaimed. "It sounds lovely."

"We'll find you a comfy seat—you don't have to make conversation if you'd rather not."

Jean couldn't now remember if she'd briefed Mrs. Melsom about her mother's social anxieties, or whether this was something that had become apparent during their tea together.

"It's the walking," her mother said, shaking her head firmly. "I'm not steady enough."

"My husband will take us in the Riley," said Mrs. Melsom. "Door to door."

"There," said Jean. "What could be nicer?"

"Well I suppose if you're coming, too," said her mother.

This wasn't the outcome Jean was hoping for.

"The invitation is for *you*, Mother," she said, shooting Mrs. Melsom a supplicating glance. "It would be so good for you to get out of the house."

She hadn't wanted to use this form of words. Nothing that was presented as being "good for you" was likely to hold much appeal. She almost wondered whether it would be worth enduring a strawberry tea and swap meet just to induct her mother gradually into a new world of extramural activities. But the immediate possibility of a free Saturday was too tempting.

"Well, you think about it and let me know," Mrs. Melsom said.

Jean felt the prospect of liberty slipping away. If she didn't settle the matter now, with Mrs. Melsom still here providing additional traction, the battle would be lost.

"You might find you enjoy yourself. And it will be something to tell Dorrie in your next letter."

Her mother wagged her hand as though waving a white flag. "Oh, all right. If you're so set on it."

Mrs. Melsom, to her great credit, refused to take offense at this ungracious response but beamed as though on the receiving end of a huge favor.

I will make it up to you somehow, Jean thought. She had no great confidence in the long-term success of the experiment. It was too much to hope for that her mother might make and keep a friend, and find some source of entertainment or comfort beyond herself and their four walls.

"I suppose you'll be off gallivanting with your new friends while I'm out," said her mother astutely as soon as the door was closed on the visitor. "They seem to be making quite a project of you, for some reason."

"If I am 'gallivanting,'" said Jean, magnanimous in her victory, "surely it's better I do it while you are out having fun yourself than when you are on your own here."

"*Fun?*" said her mother with a kind of shudder. "A lot of silly women more like."

"I'm sure they're not all silly. Mrs. Melsom is perfectly decent."

"As long as they don't try to get me on some kind of committee. You know what those churchy women are like when they get their claws into you."

Jean laughed. "You do exaggerate! It's the Mothers' Union, not a pack of wild beasts."

"I didn't see you volunteering to get involved."

"I'm not a mother," Jean said.

16

....

Pam's Piece

THE UNOFFICIAL AUNT

Can there be any category of women more derided than the maiden aunt? Having missed out on marriage and motherhood owing to a post-war shortage of men, she is regarded as both comic and tragic. Prudish and easily shocked, suspicious of anything modern, fond of cats and the local curate, she is to be pitied but also mocked. She dithered in the margins of literature like Jane Austen's foolish Miss Bates, until Agatha Christie raised up Jane Marple to be her heroine—the maiden aunt's natural nosiness and apparent harmlessness making her an ideal detective.

But there is a new breed of unmarried women at large now—modern, educated women with money and careers of their own—and hard-pressed parents are reaping the benefits.

These women have the time and energy to be "unofficial aunts" to their friends' or neighbors' children. What could be more rewarding and mutually beneficial?

The young person acquires a wise counselor and confidante, unburdened by parental expectations. The childless woman enjoys a fleeting taste of the joys of parenthood and acquires a greater understanding of the younger generation. The parents gain some time for their own pursuits. Everybody wins!

....

The jaunty notes of Rondo Alla Turca filled the church of St. Mary le Strand, the vibrations from the piano rattling the flowers in the slender wooden plinth below the lectern. Left over from the previous week's wedding, Jean thought, fanning herself with the printed program. They had walked through a mush of paper confetti at the entrance. Beside her sat Margaret, swinging her legs, encased in white socks and navy T-bar sandals, in time to the music. On her lap was a bag of toffees. Jean had taken the precaution of unwrapping them all beforehand so they wouldn't rustle. Now, they had softened and fused in the heat, and were proving difficult to pry apart.

Her father had taken her to just such an afternoon concert when she was a girl. She hadn't enjoyed the music much then—and didn't now, in truth. It was the experience of a special day out with just her father that was precious to her in its rarity. A piano recital had seemed a good idea to inaugurate these outings with Margaret—something to encourage her in her music lessons—but she sensed the little girl was bored.

It was rather a long program and the pews were hard. The rest of the audience were mostly even older than Jean—regulars, perhaps—and there were no other children. She would probably rather be back home playing with the rabbit, Jean thought. Perhaps this is not a treat to her at all but an awful chore, to be suffered to please her mother. And yet when she had arrived at the house in Sidcup at midday to pick Margaret up she had found the little girl dressed in her best clothes, in a state of eager expectation.

Gretchen herself seemed almost equally excited on their behalf and Jean felt a momentary twinge of guilt that she was being excluded from their adventure.

"Will you be all right without me, Mummy?" Margaret asked as they were about to leave, her voice suddenly serious.

"I will try to cope as best I can." Gretchen laughed, kissing her daughter's shiny cheek.

"If you get lonely there's always Jemimah."

"Thank you, I'll bear it in mind."

There was a brief pause after the Mozart before the Rachmaninov while the pianist left the transept to gather herself together, perhaps, or have a drink of water. The air was dry and dusty; particles shimmered in the shafts of light from the high windows, catching in the throat.

"Is it over?" Margaret whispered over the applause in a voice that seemed to carry more hope than regret.

Jean stood up, gesturing Margaret to follow her, and they crept out of the pew and down the aisle, slipping through the heavy west door into the dazzling sunshine and sudden clamor of the street.

"I'd had enough, hadn't you?" Jean said when they were safely away from the silent precincts of the church.

She had never walked out in the middle of a recital or any other kind of performance before and felt almost dizzy at her own daring. Even if you weren't enjoying yourself it was still a waste, and therefore a sin against thrift—the only kind of religion Jean practiced.

Margaret nodded. "I liked that last tune but it was quite long."

"You could play like that one day, you know."

Margaret shook her head, screwing up her face in horrified denial.

"That woman in there was once just like you—learning her scales, doing her practice; she wasn't born playing like that."

"I don't like playing in front of people. As soon as people start listening I make mistakes. I like singing. You don't have to make the notes; they're already inside you."

She was full of these charming and unexpected comments—at once innocent and profound. Questions seemed to bubble up out of her, prompted by anything or nothing. "Do you think Jemimah likes me? I mean, do you think rabbits can actually like people?" "When you look at the sky do you think you see the same color as me?" "If you've had one baby does it mean you can definitely have another one?" Jean wasn't sure how to answer this last one without getting into complicated matters of human fertility, far beyond her remit as unofficial aunt. Given Margaret's own curious provenance, it was safer to say, "Not always. Babies don't always come along when you want them to."

They walked along the Strand in search of refreshment. Margaret was carrying a small shoulder bag—a child-sized version similar to one used by Gretchen—swinging it at ankle-height. Now and then it caught Jean on the back of the leg.

"That's a dear little bag," said Jean, sidestepping to avoid another swipe. "What do you keep in it?"

Margaret hoisted it over her head and across her body like a postman's sack before opening it up to display the contents.

"Handkerchief, purse, toffees, notebook, pencil."

"What's the notebook for?"

"It's for when the angel voices say a word I don't know, so I can write it down and look it up later."

"Oh," said Jean. She hadn't meant to ask about her voices. Gretchen had said it was best to make nothing of it, but the matter had come up quite naturally. "Have you heard from them lately?" She might have been asking about a pen pal or distant relative.

"They've been a bit quiet since I got Jemimah. I think they're jealous."

"Possibly," said Jean, struggling to imagine the human weaknesses of these phantom whisperers. Perhaps it was just loneliness speaking. Perhaps Jemimah really might be a "cure."

Margaret took out the spiral notebook and flipped it open at the most recent entry.

"Administrator, malfeasance, ormolu," she read, stumbling over the syllables.

"Good heavens. I'm not sure I understand all of those words myself," said Jean, wondering again how Gretchen could accept this bizarre phenomenon with such equanimity. If it was down to her she would be all over it until she had these "angels" under a microscope. "You'll have a splendid vocabulary if this keeps up."

"My teacher Mrs. Garpitt said I've got a reading age of thirteen," Margaret replied.

Jean could tell she was desperate to tell someone of this accolade but at the same time embarrassed to be thought boastful.

"At least, I'd say," said Jean. "Shall we have tea at Simpson's? I've got a terrible thirst after all those toffees."

She was rewarded with a broad smile.

The waiter showed them upstairs to the ladies' dining room, to a table on the far side of the large, high-ceilinged room, at some distance from the concentration of other diners. Jean had a suspicion they were being put out of the way and was rather gratified when Margaret pointed toward a group of elegantly dressed women near the window and said in his hearing, "That was where we sat last time."

It was some years since Jean had eaten anywhere smart and she had to hide her surprise at the prices—five shillings for a slice of strudel!

She ordered a pot of tea with scones and jam and Margaret chose a strawberry millefeuille from a trolley of pastries, with a glass of milk. The sight of the strawberries reminded her of her mother and she wondered how she was coping in the village hall.

Her stomach gave a squeeze of anxiety at the prospect of the recriminations that might follow an unsuccessful afternoon.

The scone when it arrived was warm, crumbly and scented
with rose water. It came with a dish of strawberry jam and some
double cream whipped almost to butter. I could easily make these
at home, Jean thought, but I never do. She would always rather
be in the garden than in the kitchen in the summer. Margaret
was deconstructing her millefeuille, eating it from the top down,
one layer at a time.

"You could just attack it with a fork," Jean suggested, observing her struggles.

"But all the insides will squish out," said Margaret. "It is lovely,
though." She rolled her eyes appreciatively.

She had managed to get cream all over her fingers and a smudge
of icing sugar on her cheek. It was a delight to Jean to witness
her childish pleasure in things; that interlude between the dawning of consciousness and the onset of self-consciousness was so
brief. Margaret was now ten; there were perhaps two more years
at most.

"What would you like to do after this?" Jean asked, helping
herself to more tea. An art gallery might be pushing things. You
could have too much culture.

Margaret looked shy. "Shall I tell you what I'd like to do
most?"

"Yes, please do."

"I'd like to go and surprise Daddy at his shop."

"Oh." This wasn't what Jean had been expecting and she had
no ready excuse to hand, so she said, "Well, all right. If that's
what you'd like. But if he's busy with customers we'll have to
keep out of the way."

When the bill came, Margaret produced a small beaded purse
from her shoulder bag and tried to give Jean a shilling.

"Mummy gave me some money to pay for things," she said.

"Oh no," said Jean, laughing. "That isn't how it works at all. This is my treat."

Margaret accepted this as she did all of Jean's utterances and dropped the coin back in her purse.

It was only a short walk to Bedford Street and Jean felt her spirits lift at the first glimpse of the bottle-green shop front and the gold painted sign. A Silver Cross pram was parked on the pavement outside; a baby in a blue knitted romper was kicking vigorously at his blankets and chewing on his fist. One cheek was fiery red with toothache. Jean and Margaret stopped to chatter to him until the mother emerged from the shop next door and bore him away.

Howard was in conversation with a man by the till and didn't notice the visitors peering through the window. Even when they opened the door, setting the bell jangling, it was a second or two before he recognized his own daughter, and then his face broke into a smile of surprise and pleasure.

"I don't know what she'd like," the customer was saying, peering helplessly at the velvet trays of necklaces and bracelets laid out on the display case. "They all look much the same to me."

"Perhaps this lady can advise you," said Howard, indicating Jean. "She can bring a feminine perspective."

The man, who was in his late twenties, perhaps, with a haircut of military severity, looked at her with helpless gratitude.

"But be warned, she has very expensive taste," he added.

"That is quite untrue," Jean assured the customer, who was now looking rather confused. "I know next to nothing about jewelry. But I can tell you which one I think is the prettiest."

She indicated a delicate silver bracelet, dotted with moonstones— the cheapest of all the exhibits, though this was not, for once, a consideration.

"I like this one," said Margaret, pointing a nibbled finger at a more ostentatious and costly ruby pendant.

"That's lovely too," Jean agreed, realizing that she had hardly done Howard a favor by recommending the one with the modest price tag.

"Yes. Perhaps a ruby," the young man said. "I think it sends the right signals."

Howard's lips twitched and Jean looked away, feigning sudden interest in a display of gentlemen's wristwatches.

"There are actually matching earrings," said Margaret. "You could get those, too."

"Good heavens, Margaret," said Howard. "I'm afraid this young lady is my daughter," he explained. "And therefore not an entirely disinterested party."

"Quite the saleswoman already!" said the man, and almost seemed persuaded to take them until it occurred to him that he couldn't now be sure whether his fiancée had pierced earlobes. The fact that he couldn't remember this detail troubled him. "You'd think I'd have noticed a thing like that," he said, shaking his head as Howard polished the ruby pendant and put it in a velvet box.

The box went inside an elegant green bag with handles of satin ribbon. Jean felt a surge of envy for this unknown young woman, soon to be the recipient of such a lavish gift. Although she could not imagine any circumstance in which she would be able to wear a ruby pendant, it would be an exciting addition to her drawer of treasures.

Margaret was staring with unembarrassed interest as the man produced four new five-pound notes from his wallet and laid them on the counter with what was almost a shiver of reluctance. Jean could sense his anxiety at parting with such a large sum of money all at once. It would take her nearly a month to earn it.

"Well done, you two!" said Howard when the customer had gone on his way, carrying the dainty bag a trifle self-consciously, having failed in his attempt to squash it into his pocket. "That's the best sale I've made all day."

"I take no credit," said Jean. "I don't think I have any knack for selling."

"I'm not sure I have, either," Howard admitted. "Which is unfortunate."

"I think to be a convincing salesperson you have to be a spender yourself. I'm far too careful."

"I used to like buying toys, but now I've got Jemimah I don't need anything else," said Margaret piously.

"Oh yes, Jemimah's been a great success," Howard said to Jean. "I can't think how we got by without her. Now, we just sit around bitterly regretting the wasted rabbit-less years."

Jean smiled. He had such a droll way of speaking that it was a pleasure to be teased by him. She thought again of their first meeting; how awkward and unimpressive she had found him, and how unworthy of his pretty young wife. Now, she felt the good fortune was all on Gretchen's side. He was by some stretch the nicest man she had ever met.

It also occurred to her that his first impression of her might not have been especially favorable. She had no illusions or anxieties about her own lack of physical beauty; her ordinariness, in fact, grew less irksome with every passing year. It had been dispiriting to be plain at twenty, but by forty it hardly mattered. Time had caught up with most of her prettier contemporaries and those with the most to lose seemed to feel its depredations the hardest.

The arrival of another customer, a woman whose immaculate hair, hat, gloves and fashionable suit seemed suggestive of a promising combination of wealth and vanity, signaled to Jean that it was time to depart. Affecting the air of satisfied shoppers, she and Margaret slipped out with a discreet goodbye.

"I wonder if Mummy's been all right," said Margaret, twirling her handbag as they walked down Bedford Street in the direction of Charing Cross. "She promised she'd make *spitzbuben* for tea."

"What's *spitzbuben*?"

"They're jam cookies."

"I've learned so many new words today," Jean mused. "Ormolu. *Spitzbuben*. I shall need a notebook of my own to keep track of them."

"You must decide where you want to go on our next outing," said Jean as they approached 7 Burdett Road. "Maybe the zoo, if you haven't been recently?"

"I'd like to go swimming," Margaret said. "But only if you come in the water with me. It doesn't count if you just sit on the side and watch."

"I'm happy to go swimming," said Jean.

"Mummy doesn't like it, so we never go."

Maybe it was something to do with being Swiss and landlocked, Jean thought. Although there was surely no shortage of lakes.

She offered this theory to Margaret, who considered it judiciously and then said, "No. She just doesn't like getting her hair wet."

At first it seemed as though there was no one at home. The side gate—the usual point of entry—was bolted, but when they rang the doorbell and peered through the stained glass, there was Gretchen coming down the stairs towards them with a basket of ironing under one arm.

"You're all hot," said Margaret, disengaging herself from her mother's welcoming hug.

"Sorry," she replied a little breathlessly, fanning herself with the skirt of her pinafore. "I've been busy."

"Did you make the *spitzbuben*?"

Gretchen's face fell. "Oh no. I didn't. I got caught up with other things."

Margaret screwed her face into the most furious knot of displeasure.

"I'll make them this evening, when I've done the ironing," her mother promised.

"But I wanted to give Jean one."

"Poor Mummy," said Jean, feeling that Margaret was being rather unreasonable. Spoiled even, though it pained her to think the word. "She's been slaving away all afternoon while we've been out having tea at Simpson's."

"Really—Simpson's? Margaret, you little monkey! You hardly need *spitzbuben* as well."

Margaret looked suitably sheepish. She was a good-hearted girl really, thought Jean, and was easily corrected.

"And we called on Daddy at the shop. We helped him to sell a ruby necklace for twenty pounds!"

Gretchen glanced at Jean. "Oh, did you? That's a nice idea. I bet he was surprised to see you."

Jean hoped it was apparent that the nice idea had been all Margaret's, but it would have been making too much of it, she felt, to raise the matter. She couldn't linger anyway; there was her mother and the postmortem of the strawberry tea to be faced, so she said goodbye to Margaret, who was eager to get outside and commune with Jemimah.

As soon as the two women were alone though, it was Gretchen who brought it up again.

"I'm so glad you went to see Howard," she said. "He likes you very much, you know, and it's so good for him to have a woman friend to talk to."

She was so emphatic in her approval that Jean began to suspect her of meaning quite the reverse. It was funny, too, that Howard had described the benefits of Jean's influence on Gretchen in much the same terms. She remembered her mother's jealous remark: "They seem to be making quite a project of you, for some reason."

17

September 1957

Dear Jean,

I wonder if you would be free to come on a little family outing next Sunday to Howard's Aunt Edie near Maidstone. We go every year to harvest her apples and cobnuts. She has a wonderful garden for tennis and a picnic and it's always a lovely day out.

I do hope you can join us.

With good wishes,

Gretchen

The day after this letter arrived saw Jean once again paying court to Mrs. Melsom. She took with her a gift of runner beans and tomatoes from their own vegetable patch, and some plums and red currants, which Gretchen had foisted on her the week before. Mrs. Melsom was out in her front garden, kneeling on a hassock filched from the church to weed the flower beds. At Jean's approach and in spite of her protestations, she hauled herself up to standing using the garden fork.

"I've a little favor to ask," Jean said as soon as the offering of fruit and vegetables had been accepted. "I'm away for the day next Sunday and wondered if you'd be able to just look in on Mother at some point. She doesn't seem to take to anyone but you." She almost blushed at her own shamelessness.

Mrs. Melsom wiped soil-dusted hands on her skirt and leaned on the fork for a moment to recover her breath.

"Of course, dear. I was only saying to Mr. Melsom that we should take her out for a drive in the Riley one day."

"Well, that would be wonderful. She had such a lovely time at the strawberry tea."

This was not too violent a distortion of the truth. Mrs. Swinney had not been nearly as critical of the event as Jean had feared, declaring it, "Bearable, I suppose."

"Did she? I'm so glad. I wasn't sure. I thought it might have been a bit noisy for her, but she seemed to enjoy the strawberries."

"Oh yes, there's nothing wrong with her appetite," said Jean, wondering if Mrs. Melsom was hinting at a degree of over-indulgence. Although keenly alert to her mother's faults, it still pained Jean to think others might notice and judge them.

It was left with Mrs. Melsom to discuss with her husband the possibility of a drive out into the countryside on Sunday. Jean went home with her usual unsettling combination of a light heart and a heavy conscience, made heavier by her dawning awareness that the impetus behind these plans and schemes was, above all else, the thought of seeing Howard.

On the appointed morning, Jean's mother, having been briefed and coached into a positive frame of mind for most of the previous evening, woke after a poor night's sleep and seemed about to cry off the outing. It took all of Jean's patience and encouragement to cajole her into compliance, until at last she was dressed and brushed and painted and loaded into the Riley, as though into a tumbrel for her final journey.

When Jean arrived at the Tilburys', Howard was on the drive-way, pumping up one of the tires on the Wolseley, while in the kitchen Gretchen packed a picnic basket with enough food for ten hungry men. Veal and ham pie, chicken, chopped-egg sandwiches, the infamous *spitzbuben*, split scones, Aunt Edie's favorite *zopf* bread—a Swiss plaited loaf that was one of Gretchen's specialities—and tomatoes and plums from the garden.

She was wearing one of her own creations—a cotton lawn sundress with a gathered skirt in a bold poppy print. Jean, who had inferred from the invitation that manual labour and tree climbing would be required, was dressed in twill trousers, a short-sleeved shirt and gym shoes.

"I feel a bit of a mess," she said. "I thought I'd be shinnying up tree trunks."

"Oh, I always leave that to Howard and Margaret," said Gretchen. "But you look fine. Aunt Edie's very informal."

Margaret wandered in, clutching two tennis rackets and looking whey-faced and queasy; quite unlike her ebullient self. She watched her mother's preparations for a minute or two without enthusiasm.

"I can't find any tennis balls and I've got a tummy ache," she said.

"The balls are in the cupboard under the stairs," said Gretchen. "I saw them there the other day. Are you all right?" she added, taking in her daughter's wan expression. "You're very pale."

Margaret responded to this inquiry by dropping the tennis rackets and bolting from the room with a hand over her mouth. The sound of pounding feet on the stairs was followed moments later by distant retching.

The two women exchanged looks of alarm and Gretchen hurried to investigate, leaving Jean standing in the kitchen feeling upset. The outing would surely not go ahead now, postponed for another day, requiring another favor from Mrs. Melsom, pushing Jean's level of indebtedness even further into the red.

Howard came in from the driveway holding out hands smudged with grease.

"All set," he said. "Tires pumped. Oil and water topped up. Tool kit in the trunk. How are things coming along in the catering division?"

"There's been a setback," said Jean. "I think Margaret's been sick. She said she was feeling poorly and then rushed upstairs."

"She didn't eat her breakfast this morning," said Howard. "I thought that was odd. Poor old Maggie."

Gretchen rejoined them, looking harassed. "Well, she's not going anywhere," she said.

"Poor thing," said Jean, trying to master her own disappointment at the cancellation of the trip, in the face of Margaret's greater misfortune. "Is she all right?"

"An upset tummy, I think. I've put her to bed. What a pity—it's such a lovely day, too."

"I'd better run down to the phone booth and see if I can get hold of Aunt Edie," said Howard. "Postpone for another day."

"Oh, you can't let her down at the last minute," Gretchen protested. "She'll have been to all sorts of trouble. And the apples have got to be picked. You two go—I'll stay here with Margaret."

"But that's such a shame for you, Gretchen," said Jean. "Why don't I stay with Margaret?"

She felt she knew the little girl quite well enough by now to make this offer. Since the trip to Simpson's they had had two subsequent outings—once to the swimming baths at Beckenham, where Jean had shown a commendable willingness to get her hair wet, and once to the Swinneys' house, where they had made cinder toffee. Both events had passed off successfully and even Jean's mother, initially suspicious of any new acquaintances, had conceded that Margaret was a "dear little thing."

"Oh no. I wouldn't leave her when she's unwell. You two must go. The picnic's all made and Aunt Edie will be so disappointed if no one turns up." She looked from Jean to Howard, beaming with pleasure at her sacrifice.

Jean felt a flutter of uncertainty. Was Gretchen really packing her off for a jaunt with her husband?

As if reading her thoughts, Gretchen said, "You can put up with Howard for a day, can't you, Jean?"

"I'll try not to bore her to tears," said Howard humbly.

"And Aunt Edie is tremendous company. You'll love her."

"She won't think it odd—her nephew turning up with some strange woman?" Jean remarked.

"Oh no. She's a game old bird," laughed Gretchen.

She continued to wrap packets of sandwiches in greaseproof paper and tuck them into the already full hamper as Howard washed his hands at the sink.

"We surely won't need all this food now?" said Jean, aghast. "You must keep some of it for yourselves."

"Well, Margaret certainly won't be eating anything," said Gretchen, finally consenting to remove one slice of pie and a tomato from the banquet.

Having satisfied herself as to the sufficiency of the provisions, she fastened the buckles on the basket and began to scurry around collecting together the remaining equipment for the outing. Wooden crates for the apples, picnic blanket, tennis rackets and balls were all soon stowed in the trunk of the Wolseley and they were ready to go. Gretchen seemed quite invigorated by her efforts on their behalf and almost eager to see them off. Either she was relieved to be ducking out of an irksome family duty, which seemed most unlikely given her apparent enthusiasm for the outing, or . . . Jean was at a loss.

Even now, as the car was reversing out of the driveway, Gretchen came running after them, brandishing a wide-brimmed straw sun hat, which she passed through the front window to Jean.

"You'll need this or you'll burn," she panted. "It's going to be a scorcher."

As they drove off, at Howard's usual sober pace, Jean could

see Gretchen's diminishing figure in the wing mirror, waving goodbye and then turning back to the house, almost with a skip.

Even as an idle daydream, Jean had never dared to imagine an opportunity like this—to be alone with Howard for a whole day, with the complete and cheerful approval of Gretchen. She could hardly believe her good fortune.

It was warm and stuffy in the car, and Howard wound down his window, resting an elbow on the car door.

"Tell me if it's too breezy for you," he said, glancing at her hair whipping in the wind.

A silence descended—the not entirely comfortable silence of two shy-ish people who feel bound by politeness to make conversation but can think of nothing brilliant to say.

They proceeded for some miles, lost in their own thoughts, until at last Jean said, "I'm sorry, Howard. I'm very poor company. I'm no good at small talk."

"That's all right," he replied. "Neither am I. We shall have to make do with big talk, or no talk at all."

This seemed to break the spell of awkwardness and they exchanged a smile of relief before turning back to face the road ahead.

"Your wife is very unselfish," Jean said. "Most women would have been bitterly disappointed to miss a day out like this."

"Yes. Gretchen's a very uncomplaining sort. And she'd do anything for Margaret, of course. She's what you call 'a devoted mother.'"

"Did you ever think of having more children?" Jean asked. "You seem to be making such a good job of parenthood."

If it was an impertinent question, Howard gave no sign of taking offense.

"At one time," he replied. "In the early days we thought it might be nice for Margaret to have a brother or sister. And I think Gretchen assumed I would want a child of my own, so to speak.

That was never a concern for me—I feel Margaret is as much mine as any child could be."

"Of course."

"But it didn't happen. And somehow Gretchen wasn't surprised. I don't think she ever really believed she could have a child in the normal way."

"She's still young enough," said Jean. "She's not even thirty."

"But I'm not," said Howard. "And Margaret is too old now for a new baby to be much of a playmate."

"I suppose so."

"And in any case, it couldn't happen now," Howard said. His voice was barely audible above the noise of the engine.

"Oh." Jean remembered the single beds and the gap between them—close enough for hand-holding, but no more—and blushed.

"Gretchen and I haven't had that kind of relationship for some years now."

"I'm sorry. I didn't mean to pry. You always look like a perfect couple to me."

"Is there such a thing? I doubt it. But yes, we get along very well in our way."

"Gretchen is absolutely devoted to you," Jean insisted.

"Has she said so?"

"She doesn't need to—it's perfectly obvious."

She realized as she said this that it wouldn't do. What could she really know of Gretchen's feelings, when she could hardly bear to interrogate her own?

"I don't doubt that she loves me—like a brother, or a favorite uncle."

"Oh, more than that, surely!"

"Perhaps I'm exaggerating, but only a little. Not like a wife, anyway."

"Some men might take that as a license to stray."

"No doubt. But it would be shabby behavior, in my view."

"In any case, who can know what other wives are like? Or husbands, for that matter. Your . . . arrangement may not be unusual."

"You are very wise, Jean, but I sincerely hope you are wrong in this instance."

"Why?"

"Having experienced a proper marriage—if you'll allow that there is such a thing—at the beginning, I can only say that it would be a great pity if many people had to settle for what is a pale imitation."

"Some of us have to settle for far less than that," Jean retorted with some warmth. She wasn't sure anymore whether she was agreeing or disagreeing with him; it was as if he had taken a sledgehammer to a stained glass window. "Companionship and affection and family life—these things can't be easily discounted." She was aware that her voice was shaking. It was both a relief and a kind of torture to speak frankly for once.

"You are quite right. I'm not blaming Gretchen, by the way. I blame myself. I often wonder if she'd have done better to wait until she met someone she could fully love. But I was there, on the spot, so to speak, when there was a certain amount of urgency to provide Margaret with a father and a respectable upbringing. Her mother certainly thought so."

"You're not suggesting she was pressured into marriage against her will?" Jean protested. "Nobody who has seen you together could possibly think so."

"No, no, nothing as brutal as that. She accepted me gratefully, but now I think I did her a disservice in proposing when she was so vulnerable and her mother was dying. It was hardly a free choice."

"You talk as if the good fortune was all yours. Because she is young and pretty. But she is lucky to have you, too. Kind, decent men are scarce."

Of course he was better than just kind and decent, she

thought—words that hardly stirred the soul. He was the best man she knew and Gretchen the luckiest woman. But this could not be said.

"Are they?"

"In my experience."

She could call to mind only three—Roy Drake, Dorrie's husband, Kenneth, and Howard himself. Even her own father had fallen short in the end. To her dismay she found her eyes beginning to smart, and she turned away and stared out of the window at the green hedgerows until she had mastered herself. It wasn't sadness that prompted the threat of tears but a general sense of emotional fullness that always accompanied any attempt to discuss her inner life.

"I'm sorry to hear that, Jean," Howard said. "I'm sure you deserve much better."

"I don't know about that. I probably got exactly what I deserved. I seem to be attracted to precisely the sort of man who isn't husband material. Not my husband, anyway." She gave a hollow laugh.

"I hope I haven't upset you," he said. "I felt I could talk freely to you. I don't know why."

"You can. I'm glad you did."

"I suppose you give the impression that you don't judge people."

Jean had never thought of herself in this light before; sometimes, in fact, she caught herself out in some act of lofty disapproval and felt ashamed. Howard's confident assertion of her goodness made her the more determined to live up to it and be the broad-minded, tolerant person he thought her. I love him, she thought with a kind of wonderment. I never intended to, but now I do. The relief of admitting it to herself and accepting it as a fact that couldn't be dismissed or changed was like throwing off chains.

"Well, thank you. That's a nice thing to say," she said, keeping her voice steady.

It seemed impossible that he wouldn't notice her transformation, but he just gave her a quick smile and kept his eyes on the road, as a sensible man would.

They had left the suburbs behind now and were driving through the Kent countryside of sunken lanes and hedgerows tangled with honeysuckle and brambles and teeming with butterflies. At Shoreham, a stream ran through the middle of the village. A gang of children was wading bare-legged in the water with jam jars and nets; they turned as one and stared after the car with tribal hostility as it passed over the bridge.

The house was on the edge of the village, in a large, unkempt garden consisting mostly of shaggy lawn, with fruit trees and beds of straggling wildflowers. Beyond the trees a rustic tennis court had been shaved into the grass.

Aunt Edie was reclining on a wooden sun lounger, swathed in shawls in spite of the heat, which by now was shimmering, intense. She was drinking cider from a bottle and reading a Dashiell Hammett. It was hard to see exactly what she looked like, as her face was so crowded; as well as a yellow sun visor, she was wearing a pair of modern cat's-eye sunglasses over her regular spectacles and had a large sticking plaster across her nose. An elderly spaniel lay at her feet, stirring itself to aim a few dutiful yaps at the visitors before slumping back beside her.

"Hello, Auntie," said Howard, bending to kiss her powdery cheek. "This is Jean," was the extent of his explanation for Jean's substitution for his wife and daughter, and all that Aunt Edie seemed to require.

"You'll be thirsty, I expect. Help yourself to cider—you know where it is," she said, waving an arm toward the open back door.

While Howard went to fetch the drinks, Jean spread out the woolen blanket on the tussocky grass and sat, cross-legged, awaiting interrogation, but her hostess was serenely incurious. Jean was glad now of Gretchen's sun hat, as there was no shade where they sat and the trees were quite useless in this regard, with their lowest branches dipping almost to the ground. She was grateful, too, for the element of concealment, in case her recent upsurge of feeling was readable in her face.

"I like your getup," Aunt Edie said, laying aside her book and peering at Jean over both sets of glasses. "Very practical. I've never worn a pair of trousers. Do you think it's too late to start?"

"Not at all," said Jean. "I think you'd look elegant in trousers."

"Useful for cycling, I should think."

"You're not still roaring around the village on your bicycle?" said Howard, catching the end of this exchange as he returned with two bottles of cider. "I thought you were going to get rid of it after your accident."

Aunt Edie's hand strayed to her bandaged nose. "I admit, I was a bit shaken up. But I've decided I can't quite do without it. It's so useful for going to the library and so forth."

"Aunt Edie was in a collision with a horse trough," Howard explained. "It was the trough's fault, apparently."

She swatted him with Dashiell Hammett and he laughed.

"I wish my mother was as intrepid as you," said Jean.

She took a long swig from her bottle and gasped as it tore at her throat. It was strong and fiery and like no cider she had ever tasted.

"My aunt is one of a kind, I'm afraid," said Howard. "Comparisons are futile."

"Where are the gorgeous creatures today?" she asked, registering at last the change in personnel.

"Margaret was taken poorly this morning, so Gretchen has stayed behind to look after her. Both send their love."

"I have some bits and pieces for them. Don't go home without reminding me. I've been having a clear-out."

"Oh dear," said Howard, who had evidently been the beneficiary of this largesse before.

"Well, it will all be yours to deal with one day," said his aunt. "I'm just trying to cull as much as I can now."

"Oh, you'll outlive us all, surely."

"I will not," she replied tersely. "If you think I'm going to become one of those ancient old crones with a whiskery chin you can think again. I've got a loaded pistol in my bedroom. I shan't tell you where in case you try and get it off me. But I'll be using it when the time comes."

"You'll probably miss and shoot the paperboy or someone," said Howard mildly.

Jean was finding this exchange quite stimulating. She couldn't imagine such a conversation arising at home. Her mother shrank from any mention of death with violent superstition, as if to breathe his name was to invite him in. She took another tentative sip from her bottle and shivered.

"Is this last year's cider?" Howard asked, noticing Jean's struggles. "It's stronger than I remember."

Aunt Edie took the bottle from him and rolled her eyes. "You've picked up the apple brandy, you clown. You'll both be pie-eyed."

Jean lay back on the blanket and began to giggle. She felt quite light-headed.

It took them two hours to strip the trees of all but the most unreachable apples, which were left for Aunt Edie to gather as they fell. She wasted nothing: the best unblemished fruit was wrapped in newspaper, packed in crates and kept in a cool stone shed for use over the winter. The second best would be given to friends, exchanged with neighbors for potatoes and beans, donated to the village school, made into pie filling and bottled or kept for imminent consumption. The windfalls and damaged apples were sent to the farm for pressing.

Tree climbing was a new and exhilarating experience for Jean. With no brothers or male cousins, she and Dorrie had never been introduced to rowdy outdoor games. They had spent their child-hood in a second-floor flat in Gipsy Hill; by the time they moved to the house and garden in Hayes she was already an adult. Aunt Edie's trees were perfect for a beginner, with a framework of ac-cessible branches radiating like spokes from the trunk to provide steps and handholds.

Jean scrambled up as high as possible, made bold by brandy, until the boughs were too slender to take her weight. From her perch she dropped apples down to Aunt Edie, who was much nimbler than her previous prostration on the lounger had seemed to promise, and adept at catching them in a shawl tied around her waist. Chester, the spaniel, quivered and panted at her side.

Howard, with a basket contraption on his back, tackled the clusters of fruit on the outermost branches using a stepladder and fishing net. The cobnuts, being altogether less fragile, were thrown, shaken or knocked into the long grass, and then gath-ered into piles with a leaf rake and shoveled into burlap sacks.

For Jean, anesthetized by fierce sun and strong drink, the whole experience took on a misty, trancelike quality. When she finally climbed back down to earth she was surprised to notice her shirt torn and her bare arms striped with scratches. She had felt nothing.

Howard was astonished to learn that she had never eaten a cobnut, a deficiency he was determined to put right. While she unpacked the picnic, stepping uneasily into Gretchen's role, How-ard disappeared indoors and returned with a dish of salt and some nutcrackers.

"A cobnut has many layers," he said with great solemnity, "and you have to unwrap them all to reach the prize. Observe."

He stripped off the leafy outer case, cracked and discarded the shell, scratched off the woody skin and then finally rubbed away the inner membrane to reveal the kernel, naked and marble white. This he dipped in salt and presented to Jean on his open palm like a pearl on a cushion.

"So much effort for such a tiny morsel," said Jean. "Even worse than peeling a grape."

"There are no shortcuts," Howard insisted. "You have to re-move every layer or it tastes bitter."

Jean crushed the polished, ribbed nut gently between her teeth, allowing the flavor—a combination of buttery sap and new wood—to fill her mouth.

"It is lovely," she sighed. "But you would tire of peeling them long before you tired of eating them."

"It's self-limiting," Howard agreed. "You could hardly gorge on them. But that's part of the appeal."

He continued dutifully preparing a little mound of these delica-cies for Jean and Aunt Edie to share, taking none for himself.

"Gretchen has gone quite mad," Aunt Edie protested as Jean plied her with veal and ham pie, chicken, *zopf* bread, sandwiches and tomatoes from the hamper. "Does she think she is feeding the whole village?"

"This is only half of it," Jean said. "You need to leave room for the cake and biscuits."

"I have a horror of waste," said Aunt Edie with some asperity. "I can't help it."

"Well, Gretchen has a horror of want," said Howard. "Years of doing without take people in different ways, I suppose."

Jean felt a fresh surge of love for Howard for having defended Gretchen so tactfully against a mean-spirited remark, even when she was not there to appreciate it. It was the essence of the man, she thought, and absolutely typical of her twisted bloody luck that the very quality she admired most in him—loyalty to his wife—was the one that put him forever out of her reach.

He lay beside her on the blanket, defending the hamper from incursions by Chester and stroking the spaniel's silky ears. There was something intimate about sharing this bed-sized space; he felt it too, she was certain. The heat had stolen their appetite and they could hardly do justice to the picnic. Out of respect for Margaret, Jean forced herself to try one of the *spitzbuben*, a pair of cookies sandwiched with jam, which attracted a trio of persistent wasps. Having dispatched these pests with a rolled napkin, Howard removed the remains of the food to the cool of the pantry.

"I may fall asleep," Aunt Edie said to Jean while he was out of earshot. "But I expect you two will be able to entertain yourselves one way or another."

Jean wondered if there was any undertone to this remark and looked up sharply, but the old woman's expression, as far as it could be read behind its scaffolding of spectacles, was neutral.

"It's a pity Gretchen and Margaret couldn't come," she said firmly. "They're such fun."

Aunt Edie stared at her. "Margaret is an angel, of course, but for all her charms one would hardly call Gretchen *fun*."

She shut up smartly as Howard reappeared and closed her eyes. Jean thought she must be shamming, but within seconds a faint purring came from her parted lips.

"I see you've been keeping Auntie entertained," said Howard, picking up one of her trailing shawls and draping it across the top of the sunlounger so that it shaded her face.

"She was finding me scintillating company right up to the point where she fell asleep," Jean replied, fanning herself with Gretchen's hat. There was no breeze and the air was like molten metal.

"Let's find some shade," Howard suggested, helping Jean to her feet. "We could play tennis if it was a bit cooler, but I think it might kill me if you make me run around like you did on the badminton court."

"I seem to remember I was the one doing the running."

"The return match is very much overdue."

They walked between the fruit trees to the far end of the garden, past the shorn rectangle of tennis court, marked out with white paint.

"Who laid this out?" Jean wondered aloud. "Not Aunt Edie, surely?"

"She has an admirer in the village called Wally Noakes. He's about eighty but he does various manly jobs like pumping up her bicycle tires and mowing the lawn now and then, in exchange for . . . I don't know what."

"I do like her," said Jean. "She's very determined and spirited. She doesn't play the dotty old woman."

"I'm glad you like her. She's the only blood relative I've got."

"What will happen when she's too old to manage by herself? Will you have her to live with you?"

"I don't know. I suppose that would be up to Gretchen."

Howard had clearly never considered the matter. Care of the elderly was a woman's business, thought Jean, and not something men allowed to clutter their minds.

"Perhaps she'll get some kind of nurse to live in. Or maybe she really does have a pistol hidden among her corsets."

Beyond the tennis court at the farthest boundary of the garden was a stone bench, freckled with lichen, beneath a wooden arbor. An elderly wisteria gripped one of the weathered uprights in its coils and formed a canopy of leafy fronds, offering a pool of shade. Howard produced a clean handkerchief from his pocket and seemed about to lay it out on the bench for Jean's benefit, but she shook her head; her trousers were already scuffed with grass and bark, her shirt torn and grubby.

The bench was narrow; even when they sat at opposite ends the gap between them was barely a hand's span. Less, Jean thought, than the gap between two single beds. Howard offered her one of his cigarettes, lit with a match rasped along the rough stone, and they smoked in silence for a few moments.

Jean felt something dangerously close to happiness stealing over her; a realization that there was nowhere else she would rather be, and nothing she wanted that she didn't already have. But the moment of perfect contentment was no sooner acknowledged than it began to recede; already she was outside the moment, chasing it into the past. The silence continued, well beyond the point where it was comfortable.

"Gretchen and I were discussing you the other night," Howard said at last.

"Oh, really?" said Jean, blinking at him through the smoke.

"We agreed that you were a good thing."

She laughed. "Why thank you. I'm not sure about being a thing, but I'm glad I'm a good one."

"You've stirred us out of our routine."

"I have? I thought it was the other way about."

"Surely not. Your job must be infinitely various."

"No—it's remarkably repetitive. The same pages to be filled each week. It wasn't really interesting at all, until Gretchen."

"Well anyway. Our paths crossed and we're the better for it."

"Yes."

For a minute Jean allowed herself to contemplate an alternative reality in which they had never met and her life consisted of no more than the *Echo*, Mother, house, garden for all eternity. Considering the thousands of insignificant chances and choices and paths not taken that had led to their meeting, it was nothing less than a miracle.

"It's been a lovely day," she said, inadequately.

"It's not over yet. There's a game of tennis to be played first."

Jean had cooled down somewhat and was in any case happy to fall in with anything Howard suggested.

"I suppose you're going to pretend you haven't played since school," he said as they warmed up with a few gentle ground strokes.

"It's quite true," Jean replied as the ball glanced off the edge of her racket and away into the long grass. "But what I lack in practice I make up for in competitiveness."

"You would never tactically lose out of politeness?" he inquired, lobbing another ball gently into her half.

"Never," she replied. "I wouldn't think it polite to hand someone a victory they didn't deserve."

"Even a child, like Margaret, who might need the encouragement of a victory?"

"Children are a special case. But I'd rather teach her well so that she'd soon be good enough to win fair and square."

"Well then, let's play and give each other no quarter."

Howard won two sets easily without needing to exert himself. Jean only hit her stride in the second set, managing to get a few first serves in and hit an occasional winner, but by that time she was too hot and breathless to play on. When she looked at her watch she was surprised to see that it was nearly five. The hours in Howard's company had sped past. It would be six before they reached home even if they left now. She felt duty tugging at her with its remorseless grasp.

Seeing her glance at her watch, Howard said, "This might be a good time to make a move. If we get caught up with tea we could be hours."

"Yes," Jean agreed, both grateful and despondent. "There's Margaret to think of."

"And your mother."

Jean nodded. "I won't forget today."

This was no idle remark. In the days ahead she would think of little else, replaying their conversation and luxuriating in every remembered detail of their surroundings.

"We must hope there will be others," said Howard.

"Yes, why not?" said Jean, knowing exactly why not.

The absence of Gretchen, so unexpected and fortuitous, could hardly be depended on in the future, but this was not something that could be said, or even thought, by anyone with a conscience.

They rejoined Aunt Edie, who had been woken by the arrival

of Mr. Noakes bringing a basket of eggs and a jar of honey, in return for which he received a box of the second-best apples. He had brought a folding canvas fishing stool with him, perhaps accustomed to being offered no seat, and was now perched beside the sun lounger, displacing Chester, who had been bribed with a mutton bone. They were holding hands and leaning toward each other but jerked apart as Jean and Howard approached. Aunt Edie seemed quite flustered in his presence, her previous languor deserting her.

"This is Mr. Noakes, who I might have mentioned," she said. "He looked after me when I came off my bicycle."

"I'm very pleased to think you are keeping an eye on her," said Howard.

"It's a privilege," said Mr. Noakes, looking at Aunt Edie with misty devotion. "I would do more if she'd let me, but she's very independent."

"He's been very good to me," she replied. "I don't know what I'd do without him." She squeezed his hand and this time she didn't let go.

"It comes to something when your eighty-three-year-old aunt makes you feel you're playing gooseberry," said Howard when they were on their way.

Alongside the remains of the hamper, four crates of apples and a sack of cobnuts were stacked in the boot. On the back seat were the promised spoils of Aunt Edie's clear-out—a musquash cape, a satin evening dress and three pairs of shoes last fashionable in 1920 for Gretchen; a jewelry box of tangled chains, broken strings of pearls and coral bracelets for Margaret. To Jean she had given an emerald pin brooch missing one of its stones.

"I'd always assumed she found him a nuisance, but apparently not."

"They certainly seem delighted with each other," Jean agreed.

"I've never seen her so flirtatious," said Howard. "It made me feel quite uncomfortable. I don't know why."

"Perhaps you feel they are too old for that sort of thing."

"Maybe. It seems a bit undignified. But romance shouldn't be the preserve of young people, should it?"

"No, certainly not." Jean felt the injustice of any prejudice that might one day apply to her and was determined to smite it. "I'm sure inside they feel the same emotions as an eighteen-year-old. The yearning for approval and love doesn't change. The aging body is just cladding."

"You put it so nicely," said Howard. "And imagine if dignity was all we had to look forward to in old age!"

They drove in silence for a while through the sunken lanes with exposed tree roots and overarching branches—great cathedrals of beech and oak with their vaulted roofs of sunlit green.

"If you leave me that brooch I'll mend it for you," Howard said finally. "It needs a new stone."

"You don't need to go to any trouble," said Jean. "It's fine."

"It's no trouble," he replied, shaking his head. "I'm a jeweler. Anyway, I'd like to. It's one thing I can do for you."

"In that case, thank you."

"Aunt Edie's gifts are kindly meant but often more trouble than they're worth. I dread to think what Gretchen will have to say about that fur. And the shoes."

"The silk dress will probably be all right. She'll be able to turn it into something fabulous."

"She will be too busy making strudels."

"Likewise." They had insisted she take one of the crates of apples, enough to last all winter. "Although the English equivalent in my case. Turnovers, perhaps."

There were still hours of daylight left and yet there was a melancholy sense of approaching dusk and the fading of a perfect day, which brought tears to Jean's eyes. Tomorrow she would be back at her desk, writing Pam's Piece and Household Hints and The Garden Week by Week. There was no possibility that circumstances would align themselves in just this way again to allow her another similar outing with Howard. It would survive only in memory; to be taken out and turned over now and then, like one of the treasures from her dressing-table drawer.

They had reached Shoreham now; even after so many hours the children were still playing in the stream. One of the girls—no more than eight or nine herself—was carrying a huge baby on her hip, staggering under the weight of him. They looked just like the sort of scruffy, neglected children Jean would have been forbidden to play with or even approach when she was young, and even now they exerted a powerful fascination. She took a deep breath, which emerged as a sigh, and Howard glanced at her.

"Are you all right, Jean?" he asked. "Have I said something to upset you?"

"Oh no, of course not. I was just giving in to introspection." She forced her face into a smile, but it was effortful and rigid and would have fooled no one, least of all Howard.

After a moment or two he said, "My wife has a theory. Everyone has a secret sorrow."

"Really?" She managed a laugh that sounded more like a sob. "What's yours?"

"I've already told you mine."

"Oh. I see. Then what is Gretchen's?"

She recalled now that occasion in their garden—her stricken face when she believed herself to be unobserved.

"I don't know. Perhaps the counterpoint of mine. But it's you I am interested in. You never told me yours."

"I have had it drummed into me not to dwell on my disappointments."

"Who is this stern drummer?"

"My mother, I suppose."

"Does she live by this creed herself?"

"She certainly never talks about things in that way. But you could hardly call it a success." She gave a brief, bitter laugh.

"Well then?"

"You might think badly of me."

"Jean, I don't think there's anything you could tell me that would alter my opinion of you."

"You're the first person I've ever told," she said, blushing from both the warmth of his compliment and the enormity of what she was about to do. It violated every code that she had been brought up to live by, but the urge to tell him was unstoppable. Decorum, secrecy, self-control were all blown away by the force of this need to confide. "It's a funny coincidence really, but around the same time Gretchen discovered she was expecting Margaret, I found out I was pregnant, too. Only in my case it was more of a disaster than a miracle."

Howard said nothing, his eyes on the road.

"So I did that terrible thing that unmarried women do when they can't keep the baby."

"Did you do it yourself or go to an abortionist?" There was no disapproval in his voice, only curiosity and sympathy.

"I went to this woman in Stockwell. She made me lie on an old door resting on a couple of trestles. It had blankets over it but I could tell it was a door because it still had a handle—digging into my side."

Even at a distance of over a decade she could still remember every detail about that day. The street was called Southville, in a part of London that was unfamiliar to her and that she had never since visited.

He had drawn her a map with a casual efficiency that suggested previous experience. Union Grove, Paradise Road; even the street names had mocked her. The left-hand side of the road was a bomb site—a pair of surviving shops stood out from the rubble like old teeth; containers from an old factory spilled out onto the pavement.

"You're lucky to be alive," said Howard.

"I remember there was a dead fly on the mantelpiece—it seemed like a terrible omen. But the woman was so matter-of-fact about everything. She said, 'I've done this many times and it'll soon be over and you can get on with your life. I've never lost a girl yet.'

"I was so naïve; I thought she'd just flush it out and it would all be gone, but it wasn't like that. I had to go back home to my mother and pretend nothing had happened, and then in the middle of the night the cramps started."

She had crept to the lavatory, carrying the towel she used to protect the bedsheets. As she lowered herself onto the seat there was a sensation of something bursting and a torrent of blood, and clots like raw liver hit the sides of the bowl.

"Oh, Jean. What an awful experience."

"My mother found me on the floor. She was very good—she must have called the doctor. He'd been quite kind to her after my father died, but he wasn't kind to me." *I know what you're about, young lady. If it wasn't for your mother, I'd see you prosecuted—you and the person who did this to you.* Even in her state of near delirium Jean had felt the burning shame of his judgment and the injustice that she had to bear it alone. "He seemed to take great pleasure in telling me that I'd probably never be able to have another child."

Howard shook his head and his hands clenched the steering wheel, but he didn't interrupt.

"We moved not long after that, so that was the last I saw of him, thankfully."

"Had you ever considered keeping the baby? The father wasn't willing to . . . take responsibility?"

"No. He wasn't really . . . available, as it turned out."

"Married already?"

"Oh yes. Anyone but me would have worked that out

straightaway. He had a wife and children. I wasn't even his only girlfriend."

They had used to meet in the White Swan in Crystal Palace, not far from the Swinneys' flat in Gipsy Hill. If Frank was early, which he seldom was, he would wait inside enjoying a pint until she arrived. More usually he was late and Jean, who was not comfortable sitting alone in a pub, would stand outside, checking her watch and fretting. Sometimes, more often than she liked to acknowledge, he failed to turn up at all.

"He did pay for the abortion, though."

"Is that the best you can say for him?"

"Pretty much."

He had finally turned up at the pub after an absence of three weeks, when she had almost given up. "Hello, lovely lady," he said and, registering a certain brittleness in her response, "You're annoyed with me, aren't you?"

"I was worried when you didn't show up. Twice."

"Silly girl."

He had kissed her fiercely—it was the sort of kiss designed to stop a woman from talking and there was no passion in it. They'd left the glow of the pub and crossed into the park, past the stone scars of the old Crystal Palace.

"What did you want to go worrying for?"

"Because I'm pregnant."

She had watched the words land on him like a woman's blows— a nuisance but doing no real damage.

"How can it have happened?"

"It must have been at Worthing, when the thing came off inside me."

That trip to the coast had been the high point of their relationship, really, never to be repeated.

They came to a bench, still damp from earlier rain. He spread out his newspaper for her to sit on, accepting the wet seat as his due. With the small change of decent behavior he had always been generous.

"How did you meet?" Howard asked.

"He came to the door one day selling insurance. I mean, I assume he *was* an insurance salesman. It's hardly something you would invent to impress. I can't even use the excuse that I was young and innocent. I was twenty-nine. I really ought to have known better."

"It must have left you with a very low opinion of men," said Howard.

"Oh, I don't know about *men*. It took me a couple of years even to revise my opinion of Frank—I was so infatuated. I only knew I'd finally recovered when I saw him from a bus window on Piccadilly and didn't feel a thing. There was a time when I'd have jumped off a moving bus to chase after someone who merely looked like him. You see, Howard, I wasn't always the sensible woman you see today."

"I'm only sorry you had to live through it all to become her."

She gave him a grateful glance. Never before had she considered that all these experiences that had nearly demolished her had built her into something better.

"Thank you for listening. I'm sorry for going on."

They were crossing the common now and nearly home. Jean felt a weightlessness; the deep relief of the confessional.

"You didn't *go on*. I'm glad you could tell me."

"My only regret is the baby. She'd be ten now." Jean blushed. "I don't know why I say 'she.'"

The reflective silence that followed this remark lasted the few minutes that remained of the journey.

18

....

Pam's Piece

With orchards and gardens bursting with delicious Kentish apples, now is the time to fetch out those favorite recipes. Spiced Apple Cake is simple to make and a nice change from a pie. It works well served warm with custard, or cold with a cup of tea in place of a traditional fruit cake.

3 apples, peeled, cored and sliced
2 tsp golden syrup
1 tbsp butter
1 tsp ground cinnamon

Sponge mix:
4 oz butter
2 tbsp golden syrup
4 oz caster sugar
2 eggs
4 oz self-raising flour
1 tbsp milk

Simmer the apples with the syrup, butter and cinnamon for a few minutes until tender but not mushy. To prepare the topping, soften the butter and golden syrup in a bowl over a basin of hot water. Remove from the heat and beat in the sugar and eggs. Fold in the flour, adding milk to give the consistency of lightly whipped cream. Place the apple chunks in a greased pan or ovenproof dish and pour over the topping. Bake at Gas Mark 4 for 25 to 30 minutes until the sponge is golden brown and springy to touch.

....

Jean pulled the sheet of paper from her typewriter and added it to the pile. She now had enough apple recipes to make a page and could personally vouch for every one, having tested them all in her own kitchen over the previous weeknights. On the corner of her desk sat an open cake pan displaying the unclaimed remnant of a batch of turnovers. Even the greediest of her colleagues, the beneficiaries of all this experimentation, could no longer be tempted and passed her desk with averted eyes.

The phone rang. Locating it under a drift of foolscap, Jean heard the clipped voice of the switchboard operator announcing, "Mr. Tilbury for you." It was not unknown for him to call her at work—at Gretchen's suggestion this was sometimes the way arrangements were made or confirmed—but it was the first time they had spoken since their visit to Aunt Edie's nearly over a week ago now.

Remembering the intimate and confessional tone of their last conversation, Jean was suddenly shy and full of regret. Until now she had never told anyone about the abortion. Her mother knew, of course she did, but had chosen not to know and it was never spoken of, not in the hospital, or later when Jean came home to convalesce, or ever since.

Dorrie, who had left for Kitale two months earlier, was no

longer available for sisterly confidences and it was hardly the sort of news for a letter. And now, having kept her own counsel for over a decade, she had settled on the one person in the world she wanted to impress. The heat and the apple brandy must have fogged her judgment.

There was no time to subdue the fluttering of panic; the switchboard operator had already connected him.

"Hello, Jean, I hope I'm not disturbing you," came his familiar diffident voice.

"Not at all," she replied. "I am typing up apple recipes and very ready to be distracted."

"Apples?" he said. "Whatever gave you that idea?"

"I have to take my inspiration where I find it."

"Well, speaking of the spoils of that afternoon, I have fixed that brooch of Aunt Edie's and wondered if I could drop it off on my way home."

"Do you mean here?" She remembered that Thursday was his half-day at the shop.

"Yes, I meant the office—if that's convenient?"

"That would be fine. It's very good of you."

"My pleasure. I'll be there in about an hour."

She hung up and fanned herself with her notebook, relieved that she had handled the conversation without betraying any inappropriate pleasure at the prospect of seeing him.

For the last few nights she had been troubled by insomnia. The dark thoughts that woke her at 3 a.m. and chased away all hope of sleep until just before dawn issued from a strange form of guilt. Not the conventional kind, for past wrongs regretted, but anticipatory guilt, for things that might yet be done.

Since Howard had told her that he and Gretchen no longer had a sexual relationship, Jean had allowed herself to imagine what it would be like to make love to him herself. Or rather, to be made love to, since even in her fantasies she was always the pursued, not the pursuer. She was able to square this with her conscience by reasoning that a) the mind cannot be policed—thoughts will roam where they will; b) she had no intention of revealing or acting on her feelings; c) there was no betrayal of Gretchen involved in these fantasies, since she had apparently renounced any sexual interest in Howard.

At ten to two, Jean went to the ladies' room to check her appearance in the small mirror tile above the sinks. She combed her hair and re-powdered her pink cheeks and nose. She wore no other makeup—previous experiments with cosmetics had always made her look painted and clownish, and they were now consigned to her drawer of treasures, to be admired as artifacts but never deployed. In her general appearance, however, she felt more confident than usual, as she was wearing Gretchen's dress, which always prompted compliments.

She was drying her hands on the broken roller towel when the door opened and one of the secretaries came in, red-eyed and wretched-looking, and plunged into a stall, slamming the door. Jean recognized her as the pretty one who was often tangled up with the lad from the print room.

In the weeks and months after Frank's desertion Jean herself had cried in that very room and would have been grateful for a kind word from a motherly female colleague. Even so, she could not bring herself to be that woman and ask the weeping girl what was wrong, but slipped out of the washroom, leaving her to her private misery.

In the forecourt, a reason for the girl's distress became apparent. The lad from the print room was in huddled conference with the newest recruit among the secretaries. She had her back to the wall and he was standing over her, whispering in her ear and brushing strands of hair away from her face in a gesture of ownership.

Jean glared at them as she passed and then felt ashamed. We are all fools, she thought.

Howard was waiting just outside the gates, standing by his parked car. Jean was aware that any self-consciousness on her part could very well set the tone for all future encounters. It was vital to behave normally, whatever that meant. Howard himself showed no signs of awkwardness.

"Sorry to have dragged you away from your desk," he said, producing a green velvet pouch from his inside pocket and handing it to her. "It just seemed easier to come here."

Jean loosened the cords and tipped the slender gold pin into her palm.

"You'll notice I've done something a bit devious," he said, turning it over so that she could see the design. He had a craftsman's pride and interest in the details of his creation, which she found touching. "It used to have two emeralds either side of an opal, but one of the emeralds was missing, so I switched it around, so you've now got two opals around a single emerald. It's easier to replace an opal."

"It's lovely, Howard. You would never know it had been repaired. You must let me pay for the stone—and your time."

"Out of the question. I'm only making good an otherwise quite useless gift from my aunt."

"I'll always think of her when I wear it," Jean said.

She pinned it to her dress, meeting some resistance from her bra and petticoat before the job was done.

"Is that the frock Gretchen made?" Howard asked.

"Yes. It's by far my favorite—she made it so beautifully."

"It suits you very well."

"People always admire it."

Jean noticed the way he had managed to praise her appearance while at the same time acknowledging Gretchen, to demonstrate that there was nothing furtive in his compliment.

They were still standing, somewhat provisionally, on the pavement, now and then having to stand aside for other pedestrians and in full view of the large upper windows of the editorial offices. Out of the corner of her eye Jean could see Muriel from Accounts gazing down at her with undisguised curiosity.

"I'm keeping you from your lunch," said Howard, following the direction of her upward glances.

"Not really," said Jean.

She had now missed the trolley, which delivered sandwiches and cake and tea to the offices, and would have to go to the bakery in the high street instead. Their conversation, so natural and open at Aunt Edie's, now felt stilted and evasive. It was no mystery: by confiding in each other they had set up a false intimacy, which excluded Gretchen and placed them in a perilous position of near conspiracy, from which she could sense Howard retreating. His reference to Gretchen was his way of signaling his rededicated loyalty.

"Howard," said Jean quietly. "All those things I told you about myself. I didn't expect you to keep anything secret from Gretchen. You mustn't think . . ."

He put his hand on her arm and shook his head so urgently that she stopped.

"Don't," he said. "We don't need to say anything. We understand each other perfectly as it is. There's nothing to be said. Or done."

For a moment their gaze held and Jean could read in his unhappy expression all that he was feeling and at the same time the impossibility that he could ever act on it, or even speak of it. But it was enough.

"Nothing," she promised, her heart singing as she watched him get in his car and drive off, home to his wife.

19

Dear Miss Swinney,

I am taking the unusual step of writing to you regarding the ongoing tests on Mother and Daughter. They failed to attend the scheduled appointment for the serum protein electrophoresis test and Mother has not responded to my follow-up letter of inquiry.

I wonder if you could use your influence to iron out whatever seems to be the problem and reassure her that this procedure is very simple (for the patient at least; the analysis is rather more complex, but that is our business), requiring no more than a blood sample. All of us involved in this experiment are very excited by the findings so far and keen to press on as far as the science will take us.

If hardship is an issue, we may be able to assist with travel costs. Perhaps that is also something your newspaper might consider.

I await your early response.

   Yours,

      Dr. Stewart Bamber

They met as before under the clock in the ticket hall at Charing Cross. Jean noticed with dismay that since their last meeting

Gretchen had a new short haircut, which suited her but made her look a lot less like Margaret. For the purpose of a striking portrait of mother and daughter to accompany her story, dissimilarity was not ideal.

It took her a moment or two to subdue an attack of wholly unreasonable indignation that she had not been consulted. Howard had so thoroughly displaced Gretchen in Jean's consciousness lately that she was almost surprised to be confronted with the origin and purpose of their meetings.

Since receiving Dr. Bamber's puzzling letter, it had taken her an inordinate amount of time to bring matters to this point. Previously, appointments had been arranged by calling Howard at the shop; this time Jean preferred not to use him as an intermediary unless absolutely necessary. In any case, it was Gretchen she needed to talk to in order to discover what lay behind this fresh resistance to further tests. The only solution seemed to be to call on Gretchen uninvited and hope to find her at home.

Accordingly, at eleven o'clock on a Monday morning, an hour when Jean judged Margaret and Howard would be out and Gretchen most likely working at her dressmaking, she left the newspaper office and caught the bus from Petts Wood to Sidcup. It was late September; the trees still wore their summer colors and the fogs of autumn were only a distant threat, but the air was cool and damp. The Tilburys' elderly neighbor was polishing the tiles of her doorstep with red wax; she sat up and nodded at Jean as she opened the gate.

"Mothers' meeting?" she inquired, which struck Jean as an odd and rather rude comment, so she said, "Hardly," and gave a thin smile in reply.

The side gate was locked, so Jean pressed the doorbell for just longer than was polite and waited, rehearsing various phrases of friendly concern, which turned to frustration as it became apparent that they would not be needed. Never without a note-book and pen, Jean wrote a brief message and posted it through the letterbox:

> *Dear Gretchen,*
>   *I called to see you this morning for a chat, but no luck. I will try again tomorrow at the same time. I hope there is nothing amiss.*
>   *Jean*

She was at the end of Burdett Road, walking briskly to burn off her irritation at a wasted journey, when she heard her name. Turning, she saw Gretchen hurrying toward her, pulling a cardigan over her dress. Even now she looks lovely, Jean thought. You could call on her uninvited on a Monday morning and still not catch her with nails unpainted and hair unbrushed.

"I'm sorry," Gretchen panted as she came within range. "I was in the bathroom and I came down to find your note." She was holding the crumpled page in her fist. "Is anything the matter?"

"Not with me. I was going to ask you the same thing," said Jean. "You missed your appointment with Dr. Bamber; he wrote me a rather peevish letter when you didn't reply to him."

Gretchen shook her head impatiently. "Well, I couldn't make that date. Margaret was still a bit off color from that sickness. I thought I'd told Howard to phone and cancel it, but perhaps I didn't. Anyway, I don't understand why they couldn't use the blood from the first tests."

"Well, I gather this electro . . . whatever it's called . . . is quite elaborate to run. You have to fast overnight and the blood needs to be analyzed within a day of sampling. I don't understand the exact process, but . . ." She tailed off. This is what you signed up for, she wanted to add. You approached us, not the other way around.

Instead, she shrugged. "I was worried that something might have happened to change your mind about the whole business."

"No, no, nothing's *happened*. I'm just tired of being poked and prodded and not believed. It's all taking so long."

Jean felt a rising impatience. She bit down on a number of sharp retorts. There was nothing to be gained by growing irritable and everything to be lost. She needed Gretchen's cooperation far more than Gretchen needed her.

"Look, I know this is difficult for you," she said, mastering the temptation to expound upon her own frustrations. "If there is any way I can make things easier for you, please tell me. You know I believe in you, Gretchen. And for what it's worth I think Dr. Bamber does, too. But science has no business with beliefs. There are only two more stages left now—this serum test and a skin graft. And then it's done."

"All right. I'm sorry. I didn't mean to be an awkward patient. I'm grateful for all the trouble you've gone to."

"There's no need for gratitude," Jean replied crisply. "We're all on the same side."

Low, rolling clouds were gathering and a few fat drops of rain hit the pavement between them. Jean wondered if Gretchen would invite her back to the house so that they could conclude their discussion inside, but she showed no sign of it.

"Phone Howard and tell him when the next appointment is and we'll be there," she promised, lifting the back of her cardigan up over her head to protect her hair.

"I can tell you now," said Jean, bridling at the high-handed way Gretchen treated Howard as her secretary. "This Friday morning. I'll meet you at Charing Cross at nine. Don't eat or drink anything except water overnight."

The matter settled, they parted, the rain coming down in earnest now. Gretchen ran back up the road with her arms over her head, while Jean trudged to the bus stop with a vague sense of

dissatisfaction that had almost nothing to do with her having set
off that morning without an umbrella.

Now, as they embraced in the ticket hall and made their way
out onto the Strand with Margaret between them, the irritable
mood of their previous meeting seemed to have been forgotten.
By way of experiment, Jean was wearing the emerald and opal
brooch pinned perhaps incongruously to the lapel of her shabby
raincoat. She was curious to know whether or not Howard had
made a secret of this gift of jewelry; its symbolic value seemed
to depend on this factor. However, as soon as the two women
had greeted each other, Gretchen had peered at it and said, "Is
that Edie's old brooch? Howard's done a jolly good job. It looks
as good as new now."

"Yes," said Jean, both disappointed and relieved. If the gift's romantic significance was somewhat diminished, Howard's integrity
at least was not. "It was so kind of her—and him."

"Aunt Edie's an absolute menace with her so-called presents,"
Gretchen retorted. "They're always broken or incomplete, so you
end up spending money you can't spare on something you never
wanted in the first place. I sent those awful old shoes straight to
the rummage sale."

"What about the fur coat?"

"I'm keeping that," Gretchen conceded. "It smells of camphor
but you never know."

This time when they reached the annex in Agar Street the
receptionist had evidently been briefed to look out for them, as
they had hardly crossed the threshold when Dr. Bamber himself appeared and swept them away to his office. A coal fire was
burning in the grate and his desk was covered with open books
and papers. It was more like the study of a busy academic than a
medical practitioner.

"It's very good of you to come all this way again," he said

smoothly, stirring the coals and sending an avalanche of ash through the grate. He aimed his smile at mother and daughter. "How are you?"

"Hungry," whispered Margaret, who had been introduced only that morning to the concept of a fast and was not impressed.

"Then let's not waste any time—as soon as we have taken the blood there will be tea and toast."

A spark flew out of the fire and landed, smoldering, on the hearthrug. Dr. Bamber stamped on it with his shiny brogues.

"I'm sorry we missed our appointment," said Gretchen, tugging off her white gloves one finger at a time and tucking them into her handbag. "I hope it didn't put you out."

Dr. Bamber batted her apology away. Jean was aware of a subtle shift in the balance of power in Gretchen's favor. At their first encounter the men of science had treated her with a certain polite loftiness, the presumption being that she was at best a curiosity and at worst a charlatan. Gretchen had been diffident and grateful for their expertise. With the evidence of each successive test, however, their interest and her status had grown. Now, apparently on the brink of being proved a phenomenon to rival a unicorn or a mermaid, she seemed to have developed a queenly indifference to the whole process. It was most odd.

"Perhaps you could explain to Mrs. Tilbury how this test works. I'm concerned that she's being treated rather like a laboratory rat."

"Oh, surely not," Dr. Bamber protested.

"I didn't put it quite like that," Gretchen said, smoothing his ruffled feathers. "I only felt I was being kept somewhat in the dark."

"Then we must provide illumination." He picked up his fountain pen and began to fiddle with the cap. "There's nothing I like more than talking about my field, but most patients find the detail rather dull."

"Maybe Mrs. Tilbury should be considered more of a volunteer than a patient. Since she's not unwell." Jean's distrust of doctors, even the helpful ones, was never far from the surface.

"Of course. What we are doing is a serum protein electrophoresis test. Serum is the liquid left behind when the red and white blood cells have been removed from the blood. It contains proteins—albumin and various globulins, alpha, beta, gamma. These carry different electrical charges and they will move in fluid to display a distinctive pattern. We usually use this test to diagnose disease, but in this case we are only interested in *comparing* the two patterns—yours and Margaret's—for any variation." He beamed. "So all we need is a small sample of blood from you both and we can get to work."

"I see," said Gretchen serenely. "Thank you."

Margaret's brow had been furrowed with concentration while this explanation lasted. Jean couldn't help wondering if the angel voices, keen curators of esoteric vocabulary, were filing *globulin* and *electrophoresis* away for another day.

There was a tap on the door and, as if she had been awaiting some secret signal, a nurse appeared to take mother and daughter to the phlebotomy department.

As soon as Gretchen and Margaret returned from the lab, Dr. Bamber's secretary appeared with the promised refreshments. With only three chairs and two slices of toast between four people, there was no chance of a convivial tea party developing. As non-fasters, Jean and Doctor Bamber abstained from toast, and he drank his tea standing up, looming over the three visitors, rocking back and forth on his heels in his awkwardness.

Gretchen, in any case, was not disposed to linger. She drank her tea quickly, gave half her uneaten slice of toast to Margaret and started to button her jacket as a sign of readiness to depart. Outside on the pavement, she turned to Jean with the unmistakable hesitancy of someone about to ask a favor.

"I wonder. Tell me if you think it is a bit of an imposition."

"What?" said Jean.

Gretchen looked at her watch. "I've got a few errands to run while I'm up in town. It seems a bit of a waste not to do them while I'm here, but Margaret really needs to get back to school."

"No, I don't," said Margaret. "It's English comprehension and I'm already the best at that anyway."

"You can't keep having days off."

"You'd like me to take Margaret back to school?" said Jean, recognizing from her own dealings with Mrs. Melsom that there was a tendency for the petitioner in these situations to rely on inference. "It would be a pleasure."

The work was piling up on her desk; pieces unfinished, pages unfilled, deadlines advancing . . . But never mind. She would take it home with her and catch up when her mother was in bed.

"Oh, *would* you? That would be so helpful." She took a pen and a notebook from her handbag and began to scribble directions. "It's only five minutes from the station."

"I know where it is," said Margaret with dignity. "I bet I could get there by myself from here."

"Yes, I'm sure you could. But there are some peculiar people about."

"I bet you are just going to sneak off and have lunch with Daddy without me," Margaret said, and from Gretchen's blushing denial it almost seemed to Jean that she might be.

"I'm not. I promise."

Having satisfied herself that Margaret's satchel contained her packed lunch and an explanatory note for her teacher, Gretchen set off along the Strand at a brisk trot, her new short haircut swinging.

Never throw away an old plastic raincoat. The hood cut off will make a useful toiletry bag. The large back panel may be used to line a suitcase to ensure safety from damp should the case get wet when traveling.

20

In late October Jean booked a week's leave to take her mother away to the coast. In previous years they had been in the habit of going up to Harrogate to stay with Jean's aunt and uncle for a week. They were the last link with her father's side of the family and even after all these years her uncle still seemed moved to try and compensate for his brother's desertion. He would give Jean the use of his car for day trips and never allowed them to pay for anything while they were his guests.

However, his health had been declining in recent years, a combination of emphysema and blocked arteries leaving him with poor breathing and mobility. Jean's aunt had made it clear that they could no longer play host, but he continued to send twenty pounds for Christmas and birthdays. These generous gifts represented Jean's mother's only source of spending money.

For the last few years then, they had been forced to resort to the more costly option of hotels and boardinghouses. These trips used to take place in early September, when children were back at school and resorts quieter. This summer, however, Jean had been engrossed with the Tilburys and the weeks had slid past. It was now nearly autumn and nothing was arranged.

Her mother made no reference to this oversight, and somehow

her silence on the topic had allowed Jean to avoid tackling it, but it was one of those nagging thoughts that returned to plague her during bouts of sleeplessness. Lying awake at 3 a.m. when nothing practical could be done, she would burn with guilt at her own indolence and procrastination, and vow to call in at the travel agent in Petts Wood at the first opportunity. By morning she would have forgotten.

The truth was, these holidays were never much of a treat for Jean, involving as they did unbroken exposure to her mother's considerable needs, dislikes and eccentricities, which seemed to increase in proportion to their distance from home. However, she knew that her mother looked forward to these trips, and complaining about the weather, the food, the mattress and the journey was for her no small part of the pleasure. Jean was also aware that the process of hawking someone infirm and nervous from taxi and train and bus to hotel was getting more difficult with each passing year, and that the tradition, once allowed to lapse, might never be revived.

Finally, it was the discovery that the Tilburys themselves were going away for a short break to the Forest of Dean that persuaded Jean that she would not be missed, so she booked two rooms at the Stanmore House Hotel in Lymington. The timing was convenient: the results of the electrophoresis serum test had shown a perfect match between mother and daughter, and a skin graft had been performed from one to the other.

Dr. Lloyd-Jones's expectation was that if Margaret was indeed the product of parthenogenesis, she would comprise no genetic material not originally from Gretchen and the graft from daughter to mother would take. If the new skin started to shed it would suggest the presence of at least one incompatible antigen, implying the existence of a father. All that remained was to wait and see whether or not the skin was rejected by its new host.

In the days before their holiday, Jean had worked long hours with obsessive focus and pace to clear her desk and produce pieces in advance for the following edition. As well as her regular pages, she compiled a recipe section to mark National Soup Week, and in a nod to falling temperatures, wrote a light-hearted column *celebrating* the vest. It was a while since she had found time for any serious gardening to use as the basis for her column, so she resorted to calling in at Oaklands, the garden supplies shop opposite the church, and interrogating the owner for his seasonal tips.

She left Roy Drake the telephone number of their hotel in Lymington in case of any developments in the matter of the skin grafts and he promised to pass on any news without delay. Dr. Lloyd-Jones had told her not to expect anything to happen in her absence. Mother A and Daughter were not expected to have their dressings removed until their return from the Forest of Dean. A definitive result was likely to take weeks rather than days.

All the same, it was with a sense of reluctance, quite at odds with the holiday spirit she had been trying to instill in her mother, that Jean boarded the train at Waterloo. At the first effortful tug of the engine she had sighed so gustily that her mother had glanced up in concern and asked if she felt unwell.

"No, not unwell. Just the usual anxiety that I've overlooked something," she said.

"It will do you good to get away. You work too hard at that job. Always dashing around."

Jean refrained from pointing out that without her wages—the fruits of all this inconvenient "dashing around"—there would be no holiday. Instead, she took silent refuge in her notebook, reviewing the transcripts of her initial interviews with Gretchen, Howard, Alice and Martha, the floor plan of St. Cecilia's and her jotted observations since. One page was divided into two columns headed Virgin Birth +/-:

+	−
H's confidence in G's honesty	*M's assumption G was lying*
A's assumption G is truthful	*G's impatience—why now?*
My first impressions	*G's hidden sadness—irrelevant?—*
Blood test	*but shows ability at concealment*
Taste test	*Drugged sleep—opportunity?*
Saliva test	*But timing is wrong plus Kitty?*
Serum test	*Brenda?*

Her mother, opposite, was crocheting another lace doily, the oatmeal-colored circle turning and growing quickly under her hands like potters' clay. They had dozens of these at home, little puddles of string under every vase and lamp and ornament, with still enough to fill an entire drawer in the sideboard.

As she watched, her mother glanced up at her and quickly down, the light catching her glasses and turning them to dazzling mirrors, and it occurred to Jean with a jolt that she had no idea what color her mother's eyes were. She must have known once, but it was years—a decade, perhaps—since they had made proper eye contact.

They had both been witnesses to each other's disappointments and tragedies, but it had always been understood by Jean that it was weak and shameful to dwell on them and so their conversation never strayed far from the surface of things. Sometimes Jean had the sensation that they were adrift in a perilously overladen boat; a moment of emotional turbulence would be enough to capsize them.

Her mother put down her crocheting and removed her reading glasses, blinking hard to bring into focus the Surrey countryside as it flowed past: neat farms, tamed hedgerows and plowed fields of crumbled soil.

Gray, Jean thought with surprise. They are gray.

Dear Dorrie,

Mother and I are at Lymington for a week's holiday. The picture on the front shows the main street. Our hotel is on the right with the pillars. It is low season and very quiet, which suits us. There is a pretty cobbled street of quaint shops leading down to the harbor, which looks across to the Isle of Wight. We sit and watch the boats for hours.

The walk up is a bit of a challenge for Mother, but yesterday an old boy in a Bentley took pity on us and gave us a lift back to the hotel. She has talked of little else since. On Monday we took a coach trip to Bucklers Hard, a charming row of fishermen's cottages leading down to a river. We have been lucky with the weather so far.

Love to Kenneth and the twins.

Jean

Dear Margaret,

By the time you read this we shall both be back home, but never mind. I hope you are enjoying the Forest of Dean and that Jemimah is behaving herself at Lizzie's. We are staying in a place called Lymington on the edge of the New Forest, which is in fact very old. We could see wild ponies from the train on our way down.

Our hotel has a resident cat, who has her own favorite armchair in the lounge. If you leave your bedroom door open she comes slinking in and goes to sleep on your pillow.

There are at least half a dozen tea shops within walking distance of our hotel and we try a different one each day. None can quite compete with Simpson's—or homemade spitzbuben.

Your friend,

Jean

Toward the end of the week the weather changed and a series of fronts swept in from the west bringing wintry rain, which kept

Jean and her mother indoors. They rose as late as permissible and after a cooked breakfast moved into the lounge, where they played rummy and read the selection of out-of-date magazines. There were a number of other residents, similarly marooned by the bad weather, but the room was large and the arrangement of furniture—remote islands of wing-backed armchairs around low coffee tables, separated by vast expanses of carpet—did not encourage them to mingle. By silent consensus, everyone kept to the seats they had originally claimed, exchanging in passing no more than a nod or smile of fellow feeling at the perversity of the English climate.

Among the mostly elderly clientele were a mother and daughter about ten years older than the Swinneys. The old lady was plump and moon-faced, hard of hearing and lost in confusion. The daughter was thin and round-shouldered with skin ravaged by eczema. The corners of her mouth sagged, and her drooping cardigan, raw, ringless fingers and darned stockings spoke eloquently to Jean of self-denial. In the quiet of the lounge, above the swishing of magazine pages and the slap of playing cards, Jean could hear her patiently answering the same bewildered questions over and over.

"We're just waiting for the rain to pass . . ." "No, we've had lunch. We're just waiting until it's stopped raining . . ." "When it clears up. Then we'll go out," the daughter said, raking the flaming skin of her arms with chewed nails.

Jean's mother, who enjoyed trying to listen in on the conversations of other guests and felt entitled to comment on anything overhead, said, "She needs to stop scratching. It'll get infected."

The woman glanced up and blushed.

"Mother!" Jean hissed in reproach, shrinking behind the wings of her armchair.

The room was so very hushed that most people spoke only in whispers, leaving the disinhibited few, of whom her mother was one, brutally exposed.

"If this weather's in for the week we might as well go home tomorrow," one of the other guests was saying to her husband in a low voice.

"That lady's had enough," Jean's mother commented, causing several heads to turn.

In one corner an old man in green tweeds had fallen asleep over his tea. The cup and saucer rattled perilously between his fluttering hands as it rode the gentle rise and fall of his stomach like a small boat on a rolling sea.

"Can you hear snoring? I can hear snoring," her mother remarked as Jean dived to rescue the cup before it deposited its contents in the old man's lap.

On her way back to their island, Jean caught the eye of the downtrodden daughter and they exchanged rueful smiles, but this moment of shared experience gave her no great comfort. Instead, it provided a glimpse of a future that was anything but rosy. "I'm not like her," she wanted to announce to the room. "I have a career and colleagues who respect me, and there is a man who admires me and knows my worth!" But these certainties had lost some of their bite here, so far from home, and Jean felt something close to panic the next morning when they awoke again to the clatter of rain at the window and the prospect of another day of enforced idleness.

In a fit of desperation, she booked them at the last minute onto a trip to Beaulieu, even though neither of them had any great interest in traveling.

Through the misted windows of the coach the New Forest was a bleak landscape of beaten gorse and clumps of tattered trees under leaden skies. Jean's mother had got her feet wet on the short walk across the pavement to the pick-up point and this was now the focus of much grumbling. Jean herself, who had been holding but not benefiting from the umbrella and was thoroughly bedraggled, hunched in her seat and smoked furiously.

At Beaulieu, her mother could not be persuaded to leave the

bus. It was too wet and cold; the prospect of walking even a few steps defeated her.

"I'm quite happy here looking at the view. You go," she urged Jean, who needed no prompting to seize a few moments to herself.

She strolled around the shed of vintage cars with the line of other visitors, enjoying the temporary respite from her mother's stream of comments. Loneliness made some people withdrawn in company, she thought, but others like her mother grew vocal when given an audience, spilling out opinions and observations without any thought for how they might be received.

The allotted hour was longer than was really needed to view the small motorcar collection and those few rooms of the house open to the public, but Jean was in no hurry to return, savoring the silence and the opportunity to wander unencumbered. Her mother had a way of clutching and leaning on her arm as they walked, as if liable to topple over at any moment and determined to take Jean down with her if she did.

When she made her way back to the bus at the appointed time, she found it ready to depart, the engine running and the other passengers waiting and restive. She stumbled down the aisle to her seat, raked by disapproving looks.

"I thought something must have happened to you," said her mother. "Everyone's been waiting."

It had grown cold in the bus with the engine off and she had shrunk inside her coat, the collar up to her ears.

"I'm not late," Jean whispered back, offering up her watch face in evidence. "Everyone else was early."

It would have been easy enough to apologize, but she was too mortified.

The driver took a circuitous route back through Brockenhurst and Sway, "to enjoy the scenery," he said mirthlessly over the whine of the windscreen wipers and the machine-gun rattle of rain on the metal roof. Between the fug of cigarette smoke within and the boiling skies without, the picturesque views stood no chance.

"Well that was a disappointment, I must say," was Jean's mother's verdict as the guests trooped back into the hotel, shaking out their umbrellas, filling the lobby with clouds of vapor and a mushroomy smell of wet raincoat.

This remark prompted general agreement from the company. They began to exchange other reassuring banalities about the weather and the risks of off-season travel until the icy reserve of the past few days was thoroughly melted and they moved into the lounge as a united band, grumbling cheerfully. Later, Jean's mother would describe it as the best day of the entire holiday.

The exertions of the outing must have exhausted her, as she went to bed early. They had eaten their last meal in the dining room—tomato soup, fishcakes with sauté potatoes and peas and sherry trifle—and played cribbage with a retired bank manager and his wife who were part of the Beaulieu contingent. It emerged in conversation that they lived less than thirty miles away in Blandford Forum and had been coming to the same hotel every year since the end of the war. Jean, for whom seven days in the place had seemed an eternity, found herself depressed and repelled by their complacency.

They had never been to London and had no desire to go. They had heard it was overrun with traffic and delinquents and they wanted none of it. Other manifestations of progress, the television and the car, were given equally short shrift. The first was a threat to family life; the second was a blight on the countryside and a menace to public safety.

It occurred to Jean to wonder why such sworn enemies of automotive traveling had settled on a trip to Beaulieu, but she was too polite to challenge them. Besides, their opinions were delivered with the sort of assurance that has never experienced dissent and might not even recognize it. Instead, simmering inside, she began to formulate a Pam's Piece on provincialism, which would of course be unprintable but soothed her bad temper.

In Jean's mother they had found a somewhat anarchic soul mate; she was inclined to agree with everything they said but occasionally misheard and ended up roundly seconding a quite contrary viewpoint. More than once Jean had to step in and politely steer her back on track. It all made for effortful conversation and Jean was relieved when her mother, wearied by the day's novelties, declared herself ready for bed.

"Well, they were a very nice couple," she said on her way upstairs, taking Jean's grunt for agreement. "It's a pity we didn't get to know them at the beginning of the week."

Once Jean had overseen her mother's lengthy preparations for bed, from the discreet vantage point of her adjoining room, and satisfied herself that she was settled with her hairnet in place and a Georgette Heyer to soothe her to sleep, she made her escape.

The storm had blown away leaving a ragged sky and it was warmer now than during the day. A few wounded shreds of cloud blew across the moon, which lit up the street with its great wax face as Jean walked down toward the pier enjoying the last cigarette of the night.

A group of working men was just emerging from the King's Head, boisterous with drink, as she approached. They greeted her with beery good humor, dragging each other out of her path with exaggerated gallantry that was closer to mockery than good manners. Jean, who was used to being outnumbered by inferior men, refused to be intimidated.

"Good evening," she said briskly, causing general convulsion.

"She said 'Good evening!'" one of them called after her departing back.

The harbor was quiet, the small boats gently nudging and dipping in the moonlight. Across the Solent the Isle of Wight was visible as a dark mass, Yarmouth a scatter of lights at the shoreline.

Jean sat down on a bench to enjoy the view and let her thoughts roam in the direction of Howard, wondering where he was and if at this very moment he might be outdoors and looking at the same stars.

She was aware of somebody coming to stand behind her, a little closer than was polite, and turned to see the confused old lady from the hotel. There was something odd about her appearance; it took Jean a moment or two to realize that she was wearing a nightgown and carpet slippers under her coat. Her bare legs were tracked with ropy purple veins.

"Hello," said Jean, looking around for the daughter. "You've come out for some fresh air like me."

"No," came the reply.

"Will you be all right getting back? It's a fair walk."

The woman stared at Jean with mystification and a degree of hostility. "I suppose you're going to tell me you're Nora. Little tart," she added.

Her prospect of a quiet half-hour dashed, Jean surrendered to the responsibility of getting the old woman safely back. For a moment, stung by the irony that she had exchanged the modest demands of one geriatric for the much more urgent needs of another, she had considered leaving her to it, but there, a few feet away, was the black oily water plucking at the harbor wall.

"I'm going back now. Shall we walk together?" Jean offered her arm.

The woman allowed herself to be guided away from the pier and up toward the town, their progress impeded by her tendency to stop every few paces and turn, stiff-necked, towards Jean with some new query.

"Who the hell are you?" she would say. "You look like Nora but you don't smell like her."

As the elegant pillars of the hotel came into view at last the fretful figure of the daughter appeared on the steps, casting anxious glances up and down the road. She swooped on them, almost frantic with relief and reproach.

"Oh, Mother, where on earth have you been? I've been out of my mind. I only left her for a minute to get some clean towels. Oh, you are the limit. Thank you so much," she babbled.

"I found her down on the edge of the pier," said Jean, who felt the matter of tragedy narrowly avoided warranted a mention.

The daughter rolled her eyes. "You are kind. I can't thank you enough. Now come on, Mother. You're as cold as ice."

The old lady, who up to this point had been meekly linking Jean's arm, suddenly wrenched herself free and gave her daughter a terrific shove, sending her sprawling onto her back, and stomped past her into the hotel.

For a moment it seemed as though the fall had knocked her out or worse, as she lay motionless, crumpled up against one of the pillars with her skirt up over her knees. Presently, however, she gave a moan and drew her legs toward her, raising her hand to explore the back of her head for damage.

Jean squatted beside her, an embarrassed onlooker in a domestic drama that had now become horribly public.

"Are you all right? Do you need a doctor?"

From behind her hands the woman gave a muffled sob.

A young couple, out walking their dog, had now stopped to offer assistance; Jean had a sudden fear that they might assume the woman was drunk. At this angle and in this state of dishevelment she did look quite unlike the respectable spinster of previous days.

"Do you need some help?" the man asked, tugging at the dog, a fox terrier, who was now pulling on the lead.

"She's had a nasty fall," said Jean, feeling that the real story of maternal violence was hardly hers to relate. "I'll look after her. We're both staying at the hotel."

Shrugging their assent, the couple moved off, giving Jean a doubting backward glance.

The woman had shuffled herself into a sitting position against the pillar but made no move to get up.

"Will you let me help you in?" Jean said, putting a tentative hand on her arm. "I'll bring you a cup of tea or something."

At this gesture of kindness, tears filled her eyes and rolled down her face.

"That was quite a bump. Does she often do this?" Jean asked.

The woman nodded, sniffling. "She's so strong. She'll kill me one day. If I don't kill her first."

"Oh, surely not," said Jean. "You are so patient with her." She held out her hands and lifted her to her feet, noticing, as the wide cardigan sleeves fell back, arms smudged with bruises.

"I wish one of us was dead. I don't care which."

"You mustn't think like that. Is there no one who can help you with looking after her?"

An idiotic question, Jean knew, because it was the sort of thing people said to her, as if she wouldn't have already considered the idea, if such a person existed.

Once vertical, however, the woman seemed to master herself, straightening her clothes, now streaked with grubby water from the pavement, and mopping her face with a balled-up handkerchief.

"I'm quite all right now, thank you," she said, looking anywhere but at Jean. "I'm sorry to have been a nuisance."

"Won't you let me get you a cup of tea or something stronger?"

"No, thank you. I must go and see to Mother. She'll be wondering where I am."

Wincing, she straightened up and proceeded into the hotel.

21

Dear Miss Swinney,

Thank you for your letter, which has just reached me after a considerable delay. It went to my old address and I'm afraid the new tenants have only now got around to sending it on. It was not the only piece of mail they had been sitting on. Most annoying. Anyway, it made interesting reading and stirred up plenty of memories—not all of them good.

I do remember Gretchen. She was rather quiet but very pleasant. Unfortunately, I didn't get to know her all that well because there was another girl—Martha—in the bed between ours who was a bit of a bully and very possessive. She used to get quite sulky if Gretchen tried to be friendly to anyone else but her. I had to wait until the nurse was giving Martha a bed bath with the curtains drawn and then I would creep round to have a chat with Gretchen, because I was the only one who was well enough to get out of bed.

The two of them were as thick as thieves. You could hear them whispering at night—not especially quietly—when they couldn't sleep. I had to put cotton wool soaked in olive oil in my ears! Martha got into terrible trouble at one point for persuading Gretchen they should take triple the dose of sleeping pills. One *of the nuns accused her of attempting a suicide pact, but of course it had been going on for weeks, so it was nothing of the kind. I think it was just attention-seeking myself.*

I must admit to being a bit taken aback by your suggestion that Gretchen fell pregnant while at St. Cecilia's. Under the noses of Matron and the nuns, not to mention the rest of us on the ward? I can't see how it could possibly have happened. I didn't keep in touch with Gretchen after she left, but I used to get a Christmas card from Kitty, the fourth girl on the ward. She was stuck in an iron lung for her polio and we got quite friendly because I could get up and chat to her. I think she appreciated the company. No doubt you have already tracked her down as she's in your part of the world, but in case you haven't here is her address:

> *Miss K Benteen,*
> *The Grange,*
> *Locksbottom,*
> *Kent*

I don't know if she'd be able to add anything to my reminiscences.
Please remember me to Gretchen, and to Matron, who was always very kind to me, and give them my best wishes.
Yours sincerely,
Brenda van Lingen

This letter, which was awaiting Jean on her return from Lymington, sent her hurrying back to Alice Halfyard's diary, with a guilty jolt that she had allowed her focus on the investigation to slip. But the positive outcomes of the various medical tests had made her complacent and her emotional involvement with the Tilburys had distracted her.

There, on August 20, was the reference to the deliberate overdosing of Gretchen and Martha, confirmed now by Brenda as a regular occurrence and not the one-off event Alice had believed it to be. She checked the dates against Margaret's birth—April 30. She had not been premature, so conception must have occurred some time between early July and the beginning of August. The possibility that for at least some of those nights she had been all but unconscious seemed too much of a coincidence to be ignored. Clearly, Martha and Brenda would have heard nothing, for different reasons, but Kitty?

Jean felt a certain reluctance to pursue the fourth member of this curious fellowship but knew that she must. It was pure squeamishness—a fear of confronting serious illness—that made her hesitate and while she delayed, something else happened that threw all other plans into confusion.

22

"That man's here again."

Jean's mother was standing at the front-room window, count-ing in the sacks of coal as they were carried past to the bunker in the back garden, convinced that it was only her vigilance that kept tradesmen honest.

"What man?" Jean asked, but her heart had got ahead of her, already knocking at her ribs.

On the street outside, just beyond the dray from Hall & Co., was the green Wolseley. Howard sat behind the wheel, motionless, for so long that Jean wondered if he might be about to change his mind and drive off.

They had been back from Lymington for a week and there had been no communication from the Tilburys apart from a postcard from Margaret of the Forest of Dean. She had described a visit to a ruined abbey and her frustration at not being allowed to swim in the river because of the dressing on her skin graft.

Work had claimed all of Jean's attention; she had been too busy catching up after her absence, and chewing over the contents of Brenda's letter, to feel more than a trace of uneasiness at the silence, but here was Howard now, calling unannounced on a Monday evening. He showed no sign of moving and in any case it would be easier to talk away from the inquisitive gaze of her mother, so Jean hurried up the driveway, drawing her cardigan around her against the chill evening air.

He looked up as her shadow darkened the window and gave a wan smile, then reached over to open the door.

"Is everything all right?" Jean asked as she slipped into the seat beside him, convinced now that it wasn't.

"Gretchen has run away."

She stared at him in astonishment, momentarily lost for words. Of all the many varieties of bad news that were possible, this one had not occurred to her.

"What do you mean? How? Where?"

"I mean she's left home. She doesn't want to be married to me anymore."

There was a roaring, whooshing noise in Jean's ears and the rushing sensation that comes just before a faint. But she didn't faint, of course.

"No. Surely not. What about Margaret?"

"Margaret is away on a school trip, so she doesn't know yet. Which is no doubt why Gretchen chose this week to leave."

"I can't believe it, Howard. She must be having some kind of breakdown."

"Maybe. Though she seems quite collected."

"But you've just been on vacation. Did something happen while you were away?"

"Oh no, it's been going on much longer than that."

Jean was aware of her mother, having dismissed the coalman, peering at them through the front window, in agonies of curiosity.

"Shall we drive?" Howard asked.

"Yes, do."

It was easier to talk while moving, with eyes on the road ahead.

"Do you know where she's gone?"

"Chelsea, I believe."

A confused sense of dread, a foggy state of both seeing and not quite seeing, which had assailed Jean from the start of their conversation, now gave way to awful clarity.

"Oh, God," she said, sick with guilt as if she had deliberately conspired in the betrayal. "Martha."

"I think I always knew," said Howard. "Not about Martha herself, but that her aversion wasn't just to me but to all men. It ought to make it easier. But it doesn't."

They were driving through the common now, toward the countryside, with no declared aim other than to keep moving.

"I didn't know they had even made contact. Gretchen never said."

"That little painting of the tangerines that you brought back—it had Martha's address on. I knew Gretchen had got in contact and been to visit her—once—but I thought nothing of it. A reunion of old friends, that sort of thing. But they've been meeting in secret since."

"This is all my fault," said Jean. "It was me who brought them back together. I never imagined."

She had a sudden memory of the three of them, Howard, Gretchen and Margaret in the garden; badminton and afternoon tea, dressmaking and piano practice; the ordinary miracles of family life that she had blundered into and destroyed. It had all been an illusion; the real Gretchen was not the happy housewife with the sunny smile but the other one with the stricken expression, guarding her painful secret.

"No one is to blame," Howard said. His hands on the steering wheel clenched and released. "Except perhaps me for going ahead with the marriage when I knew that she didn't love me the way I loved her. Suspected it anyway."

"Howard, you are too hard on yourself," Jean protested, tears springing to her eyes.

"She told me she had never really stopped loving Martha, even though she never expected to see her again."

"That was cruel of her."

"She didn't mean it to be. She said she loves me too, and I believe her."

"But what about Margaret? Gretchen would never do anything to hurt Margaret and she must know this surely will."

"She's beyond reason. Her feelings for Martha have driven out all other considerations."

"But people deny their feelings all the time," Jean said. "Isn't that what parenthood is all about—sacrificing your happiness for your children's?"

"I suppose she would say that's what she has been doing these ten years—and she can't do it anymore."

"You are so reasonable, Howard. You should be raging and storming and demanding that she comes home."

"I did try a version of that," he admitted. "But it's hard to rant at someone who is already on their knees, weeping their apologies. I felt like a brute."

This image of Gretchen, abject and pleading, was too much for Jean.

"Don't," she said with a sense of guilt that was out of all proportion. "This is all my doing. I've brought this chaos into your lives."

She felt a powerful and irrational hatred for Martha, her filthy kitchen, her pretensions to art, her scarlet lipstick, her scheming. And as she contemplated the wreckage of this once happy marriage, a dark corner of her soul registered that Howard himself was now, if not legally, then at least morally free, and her heart bounded with selfish joy.

"Well, if she's gone to stay at Martha's she won't stick it for long. The place is a slum," she said with uncharacteristic spite.

It was impossible to imagine the poised and fastidious Gretchen at home among that clutter.

"Really?" Howard's face fell and Jean immediately regretted her remark. Of course it hardly flattered him to know what a reduction in circumstances she was running to. "I just can't imagine her being happy there," Jean added lamely.

The sky was darkening and they were passing Biggin Hill now, the airfield on their left, following the same route they had taken to Aunt Edie's, weeks ago when life was straightforward. It seemed as though Howard might drive all night if she let him.

"Is there anything I can do that might help? Anything at all?" she asked, conscious that her intervention so far in the Tilbury marriage hardly recommended her for the role.

"She'll need money," Howard replied. "I wouldn't like to think of her struggling or dependent on . . . someone else."

"Only you would think like that."

"I wonder if you would go and see her, give her some cash and check that she is all right. I know she won't want to face me. I don't even have an address for her."

"Of course. If you think she'll see me."

"She'll have to see someone. Margaret comes back on Saturday. She needs to be told."

"Poor Margaret," Jean burst out. "This is desperate."

Howard pulled over to the side of the road. In the pool of light from a streetlamp his face looked pale and waxy. He flipped open the glove compartment and took out a stiff white envelope addressed, with touching formality, in his neat handwriting, to Mrs. H. Tilbury. He passed it to Jean.

"It's just twenty pounds. Of course there's more if she needs it. I didn't put in a letter. I started one, but . . ."

"I'll go tomorrow morning," Jean promised.

"What about work?"

"You and Gretchen *are* my work."

Chimneys can be kept reasonably clear of soot if potato parings mixed with a little salt are burned in the grate at least once a week. This will form a glaze inside the chimney and prevent it from becoming clogged.

23

"Where are we with this Virgin Mother story? It seems to have been dragging on for months." Roy Drake shifted, wincing in his swivel chair as Jean explained the unwelcome developments in the Tilbury story. He had pulled his back over the weekend digging in his allotment and pain was adding to his displeasure.

"None of the tests so far have proved the involvement of a father. They've done the skin grafts—now they're just waiting to see if they take."

"You'd think these doctors could work a bit faster. If they treated their patients in this leisurely fashion they'd surely all be dead."

"I didn't realize it would all be so time-consuming."

"It was supposed to be an Advent miracle story. It's nearly November and we're still nowhere."

He tossed her his cigarettes and they sat for a moment recuperating in silence as the first hit of nicotine worked its magic.

"Things have got a little more complicated. Mrs. Tilbury's . . . left home."

Roy's eyebrows shot up. "Found herself another fellow?"

"Oh no," said Jean, relieved that on this point she had not been required to lie.

Although she looked up to Roy and admired him more than anyone she had ever worked with, still she could not bring herself to expose the details of Gretchen's defection to his sharp, journalistic eye. Unlike her, he had no feelings of loyalty to the family and might think this development fair game. To her mind it would be unthinkable if the real story of Margaret's mysterious origins was eclipsed by a sensational sex scandal. It would be awful for Gretchen, of course, but her sympathies now lay firmly with Howard and Margaret. It was them she had to protect at all costs.

"It just makes it awkward to get hold of her at the moment, but I'm sure it's only temporary."

"Do you think it's the pressure of all these investigations?"

"I'm sure it hasn't helped. It's on my conscience."

"You can't blame yourself for the way things have gone. She came to us. And every marriage has its fault lines."

"I suppose so. But she hid it so well. It makes me wonder what else she's been hiding."

The paradox was that while Gretchen's sexuality made it more likely that she had never had relations with a man until Howard, her dishonesty made her a less credible witness.

"I see. You think she might have been hoodwinking us all along?"

The phone on his desk rang and he silenced it with a twitch of the receiver.

"I only know that I feel a bit less confident in Gretchen personally, and yet test after test has vindicated her." She gave him an apologetic smile.

"Well, get out there and do some more digging. It's not too late. And take a word of friendly advice from an old man. Keep the husband at a distance while this plays out. Newly abandoned men tend to look for consolation wherever they can find it."

Jean felt herself reddening under his scrutiny.

"Don't tell me he's already . . ."

"No, no, nothing like that," Jean insisted, her blush deepening.

He expressed his relief by blowing out a long plume of smoke.

"He's the most decent, honorable type you can imagine—apart from you, of course."

"I'm glad to hear it. I'd begun to wonder whether there wasn't something more personal in your commitment to this story."

A shadow darkened the room. Muriel from Accounts stood outside the glass-paneled door with a sheaf of invoices. Roy raised an open hand to indicate five minutes and she retreated.

"Well, there was. Is. But it was the whole happy family thing. I wanted a little of what they had. And they were so willing to share. Even Margaret."

"The little girl."

Jean nodded. "I thought I'd buried all those maternal feelings long ago, but . . ."

Roy Drake, father of four, placed his large freckled hand on her shoulder. "It's all right, old girl. I understand."

24

Jean's first visit to Luna Street had been in the summer. Children had been playing football and vandalizing cars on the street, and babies had been put out to air in their carriages on doorsteps. On a cold Tuesday morning in late October it was deserted. Frost still glittered on the pavement on the shaded side of the street.

The slanting autumn sunlight exposed the smeared windows of number 16. A glass panel was missing from the front door, a piece of plywood nailed over the gap in the sort of temporary repair that was likely to become permanent. It was not the only house in the street to boast this sort of improvisation.

As she had walked from Sloane Square, Jean had caught a glimpse of herself in a shop window and was dismayed to see reflected there a stooping, middle-aged woman in a shabby raincoat, with unstyled mousy hair, neither straight nor curly and streaked with silver. This image of round-shouldered drabness was quite at odds with Jean's sense of herself as a brisk and respectable workingwoman, and reminded her why she generally avoided mirrors.

Drawing herself up straight, she now rang the doorbell and after a long delay heard the slap of approaching feet. It was Martha who answered. She was wearing a belted dressing gown as though just out of bed, but her face was made up, her hair tied back in that cleaning woman's bandana.

"Ah," she said by way of welcome. "I thought someone would be along sooner or later."

"It's Gretchen I've come to see."

"She's not here at the moment, but come in anyway."

Martha led the way down the passage and into the studio. The doors to the kitchen and bedroom were—perhaps strategically—shut against the intimate evidence of shared occupancy. There were already touches of Gretchen about the place—the dead plant replaced with a jam jar of fresh flowers, the floor swept, the clutter corralled if not exactly tidied. They sat as before on the low couch, but this time there was no offer of coffee and no gift of florentines.

"Do you know when she'll be back?"

"No. She comes and goes as she pleases. She's not a prisoner, you know."

"I never imagined she was. I've brought her some money. From her husband."

Martha raised her eyebrows, clearly not expecting this degree of compliance.

"Well, that's useful," she conceded.

Jean had taken the envelope from her bag but kept hold of it, reluctant to surrender it to anyone but Gretchen.

"You can leave it with me. I won't steal it, if that's what you're worried about."

"I was hoping to talk to Gretchen herself."

"She doesn't want to talk to anyone."

"I can imagine. But there is a conversation to be had about Margaret, sooner rather than later. Do you know what she intends?"

"I expect she'll want her here." Martha shrugged as if it was a matter of no great moment, one way or another.

"There is scarcely space here for a child," Jean said, feeling that there was something surreal in this discussion, conducted without any of the relevant parties present.

"We might need to find somewhere bigger at some point, I suppose."

"She is due back on Saturday." Jean's voice gave a squeak of impatience. Martha's nonchalance was beginning to rile her.

"I know you don't approve of me, Jean," Martha said, folding her long legs under her on the couch. "I'm used to it. People have disapproved of me as long as I can remember."

"One can hardly 'approve' the break-up of a family," Jean replied stiffly.

She hated being aligned with the forces of narrow-mindedness and conservatism, even though that was where she felt most at home. She had quite admired Martha at their first meeting and she was intrigued rather than alarmed by lesbianism. As a touchstone, she imagined her mother's opinion—and rejected it. She would be disgusted—therefore, Jean chose not to be. But none of this could be said.

"She was mine before she was his," Martha was saying.

"But now there's a child to consider."

"I *meant* the child."

Jean blinked, confused.

"She was named for us, you know. Martha and Gretchen."

Jean was utterly unprepared for this and had no idea what to say. "No, I didn't know."

In the silence that followed this exchange a pin-drop of sound came from behind the closed door. It was less than a breath, but Martha's quick glance confirmed that she had heard it, too.

"She's here, isn't she?" Jean said.

Martha hesitated, on the edge of a denial, and then the bedroom door opened and Gretchen stood there. Her loveliness was never off duty and she wore it like armor today.

"It's all right," she said to Martha, who had sprung up, as though to her defense. "I want to talk to Jean."

There was something defiant in the tilt of her chin.

"Do you want me to stay?"

"No, I'd like to talk to her alone. You go."

Gretchen squeezed Martha's hand and waited until she had swept up a purse and keys from the table and left, closing the front door behind her.

"Oh, Gretchen," was all Jean could say.

"Don't be angry with me, Jean," she replied with downcast eyes. "I can't help it."

Without the fortifying presence of Martha she looked much less assured.

"I'm not angry, Gretchen. It's nothing to do with me. Even Howard's not *angry*."

"Dear Howard." She perched on the edge of the couch as though not quite at home. "Is he all right?"

"Well, I don't know about 'all right,'" Jean replied. "He's very concerned about Margaret. And you. He asked me to give you this."

She handed over the envelope and Gretchen opened it in front of her, shaking her head as she counted the money.

"He's very generous," she said. "I didn't expect anything."

"Do you really mean to leave him and live here?"

"Yes."

"And what about Margaret?"

Gretchen seemed nonplussed by this question.

"Well, she'll be here too, of course, with me. Where else would she be?"

"But school? Will she have to leave her friends and start somewhere new—around here?" Jean waved an arm to signify the hinterland of Luna Street.

"Oh no, I don't think so," said Gretchen as if this was the first time she had given any thought to the matter. "She's in her last year—it would be too much upheaval. I'll take her back to Sherwood Park each morning on the train and pick her up. I think that'll be best. Don't you?"

"Best?" Jean echoed, struggling to adjust to this new casual, thoughtless Gretchen. "No, what would be best for Margaret is what she already has."

Gretchen flinched as though Jean had flung a glass of water in her face.

"But I can't," she said in a stricken voice. "I've never loved anyone but Martha. All these years with Howard—I tried, I really tried. And it's not fair on him, either. He deserves someone who can love him properly."

For an uncomfortable moment it occurred to Jean that all along Gretchen had been auditioning her for the role of Howard's comforter; coaching her, finding excuses to throw them together—the thought revolted her. She shook her head.

"You can't really be suggesting that you are doing this for Howard's benefit. He is heartbroken."

"Don't say that," Gretchen pleaded. "I can't bear to think of him unhappy. But I can't lose Martha again now that I've found her."

"That's what I don't understand. If you wanted to find Martha you could have done it years ago. She's not been in hiding. It took me no time at all."

Gretchen shook her head at Jean's simplicity.

"It wasn't finding her that was the problem. It was proving myself. And you did that for me."

"Oh?"

Through a mist of incomprehension, a distant gleam of light.

"When I found out I was going to have a baby I went to see her in Chatham at her parents'." I thought of the baby as ours—it had come to me while we were in St. Cecilia's together. I thought she was the one person who would understand. But she wouldn't believe me. She thought I had been with a man and nothing I said would persuade her.

"We had a terrible row. I said I would prove my innocence one day and she would have to kneel at my feet and apologize. Then she told me to get out and shut the door on me, and I never heard from her again until this summer, when you went to visit her and told her you believed my story."

"So all this was for her?" Jean said.

"When I saw that article in your newspaper it seemed to call out to me. I thought if you could prove I was telling the truth, my picture might be in the paper and Martha would see it and feel sorry for all the things she said."

"I see."

"It hadn't occurred to me that I might see her again. I assumed she would have forgotten me and found someone new. I just wanted her to know the truth. That was all."

"And did she?"

"Did she what?"

"Kneel at your feet and apologize."

Gretchen laughed, embarrassed. "Well, not exactly. Martha's not really the kneeling kind."

I bet she isn't, thought Jean.

"But she believes me, and that's what matters."

"And do you think you'll be happy here? And Margaret?"

Jean cast a disparaging eye around the room. Even Gretchen's efforts to make the place more homely could not disguise its seediness.

"I know it's rather crowded and messy, but that's because Martha works so hard. But I can help her to make it nice. And if I'm happy, Margaret will be happy. I'll explain it to her. She and her friend Lizzie are inseparable. I'll explain that it's the same for Martha and me—she is my best friend and we have to be together. She'll understand."

"You make it sound so simple."

"It is—why can't it be? I love Martha and I love Margaret, but I love Howard too, and even you, Jean. Especially you, because you brought Martha back to me."

Jean received this declaration with a stony face.

"I've trusted you and defended you against people who assumed you were a liar or a fantasist. And all this time you were deceiving me."

"I wasn't!" Gretchen's voice was shrill with protest. "Everything I told you about Margaret's birth is true. I never lied about that."

"You were playing a different game. And you haven't been honest. How can I know what to believe?"

"Can't you be happy for me?"

"I'm more concerned for Margaret's happiness."

She had gone too far, trespassing on a mother's territory. Gretchen blinked, wounded.

"I've always put Margaret first in everything," she said, the words thick with stifled tears. "You can't accuse me—"

"I'm sorry," said Jean. "I spoke out of turn."

She was only now beginning to realize that her own relationship with Margaret was in jeopardy—dependent as it was on Gretchen's goodwill, which could be withdrawn at any moment. The thought of being frozen out, replaced by Martha as unofficial aunt, was too much to bear. But Gretchen was not in a vindictive mood and seemed to crave only approval. She took Jean's hand between hers and squeezed it.

"We're still friends, aren't we?"

Jean nodded.

"And you'll look after Howard, won't you? He admires you so much."

"I don't suppose I shall have any reason to see him if you are no longer living there," Jean said, in part to test out her suspicion that Gretchen had deliberately thrown them together in order to ease her own escape.

"Oh, but you must! He has so few friends. Will you give him a message from me?"

"I think you need to talk to him yourself. About your plans for Margaret. I can't do that for you."

"But it was so painful last time. I can't bear it."

"You must. May I give him this address?"

"Yes, I suppose so. Will you give him my . . . love . . . or whatever you think."

At the scrape of a key in the lock, which signaled the return of Martha from wherever she had been waiting out this interview, Gretchen immediately stood up and Jean sensed herself dismissed.

The two women stood shoulder to shoulder on the front step to wave her off, or perhaps, Jean thought, to block the doorway against her return. She left with a strengthening resolve. Gretchen had forfeited all claim to Howard through her own recklessness and engineered his friendship with Jean for her own selfish ends. There was no need for any agonies of conscience on her part.

If he reached out to her in his loneliness, she would be ready.

25

Dear Howard,

I went to see Gretchen today as you asked. She was grateful for the money and touched by your kindness. I tried to make her see reason but, as you said, she seems set on this path. She was of course full of anguish at the thought of having caused you pain, as well she might be. She sent her love and will contact you soon—tomorrow—to discuss plans for Margaret.

Her address is 16 Luna Street, Chelsea.

You are in my thoughts constantly. If I can be of any further help you have only to ask.

Your friend,

Jean

Having labored over this note for far longer than its brevity warranted, Jean tore it up and started again. It had made her sound needy and emotional and a little too eager to step into Gretchen's shoes.

Dear Howard,

I have been to see Gretchen today and given her the money, for which she was grateful. She sent her love and will contact you soon about her plans for Margaret. Her current address is 16 Luna Street, Chelsea.

I hope you are well, in the circumstances.

Yours,

Jean

She was surprised and disappointed to receive no reply, even to ac-knowledge her effort, and as the days passed she began to wonder if she had all along misread his feelings for her. But she had surely not mistaken the connection between them. It had been there in that pledge of silence when he had given her the emerald brooch weeks *before* Gretchen's desertion. He couldn't now be bound by vows that had been so violently broken.

Each night before bed she would take the brooch from its velvet pouch and contemplate its careful and loving workmanship. Then she would close her eyes and replay the still-fresh memories of the day at Aunt Edie's, when their love was unspoken, real and perfect. Tomorrow, perhaps, he will call, she thought, like any lovesick girl, but tomorrow came bringing nothing.

"What's wrong with you? Are you going down with some-thing?" her mother said, watching Jean prod listlessly at her dinner of roast heart and mashed rutabaga.

"I don't know," she said, laying down her fork, the food untasted.

The least squeamish or fussy of eaters, tonight she found the sight of lambs' hearts, the valves and chambers still visible in all their anatomical detail, suddenly repulsive. Her throat bulged with the effort of not retching.

"I think I'll just have some bread and margarine."

She stood up and wrenched open the refrigerator door, feel-ing the gust of cold, sour air on her hot cheeks with relief.

"I wonder if you're going through the change," her mother mused. "It takes some women badly."

"I'm not even forty," Jean said into the fridge, her teeth gritted. "Surely not."

"You've not been yourself since Lymington."

Jean, who took pride in her ability to conceal unruly emotions, could still on occasions be surprised by her mother's acuity. She was not, then, as inscrutable as she liked to think.

"I suppose I was a bit out of sorts," she conceded, scraping margarine across the heel of a white loaf. "The weather didn't help."

"You haven't seen much of those friends of yours lately. The Jews."

"They're not Jews. I said he was a jeweler. Gretchen's a Catholic, I think. Lapsed."

"Them, anyway. I wondered if you'd fallen out."

"They've been away."

Although the temptation to talk about the Tilburys in any context was almost overwhelming, and it would have been a pleasure just to say Howard's name aloud, she felt an odd instinct to protect Gretchen from the criticism that would surely follow. And she had no wish to expose Howard to either pity or scorn, the only foreseeable responses to his predicament. So she said nothing and the moment for confidences passed, unused.

"Perhaps you need a day in bed with a hot-water bottle," her mother suggested, her remedy for every kind of feminine complaint.

"I can't take any more time off work," Jean replied. "It mounts up."

"You are probably worn out from looking after me. I'm sorry I'm such a nuisance."

"Oh, you're not really," said Jean, moved by her mother's forlorn tone. She gave her freckled, knobbly hand a squeeze, noting the contrast with her own small, delicate fingers. "Don't say that."

"At least I'm not as bad as that old dear at the hotel." She cheered up at this recollection of someone else's greater misfortune. "If I ever get like that you must put me in a nursing home."

"You know very well you'd hate that," Jean replied, unable to take much comfort from the comparison. As far as she was concerned, the only thing that divided them was the distance of a few years.

"Well, I don't want to become a burden."

"Don't think like that. We get along all right, don't we?"

"I try," her mother replied ambiguously. "If you're not going to eat that, I might as well have it."

She steered the lamb's heart onto her plate with the tip of her knife.

"Please do," said Jean, looking away to avoid witnessing the first incision.

"Perhaps we could have a fire tonight, now that the clocks have been turned back. I made some spills."

They usually tried to wait until All Souls' Day before lighting the first coal fire of winter—once having succumbed there was no going back until the following March—but there was a chill to the newly dark evenings now. They had held out longer than most of their neighbors; Jean had noticed the chimneys smoking on her way back from work for the past few days.

"I don't see why not. The coal bunker's full."

"It's a good thing the chimney's swept and ready."

As every year, her mother insisted on getting the sweep round in spring rather than waiting until autumn when the prices might have gone up. She took some pride in this sort of foresight, paying in advance for a far-off future benefit. To Jean's mind it took a particularly dark outlook on life to greet the arrival of warmer weather by making preparations for the onset of winter.

After dinner had been cleared away Jean filled the coal scuttle and set the fire going with a base of newspaper spills. They settled down together to listen to Paul Temple on the *Light*

Programme—her mother's favorite. The glamourous Steve, with her creamy voice and her chauffeur and butler and her pre-dinner cocktails with Sir Graham Forbes of Scotland Yard, was like no journalist Jean had ever met, and seemed in fact to be a complete stranger to the typewriter. It was hard to imagine *her* cycling through the rain to Petts Wood to write a column about prolonging the life of your dusters with paraffin or stiffening a petticoat with sugar water.

She found her attention wandering, soothed by the mellifluous voice of Marjorie Westbury as Steve, imagining, just a few miles away, Howard alone in the house in Burdett Road preparing a simple supper for one. She supposed he could cook, although she had seen no evidence of it. Gretchen had always seemed to be the proper *hausfrau*, with her *Sachertorte* and her *zopf* bread. Perhaps he would stay up in town after closing the shop and eat out, at some cheap establishment in Soho, with nothing to hurry home for.

This picture of Howard, standing at the stove stirring a pan of scrambled egg, or trudging the streets in the cold and dark, was so persuasive that it made her eyes smart. It struck her as monstrously unfair that Gretchen should be enjoying her freedom and the pleasures of a new lover, while she and Howard, out of some misguided sense of decorum, remained aloof and lonely. Even though she has betrayed him, he won't betray her, she thought sadly. He would never be—what was the word he had used?—"shabby."

These melancholy reflections were interrupted by the strains of *Coronation Scot* heralding the end of Paul Temple. Her mother, drowsy from the heat of the coal fire, opened her eyes, blinked and said, "Very good." If challenged, she would deny that she had been asleep but would be unable to furnish Jean with any details of the plot.

"Oh, I don't bother about the story," she would say. "I just like their voices."

Jean went out to the kitchen to make her a mug of Allenburys and to smoke her last cigarette of the day, noticing on her way an envelope on the front doormat. It had not been there earlier. She picked it up, her heart clubbing in anticipation as she recognized the neat slanted handwriting and the stiff white envelope that she had recently delivered to Gretchen.

Patience, she thought, laying it aside while she put a match to the stove and measured a mugful of milk and water into a saucepan. Bad news could wait, and good news improved with keeping. She lit her cigarette from the stove and at last sat down at the kitchen table to open her letter:

> *7 Burdett Road*
> *Sidcup*
>
> *Dear Jean,*
>
> *Thank you for your kindness in going to call on Gretchen. She has telephoned me as promised and we are agreed that I will have Margaret on Sundays, and the rest of the week she will stay with her mother in Chelsea. Margaret was naturally a little confused and upset by the new arrangements, but children are resilient creatures and she seems to be bearing up.*
>
> *The house is very quiet without them and I find myself working later, and sometimes sleeping at the shop to avoid returning to it. Obviously, something must be done in time to address the inequality in our living standards, but Gretchen is in no hurry for any further upheaval and so we proceed as we are for now.*
>
> *One unfortunate by-product of this unhappy situation, dear Jean, is that a certain awkwardness has crept into our friendship and that I regret more than I can say. I quite understand if you feel uncomfortable in my company now that Gretchen is not around, but I want you to know that in your company I always feel only pleasure and comfort and perfect ease.*
>
> *In short, I would very much like to see you and wonder if you*

would be able to meet me for lunch on Saturday in town. There is
a decent place near the shop. If you prefer not to meet, there is no
need to reply—I will be at the shop all day anyway—but I hope
you will think our friendship is sturdy enough to survive a crisis
that was not of our making.

   Yours,
      Howard

Jean sat so long at the table rereading these words in a daze of happiness that the milk boiled up all over the stove, into the gas jets, and left a burned ring on the bottom of the pan. But that was fine, because there was no chore in existence that could dampen her spirits now. He wanted to see her. Life was suddenly beautiful, precious and full of meaning. She cleaned the hob and made a fresh mug of Allenburys, and when it came to bedtime astonished her mother by throwing her arms around her and squeezing her tightly.

26

....

Pam's Piece

THE JOY OF MAIL

In our increasingly hectic lives, and with more and more of us having access to a private telephone, the art of letter writing may soon be in danger of dying out. This would be a great pity, as a thoughtful and well-written letter can bring immense pleasure to the recipient, and can be revisited again and again in the way that a phone call cannot. There is nothing quite like the sound of an envelope landing on the doormat and the thrill of recognizing the handwriting of a dear friend or distant relative.

The telephone is a shrill and demanding taskmaster: "Deal with me now!" it shrieks, like a fractious toddler. Whereas a letter may be read and replied to—or not—entirely at the convenience of the recipient. And at only 3 pence for a postage stamp, providing carriage from Land's End to John o' Groats if necessary, there can hardly be a cheaper or nicer way of making someone's day.

How many of us, though, restrict our letter writing to dutiful thank-you notes, seaside postcards or annual bulletins at

Christmas? It shouldn't be impossible to set aside half an hour a week to devote to correspondence. It will not take long for the habit to become ingrained and the effort will be rewarded many times over when the replies start coming in. Everybody stands to gain—except perhaps the overburdened postman!

....

Dear Howard,
   I'm so glad you wrote. Of course I'll come.
Your friend,
   Jean

The next three days passed in a frenzy of industry and efficiency both in the office and at home. Ashamed of having let her work on Gretchen's story lapse, she decided to rededicate herself to the investigation, finally taking the initiative to write to Kitty Benteen to arrange a meeting, using Brenda's letter as an introduction.

She also telephoned Anselm House Prep School, Broadstairs, to ask if she might visit again, after school hours, to get a more thorough look at the former wards. (In this manner she hoped to bypass the headmaster, who she felt was less likely to indulge her.) Susan Trevor, the secretary who had been so helpful on Jean's first visit, was about to go on leave to have an operation but made an appointment for the week of her return.

Optimism was a new mood for Jean, and it gave her energy for work and enthusiasm for even the dullest household chore. In the evenings, after dinner was cooked and eaten, she would launch immediately into some long-postponed task—clearing out the pantry, resewing worn sheets sides to middle, polishing the brass door handles, switching to winter drapes.

"Why don't you have a rest?" her mother would bleat from her armchair at nine o'clock as Jean dragged the furniture into the middle of the room to sweep behind it, slamming the Ewbank into the baseboard, or jumped up on a chair to wipe cobwebs from the picture rails.

"I don't need a rest; I'm fine," Jean would call as she whisked past, convinced that if she did everything at double speed she could trick time into hurrying to meet her.

On Friday she left work a little early in time to call in at Deborah's (Ladies' Fashions of Distinction) and bought herself a claret-colored wool dress with a pleated skirt, which she had seen on a mannequin in the window. Gretchen's dress, although perhaps more elegant, brought to mind too forcefully its absent creator and was therefore ruled out. Claret was a much bolder choice than her usual safe gray or navy and she wondered if it would provoke raised eyebrows indoors.

The only area in which Jean had failed to triumph was achieving a leave of absence for the afternoon. She had taken a detour past Mrs. Melsom's on her way to and from work, but they were evidently away. There was no Riley in the driveway, and the curtains upstairs and down were half drawn, and the mail slot taped shut—measures more likely to attract burglars than to repel them, in Jean's view.

Her hope rested on the fact that it was some while since she had gone "gallivanting" on a Saturday and on her weeklong tour of duty in Lymington, for which she felt some credits were due. Even so, she was not confident enough to bring up the matter much in advance, leaving it to the morning itself to present it as a *fait accompli*.

"I haven't seen that before," her mother observed as Jean appeared at breakfast, a trifle self-conscious in the claret-colored dress. "Is it new?"

"Yes. I bought it at Deborah's yesterday." She swished the skirt to and fro to show off the pleats before covering it with an apron to protect it from splashes.

"Very smart. What's the occasion?"

"Nothing special." Jean turned her back and began to busy herself at the stove preparing oatmeal. "I'm meeting a friend in town . . . if you can manage without me for a few hours."

"Oh. I daresay I can. You won't be out all day, I suppose."

"No. Just lunch. I'll be getting the midday train. If there's anything you need I could pop into Derry & Tom's afterward."

This was a tactical move, turning it from a jaunt into an errand. But her mother was not so easily played.

"I don't think so. Who's the friend? Anyone I know?"

Jean sighed. She had no appetite for the conversation that would surely follow, but she couldn't tell the kind of lie that might need elaborate embroidery in the future.

"Howard," she conceded.

"On his own?"

Here we go, thought Jean. "Yes, on his own."

"Goodness, how modern. Where's his wife? Doesn't she have something to say about this?"

"She's in no position to, since she has left him," said Jean in a crisp voice.

"Oh." Her mother drew out the lone syllable—rich with inference—almost to the snapping point. "Well, be careful. That's all I'll say."

Jean flopped the oatmeal into two bowls and set them down on the kitchen table with some force.

"Quite unnecessary. I'm not in any danger."

She could feel her cheeks burning. No one else had the power to rile her in quite the same way. When Roy Drake had cautioned her in almost identical terms it had seemed only old-fashioned and endearing. From her mother it was poison.

"He's still a married man, remember."

"We are just having lunch. I don't see why I should have to forfeit his friendship just because his wife has run off."

"It's none of my business," was the wounded rejoinder, and they proceeded to eat their oatmeal in silence.

Before she left for the train, Jean went to Harrington's to buy a small piece of beef for Sunday, and picked up potatoes and vegetables from the farm shop opposite the church. She couldn't do any dirty housework in her finery, so she contented herself with ironing and folding the laundered sheets and towels, putting some elderly tea towels to soak in borax, intending to deal with them on her return. Then she made her mother a ham sandwich for lunch, which she left on the side, covered with a linen napkin.

The wintry atmosphere of breakfast had not quite had time to thaw when Jean set off. Their disagreements and subsequent reconciliations always followed a pattern: sharp words; withdrawal for sulking and licking of wounds; silence; frosty civility; concessions on both sides; resumption of friendly relations. On this occasion they had reached the stage of frosty civility and they parted with a cool, "Goodbye then, Mother."

"Oh. Are you off? Goodbye."

And then Jean was hurrying down the hill to the station in her smart shoes that pinched, a brisk wind whipping the fallen leaves around her ankles and tugging at the flaps of her drab raincoat, which was shielding the claret-colored dress from the threat of showers.

Howard was in his workshop when she arrived. Through the shop window she could see him in profile framed in the doorway. He was quite absorbed, applying solder to the sawn edges of a silver ring with pointed tweezers, biting his bottom lip with concentration.

It was less than five months since she had first set eyes on him here and yet she found it impossible to recapture the critical detachment of that meeting, when he was just an unremarkable, oldish man who meant nothing. Now, there was no one to compare to him; when he looked up from his work and broke into a smile of welcome it filled her with joy and wonder.

She had worried about this moment: the navigation of hellos and goodbyes was fraught with hazards. But with Howard there was nothing but warmth and kindness and the certainty of some feeling not yet declared, but even so accepted and returned.

"I've missed you," he said simply when he stood beside her on the pavement, having shut up the shop and turned the sign to Closed.

"Likewise."

"Are you hungry?"

"No. Not even slightly."

"Me neither. But never mind. Let's at least go somewhere we can sit and compare our symptoms. Come on."

He walked briskly down Bedford Street, Jean just keeping up. After a few turns she was quite disoriented, with no idea where they were in relation to the shop or the Strand, or anywhere else. It was a strange and liberating experience to surrender all autonomy and be guided entirely by someone else.

Presently, he stopped outside a small Italian restaurant with pots of standard bay trees guarding the door. Its front window was no larger than that of the jeweler's shop. Inside, however, was a mysteriously spacious dining room, lit by candles in wax-spattered wine bottles. Jean had the impression of polished wood and checked tablecloths and the lively clamor of lunchtime trade.

The proprietor greeted Howard with the familiarity due to a regular customer and showed them to a corner table. It was only on stopping to make way for what turned out to be her own advancing reflection that Jean realized that one whole wall was made of mirrors and that the restaurant was only half the size that she had first assumed. She was glad to take off her coat at last, but Howard was no more aware of her smart new dress than he had been of her dowdy raincoat. I could have worn anything, she thought, with dawning relief, and he wouldn't have noticed or cared.

Without being asked, the waiter brought them a little dish of shiny green olives, a new experience for Jean, who discovered that she liked the idea of them much more than the flavor. They seemed to hail from the same world as Paul Temple and cocktails with Sir Graham and yet tasted like the smell of old gym shoes. More to her liking were the long twigs of salty bread in paper packets, which provided something to do with nervous hands while waiting for the menu.

They ordered minestrone soup and grilled sardines, which they agreed was enough for their impaired appetites, allowing for the possibility of dessert.

"Are you all right, Jean?" Howard asked as she shifted to one side and then the other.

"Yes. I'm just trying to avoid my reflection over your shoulder. It's very disconcerting. I was trying to move so you'd block the view."

Howard smiled at this, but obliged by adjusting his seat. "Some women would take it as an opportunity to preen."

"My mother used to say the Devil would creep up behind me if I stared at myself for too long. I used to run past mirrors with my hands over my eyes."

"The lies they told us."

"I could never lie to a child like that," Jean said with sudden warmth. "Could you?"

He considered. "I'm trying to remember whether I ever have. I don't think so. Although recent conversations have certainly been testing."

"Oh dear. How is Margaret? I often think of her."

"It's my day to see her tomorrow, so I'll find out. I pick her up from Luna Street at ten and take her back at six, so the whole day is ours."

"Have you been inside?"

"No, I prefer not to. But Gretchen comes to the door and it's all very . . . cordial."

His face clouded and Jean could tell that the maintenance of this civilized behavior was not without effort.

"What will you do tomorrow?" she asked, tearing open another packet of breadsticks, showering the table with crumbs.

Howard was fiddling with a packet of Lucky Strikes.

"She wanted to go swimming, but she can't because of keeping the dressing dry. So we're going to drive down to Aunt Edie's and have a bonfire in the garden. You could come if you like," he added, suddenly hopeful.

"I can't leave Mother two days in a row," said Jean, pierced with regret. "It sounds fun, though."

Always her mother, the obstacle to any such spontaneous act.

"She was quite taken with you—Edie."

He offered her the last of the olives and she took it to please him, wondering if like tea without sugar it was a taste that came with practice.

"I can't imagine why. All I did was guzzle her apple brandy and almost pass out on her lawn!"

They laughed at the memory—that day seemed long ago now, chased into the past by the dramas of recent weeks.

"That wouldn't necessarily have counted against you."

The waiter arrived with the soup and they ate for a while in silence.

"Have you told her about . . . Gretchen?" Jean said presently.

"Yes. I couldn't keep anything from her; she's far too sharp."

"Was she very shocked?"

"No—nothing rattles Aunt Edie." He laid down his spoon

and looked at her. "In fact, she said: 'Gretchen was never going to make a Tilbury. That other girl would have been much more suitable."

"Girl." Jean shook her head. "I'll be forty next month."

"Then we must do something to mark the occasion. There are few enough reasons to celebrate, so we must seize them where we can."

"We've never made much of birthdays," said Jean. "My uncle in Harrogate sends me a money order and I get a card from Dorrie, but that's about it. Perhaps I'll exert myself and bake a cake."

She remembered as she said this that baking was another area, along with not being forty, in which Gretchen had the advantage.

They finished the soup and the waiter brought them grilled sardines, crisp and crusted with salt and quite unlike the limp and soggy tinned fish that Jean was used to. She had expected potatoes and vegetables as a matter of course, but none were forthcoming and Howard didn't seem troubled by this omission. Instead, she ate the sardines unadorned by anything but a squeeze of lemon and was surprised to find them not only delicious, but also quite sufficient. She wondered how her mother would react if she took to serving an unaccompanied slab of fish or a pork chop for dinner.

Howard tried to persuade her to have dessert, but she was comfortably full and conscious of passing time. Instead they had coffee, dark and silty in dollhouse-sized cups, with a hard almond cookie, which seemed likely to fetch out a tooth and had to be abandoned for a cigarette instead. Everything about the meal was foreign and unsettling, suggesting that there were, just possibly, different ways of doing things. It was with some surprise that when they emerged once more it was to the fog of a London street rather than a sunny Italian piazza.

"I suppose I must be getting back," said Jean, already squaring up to the emptiness that would take hold of her when they had said goodbye.

"Must you so soon?" said Howard as they loitered under the restaurant's awning. "I could swear you only just arrived. Time does strange things when we're together."

"And when we're apart," Jean agreed, daring to look him in the eye as she said this.

"Let's walk for a bit," he said, taking her hand. "With a bit of luck we'll get lost in the fog."

Just a few minutes more, Jean promised herself, and then I'll go home. She could feel the pressure of his hand, gently squeezing hers as they walked through the milky grayness. Other pedestrians, appearing as distant smudges, loomed into focus briefly as they passed before being swallowed up again.

"Where are we going?" she asked at last.

"I don't know," he admitted. "I just know that if I stop walking, you'll leave."

"But you know where to find me again."

They had turned into a narrow street, empty of cars, and walked the length of it before realizing it was a dead end, leading nowhere but to the back stairs of restaurant kitchens and a high brick wall at the rear of a theatre. There were empty wooden crates and steel dustbins on the pavement and in the gutter carrot tops and bruised cabbage leaves and other detritus of a fruit and vegetable market. As if given courage by their solitude, he drew her toward him and they stood pressed together for a moment.

"I must go," Jean said, laying her head on his shoulder.

"I know."

"Will you stay at the shop tonight?"

"Yes—there's a camp bed in the workshop. It's like a bed of nails but it's better than the empty house."

"You must miss her terribly. I wish I could help."

"You do help." He put his hands on her shoulders and moved her away so that he could look at her. "May I see you again soon?"

"Of course." She laughed lightly to disguise a bubbling up of emotion that might embarrass them both. "You can call me at the paper. Or at home, but of course that's not so private. And now I really must go, only I don't know where I am."

She looked at her watch and gave a yelp of alarm. Four o'clock. It would be five, perhaps later, before she reached home. She could imagine the reception that awaited her.

Howard led her through the foggy streets to the Strand, where the traffic was crawling along, inch by inch, the streetlamps creating cones of milky light, and they said a hasty goodbye.

The train was even slower than usual, stopping at stations for so long it almost seemed it must have broken down before lurching off again at a stately pace, never quite gathering speed. But even her guilty anxiety couldn't quite take the shine off the day. The memory of it was all still there to be taken out of its box and inspected from every angle later.

Out in the suburbs the fog had dissolved, leaving just a gauzy halo around the street lamps as Jean toiled up the hill from the station, her smart shoes biting with every step.

She could tell as soon as she came in sight of the house that something was not right. There were no lights on, even though dusk had fallen, and the front room curtains were still open. She fumbled and jabbed her key at the lock with clumsy hands.

"Mother, where are you?" she called into the cold and unlit hallway, but only the hollow scraping tick of the grandmother clock came back in reply.

A chilly draft licked at her ankles and she traced it to the open back door. Peering out into the twilit garden she saw a row of white tea towels swinging stiffly on the washing line and her mother, a pale shape, stretched out on the grass below as though asleep.

27

The arrival of an ambulance in the Knoll on a Saturday evening brought the neighbors to their windows. Jean was conscious of this silent audience gathering to watch the unfolding drama as her mother was carried up the driveway on a stretcher. Their curiosity would have to go unsatisfied for a while longer.

Jean had crouched beside her on the lawn awaiting the ambulance, having fetched her a blanket, a pillow for her head and a hot-water bottle. The ground was damp and her hands icy.

"I'm glad you're back," she croaked, looking up at Jean with watery eyes. "It's terribly cold out here."

She had been trying to hang out to dry the tea towels—those damned tea towels!—that Jean had left to soak rather than risk splashing her new dress. Somehow in reaching up for the line to hang up the last one she had lost her balance and toppled forward. There was a raised lump on her forehead, puffy with fluid, and pain everywhere that made movement impossible.

Tears leapt to Jean's eyes as she imagined the frightened cries for help going unanswered while she was dawdling in the fog with Howard. But, at the same time, the clamorous inner voice of self-justification kept up its pleading: why was her mother out in the garden on her own, troubling herself with laundry—a chore she would never bother to attempt while Jean was on hand? And now she probably had a broken hip and double pneumonia, either of which would be enough to carry her off, and it would be all Jean's fault.

The thought of losing her mother, source of so much resentment and self-sacrifice, caused her heart to gallop in frantic denial. How would she tell Dorrie? How would she live out the rest of her years—an orphan—in the empty house?

It was only a short journey to Bromley & District Hospital and the ambulance man, at the head end of the stretcher, kept up a flow of reassuring chatter, even though the patient was unable to respond with more than a blink and a flutter of her fingers.

"She will be all right, won't she?" Jean whispered, from the foot end, when at last she could bring herself to meet his eye.

"Oh yes," he said with massive, beaming confidence. "She's tough, aren't you, Mother?"

Standard-issue reassurance that did for everyone not yet deceased, no doubt, but Jean was grateful for it.

On arrival at the emergency department her mother was borne away and Jean felt herself dismissed. The smell—nauseating gusts of sickness, rubber, disinfectant and cooking—still made her queasy. Her recent happier visits to Charing Cross Hospital with Gretchen and Margaret couldn't quite efface those earlier grim memories of being a patient herself.

In the waiting room, half a dozen people, relatives of other recent casualties, similarly abandoned, sat gazing into space. Occasionally, a door would open and they would sit up hopefully as a nurse appeared and then slump back again as she passed through without breaking her stride.

In one corner an elderly clergyman was trying to cough discreetly into a handkerchief, his lungs bubbling and crackling. Opposite Jean was a young man, with quiffed hair and a cigarette behind his ear, dressed up as though for a night out. He seemed hugely self-conscious and ill at ease, his neck red with embarrassment, one foot tapping uncontrollably. Jean remembered the awkwardness of youth and pitied him.

One woman was attempting to distract a grizzling infant with nothing but a door key on a leather fob. Within seconds its potential to fascinate was exhausted and the child's whining redoubled. The woman stood up, hauling him onto her hip, and began to pace.

"He's not mine; he's my daughter's," she announced with a preemptive glare.

The young man looked up and Jean recognized him now as the Romeo from the print room. She nodded at him and he nodded back, but not before she saw a flicker of alarm cross his face—a fear of being acknowledged in public by a middle-aged woman. Jean sighed. The cigarette behind his ear reminded her that she had smoked her last one with Howard at lunchtime, a lifetime ago. The realization that she had none left and tomorrow was Sunday brought on an unassailable craving.

Leaving the hospital, she crossed the road to the pub. It was dark outside and cold, too, after the heated stuffiness of the waiting room, and she shivered in her thin raincoat. The pub was bright and crowded with drinkers enjoying their Saturday night. Jean bought twenty Players. Even though she often ran out and had no intention of giving up the habit, she couldn't quite bring herself to buy in bulk. It seemed to demonstrate too hubristic a faith in the future.

By the time she got back to the hospital a nurse had appeared and was calling her name. Her heart lurched in fear, but the news was reassuring: her mother had been admitted to the geriatric ward and was drinking a cup of tea. She was cold and bruised but otherwise uninjured. There were signs of a chest infection, which needed monitoring.

"Can I see her? Does she know I'm here?"

The nurse looked at her watch. "Visiting hours are over now. You can come back tomorrow at three."

"All right. Will you give her my love?"

The nurse smiled and turned to the next name on her list.

Jean was letting herself into the house for the second time that day when her neighbor Mrs. Bowland came hobbling up the drive to intercept her.

"My dear, is there any news of your mother?" she asked with her head on one side in an attitude of concern. "I saw the ambulance."

She must have been sitting by the window all evening, hoping for a tragedy to feast on, thought Jean, and then felt unworthy. Her mother was not popular in the street, having frozen out all early attempts at friendship, but the Bowlands had certainly tried, so perhaps her sympathy was genuine.

"She fell over in the garden earlier and gave herself a bit of a knock. Nothing broken, apparently," she replied, finding herself adopting the same brisk tone as the nurse.

Now she wouldn't need to bother telling the other residents of the street. Once one knew, they all knew.

"Well, it's so easy to fall at our age. And it rather knocks your confidence," Mrs. Bowland remarked.

"Oh dear—she never had much of that to begin with," Jean said.

Once inside, the door closed, she felt suddenly weary and sat down hard on the stairs. It was nine o'clock; she had eaten nothing since those sardines at lunchtime and her stomach growled. There was a time when the prospect of an empty house would have been precious beyond imagining; a whole evening to spend or waste in solitude just as she chose. But she was too tired and anxious to enjoy it and her feet were so sore from walking in shoes that pinched that she could think of nothing more luxurious to do than collapse on the couch and examine her worries, one by one.

28

When Jean arrived on the ward the following afternoon for visiting time she found her mother sitting up in bed with an expression of rapt concentration on her face as she eavesdropped on the whispered conversation taking place at the next bed.

"Shh!" she said, cutting off Jean's greeting. "I'm trying to listen."

"Well hello to you, too," said Jean, relieved to see her mother's spirit undimmed by her surroundings.

She had brought with her a carpetbag containing slippers, shawl, the brushed-cotton nightgown from Peter Jones and a tablet of lavender soap delivered that morning by Mrs. Melsom. News of the accident had spread via the Bowlands to the congregation of St. Mary's, at which Mrs. Melsom was a volunteer. She had hurried around directly with her gift, wrapped in blue tissue paper.

"I always think it's nice to have something to put under your pillow to mask the hospital smell," she said, pressing it into Jean's hand. "I know your mother likes lavender."

Does she? thought Jean, ashamed to realize that she knew nothing of these preferences. But she was touched by the gesture—one of those small, untrumpeted acts of kindness, passed from person to person, that bind a community together.

"Soap? Funny thing to bring," said her mother, laying it aside unopened.

"How are you today? Nothing broken, they say."

"If you believe that you'll believe anything. Look at me!" She threw the bedsheet back with surprising strength and lifted her cotton gown to reveal a livid purple bruise from hip to knee—and much else besides.

"Yes, well, cover yourself up," said Jean, flustered, replacing the sheets.

It was something she had noticed before about people in hospitals; in the face of illness and shared quarters they rapidly abandoned all modesty.

"It's agony, I might tell you," her mother remarked.

"It looks it. Do they give you anything for the pain?"

"Probably. I don't know. It's a madhouse." She leaned, wincing, closer to Jean and spoke from the corner of her mouth. "There was a man in here last night—going from bed to bed. He put his hand right under the covers. I soon sent him packing."

For a moment or two Jean was quite dumbfounded, speechless with outrage.

"A man? On the ward? Why didn't you call out or say something?"

Her mother gave a scornful laugh. "No one would believe me . . . Anyway, then there was a sort of fire drill, and we all had to get up and go outside in the rain in our nothingness. What a performance." She chuckled to herself at the memory.

Jean looked around at the other occupants of the ward—comatose, heavily bandaged, intubated or otherwise immobilized—and caught up at last.

"Goodness. Quite a night, then."

"I'll say."

All the same, she felt obliged to mention her mother's remarks to the head nurse before she left.

"She seems a little confused."

"They all get like that. It's the diamorphine."

Jean smiled, not altogether reassured.

"She thought she'd been interfered with. By a man."

Matron shook her head. "She also thinks Queen Mary is in the bed opposite."

"It must be so distressing—perhaps she'd be better off without the diamorphine."

The head nurse looked at her over her glasses. "You only say that because you are not in pain."

Jean accepted the rebuke. "How long will she be in here, do you think?"

"I can't say. At the moment she can't even use the bathroom."

The look in her gray eyes was neither stern nor kind but some combination of the two—a calm, unassailable confidence that she was in charge and knew what was best. It was oddly soothing and reminded Jean of someone; she had been in the presence of this phenomenon before, but she couldn't now recall where.

She went home feeling somewhat disconcerted by the conversation with her mother. Something about it kept tweaking at the edge of her mind, refusing to reveal itself, as she prepared her dinner of cheese on toast. It was there as she washed up her single plate and knife and fork, and as she sat at the kitchen table to write a brief letter to Dorrie explaining about the accident and that there was no cause for alarm, but she couldn't coax it into view.

The next day when she arrived for evening visiting hours after a long day at work, she found her mother slightly worse.

Someone had brushed her hair back off her face, destroying what was left of the curl, and giving her a severe and somewhat masculine appearance, which would have horrified her if she had been able to see it. Looking around, Jean noticed with dismay that the other patients had been treated to a similar grooming regime and now looked like members of the same androgynous tribe.

She was thankful that there were no mirrors within range. For a recluse, her mother had always been particular about her appearance, fretting over her diminishing looks, taking great comfort from her remaining advantages—slender ankles, straight teeth—and frequently reapplying lipstick and powder, even though there was no one but Jean to appreciate it.

Today her confusion was deeper, robbing her of confidence and causing her to retreat into silence, with occasional bursts of chuckling. Inquiries as to what was amusing her produced the mysterious one-word explanation—"Badgers." She seemed fascinated to the point of obsession by the woman in the opposite bed, an unlikely source of entertainment, as she was mostly asleep and snoring. If a nurse approached, momentarily blocking the view, she would crane her neck and wave her imperiously out of the way in case she missed something important. Jean, by contrast, she barely noticed.

The nurse on duty expressed surprise when Jean mentioned her concerns. From their point of view, Mrs. Swinney was an ideal patient—placid and untroublesome, grateful for small attentions, where others were restless and obstreperous.

"But she's not herself," Jean protested. "She was perfectly sane when she arrived. Now she hardly knows who I am."

She remembered with shame her previous irritation with her mother's irksome habits and predictable conversation. What trivial dissatisfactions these now seemed.

The nurse looked disappointed. There was a hint of reproach in her voice.

"I'll tell the doctor what you've told me. But *we're* all really pleased with her progress."

Jean cycled back to the empty house and a supper of beans on toast. She was getting used to having the place to herself and a little flexibility was creeping into her routines. Her evening meal could be anytime and consist of anything—bread and jam if she fancied it—and bath night could be whatever night she chose. She could listen to the record player, the radio or neither without any negotiation and after nine o'clock.

By the time she returned from the hospital in the evening it was hardly worth lighting a fire, so she took a hot-water bottle up to bed instead and left the grate unswept. In an exceptionally bold act, she threw out the threadbare brown rug from the sitting room, which had come with them from the flat in Gipsy Hill with the rest of their belongings. Jean had always hated it, because it curled at the corners to trip the unwary and darkened an already dark room.

She replaced it with a pale blue carpet from Nash's of Orpington in a defiantly impractical shade that matched nothing. Its newness was a dazzling reproach to its surroundings, which now looked evermore tatty and forlorn. But it was difficult to enjoy even these small liberties untarnished by feelings of guilt and remorse, while her mother was so lost and strange.

In those undisturbed evenings she turned back again to Alice Halfyard's diary, rereading the entries covering the dates when Gretchen had been a patient, and then idly—and because she rather enjoyed Alice's brisk prose—reading on into the days and weeks beyond. Gretchen's place in the ward had been taken by a girl called Ruth, who was being treated (unsuccessfully) with ultraviolet light therapy for psoriasis. There were occasional references to someone called V, whom Jean was unable to identify among the other inmates or staff and whose symptoms were only alluded to in vague terms.

September 19
V not tolerating the new drugs. V excitable.

October 6
V worse than ever today.

This awakened Jean's curiosity and she reread the entire diary to see if there were any other mentions. There was just one entry from May—*before* Gretchen's arrival:

May 24
Startled to find V waiting for me today in the rain.
Absolutely soaked through like a faithful dog. I managed
to conceal my alarm.

But there was no record of an admission or discharge date, which puzzled her. V had clearly been a long-term patient throughout the period of Gretchen's residency and yet none of the girls had ever mentioned her. Jean decided to query this with Alice herself and made several attempts to telephone her, during office hours and in the evening, but there was no reply.

Howard, and the memory of their lunch and that strangely *intimate* walk in the fog, was never far from her mind. He had said he sometimes slept at the shop, but when she tried ringing there one evening there was no answer, so she assumed he was back at home. Calling him during the day was problematic in a shared office of shameless eavesdroppers, so she sent a brief note, thanking him for the lunch and explaining about her mother's accident.

The following evening, Friday, on her return from the hospital, she was contemplating, without enthusiasm, the range of cans in the pantry and wondering what manner of meal might be conjured from sardines, new potatoes and oxtail soup, when she heard the flap of the mail slot. The fact that the sardines had already brought to mind the Italian restaurant and Howard himself sent her hurrying to the door. On the mat was the now-familiar white envelope. She tore into it without waiting.

Friday, 8:30 p.m.

Dear Jean,

I have just come home to find your letter with the news of your mother.

I am so sorry that our afternoon should have ended so unfortunately and that you had to deal with it alone. I will not ring the doorbell in case you have company, but I will wait at the end of the road for half an hour or so, in the hope that you receive this in time and want to talk.

Yours,

    Howard

Jean snatched up her keys and flew from the house, realizing at the end of the drive that she was still wearing her apron and slippers. She tore the apron off and stuffed it into the hydrangeas; the slippers could not be helped and Howard was the last person to mind or notice.

There was the dark shape of the Wolseley parked at the top of the road. The headlights blinked in welcome at her approach. The passenger door was open; she jumped in beside him and they clasped each other awkwardly across the hand brake.

She was aware of the bristly tweed of his jacket against her cheek and his unique scent—a combination of soap, tobacco and wool and the oily metallic smell of the workshop. Strength and comfort streamed from him like a warm current. She felt, as always in his presence, a deep sense of relief. Now she was perfectly safe.

They disengaged from their somewhat contorted embrace and looked at each other. In the shadows cast by the streetlamp outside his eyes were black and unreadable.

"My friend," he said in a kind of wonderment, taking her hand and kneading it in his. "You're here."

"Yes."

"I don't know what I'd have done if you hadn't come. Waited all night, perhaps."

"I'm just glad I didn't miss you."

"I would have come sooner if I'd known you were by yourself all this time. I've been kicking around at home with nothing to do but think of you."

"Same here."

"What a waste." He put her hand up to his lips and kissed it.

At the tap of feet on the pavement they moved apart instinctively, guiltily. The passerby was a stranger to Jean, a commuter, with overcoat and rolled umbrella, returning late from the station. If he had glanced into the car he would have seen a plain middle-aged woman in slippers and an even older man with thinning hair and heavy-rimmed glasses—such unlikely objects of passion, he could hardly have guessed at the longing that flowed between them.

"I wish . . ." Howard began and then stopped.

"What?"

"I was just thinking, I wish I'd found you years ago."

"You make me sound like a lost glove," Jean laughed.

"Well that's a good image. The missing half of a pair."

She had come running out of the house without a coat and it was cold in the car with the engine stilled and the darkness pressing at the glass. He noticed her shivering.

"We could go somewhere warm. A pub, if you like?"

She shook her head, recalling those evenings spent in the White Swan with Frank while he drank himself into a good mood and then out the other side again.

"We have two empty houses between us," she said. "Surely there's no reason for us to skulk in the car? Why should we be lonely?"

And yet the guilt was there between them like an unwanted third person, interfering, spoiling everything.

"No reason at all," he agreed. "Just say which you prefer."

Jean imagined Mrs. Bowland stationed at the front room window, observing and judging, and her defiance faltered.

"Yours," she said.

He nodded. "Mine, then."

Only a faint yellow glow leaked from the curtained windows in Burdett Road. All was still.

"Everyone's back in their hutches," Howard whispered as he let them into the house.

Jean felt a momentary tremor of unease at this act of trespass, but then he switched the lamp on in the hallway and the feeling vanished with the darkness. He led her into the sitting room and turned on the gas fire, which emitted a bluish light and a high-pitched whine and sudden, dramatic heat. She had never seen this room before, with its armchairs and television set; as a guest, she had been ushered into the front parlor, upstairs to the workshop for a dress fitting or into the garden.

They kissed, for a long time, gently at first and then less so. Then Howard pulled away and, holding her face, said, "Will you stay tonight? I don't think I can bear to take you back home."

"In Gretchen's bed?"

"No. In mine."

She remembered the single divans with their matching bedspreads and the chilly chasm between them.

He mistook her hesitation and said, "Or here," and before she could correct him, he dashed out of the room and upstairs. Moments later he reappeared dragging a quilted eiderdown and blanket, which he spread out in front of the gas fire.

"All right. Just here," she said. "Now, kiss me again."

He knelt down to undress her, his shaking hands fumbling over every button and zip and hook, until she was naked in front of him. Then he stopped and looked up at her with a troubled expression.

"I haven't done this for seven years. Will you forgive me if it goes badly?"

Jean laughed, amazed at her own boldness in displaying her body while he was still fully clothed. It was the strangest feeling, placing herself in someone else's power with complete confidence. There was nothing she wouldn't do for him.

"Well, I haven't done it for longer than that. But it doesn't matter, as long as we're kind."

And so even though they were unpracticed, they were kind and that made it all right. And afterward they lay for a long time pressed together, her head on his shoulder, his hand stroking her hip while the night deepened around them. There was no urgency to move apart; morning and work were a long way off.

Jean remembered how Frank could never lie still with her for one minute once the loving was over but would sit up, light a cigarette and start scrabbling for his clothes in one impatient movement. She'd thought it was something all men did.

"Are you tired?" Howard asked, kissing her hair. "You can sleep if you like."

"No—I'm wide awake," said Jean, not wanting to waste a moment of their time together in mere sleep.

They shifted into a sitting position with their backs to the couch, the eiderdown gathered around them, and she confessed that she had had no supper and was hungry. So he made them tea and toast, which they ate there on the floor, and when he noticed that she was shivering he fetched a soft woolen shawl for her shoulders.

"It's not Gretchen's," he said. "It's one of Aunt Edie's cast-offs. She's never worn it, I promise."

He had a gift for anticipating her vulnerabilities and reassuring her before she was even aware of them.

"You know all my thoughts without my saying them," Jean replied. "Am I really that transparent?"

"Let's see," said Howard, gazing into her eyes with a frown of concentration, his lips moving slowly as he pretended to read.

"What does it say?" she laughed.

It was so easy and natural to talk nonsense when your love was returned.

"It says, 'I would like to come back and do this again tomorrow and possibly the next day.'"

"More or less," she agreed.

"Why shouldn't we?" he asked, more serious now. "We are not hurting anyone, are we?"

"No. But, Howard, we won't tell Gretchen, will we? I'd feel so awkward."

"I can't see that I'd have any *occasion* to tell her. But I don't see any need for deception."

He was right, of course. Dishonesty could never bring peace of mind. Always he was there just ahead of her, with that lantern of decent behavior.

"I just feel guilty somehow, for stepping so quickly into her shoes. Her bed, I mean."

"She was never *in* her bed!" he protested, gathering her in his arms again. "But whatever you say."

"Did you really never make love with her? Even in the beginning?" Jean asked.

"Of course, at first. But I could tell she didn't like it—it was just something she felt she had to do, with gritted teeth, so to speak. Which made me feel like a monster. So I gradually stopped asking and the intervals got longer and one day I realized that it had been more than a year and it sort of dawned on me that we would never make love again."

"It was selfish of her to marry you, knowing that she couldn't love you properly."

"The thing that hurt most was being made to feel that my desires were unreasonable for all those years. Gretchen always insisted that sex was unimportant and meant nothing to her, but that wasn't true. As soon as Martha reappeared, suddenly her desires trumped everything. Her 'natural feelings' couldn't be suppressed for five minutes, but I'd had to suppress mine for years."

He still loves her, Jean thought with a tightness in her throat of swallowed jealousy.

"I understand," she said in as steady a voice as she could manage, "that she's still your wife and your feelings for her won't change overnight. I do understand that."

He looked at her with concentration and amazement.

"You are generous, Jean," he said, kissing her again, "but you don't need to be. It's you now."

"It's you, too," she said.

A feeling of peace swept over her as if she had reached the end of a long journey and could now rest.

"I sometimes wondered . . ." she said, drawing him to her so that he lay back with his head in her lap. He looked at this angle and without his glasses quite different, a stranger. "Whether Gretchen was trying to engineer things to throw us together. Did you ever think that?"

"It's possible. Something like it happened once before with Margaret's first piano teacher. Gretchen always made me take her home and seemed to find ingenious ways of leaving me alone with her. It was as if I was being given permission to stray. All unspoken, of course. But I wasn't the least bit attracted to the piano teacher. Or she to me, I might add."

Jean looked skeptical. The idea that someone could be indifferent to Howard struck her as highly improbable. The woman must have been some kind of imbecile.

"I didn't think I'd made much of a first impression on you myself," she said.

"You were rather businesslike and brisk with your notebook," he smiled. "And then you cut yourself on my coping saw."

"Yes. I'd forgotten that. You complimented me on my hands."

"Did I?" He picked one up and turned it over with an appraising glance. "They are rather pretty. I never imagined you'd be putting them to such good use."

Jean burst out laughing.

"I don't think I began to notice you properly until that day you came to tea and we played badminton."

"Now you are making fun of me."

"Not at all. You were such a good sport."

"That was a lovely afternoon. And I went home envying your perfect marriage."

"Ha!"

There was a silence as they separately reflected on the unravelling of that illusion.

"And then I bumped into you at Charing Cross," Jean went on, "and you insisted on seeing me home. You were so funny; I didn't want the journey to end, even though we hardly spoke. That was when it started for me."

"I remember. But it was at Aunt Edie's that I fell in love with you. I think it was when I saw you sitting in the apple tree. But I couldn't say anything."

"You didn't need to. I felt it, too."

"The next day was so gray and empty. I was like a child on Boxing Day—all the magic over."

For Jean it was pure pleasure to reminisce about the painful separation from the safe haven of rapturous togetherness. The sense of security and confidence was quite new to her. All of her dealings with Frank had been tinged with fear—fully justified, as it turned out—that she bored him; that she would do something to incur his anger; that he would leave her for someone younger or prettier.

Howard let out a sigh and rubbed his eyes with the heel of his hands.

"You look sad," she said. "Or worried."

"Because I've so little to offer you."

"I don't need anything. I just know that when I'm with you I'm happy, and when I'm not I'm miserable. That's all."

"Will you come back again tomorrow?"

"As soon as I've been to the hospital. They might send Mother home soon and then I'll be confined to barracks again."

"Then we must make the most of the time we have."

The thought of her mother, alone and bewildered, made Jean's crowded heart quail within her. The freedom to spend her nights with Howard was entirely provisional upon her mother's continued absence. Jean now found herself in the invidious position of wishing her ongoing ill health and a slow recovery. When she tried to visualize the future any more than a few days ahead there was no certainty, only fog.

29

The crooked tines of the rake made a tinny rattle as they combed the wet grass, drawing the leaves into a copper mound. Jean, defended against the autumn weather by boots and windbreaker over her oldest outdoor clothes, was spending her Saturday out in the front garden catching up with neglected chores.

In the last week the horse chestnuts and Canadian oaks in Knoll Park had given up the last of their leaves. Great drifts of them had blown into the Swinneys' driveway and were plastered over the front lawn and banked up against the garage doors. Jean had filled the metal garbage can five times and five times carried it down to the compost heap. She had already taken down the withered runner beans, dismantled their bamboo skeleton, stored the canes in the shed for the winter and dug over the earth. The rhubarb had been mulched and the onions weeded and treated to a dressing of soot.

In the kitchen a cherry cake was cooling on the rack. She would glaze it later and take it with her to Howard's for tea when he came back from work. She had hardly spent any time at home for over a week now, returning only briefly to collect the mail and clean clothes for work.

Mrs. Bowland had waylaid her on the first of these flying visits, ostensibly for news of Mrs. Swinney; also to query the pints of milk left out on the doorstep overnight.

"Oh, I've been staying with a friend," Jean said, cursing herself for overlooking this detail.

"We wondered if everything was all right," said Mrs. Bowland, "when you didn't come home."

"Yes, quite all right, thank you," said Jean, refusing to be probed. "Although Mother is still not quite her old self."

There had been a few days of what appeared to Jean complete and irreversible derangement, during which her mother entirely failed to recognize her, mistaking her variously for the ward nurse, Queen Mary and a pickpocket bent on stealing her wedding ring. She had lost all sense of time and place, with no inkling of where she was or how long she had been there. The mystery of her circumstances didn't appear to cause her any anxiety and her hallucinations—badgers romping up and down the ward—amused rather than alarmed her.

Although Jean found these developments troubling, she couldn't help noticing that losing her wits had greatly improved her mother's mood and general demeanor. She was infinitely more cheerful now than at any time in recent memory. Jean's prayers for her recovery had a flavor of St. Augustine's plea for chastity. *Please, God, make Mother better, but not yet.*

Jean carried the last load of leaves to the compost, swept the drive and returned the rake and broom to the shed, and not a moment too soon. There was a growl of distant thunder as she crossed the lawn and a few fat drops of rain began to fall.

Howard would be back from work at six-thirty and there was liver and bacon for dinner and then the cherry cake. They would sit together on the couch holding hands and listening to his jazz records on the phonograph. Then they would go upstairs and climb into Howard's single bed together, ignoring that abandoned one just beyond the gap, and make love, because you never knew what was around the corner and when something might come along to put a stop to it.

Now, though, she had a couple of hours before she was due to cycle over to the hospital for visiting time, just long enough to ice the cake and have a hot bath—on a Saturday afternoon! She had just weighed out the sugar when the doorbell rang. Mrs. Bowland again, she thought with a sinking heart. Stretching her face into a patient smile, she opened the door.

Margaret stood on the doorstep, red-eyed, her coat bulging oddly as she clutched at her chest. A fine mist of raindrops was caught in her curls like dew on a web.

"Margaret! What are you doing here?" Jean exclaimed, glancing up and down the road for evidence of Gretchen or some other companion.

Belatedly, she took in the child's bedraggled state and the bulge, now revealed to be a struggling Jemimah.

"I've run away," Margaret said, sniffing noisily and hoisting the rabbit into a more manageable position. "I didn't know where else to go. Daddy's at work."

It was some weeks since Jean had seen her and the resemblance to Gretchen, and the doll-like beauty of her face, struck her all over again.

"Come in, come in," she replied, her mind racing at this new development. "Have you come all this way by yourself?"

"Yes. With Jemimah. She was all right at first, but she got a bit wriggly. And then it started to rain."

"How on earth did you find your way here?"

"Mummy takes me to school every day so I know how to get trains and I remembered that you lived near the station from that time I came to make cinder toffee. I know your address from sending you a postcard. So I asked the lady at the newsstand in the station. She hadn't heard of you, but she'd heard of the Knoll."

They had advanced no further than the hall during this exchange.

"Let's go and put Jemimah down and then you can tell me why you've run away," Jean suggested, wondering what Margaret would have done if she had not been at home, as was very nearly the case. The thought made her feel quite dizzy.

In the kitchen, while Jemimah hopped around the linoleum, exploring her new domain and shunning the wizened carrot supplied by Jean from her depleted pantry, Margaret took off her wet coat and rotated her aching arms with relief. She had also been carrying a shoulder bag, which she now unpacked onto the table to reveal her beaded purse, toothbrush, notebook and a sack of dried rabbit food. As a running-away kit, it struck Jean as touchingly inadequate.

Jean made her a glass of hot milk, cut a slice of cake and then fetched the least threadbare of their towels to put around her shoulders.

"Now, what's all this about running away?" she said at last as she patted dry Margaret's hair.

"I hate Martha," said Margaret, her pretty face crumpling into a frown.

"Hate's a strong word," said Jean, silently rejoicing.

"Well, she hates me, too."

"I'm sure she doesn't. Who could possibly hate you?"

"She won't let me bring Jemimah in the house for even *one minute* because she's allergic to fur, *she says*. So I have to play with her out in the backyard in the cold. And there's not even any grass. It's horrible."

"Oh dear."

"And I have to sleep on a fold-out bed in the room where Martha does all her painting and it's really messy and smells of paint. But if *I* make a mess I get told off."

"Have you told your mother how you feel?"

"She doesn't understand. Martha's all nice when she's around. But if Mummy goes out she just ignores me."

Margaret took a sip of milk and wiped her top lip on her sleeve.

"One time when we were on our own I said, 'You don't like me, do you?' and she said, 'I haven't decided yet. I don't *dislike* you."

Her rendering of Martha's low, cultured voice was uncannily, almost cruelly accurate.

"Oh, Margaret, I don't know what to say. What can I do to help you?"

The girl blinked hard to try and hold down the first hot prickling of tears.

"I wish we could just go back to the way things were," she burst out. "With Daddy. It was better before."

Jean put a tentative arm around her shoulders and, meeting no resistance, gathered her into a hug. She could feel the bones of her back, fragile and birdlike, beneath the wool of her cardigan as she sobbed.

"Don't cry," she pleaded, powerless to offer any real comfort. "Everything will be all right."

But this was an assurance not hers to make and, as one of the chief beneficiaries of the fractured Tilbury marriage, she felt its hollowness.

At last Margaret's tears were cried out and she consented to mop her flaming face with a cool facecloth. This outpouring of emotion and moisture had fogged the kitchen windows.

"Good heavens," said Jean, "much more of this and we'll have to build Jemimah a raft."

Margaret had recovered sufficiently to giggle between gulps and sniffs.

"Did you tell anyone where you were going?"

"No. I just sneaked out."

Jean imagined Gretchen, frantic at the discovery and combing the streets. She would have to be telephoned and reassured at some stage, but would it really hurt her to taste a little fear, if it opened her eyes to the cost of her emancipation?

In the end it was Howard she rang, leaving that other, more difficult phone call to him. Margaret was adamant that she wanted to go home to Burdett Road. It was agreed that he would pick her up after work; Sunday was their day together anyway. The rest would have to be negotiated with Gretchen. Margaret's main concern was Jemimah.

"Where is she going to sleep tonight? I had to leave the hutch behind."

Howard promised to bring a stout cardboard box home from the shop; he would spend the evening fashioning some form of temporary rabbit-proof accommodation. It was impossible for Jean to speak openly with Margaret bobbing about beside her and interjecting every few seconds, and the anguished pauses in the conversation were heavy with unspoken regret for their abandoned plans.

Noticing that Margaret was starting to shiver in her damp clothes, Jean offered to run her a hot bath—the one she had intended to take herself but would not now need. She filled it a little deeper than the scant three inches that was her usual allocation and dug out another of their elderly towels from the airing cupboard. It was only at moments like these, when she saw her belongings through another's eyes—even those of an uncritical ten-year-old girl—that she was ashamed of how shabby they were. There was a crust of limescale around the neck and snout of the tap, and a green streak running down the enamel from the overflow to the drain. The ancient linoleum, though clean, was cracked and ridged.

"I'm sorry, it's probably not as nice as your bathroom at home," Jean said.

Having lived there all week she knew quite well that it wasn't.

"That's all right," said Margaret kindly, beginning to peel off her jumper. "It's better than Luna Street."

Jean left her to undress and returned to the kitchen, where Jemimah had been shut in with a saucer of the rabbit food from Margaret's running-away kit. She washed up the milk dish and cut herself a slice of the cherry cake—Howard could take the rest when he came—then sat at the table gazing blankly at the crossword in the Saturday paper while brooding on these latest developments.

If Margaret moved back home permanently that would put an end to staying overnight with Howard, even before her mother's eventual discharge from hospital, which would only frustrate matters further. It was a mess.

Her ruminations were interrupted by a cry from above. Jean bounded up the stairs, her heart thudding in alarm. Margaret stood in the steamy bathroom, naked apart from her sturdy white knickers. She was craning to catch sight of her back in the mirror. A patch of raw pink skin the size of a postage stamp was visible just above her waistband.

"I tried not to get it wet but it just came off," she said, holding out the towel to Jean to reveal a jellied smear of dead skin—the mortal remains of Gretchen's rejected graft.

Good uses for sour milk. Linoleum or cloth washed with sour milk comes up brighter than with water. Sour milk also makes a good bleach for discolored white fabrics. Wring out articles in water, place in a bowl and cover with sour milk. Leave for forty-eight hours. Wash thoroughly and the articles will be snow-white.

30

The coal fire in the grate was banked up and glowing a volcanic orange; the discussion in the room was no less heated.

Enthroned behind his massive desk sat Dr. Lloyd-Jones. On the other side of the room—and the argument—were his colleague Dr. Bamber and Hilary Endicott, whose article quoted in the *Echo* had prompted Gretchen Tilbury's original letter. Jean sat quietly, listening to the debate and taking notes.

"I think we can at least say that given the results of the serological tests, it has not been possible to disprove the claim by Mother A. Is that fair?"

Dr. Lloyd-Jones alone persisted with this naming convention, though all in the room knew her identity.

"No, it most certainly isn't. You asked me what criterion would satisfy me that parthenogenesis had taken place and I told you— a successful skin graft from child to mother. This hasn't been fulfilled and therefore the mother's claim is disproved. It's quite simple."

This was Hilary Endicott, formidable in tweed suiting and brown brogues. She looked as though she would be more at home on a highland grouse moor than in a laboratory, but she had in fact come up that morning from her mock-Tudor mansion in Surrey.

Jean, who was both taller and older, nevertheless felt dwarfed in her presence.

"I think the significance of the skin graft is less decisive than you allow," said Dr. Lloyd-Jones. "It is regrettable, for instance, that we didn't perform an autograft as a control."

"Well, indeed," said Dr. Endicott.

"Another possibility," Dr. Lloyd-Jones went on, ignoring this barb, "is that one of the antigens that gave rise to the incompatibility might be recessive and only present in the daughter."

"The skin graft test was not equivocal. It failed in both directions."

"But all the evidence from the blood and serum tests is consistent with parthenogenesis."

"Among other possibilities," put in Dr. Bamber. It was his first contribution to the debate so far.

"Such as?" asked Jean.

If she had to be the one to break the news to Gretchen she wanted to be able to understand as much as possible of the detail. She had naïvely assumed that the tests would provide irrefutable proof one way or another, that science would drive out all ambiguity, but it seemed that even the three most closely involved could not agree.

"Well, consanguineous mating, for instance."

"You mean incest," Jean protested, offended by both the idea and the jargon. "There's never been any suggestion . . ."

"It's just a for instance," he replied, holding out his hands in a gesture of appeasement. "I know nothing of the personal background. I am talking as a scientist."

"This would need to be excluded as a possibility even if the blood types of mother and daughter were very rare," added Dr. Endicott. "But they are not, which makes the probability of—let's call it *coincidental*—consanguinity the greater."

"Surely"—Dr. Lloyd-Jones' face was red, the broken capillaries on his cheeks and nose blossoming in the heat—"where the mother presents herself as an example of a virgin birth without any foreknowledge of the confirming blood test results, the validity of her claim is greatly increased?"

"It is persuasive, certainly, but it is not proven," said Dr. Bamber. "It would be useful to know, for example, how many—if any—cases there are of wholly segregated women—in prisons or asylums, say—reporting the phenomenon. None, as far as we know."

"If we had data for the number of recorded women-lifetimes without any instances of parthenogenesis that would give us some basis for an estimate of probability," Dr. Endicott added.

"All this is very fascinating," said Jean, raking a hand through her hair in frustration. "But where does it leave Mrs. Tilbury? I feel she's been led up the garden path with all these tests and now even you so-called experts can't look at the results and come to a consensus. What am I to tell her?"

"I'm sure it's disappointing for you," said Dr. Endicott. "You would have liked a more explosive outcome. But perhaps if she is made to understand that the medical results do not support her claim of parthenogenesis she might be prepared to change her story."

"Never," said Jean. "She has too much invested in it."

She thought of Martha—arch-skeptic—and wondered how she would react to the news. It was hard to imagine her coming down on the side of blind faith. And even harder to imagine Gretchen admitting to the commission of a colossal fraud. Jean, her confidence in Gretchen now fatally damaged, and compromised by her own involvement with Howard, was beginning to wish the story dead and buried. Any publicity generated by publication could escalate to engulf them all in a very unwelcome scandal.

She felt the blood rising to her cheeks in anticipation of the embarrassment in store. The failure of the three scientists to agree might yet work in her favor. An inconclusive result was hardly the bombshell Roy Drake had been hoping for. Maybe if she played her hand carefully he might be persuaded to park the story indefinitely.

31

Jean thought it only fair to brief Roy Drake before the editorial meeting. His disappointment and possible displeasure would be easier to bear without an audience.

"It could hardly be a worse outcome," she said. "We're no closer to the truth than we were on day one. The story's completely dead."

She watched him drop three sugar lumps into his tea and stir it with the arm of his spectacles.

"But you haven't been able to disprove her claim by any other means?"

"Well, no."

"You don't sound very certain. I thought you said she was sincere and genuine?"

"Yes, I did," Jean stammered, aware that she was not being entirely sincere and genuine herself. "I've allowed myself to get distracted by . . . domestic matters, and I stopped digging and questioning. I've been a lousy journalist."

Roy raised a hand—a faint gesture of demurral, perhaps—but did not contradict her.

"It would have been interesting to see her reaction to the failure of the skin graft."

"I wasn't there unfortunately. Dr. Lloyd-Jones said she pleaded with him to rerun the experiment. Which he wasn't prepared to do. He didn't seem to set as much store by it as the other two."

"Even so, it's still an interesting story." He glanced at his watch; the meeting was due to start in five minutes. "So, we haven't got solid scientific proof. But, equally, we haven't been able to crack her testimony. We could still run it as an unsolved mystery—"The Strange Case of Gretchen What's-her-name"—without making any claims that are untrue. Here are the facts—let the public decide."

Jean quailed. Let the public decide? One might as well throw her to the wolves.

"The marriage has broken down. I'm concerned about the effect of publicity on the child—if one of the nationals gets hold of it."

"Their marital difficulties are hardly our problem," said Roy. "She approached us, not the other way round. And divorce is not the scandal it once was. We've invested a lot of time in this and it's an unusual story of legitimate interest to our readers. And if one of the nationals does pick it up, so much the better. That's always been the hope, hasn't it?"

"But without the scientific proof . . . ?"

"Wasn't one of the doctors still open-minded?"

"Dr. Lloyd-Jones. He said . . ." Jean opened her notebook and flipped through the pages of Dutton's Double Speed Longhand to the phrase underlined three times. "It has not been possible to disprove the claim."

"Splendid. We can use that. Maybe publication will bring some other experts, or even witnesses, out of the woodwork."

"I still feel uncomfortable."

Roy shook his head. "You'll get over it. We can run it the first week of December. Nice feature for Advent. Get young Tony to do some photos of mother and child."

"All right," said Jean, defeated. "I'll get in touch with Gretchen. I've been putting off talking to her because I thought we might be spiking the story altogether."

She reddened as she remembered the other reason why she had been avoiding a meeting.

"Good man. Anything else you need to discuss?"

"No, that was all. Thank you."

She stood up to leave, feeling outmaneuvered, the result of her own dishonesty and evasion.

"I meant to say you're looking well lately. More . . . *sprightly*."

"Sprightly?" Jean's face fell.

"No, that's not the word. Relaxed. Healthy. Blooming."

He was overdoing it now, Jean thought, to compensate for *sprightly*, the preserve of aging spinsters, immemorially unloved and yet still, somehow, mobile.

"You've done your hair differently."

"Oh well, I just used a hair dryer for once."

"Anyway, it suits you whatever it is."

"Perhaps I'm more relaxed now that Mother's a little better."

"That's very good news," said Roy Drake, who had made regular and sincere inquiries about her health, and even sent her a basket of exotic and out-of-season fruit from Harrods—a luxury she had been too unwell to appreciate.

The previous week had seen some improvement. Penicillin prescribed for a urine infection seemed to have cleared a clouded mind as well. For the first time, Jean had been recognized and welcomed. Conversation had proceeded along rational and predictable lines. The delusions of recent weeks were forgotten.

Although greatly relieved by these developments, Jean couldn't help wishing that her mother's memory loss might have been more discriminating. Those dutiful bedside vigils, on top of a day's work, eating into her precious time with Howard, had all been wiped away along with the pickpockets, Queen Mary and the badgers. And soon, perhaps in a matter of days, she would be home and Jean's brief taste of freedom would be over, every absence a matter of negotiation and forward planning.

To complicate matters further, Margaret, in a reversal of the previous arrangements, was now living with Howard at Burdett Road and spending weekends with her mother in Luna Street. This solution was accepted by all parties as the most practical and conducive to Margaret's happiness. She could now walk to and from school with Lizzie, as she had been accustomed to before her removal to Chelsea, and remain at Lizzie's until Howard got home from Bedford Street.

Once, in the guise of unofficial aunt, Jean had joined father and daughter for dinner, but the awkwardness of taking Gretchen's place at the table was too much and she never repeated it. She had been unable to exchange so much as a glance with Howard that might betray them, and then withdrawn in lonely frustration to her empty house.

While this situation lasted, Saturday night to Sunday morning was the only opportunity she and Howard had to be together. From the moment they said hello—clinging to each other in the hallway as soon as the front door was closed—time, which had dawdled all week, now hustled them along toward goodbye again. They didn't go out; the pleasure of small acts of domestic intimacy—sharing a bath, preparing a meal side by side at the stove, putting clean sheets on the bed, smoking the day's last cigarette in the garden while they looked at the night sky—these were all still delightful.

"Stop, don't move," Howard said once as they half sat, half lay on the couch, Jean's head in his lap. "Listen."

The record had finished and there was nothing to hear apart from the rasp of the needle on vinyl.

"What?" said Jean.

"It's happiness. Can't you hear it?"

She put her hand up blindly and found his. "Yes," she said, in a whisper, because happiness was shy and easily scared off.

He no longer mentioned Gretchen, either wistfully, which would have been awful, or bitterly, which would have been worse. Jean knew that didn't necessarily mean she was never in his thoughts. A decade of marriage was not easily effaced. But he was not the kind of man who took any pleasure in stoking female insecurity.

The only regrets he expressed were that he hadn't met Jean earlier and been able to love her for longer. At moments like these, and in the afterglow of lovemaking, when Jean felt Gretchen thoroughly vanquished, she thought perhaps it didn't matter even if he did still love his wife a little. In her triumph she could afford to be generous.

32

The Grange, home of Kitty Benteen since the closure of St. Cecilia's in 1947, was a large and rather grand detached house in an acre of wooded garden set well back from the road leading between Keston and Locksbottom. Jean had cycled past the end of the driveway and its high walls on her journey to and from work for nearly a decade without ever giving it a glance.

Brenda van Lingen could hardly have known, when she included the address in her long-delayed reply from South Africa, just how very close to Jean's "part of the world" it was. Now, as Jean wheeled her bicycle up the gravel drive between the dripping laurels, she felt a tremor of fear and anticipation at the thought of coming face-to-face with the final member of the foursome.

She arrived punctually, as instructed by Kitty's sister and chief carer, Elsie, with whom the interview had been arranged over the telephone. Jean had been given to understand that Kitty looked forward to the stimulus of new visitors and would be disappointed if kept waiting.

"Is she able to talk comfortably?" Jean asked, embarrassed by her own ignorance.

She had seen pictures of iron lungs in the newspapers and imagined the confinement a living death.

"Talk? Lord, yes, I should say so," Elsie laughed.

"May I bring a gift? Flowers or something?"

"Perhaps not flowers. Pollen makes her nose run, which is no fun when you can't wipe it."

In the end Jean settled on a jar of hand cream, liberated from her drawer of treasures. Elsie had confirmed that this would be quite suitable. Though paralyzed below the chest, Kitty took pride in her hands, and in her brief respites from the iron lung had been known to file and polish her nails a bold shade of red.

At the stroke of four, Jean rang the doorbell and was greeted by Elsie. She was a plump woman of about her own age with blond fluffy hair, pink fluffy slippers and at—and very nearly under—her heels, a white fluffy poodle, which barked excitedly and ran around them in tight circles. Apart from this general impression of fluff, Jean's attention was caught by a large wooden crucifix on the opposite wall, bearing a painted plaster Christ with rouged cheeks and livid red wounds. There were other paintings on the walls depicting Jesus in better days, surrounded by chubby blue-eyed children, or dazzling a cowering Peter, James and John with the whiteness of his robes.

"Thank you for coming," Elsie said, helping to divest Jean of her wet raincoat and hood, which she hung from a curious pair of carved wooden antlers by the door. "Kitty's had her nap and she's quite lively."

She showed Jean into a large, brightly lit day room, in which the "lively" Kitty lay encased but for her head in the iron lung, a monstrous metal contraption like a coffin made out of an old Morris Minor. It was impossible not to be startled by the sight of a fellow human thus entombed and it took all of Jean's self-control to hide her consternation. But Kitty herself seemed quite unruffled, cheerful even.

Someone had placed a chair near her head at a comfortable distance for conversation, and an angled mirror above her, from which a rosary was hanging, gave a partial view of the room.

"Here you are. Here's your visitor," said Elsie, withdrawing with carefully planted steps to avoid the wheeling poodle.

"Hello," said Kitty, turning her neck in its rubber cuff and smiling a welcome.

Her fair hair was curled and set in the latest style, and her cheeks were rouged. She wore a pair of tortoiseshell glasses of powerful magnification.

"I'm so pleased to meet you at last," said Jean, disconcerted by the mechanical whoosh and gasp of the air pump as it did its work. "The other girls from St. Cecilia's spoke so warmly of you. And all this time you've been under my nose, so to speak."

"I'm glad to hear that. I've such fond memories of St. Cecilia's."

"Really?" said Jean, staggered by Kitty's fortitude. "None of the other girls was anything like as positive about the experience, and they surely had far less to complain about than you."

"We were all more or less immobilized, but I suppose being paralyzed I was the only one who wasn't in pain," said Kitty. "So in a way I was better off."

"Do you remember Gretchen in particular?"

"She was a nice girl. The best of the bunch. I didn't get to know her too well because she was at the far end of the ward by the window and I was at the other end nearest the door. But she was a favorite with everyone, because she was so pretty and gentle. Martha was her special friend. The beds were too wide apart for them to hold hands, so they used to hold the ends of a rolled-up towel between them. Isn't that sweet?"

"I suppose so," said Jean, surprised by this unexpected picture of Martha's vulnerability.

"Sometimes the nuns would get Gretchen into a wheelchair

and offer to take her out for a walk, but she always said, 'No, just wheel me to the end of the ward so I can talk to Kitty.' I've never forgotten that."

"Were there ever any male visitors on the ward?"

"No, we didn't see any men," said Kitty with faint disdain. "Unless you count my angel. Angels are always male, aren't they?"

"What do you mean?" Jean asked with a slight shiver, remembering the religious icons in the hall. She couldn't hear the word without thinking of Margaret.

"I had a visitation one night."

"You mean some kind of vision?"

"No, it wasn't a *vision*. That's what Elsie calls it, but she's wrong. It was definitely corporeal, because he touched me."

Jean's heart began to beat faster.

"Do you remember when this was? Was it during the time that Gretchen was a patient?"

"Yes, it was that summer. It was late July. I know that because my cousin had been to Lourdes and brought me back a vial of holy water for my birthday, which is on the fifteenth."

"So, tell me about this vision—I mean visitation."

"Every night one of the nuns would come in to say evening prayers with me—usually Sister Maria Goretti."

"Just you—or were the other girls involved?"

"Oh no. Just me. They weren't believers."

"Anyway, sorry. I mustn't keep interrupting."

There was a tightness in her chest of held breath and trepidation.

"Well, one evening I told Sister about the holy water. I didn't know whether I was supposed to drink it, dab it on like disinfectant or what to do with it. But I'd heard all these wonderful stories from my cousin about the miracles at Lourdes. So Sister took the bottle out of my cupboard where all my personal things were kept and I asked if she could bless it.

"She said she wasn't allowed to give blessings because she didn't have the authority, but it was already holy and she would use it to mark a cross on my forehead. And then she prayed over me to St. Bernadette for a sign that I would get well. Then she put my rosary on my pillow where I could see it and I went to sleep, hoping that in the morning I would be healed.

"At some point in the night I woke up and the rosary had slipped off my pillow, and when I turned my head there was an angel standing beside me."

"What did it look like?"

"It was dark and I didn't have my glasses on, so I couldn't see clearly, apart from the outline of his flowing hair."

"Did he have wings?"

"I couldn't see."

"So what made you think it was an angel?"

"Because I felt this tremendous sense of peace come over me as if the Lord had sent him to tell me that everything would be all right, just as we had prayed."

"And then what happened?"

"He picked up the rosary, which was on the floor, and laid it on my pillow, and his fingers brushed my cheek. So I knew it was real and not a vision."

At last, Jean thought. It came back to her now, that uneasy half-formed idea that had refused to come into focus at the time of her mother's delirium. There had been a man on the ward, she had said, interfering with her. But it hadn't happened; it was a hallucination. Surely a reverse delusion was equally possible where drugs were involved?

"Weren't you frightened? I'd have been terrified," she said. A man's hand on her face in the dark . . .

"Not at all. I felt quite peaceful."

"Did he speak?"

"No, he never spoke. He just touched my cheek—his skin was soft as a child's."

"And then what? Did he vanish, or fly away, or just slip out of the door?"

Kitty looked offended.

"He seemed to glide away behind me so I couldn't see him anymore."

"Did you tell anyone about it the next day? The other girls or Sister?"

"I didn't say anything to the girls—they would have thought I was making it up. Martha was very scornful of religion—for a clergyman's daughter. But I did tell Sister Maria Goretti and she said it was a sign that St. Bernadette had heard our prayers." She beamed at Jean from her metal prison.

"And you never mentioned it to anyone else?"

"I told Elsie, of course, but she thinks it was just a hallucination. But it wasn't. I was as wide awake as I am now. You don't believe me either, I can tell."

"I've been called to believe far stranger things lately," Jean replied with a noncommittal smile. There was nothing to be gained by demolishing Kitty's delusion if it gave her comfort. "Did your condition improve after this . . . visitation?"

"Yes, it did," said Kitty firmly. "It did. From that day onward I no longer felt abandoned by God, and that gave me the strength to accept my condition and live the best life I can."

Tears of admiration sprang to Jean's eyes. Kitty's bravery and stoicism were a rebuke to her own luxurious troubles.

"I'm studying theology, you know," Kitty went on. "With Elsie's help. She reads the books to me and I dictate my essays to her. I'm very blessed."

After the unnerving whooshing of the iron lung, the silence outside the house was precious as never before. Jean wheeled her bicycle back down the slushy gravel of the driveway deep in thought about this stealthy bedside angel with his gentle hands. Kitty's testimony had unlocked a door now, and Jean felt that only by returning to St. Cecilia's and standing in the room where it all took place would she come to a proper understanding of what had happened to Gretchen in the summer of 1946.

Nursing: An emergency table may be made by using an ironing board placed alongside the patient's bed. This makes a very handy lightweight table, and is the right height for drinks and plates.

33

The back door of the ambulance opened and Mrs. Swinney, supported by Jean on one side and a walking stick on the other, made a slow and queenly descent to the pavement. She stood for a moment, looking about her as if expecting some kind of reception committee, before allowing herself to be led down the driveway to the house. She had lost weight in the weeks she had been away and her muscles were thoroughly wasted. What remained of her strength seemed concentrated in the fingers of her right hand, which were now digging into the flesh of Jean's arm.

The path and step had been cleared of wet leaves and other hazards, and the house made as clean and welcoming as time allowed. Jean had only received notice the day before that her mother would be discharged and had since been trying to make good on her recent neglect of her housekeeping.

As a homecoming treat she had made a fish pie, with potatoes from Howard's garden, and a queen of puddings, using a reckless half jar of Mrs. Melsom's raspberry jam. She had considered making up a daybed in the back room overlooking the garden, to spare her mother the stairs, but it was a cold room, with an unswept chimney and a fireplace that had never been used. The garden in late November was not much to look at anyway, so she had decided against it.

They stood in the hallway, Jean's mother breathless from the journey from curb to house.

"Home again, home again, jiggety-jig," she panted and then stopped, her eye caught by the new blue carpet in the sitting room, just visible through the open door. "What's this, then?"

She approached it tentatively, as though gathering courage to dip a toe into its freezing depths.

"Oh, I bought it. It's rather nice, I think."

"What was wrong with the old one?"

"Apart from the scorch marks and the bald patches? Hardly anything."

Her mother gave the merest toss of her head to indicate that the sarcasm had been understood but not enjoyed.

"It's very bright."

"That's because everything else around it is so old and drab."

"Ring out the old, ring in the new," she sighed. "I see you've moved the furniture around, too. I shan't know where I am."

"I wanted to make the place look nice for your return," Jean said, almost believing in her indignation that this had been the chief impetus for change.

"I don't suppose I shall be spending much time downstairs," came the reply. "I'm still very unsteady since falling over. I think it dislodged something."

Jean breathed deeply, drawing on reserves of patience untested these past weeks.

"Of course, you must do whatever is most comfortable. But it would be better for your spirits to be up and about."

She wondered if one of those fragments dislodged was the memory of the sharp words they had exchanged the last time they were in the house together. She hoped not, because sooner or later she would have to bring up the vexed subject of Howard again, since it was inconceivable that she would be able to keep the relationship a secret under her mother's vigilant eye. And yet, it was still more impossible to imagine that she would enjoy the necessary freedom to see him, much less spend the night with him, now that her mother was an even more resolute invalid. The reaction to the new blue carpet, as an index of tolerance for change, was not encouraging.

After a grueling ascent of the staircase, requiring a rest stop halfway, which looked as though it might become permanent, her mother was finally helped to bed.

Jean had tried to banish the smell of damp in the room with the electric bar heater, which was only deployed in exceptional circumstances because it was both dangerous and costly. The cable was frayed, exposing bare wires, and the plug rattled in the socket. It gave off a powerful odor of scorched lint, burned onto the element, which then had to be masked with a squirt of Yardley's Lily of the Valley. The combination was not particularly soothing and triggered a sneezing fit, which left her mother quite weak and begging for fresh air.

At last she was settled, with a cup of tea and some magazines and her prescription painkillers within reach, and only now did she seem to take notice of Jean as an individual with her own separate existence.

"What have you been doing with yourself all this time, anyway?" she inquired.

I have been spending the nights with my married lover, under the nose of his neighbors, leaving the house abandoned and the milk to curdle on the doorstep.

Tomorrow, perhaps, when her mother had settled back in properly, there was a difficult conversation to be had, but not today.

"I've taken down the runner beans and written to Dorrie. And bought some new towels for the bathroom. Nothing out of the ordinary."

34

The call to Gretchen had to be made, but Jean kept procrastinating, finding ingenious reasons to defer it until some other, less onerous task was done. For as long as a meeting could be avoided, she had no trouble dodging her conscience over Howard, but face-to-face she would sooner or later have to resort to lies, or evasion, behavior she despised.

This was not the only reason for her discomfort. Since talking to Kitty Benteen, Jean had a dark sense that something less than holy had taken place at St. Cecilia's. Until she had evidence, there was no question of disclosing her suspicion, but it would be there between them, a malevolent spirit, and another barrier to honesty.

In the event, it was Gretchen who rang her, asking if they could meet as soon as possible. She sounded agitated on the phone, the foreignness of her accent suddenly apparent.

"I can come tomorrow, if you like," Jean offered.

Now that the nettle was grasped there was no point in further delay. It was a workday, but then this was work, and she still had not addressed the problem of leaving her mother alone outside these hours.

"No, it will have to be Wednesday or Friday, because that's when Martha's teaching. We'll have the place to ourselves."

Jean refrained from asking why Martha's absence was a pre-condition of their meeting, noting only her own relief. Since hearing of her tepid efforts to welcome Margaret into her house-hold, Jean had been incubating a certain hostility toward Martha and had no wish to have it tested by another prickly encounter.

"Could I ask a favor?" Gretchen added when the time and date were settled and the conversation had run its course. "You can say no if it's inconvenient. I left behind a patchwork eiderdown on my bed at home. I wonder if you could fetch it and bring it with you. It's pink and green."

"Yes, I know the one you mean," said Jean without thinking.

"I would ask Margaret to bring it on Saturday, but it's a bit bulky for her to carry."

"Of course. I'll call in tonight after work and pick it up."

"Thank you. It gets so cold here in the basement."

Later, when she remembered this exchange, Jean had a moment of pure panic. How could Gretchen not have noticed her casual familiarity with the furnishings of her bedroom? Perhaps it had been a deliberate trap, into which she had positively sauntered. In matters of duplicity she was an amateur; if she was to survive the forthcoming encounter without giving herself away, she would need to remain watchful.

The missing pane of stained glass from the front door of Luna Street was still unrepaired and had in fact been joined by a fresh breakage, also covered in plywood. In the shared hallway were a bicycle, a twin stroller and an umbrella left open to dry. Coats ballooned from the rack of hooks, almost occluding the passage. Jean decided to keep hers on as she fought her way past. It looked as though the weight of one more would bring the whole thing off the wall. It was, in any case, bitterly cold.

Gretchen was waiting for her in the doorway of the apartment, dressed in woolen trousers, thick socks, jersey and a whiskery, handwoven tabard resembling a pair of hearth rugs stitched together at the shoulders. Her once-lustrous hair was greasy and there were dark semicircles under her eyes. If this was emancipation, she didn't look well on it.

They embraced clumsily across the quilted bedspread that Jean was carrying rolled and trussed up with string. Any awkwardness was forgotten in the warmth of Gretchen's welcome.

"Come in, come in," she urged. "I'm so pleased to see you. I've made *spitzbuben*. Do you remember them?"

"Of course," Jean laughed. "It wasn't that long ago."

"It feels like it," said Gretchen, her face falling. She cheered up on being reunited with her quilt, which she untied carefully, saving the string in a neat skein. "Thank you for bringing it. It's icy in here. We can wrap it round us on the couch."

The studio had not changed much under Gretchen's stewardship. It was still dominated by easel, canvases, sketchpads, oils, rags, jars and various scavenged items that might find their way into one of Martha's paintings. In one corner beside the couch and coffee table—the living area—was a small bundle of Margaret's belongings—the limits of her territory, Jean thought with indignation.

"You look very *schick*," Gretchen said as Jean dared to take off her coat.

Underneath she was wearing the navy shift dress as a gesture of friendship, with a matching cardigan and a red silk scarf round her neck. The same could not be said for Gretchen without doing violence to sincerity, so instead Jean pointed at the tabard and said, "That's interesting. Did you make it?"

"Oh no, it's one of Martha's. She had a loom once, until she had to sell it. She wears it to paint, because it leaves your arms free. It's lovely and warm, even though it is a horror to look at, so I've borrowed it. I left so many of my own things at home."

There was the merest hesitation before the word "home."

"Perhaps you should call in and collect them sometime. I'm sure Howard wouldn't mind. They're no use to him."

"Oh well, you know." Gretchen shook her head. "Let's have tea."

She went into the kitchen and Jean could hear her clattering about over the gathering shriek of the kettle. When she returned, carrying two chunky pottery mugs and a plate of *spitzbuben* on a tray, Jean noticed for the first time that she was moving stiffly and that her wrists were bandaged with the same leather splints that Martha wore.

"Are you all right?" she asked, jumping up to help. "You look as if you're in pain."

"My joints are a bit tender at the moment," she confessed, turning her hands over and back. "I don't know why. Maybe it's the cold." She pointed to a patch of the green marbled wallpaper that was bubbly with damp.

"Is there no way of making it warmer? A kerosene heater or something . . ."

"We have an electric fire, but it's too expensive to use during the day. We put it on for an hour in the evening, but there are so many gaps and drafts in here the heat flies straight out of the windows."

They were settled on the couch now, with the eiderdown over their legs and mugs of tea warming their hands, and it was almost cozy.

"Are you short of money? I'm sure Howard wouldn't want to think of you like this."

"He already sends me a money order every week. But Martha doesn't like accepting money from Howard. She wants to support me herself."

Jean glanced around. It looked as though she was struggling to support herself before Gretchen even appeared on the scene.

"She works so hard. She's started an evening job too, taking life drawing classes in a church hall in Battersea, but it makes it even harder to paint when she's tired and in pain. I wish I could do my dressmaking to help out, but there's no room here for all my things."

"Perhaps you'll be able to find somewhere larger?"

"I don't know." She passed Jean a cookie. "These are nice, aren't they? I can still cook!"

"I suppose," said Jean, "we should talk about the *Echo* and our plans for the story. Dr. Lloyd-Jones said you were disappointed about the skin grafts. It was a blow."

"I don't understand it. I'm not a scientist." She shrugged. "I said they could do another graft until it works, but they wouldn't. All it has proved is that their test was no good. Now, Martha is starting to doubt me again and I suppose you do, too."

"Gretchen, I would have loved to prove your case. Or even to find an alternative explanation. But I haven't been able to do either and I feel that as a failure of mine, not yours. We still want to run the story in some form. As an unexplained mystery."

Under the quilt Jean felt her hand grasped by the leather splint. "You are a good friend."

"So, I'm going to send a photographer round to take some pictures next time you have Margaret. This Saturday? Obviously, we want you to look as similar as possible, so if you could do your hair the same and dress alike . . ."

"We don't have anything matching."

"Oh, nothing elaborate; just white blouse, dark skirt, that sort of thing. It's a pity you cut your hair."

Gretchen put her hand up to her bare neck.

"Yes, it was warmer before, too. I could always cut Margaret's the same."

"Oh no!" said Jean, horrified. "Her beautiful curls." She felt quite sick at the thought of any such mutilation. "And, Gretchen,

I have to warn you that once your name is in the *Echo* there is nothing to stop other papers following it up. You may have to deal with some unwelcome publicity."

Gretchen looked fearful.

"What do you mean?"

"Well, your current domestic situation is not exactly what it was when we first began."

"But you won't mention Martha's name or anything to do with her?"

"No, of course *I* won't. But others might." She relented when she saw Gretchen's troubled expression. "Ignore me. Probably nothing will come of it."

Outside in the hallway there was a sudden crashing noise and Gretchen started, slopping tea on the tabard. A moment later there was the sound of swearing and clubbing feet overhead and doors banging.

"Just some altercation between Dennis and the bicycle, no doubt," she said, relaxing again. "He comes in drunk at odd times and falls over everything. And then his wife throws him out—again—and then a few days later she lets him back in." She laughed, a catch in her throat. "Until I came here I would never have believed people could live such chaotic lives."

"This place isn't really you, is it, Gretchen?" Jean said softly.

Gretchen shook her head, staring into her lap. When she looked up her eyes were swimming.

"Jean," she said, her face collapsing. "I've made a terrible mistake."

"What do you mean?" Jean stammered.

"You were right. You were right all along. I can't do it. I can't do without Margaret."

"But there's no room for her here. You must see it's totally unsuitable."

"I know, but I miss her so much when she's not here. The

weekend goes so quickly . . . It's not even the whole weekend—it's just one night!"

Jean, who knew exactly how inadequate this pocket of time could be, could only murmur her sympathy. There was nothing to be done about it; Margaret had made her choice. As she tried to find a way of saying this that wasn't too wounding, Gretchen's sobbing intensified.

"Please will you do one thing for me, Jean? I'll never ask another favor," she pleaded, her voice thick and bubbling.

"What?"

"Please, please will you talk to Howard and ask him to take me back? I know he'll listen to you. I just want to go back to the way we were."

On the marble-patterned wallpaper, the shadow of a cloud moved across the shadow of the window and the cold room grew colder.

"But I thought Martha was the love of your life. What's happened?"

"It's not like I thought it would be. It's not like when we were in the hospital."

Gretchen pulled a handkerchief from her trouser pocket and ground it into the corners of her eyes.

"Well of course it isn't!" Jean cried. "You were just a girl then."

"Martha tries to be kind. She loves me, I know she does, but she's in so much pain it makes her short-tempered. And she hates teaching but she can't give it up because there'd be no money. And she gets so jealous."

"Of whom?"

"Not even of real people—not people we know, anyway. We never see any other people! If I read a book she is jealous of Carson McCullers or Rosamond Lehmann. Or if I listen to music she is jealous of Schubert."

"You make her sound quite demented."

"She admits it. She says she is jealous of the gloves I wear. But that wouldn't matter if only she liked Margaret a little more."

"And Margaret senses it."

"Yes, of course. Between the two of them they are pulling me in half. But Martha doesn't understand how painful it is because she's not a mother."

"But you must have known it would make Margaret miserable. I tried to tell you." She had to resist the urge to say: "It's too late. He doesn't want you anymore."

"I thought love could overcome everything."

"Then you're a fool," said Jean.

"And so are you," that stern inner voice, Duty, with its clinging gray skirts and sturdy shoes, reminded her. Hadn't she passed the last few weeks hoping and dreaming much the same thing?

"I can't stay here. I just want to go home."

Jean felt a pressure in her chest as though something heavy had been dropped on it from a height. Blood pounded in her ears.

"It's easy to say you want to go back to the way things were. But it's like unmaking a cake. Not everything done can be undone."

"Or you could say it's like mending a torn shirt—it might not be quite the same as before but it's still a shirt."

"If it's against your nature to feel anything for men, how is that ever going to work—for either of you?"

Jean had to pick her words delicately, without betraying any-thing Howard had confided about his years of unhappy celibacy.

"I want to be a proper wife to him. For Margaret's sake. I'll do whatever is necessary. Isn't that what you told me when you first came here to try to persuade me to come home? That the most important thing was Margaret? You did."

"Yes . . ."

"We were happier than a lot of married couples. And we can be again. I'll be a good wife, like I was at the beginning. If you could just tell him how miserable I am and that I ask for his forgiveness. I know he'd forgive me if he could see how sorry I am."

"Possibly. But wouldn't all this be better coming from you? I can't act as your go-between."

The idea that she should have to conspire in her own heartbreak struck Jean as the sort of prank invented by an especially twisted deity.

"No, of course I will say all this to his face, if he'll let me. But I can't just turn up if he's going to close the door in my face. If you could tell him how desperately I am regretting leaving him and how unhappy I am without him, I'm sure he'll agree to see me. He's such a good man."

Yes, he is, thought Jean. It took almost no effort to imagine the scene of reconciliation. The alternative—Howard coldly resistant to his wife's sincere, weeping repentance—was much harder to picture. And weighing heavily in the balance, of course, was Margaret, whose happiness would be complete and wonderful to witness.

"All right." Her voice sounded strangulated, even to herself. "Of course I'll tell him. I can't promise it will be today, or tomorrow. Work is very busy and . . . and my mother's just come home from the hospital."

"Oh, I'm so sorry. Your poor mother." Having achieved her end, Gretchen was very ready to repay her sympathetic dues. "I do understand. I know it's not always easy to get hold of Howard at the shop."

"It's not the sort of conversation I can have on the office phone. I'll have to choose my moment."

"Of course. Thank you so much. And if you do have any news, could you only ring on a Wednesday or a Friday?"

"While Martha's at work."

"Yes, please."

In all this time Jean had hardly spared a thought for Martha, another casualty of the whole wretched business, whose feelings would also be trampled underfoot.

"Will you stay for lunch?" Gretchen asked as the clock in the hall struck one with a thud. "It's only barley soup."

Jean could tell that this was a piece of mere politeness, a suspicion confirmed by Gretchen's evident relief at her refusal. Perhaps the soup was carefully rationed and any depletion would be noticed. In any case, it was no hardship to decline—even the Swinneys drew the line at barley.

"I must be getting back to work. I shall have to start thinking about how to write your story."

Jean threw back the eiderdown and stood up, feeling the cold air licking at her legs.

"It's funny," said Gretchen. "It hardly seems important now. I went chasing after proof, when the only two people whose opinion really mattered—Mother and Howard—believed me all along anyway." She gave a sorrowful laugh.

"I forgot to tell you—I had a letter from Brenda the other day," Jean remembered at the door. "From South Africa. She sent you her best wishes." She could not quite trust herself to mention Kitty.

Gretchen's face brightened. "Dear Brenda. We were so mean to her. For no reason at all." She caught sight of her reflection in the tarnished hall mirror, peering past the bald patches in the silvering, and winced. "I look awful. There's been no hot water to wash my hair for days. I shall have to prettify myself before I go and see Howard or he'll wonder what he ever saw in me."

35

In an extraordinary case that has confounded scientists, a
woman from Kent claims to have given birth to a baby in 1947
while still a virgin. Born in Switzerland, Gretchen Tilbury,
twenty-nine, of Sidcup, was an inpatient at St. Cecilia's Nursing
and Convalescent Home in Broadstairs for four months between
June and September 1946, during which time her daughter,
Margaret, was conceived.

Throughout this time, she had been bedbound with acute
rheumatoid arthritis and sharing a ward with three other young
women. The patients were attended by nuns and nursing
sisters. Several of these have been interviewed and confirm
Mrs. Tilbury's account.

When the eighteen-year-old Gretchen Edel, as she then was,
went to her doctor in November 1946 with sickness, fatigue and
aching breasts, she thought she must be suffering from a virus.
She was amazed to be told by the doctor who examined her
that she was expecting a baby.

"I had never even so much as kissed a man," she told
me over tea and cake in her immaculate suburban parlor. "I
thought, they'll soon realize they've made a mistake." But as the

weeks passed and the pregnancy became visible, it was clear
that there was no mistake.

   With the support of her own mother, who never doubted her
daughter's story, Gretchen resolved to keep her baby rather than
give her up for adoption. Margaret was born on April 30—a
dark-haired, blue-eyed replica of her mother . . .

Jean stopped typing, interrupted by the ringing of the telephone
on her desk. She could tell, even from the almost inaudible intake
of breath before he spoke, that it was Howard.

"Hello," she croaked, her throat raw from smoking.

In front of her, the ashtray overflowed with the evidence of
her unease. She had been putting off this conversation, but there
could be no deceiving him.

"Can you escape?" he asked. "I've some news."

From the steady tone of his voice she couldn't be sure whether
or not she needed to worry.

"And I have some, too," she said as brightly as she could manage.

"Oh? Good or bad?"

"Well, that rather depends."

"I'm outside."

"All right. I'm on my way."

"I love you."

"Yes."

They crossed the railway line to Willett's Wood and followed the
path through the trees. Over the years Jean had often escaped
here to eat her lunch, or to clear her head from the stuffiness of
the office.

Within minutes they could no longer hear cars or any man-
made sound apart from their own footsteps. It was a beautiful,
cold day. A few tenacious leaves clung to the bare branches, scraps

of red cloth against the blue sky. Frost had crusted the ridges of mud with silver; puddles of ice crackled underfoot.

"So, tell me," said Jean, lacing her hand in his and feeling his returning grip.

"I have to go and see Aunt Edie tomorrow," he said. "To help her move. Will you come with me? We could stay overnight in one of the empty rooms."

"I can't. Mother is back home from the hospital and she's still very unsteady. I can't leave her overnight."

"Oh. Well that's good news about your mother. Grim for us, though. How will I survive the weekend without you?"

"With your usual stoicism, I expect. Where is Aunt Edie going? She's not moving in with that Wally chap?"

She stumbled over a tree root and felt his arm tighten to support her.

"No, she's found a hotel in Maidstone that has boarding for long-term residents. They seem to have a few of her sort there already."

"Does she have a sort?"

"You know—educated gentlewomen of modest means."

"Goodness—what a title. I thought she was determined to stay in her house and go down in a blaze of gunfire."

"Thankfully, I think that was an exaggeration. The prospect of another winter in the house was a bit daunting. It's a beast to keep warm and there's no hot water."

"What will happen to all her things?"

"She can take a little with her. The rest will go to the auction house, the salerooms, jumble sales. The thing is, she wants to sell the house and give me the proceeds."

"That's very generous. Are you her only nephew?"

"Yes—she said it's all coming my way eventually, so I might as well have it now so that I can come to some sort of financial settlement with Gretchen."

There was a loud cracking of twigs, and a dog came bursting through the trees and bounded toward them. It was a large, muscular setter, brown and shiny as a conker.

"What a beauty," said Howard as it jumped up and planted its front paws on his chest, leaving muddy prints on his tweed jacket.

He stroked its head and ears before gently disengaging himself. The dog wheeled around and plunged back into the woods. Howard laughed and dusted himself down.

"I don't like the idea of Gretchen living in that apartment. I've not seen inside the place myself but to hear Margaret, you'd think it was a hovel."

"It's certainly not what you'd call cozy."

"So that's my good news. Good for everyone. I'll be able to set Gretchen up somewhere comfortable without having to move from Burdett Road."

"Aunt Edie's very thoughtful," said Jean, not quite meeting his eye.

He caught the lack of warmth in her tone and turned to face her, placing his hands on her shoulders and peering at her troubled expression.

"What's the matter? Have I said something to upset you?"

"Not at all." Jean tried to laugh but it emerged as a sob, which had to be quickly swallowed. "You haven't asked me what my news is."

"My God, I'm sorry." He pulled her toward him and held her tightly; she could feel her ear grinding against his. "Is it your mother?"

"No, no, that's not it." She took a long breath. It had to be done. "I saw Gretchen on Wednesday. She wants to come back to you. She realizes she's made a terrible mistake."

Jean relaxed her grip fractionally but Howard did not.

"She said that?"

"Yes, and plenty more besides. She was distraught—begging

me to persuade you to take her back. You can imagine how that made me feel."

"Oh, Jean, I'm so sorry. I don't know what to say."

"No. I'm sure you don't. It's rather awkward, isn't it?" Her voice was bright with self-command.

"I thought this Martha was the great love of her life. What's happened?"

"Apparently, it's not quite as blissful as she imagined. And not enough to make up for losing Margaret."

"Ah, so it's Margaret she misses. Not the marriage."

They had broken apart now and begun to walk again, a little gap—perhaps six inches—between their trailing hands. Jean felt it as an abyss between them, but she didn't have the courage to reach across it. Let him come to her if he wanted to.

"She wants you to be a family again," Jean said. "And to be a 'proper wife'—her words."

It was physically painful to plead Gretchen's cause, but she was determined not to withhold anything or twist it to her advantage.

"How is that possible?" Howard exclaimed. "We both know it's against her nature."

"That's really down to her to explain. You can hardly expect me to—"

"I suppose I'll have to see her."

"Yes."

"Oh, damn. What a mess."

He patted his pockets in desperation until Jean came to his rescue and offered him one of her own cigarettes. He puffed at it urgently as though he would rather smoke than breathe. Jean could sense his distress at being placed in a situation where he would be forced to disappoint someone.

She had half hoped that he would dismiss Gretchen's pleas without hesitation and proclaim Jean his only love, but this was a fantasy. Howard was the least histrionic of men. He would do the right, sober and generous thing. All the same, his failure to offer her any word of reassurance made her spirit shrivel.

They walked on in silence, their thoughts racing along on separate tracks. If he would only give her some consolation to cling to, she knew she could be brave.

"Gretchen said you can only phone on Wednesdays or Fridays while Martha's at work," Jean remembered.

"Good grief! I don't see why I need to go in for all this subterfuge just to have a conversation with my own wife!"

Howard flung his exhausted cigarette into the bushes and then changed his mind and went to retrieve it. Even at this extremity he couldn't do something unworthy.

"It depends what you decide. If you intend to take her back and make a go of things it hardly matters whether or not Martha's nose is put out of joint."

He turned to her in surprise.

"Is that what you think I should do?"

"What does it matter what I think?" she replied, betraying more indignation than she intended. "It's nothing to do with me!"

"But it affects you, too. And your opinion is important to me. I don't want to hurt anyone."

"I'm not your conscience," she said, her voice rising. "You want me to give you permission to break my heart and go back to Gretchen? Well I won't. Or perhaps you want me to beg you to throw her and Margaret aside for me? I won't do that, either."

She had never spoken so furiously to him, or anyone. The effort left her breathless. Her face burned.

"You're quite right," he replied, startled by this outburst. "I'm sorry, Jean. I didn't mean to upset you."

He pulled her to him and kissed her hot cheeks and then her lips.

If I fought for him, I could win, thought Jean. I know I could. But it would be Margaret whose face I was grinding under my heel.

"I must get back to work," she said, disengaging herself from his grasp. "Perhaps it's just as well we can't see each other this weekend."

"Can't we?" Howard sounded stricken.

"You're going to Aunt Edie's. And I can't leave Mother overnight."

"Oh yes. Damn."

"We'll talk again when you've had a chance to think and when you've spoken to Gretchen, and you can let me know what you've decided. I won't make a fuss, so don't worry."

She had recovered her composure now, for the moment, and sounded like her idea of a sensible, rational woman. She would collapse later, she promised herself, between seven and seven-thirty, when she had got home from work and done her chores.

36

Jean's last visit to Broadstairs had been in the height of summer. Today, on a wet afternoon in late November, it had that air of melancholy and neglect particular to seaside resorts out of season. The pavements were deserted; the ice-cream kiosks boarded up; shop windows misted with condensation; the sea slate gray.

She didn't like riding her bicycle in the rain, so she had left it at home this time and taken a taxi from the station to Anselm House, formerly St. Cecilia's. It was founder's day and the boys had a half-holiday, so the school was quiet.

"You can wander around at your leisure this time," said Susan Trevor, who had arranged the appointment with just this in mind. The headmaster was attending a memorial service for a former colleague; a few schoolmasters were in the staffroom playing bridge; most had gone home early. "Pop in when you've finished and we'll have a cup of tea."

Jean could tell Mrs. Trevor was the sort who had plenty to say and relished the opportunity of a fresh audience. Jean thanked her and made her way across the small entrance hall, past the trophy cabinet and the wooden boards displaying the names of past heads of school and house captains and cricket captains, picked out in gilt.

According to the floor plan marked up by Martha, the ward occupied by Gretchen and the other girls was on the ground floor, now a changing room. There were wire lockers around the walls, containing various balled-up items of sports equipment, lone rugby boots and grass-smeared cricket pads. There was a slightly feral smell of unwashed clothes and unwashed boys.

In the middle of the room were benches and coat hooks. The windows were high and barred. It was a long, narrow room and quite a generous space for four hospital beds, Jean thought; Kitty at one end, nearest the door; then Brenda. Gretchen at the other end, with Martha's bed a towel's width away. When she closed her eyes, it was no struggle in the silence to imagine the secret sharing of tangerines; the whispering after lights out; the whooshing breath of the iron lung, and the soft tread of the nuns and perhaps that other stealthy visitor.

A doorway off the window end of the room led to the boys' showers. This would have been the washroom the bedbound girls never got to use. Here, too, were high windows, latched on the inside but not barred. Not the easiest point of entry, Jean thought, but not impossible for someone agile, if the window had been carelessly left open.

She felt a shiver pass through her, as though surrounded by ghosts, and shook it off, annoyed with herself. She didn't believe in the supernatural and, in any case, the girls whose presence she imagined were all still solidly, warmly alive.

In the office, Susan Trevor served tea from a brown china pot with a quilted cozy. It must have been stewing for some time, as it emerged toffee-colored and not especially hot. Jean drank it quickly, feeling the tannin coat her teeth, while Susan kept up a stream of indiscreet chatter about the eccentricities of schoolmasters; the school's strained finances; the declining standards of discipline—chiefly lack of respect for authority, answering back, defiance—all those crimes of which age accuses youth.

If only Susan had been a ward orderly at St. Cecilia's, Jean thought. Nothing would have escaped her ravenous curiosity and the mystery would have been solved overnight. Her attention kept wandering back to that long room of sleeping girls, until she heard the whispered word "cancer," which always made her sit up, and realized that Susan had asked her a question.

"I was wondering if you were in touch with Alice Halfyard?" she repeated. "I was saying she's apparently quite poorly. I heard it from a friend of Mother's who shares the same cleaner."

"No, I didn't know," Jean admitted. "I only met her that once, last time I was here in the summer. I was intending to visit her again today."

"I hope she's well enough to see you. Poor Alice; she's had such a sad life—and now this."

Recalling their first meeting, Jean acknowledged that yes, she had sensed an air of spinsterish melancholy about Alice, but it was one that she recognized and didn't therefore trouble to investigate. And it had in any case been slightly overshadowed by those repellent dolls.

"She didn't talk about herself much," she said. But this was no excuse; she should have asked. "Why was it sad?"

"Her sister had a baby out of wedlock and then died of peritonitis when it was still quite young. Alice and her mother had to raise the child."

Jean nodded, remembering the photograph on the windowsill, which Alice had described as her family.

"She showed me a picture of them all together," she said. "I didn't realize they were sisters; Alice looked so much older."

"I think there was nearly twenty years between them. Mrs. Halfyard was quite an age when she had her." Susan lowered her voice, even though there was no one around to overhear. "Which may account for the girl being a bit peculiar. They do say with an elderly mother the eggs can spoil."

"Do they?" said Jean, who had never heard any such saying and didn't much care for it.

"Oh yes," Susan insisted. "It's well known. Anyway . . ." She poured herself a second cup, the color of stout, on top of the leaves of the old one. "That was just the beginning. Alice's sister's child, Vicky, turned out to be not quite right in the head as well, and that's putting it mildly. Had to be looked after at home in the end—under lock and key."

Jean pulled a face. "That sounds a bit gothic."

Something suddenly plucked at her memory—V: *V was waiting for me again today in the rain. Absolutely soaked through like a faithful dog.*

"And once old Mrs. Halfyard died there was no one else to help. Alice had an awful time of it."

"It's a bit ironic that Alice spent her days tending the sick and had this poor child locked up at home. Couldn't she have been looked after at St. Cecilia's?"

Susan looked puzzled for a moment and then laughed.

"Oh, you mean Victor? We only called him Vicky as a tease because he kept his hair so long—like a girl."

37

The once-neat garden on the corner of Wickfield Drive had an air of neglect, which filled Jean with misgivings. Unpruned rose bushes sagged over the wall; the lawn was ankle-high and ravaged by clover and yarrow. Mare's tail had taken over the flower beds and burst through cracks in the paving.

I'm too late, she thought with dismay as she stood on the doorstep, listening to the chimes of the bell as they were swallowed up by the empty house. She rattled the mail slot and opened the flap to peer into the unlit hallway, releasing a puff of sour, medicinal air from inside.

There was no reply from the neighbors either side, but in the house opposite she had some success. As she put her hand on the gate there was the sound of barking, growing louder, and the crump of a weighty dog hitting the far side of the door, dislodging some flakes of rendering from the exterior wall. A moment later a harassed-looking woman appeared at the front window.

"What do you want?" she mouthed as the dog continued to batter itself against the wooden paneling.

Jean gestured to the abandoned house behind her.

"I'm looking for Miss Halfyard."

The window opened an inch.

"She's gone into the hospital. Are you family?"

"No. Just a friend. I've tried telephoning a few times."

"She stayed at home as long as she could but they took her in a fortnight ago."

She gave Jean directions and closed the window, turning to bellow at the dog. The aftershocks followed Jean up the street.

The hospital for incurables sat on the clifftop, affording the staff and visitors, at least, a glimpse of a dark and wrinkled sea. The patients, confined to their beds on the upper floors, could see only a rolling cloudscape.

Alice Halfyard, a much-reduced version of the woman Jean had met in the summer, was lying in her metal-framed bed, her skin quite yellow against the white of the sheets. Although her limbs were fleshless, under the sheets her stomach formed a swollen dome.

On a trolley nearby lay the remains of lunch: a greenish soup and a pallid blancmange, barely touched. Someone had placed a vase of artificial flowers, blowsy dahlias in paintbox colors, on the bedside cabinet.

Her eyes were closed, but at Jean's approach she opened them. It took her a minute to focus and draw her dry lips into a smile of recognition.

"I thought you might come, sooner or later." She raised a brittle arm and wagged her fingers toward an empty chair.

Jean, accustomed by now to hospital visiting and the many faces of disease, was nevertheless shocked by Alice's deterioration. The traditional words of inquiry or encouragement—how are you? you're looking well—were wholly useless.

"I'm sorry to find you like this," was the best she could do.

"I'm glad you're here. Otherwise I'd have had to write you a long letter and I don't think I've got the energy." She spoke in a low, soft voice, just above a whisper.

"Can I do anything for you?" Jean asked. She glanced at the uneaten meal. "Do you want me to feed you?"

Alice shook her head. "I spent my working life in hospitals, but this is my first time as a patient. First and last."

"What have you got?" Jean knew she would have no time for evasions or false comfort.

"Cancer. Liver and now spine."

"Is it very painful?"

Alice gave the merest of nods. "I've learned so much about nursing from being on the receiving end of it. Too late to be any use, though."

"I'm sure you were very good anyway. I had a letter from Brenda van Lingen a while back. She sent her good wishes. And Kitty, too. She lives almost on my doorstep as it turns out."

"Kitty? Oh yes. How is she?"

"Physically still very limited. But quite an inspiration, really. Studying theology, with the help of her sister."

Alice managed a smile. "A remarkable girl."

"I thought so, too."

"Now, tell me about Gretchen's baby. What did the tests prove?"

"Oh. Well, the doctors themselves don't entirely agree. But the skin graft test seemed to suggest that this is *not* a case of virgin birth."

Alice gestured for a glass of water; it clashed against her teeth as Jean tried to help her to a drink.

"That's a pity," she said. "I was hoping for a miracle."

"Yes. I think maybe we all were."

"I'm sorry I wasn't more on the ball when you came to see me. I'd not long had my diagnosis and I'm afraid I was distracted by my own woes."

"That's quite understandable. I suppose you know why I'm here."

"I can guess." Alice winced as a sudden pain gripped her.

"Are you well enough to talk?" Jean said, her shame at hounding a dying woman just trumped by dread that the answer might be no and that she would be sent on her way with nothing.

"I'm as well as I ever will be."

There was still the same sharp intelligence in her gaze as she turned it on Jean.

"I wanted to ask you about Victor."

"How did you find out?" Alice's voice was a whisper.

"I noticed these references to V in your diary, but none of the patients or nurses had names beginning with V and it set me wondering."

"I don't remember writing about Vicky in my diary," said Alice, shaking her head. "I thought it was only hospital matters."

"There were no mentions of him during the period while Gretchen was a patient," said Jean. "Which is why I didn't come across them at first. Then, when I saw Kitty quite recently, she said while she was at St. Cecilia's an angel had visited her one night. Obviously, that made me very suspicious." She realized that she, too, was whispering.

"I didn't know that. She never said."

"She'd been encouraged in her belief by one of the nuns, but I don't think she mentioned it to anyone else at the time. And then this morning Susan Trevor told me you had a nephew called Victor and something she said about his long hair made me think of Kitty's angel."

Alice closed her eyes and a tear trembled at the outer edges of the seams.

"He was my sister's boy. She was a wild one—always in trouble. She wouldn't tell us who the father was—if she knew. But she wouldn't give the baby up; she didn't care what people thought. And the funny thing is, motherhood seemed to be the making of her.

"And then she got peritonitis and died when he was four, and we brought him up ourselves—my mother and I. He was such a beautiful boy—I've got a picture of him in my purse—everybody loved him. But when he reached puberty he began to change—just like my sister. He became quite withdrawn and started to hear voices."

At the mention of voices, Jean grew very still, the air trapped in her chest.

"He had these terrible rages. It was the voices tormenting him. We couldn't keep him at school; they wouldn't have him. So we looked after him at home. The doctor gave him some pills to keep him calm, but they made him blow up like a balloon."

Jean let out a long breath.

"He kept running away and getting into awful fixes. He'd turn up covered in cuts and bruises and with no idea where he'd been. It was so awful. You've no idea."

The tears were flowing more freely now and her voice was less distinct. Jean had to lean in to catch every word.

"We had to keep the door locked or he'd take off. He wasn't a prisoner," she added, seeing the expression on Jean's face. "It was just to keep him safe. If he wanted to go out somewhere, Mother or I would take him. But there was one day when I finished my shift and I came out and he was sitting on the wall outside. He must have got out and followed me." She plucked a crumpled handkerchief from the folds of her bedclothes and applied it to her eyes.

"Do you think it's possible that he might be . . ." Jean cast about for a form of words that was not too wounding, "the father of Gretchen's child?"

"When you first came and told me about Gretchen and the baby, it was such a shock, the idea of Vicky didn't even occur to me. Or maybe it did, deep down, but too deep to be faced. But when you get ill like this, and you know you're not going to get better, all sorts of thoughts start to surface."

"I can imagine," said Jean.

"But Gretchen would never . . ."

"That's not what I meant. I think she was unconscious. She and Martha used to hoard sleeping pills and take them all at once."

"You think he forced himself on her."

Alice's voice was barely audible now, swallowed up in tears.

"I have no proof. I'm asking if you think it's possible."

"Are you sure you want this?" she asked.

"What do you mean?" said Jean with a now-familiar sense of foreboding.

"Once you've taken it off me you can't give it back."

"Go on."

Jean stopped as a ward orderly approached with a trolley and removed the tray of uneaten food. Alice thanked her graciously, watching her progress from bed to bed until they were alone again. When Alice turned to Jean her face was a picture of desolation.

"I wish I could say no. But I can't."

Her freckly hand reached out across the blanket and caught hold of Jean's. The skin was dry and papery, but the nails, now digging into Jean's palm, were long and almost indecently healthy.

"I woke up in the middle of the night once and he was there in the room, standing beside my bed watching me and, you know, handling himself. I pretended to be asleep. I didn't dare confront him; he was so strong.

"After a few minutes I heard him leave and go back to his room, and then I got up and moved my nightstand in front of the door and slept like that every night from then on."

"Where is he now?"

"He died six years ago. He seemed to be getting better. I'd retired by then, so we used to do things together when he felt well enough. He liked to sit on the station platform and watch the trains.

"Then one day I came down and he was gone. I'd got careless and he took my keys out of my handbag and let himself out.

He was hit by a train on the level crossing. It may have been an accident—we don't know. He was only twenty-one."

"I'm so sorry. What a sad story."

"I felt so guilty, because I was supposed to be a nurse and I'd failed him. But it was also a relief—and that made me feel even more guilty. Mother had passed away by then and there was just me left. I used to wonder what on earth would happen to him when I was gone. For eight years I didn't have a single day without that worry."

"I'm sure you did everything you could."

"But thinking what he did to that poor girl—when she was supposed to be in my care. And now there's a child to worry about. Such a terrible, terrible wrong."

Jean returned the pressure of Alice's fleshless grip.

"Don't torture yourself about what might or might not have happened to Gretchen. We can never know for certain."

And yet I do, she thought. Everything she had been told confirmed Kitty's story of her strange night visitor. No angel, then, but this troubled boy, standing over Gretchen while she slept her drugged sleep. She could feel the burden, as it passed to her from Alice, pressing down on her, forcing the air from her lungs, as heavy as a grown man.

"Well, you must do as you see fit. He's beyond harm now and I will be too before much longer."

"I'm glad you told me," said Jean.

It was a lie of kindness. She felt a wave of nostalgia for her previous anxieties and dilemmas. What comfortable worries they now seemed. Having set out in pursuit of the truth, she had now learned something it would have been better not to know. She would never again be able to look on Margaret with the same innocent delight, unspoiled by fear of what the future might bring.

"Will you pass my purse?" Alice was saying, indicating the bedside unit behind Jean's chair. "I want to show you something."

Jean located the red leather wallet from among the few belong-ings and watched as Alice withdrew a buckled photograph with shaking fingers. It was the size of a playing card and showed a dark-haired boy of about seven holding a cricket bat. He was standing in a garden, in front of a wicket chalked on a wooden fence, and was poised to receive a delivery, caught in a moment of perfect absorption. Jean couldn't help scanning it for any likeness to Margaret, but the image was too small to make any meaning-ful comparisons.

"That's Vicky, before he got ill," said Alice. "He was such a lovely boy."

"I can see that."

"Promise me you won't think of him as a monster. He was only a child himself. And whatever he did, he did because he was ill, not evil."

"I don't."

"Whatever he may have gone on to do, he was all we had left of my sister and he meant the world to us."

38

The bell was ringing as Jean climbed the stairs carrying a tray of supper—an omelette with a slice of tinned ham—a glass of milk and Dorrie's letter, which had arrived that morning.

She had thought Mrs. Melsom's gift of a little brass handbell a kindness, but after a few nights of jumping up to answer its tinkling summons was beginning to wonder if it wasn't an act of revenge. Since her return from the hospital, her mother appeared to have developed quite a taste for a life lived in bed. No amount of hinting, cajoling or stern admonishment could tempt her back downstairs. Her legs were too weak, her balance too precarious; the armchair too uncomfortable. It was as much as she could do to totter along the landing to the bathroom. Steps would be unthinkable.

"This looks nice," she said, pouring a molehill of salt onto her plate. "You can't beat eggs," and then she stopped, realizing she had accidentally made a joke and unsure how to proceed.

Jean sat on the dressing table stool, looking at her reflection in the winged mirror—two infinite rows of Jeans with the same hunted expression swooped away from her.

"Are you not having anything yourself?"

"No," Jean replied. "I'm feeling a bit nauseous."

She hadn't eaten more than toast for twenty-four hours and even that had turned to ash in her mouth. Her visit to Alice had robbed her of all energy and appetite.

"Shall I read to you again tonight?"

She had discovered that it was impossible to think, fret or agonize while reading aloud. Housework, listening to music, reading to herself or any of the other traditional distractions did nothing to quieten the clamouring in her head. They were making great progress with *The Nine Tailors*. Of course, her thoughts could only be held off for so long; as soon as she was quiet they came swarming back.

"Yes, please."

"What does Dorrie have to say?"

Now, more than ever, she felt the absence of a sister to confide in. It might have helped to talk to someone quite unconnected with the Tilburys, who could listen without judging. In Jean's experience people tended to be divided into two camps: sympathizers and advisers. Dorrie, too much of a hedonist herself to expect much of others, was a sympathizer. She would only listen and comfort. Her mother was firmly in the other camp. Unhappiness had not softened her to the suffering of others; quite the reverse.

Her mother skimmed through the air-mailed letter, filleting for what she considered to be "news"—chiefly sickness and health, and the twins' achievements. Matters pertaining to her son-in-law, Kenneth, whom she held responsible for luring Dorrie overseas, were of no interest.

"No. It's all about this new dog. They're all besotted with him. Oh, here we are: Mary's had measles but she's all right now. Peter won a cup for chess. No other news."

"Shall I read, then?" Jean picked up *The Nine Tailors*.

"I'm still eating."

"Doesn't matter. You can eat and listen at the same time, surely?"

"Go on, then."

After an hour her mother begged her to stop; she was drowsy and wanted nothing more than to nod off. Jean closed the book and withdrew, dismissed, dreading her own company. Being left alone with her thoughts was like sharing a prison cell with a lunatic—terrifying and inescapable.

She felt a sort of rage toward Alice for handing her this burden from which there could be no relief. She could never tell Gretchen or Howard that Margaret was the product of rape, her angel voices perhaps a sign of something dark and destructive to come. It would be pointless and cruel and blight all of their lives. And she herself would never be able to look at Margaret's innocent face without the shadow of that knowledge coming between them. She would always now be watchful and fearful.

Another issue—less serious but still a tax on her spirits—was Roy Drake. She couldn't share her discovery about Victor with him—or anyone else—while keeping it from Gretchen. But if she didn't tell him, and proceeded to publish the story as planned, she would be perpetrating a deception against him and the *Echo* and all of their readers. Whichever way she turned it around in her mind, there was no way to make it good.

Two things stood out clearly, though. Margaret was owed every advantage that a united family could bring—all other considerations blew away like straws in a gale. The other certainty: if she spoke out, it must be now; if she kept quiet, it must be forever.

Jean lay on the couch in the living room as the night deepened around her. She was determined not to move from there until she had decided what to do. The coals in the grate had given up the last of their heat some hours ago and the temperature was dropping rapidly. Through the open curtains she could see a bright sickle moon and a smudge of stars. There was a sort of majesty in the indifference of the universe, but its vastness didn't seem to make her own dilemma any less significant.

The hours passed, marked by the whirr and scrape of the hall clock. At three o'clock she levered herself up, creaking and stiff with cold, and took a sheet of paper and pen from her mother's writing case in the bureau.

Home, 3 a.m.

Dear Howard,

It's only a few days since we were walking in the woods but it seems far longer. I'm sorry I didn't offer much in the way of sympathy or support after springing Gretchen's news on you— I was out of sorts and thinking only of myself. I've had time to reflect now.

Perhaps you have already made up your mind what to do, but in case you haven't, here is my view, for what it's worth. It's no exaggeration to say that the last month with you has been the happiest time of my life. I had thought I was beyond all possibility of experiencing love, but you proved me wrong in the nicest possible way.

As you know, I was always uncomfortable about the effect of all this on Margaret, but while the decision had already been made by Gretchen, it was easy enough to go along with the situation—not an admirable moral position, I admit. But the situation has now changed, and if there is any chaĺnce that you and Gretchen can find a way of living together and rededicating yourself to the marriage, putting Margaret's happiness first, then I think you should take it. She is the innocent party in all this and her needs should override all other considerations. I said this to Gretchen when she first left you and I must stand by it now.

It should go without saying that my feelings for you are the same as ever, and unlikely to change soon. It would be nice to think we could still meet as friends occasionally as we used to when I was first a visitor to Burdett Road. But I can already see that might be difficult and painful, and I will understand if you prefer not to.

Anyway, this was not easy to write and I don't suppose it's easy to read, but if I know you at all, I know you will accept what I say is true and do what is best for Margaret.
    With love,
        Jean

She put it in an envelope and addressed it to Bedford Street, in case Gretchen might already be installed at home. She hunted for a stamp—it was essential that she took it to the mailbox right now while she was resolute and gave herself no chance to weaken. There in a drawer of the bureau was the collection of un-postmarked stamps torn from previous correspondence and saved to be steamed off and reused. A momentary qualm about this practice—disrespectful to the Queen and almost certainly illegal—was allayed by her conviction that it was the sort of shrewd and thrifty thing the Queen would do herself.

She put on her coat and slipped out of the house, closing the door slowly and without a sound. It was only a few hundred yards along the road to the mailbox on the corner of Hambro Avenue. Every house was dark, curtained and hushed. Her footsteps on the cold pavement chimed in the silence as she hurried across the road and past the park railings. The trees stood out black against the velvet sky; she felt exquisitely alone, the only brave survivor of some apocalypse.

She hesitated for a second and then, fortified by a tremendous surge of martyr's joy, thrust the letter into the mailbox. A child's pink woolen glove, dropped on a visit to the park, had been picked up by a passer-by and mounted on top of the railings. It gave her a ghostly salute as she passed.

39

"Do you think the religious symbolism is a bit heavy-handed?"

"Yes—and very possibly blasphemous."

Jean and the picture editor, Duncan, were in his office examining young Tony's contact prints of Gretchen and Margaret. He had taken a reel of naturalistic shots of the pair sitting together on the couch at Luna Street, looking at each other and laughing. Margaret's hair had been clipped back to more closely resemble her mother's and in many of the shots their expressions were identical. He had also staged a photograph of Margaret by herself, mirroring the childhood portrait of Gretchen at more or less the same age.

The little girl had played her part with enthusiasm, mimicking, with a hint of mischief, her mother's uplifted gaze and wistful expression. Young Tony had then overreached himself, having Gretchen assume a Madonna-ish pose with prayerful, downcast eyes while curiously lit to create a glowing halo around her head.

"We can ditch that one right now," said Jean. Any suggestion of divine intervention made her feel queasy. "We're not trying to claim it was a miracle. Our line is that it's an unexplained mystery."

"Is there any other kind?" Duncan wanted to know.

Jean shot him an impatient look.

"It's a great image—very seasonal, too. I can't see why you wouldn't use it."

"I've got to know this family. They've had a difficult time recently." She cringed inwardly at the understatement. "I don't want them to become an object of fascination to religious cranks."

"If one of the nationals picks it up it will be out of your hands."

"Yes, I know."

Jean felt a familiar boiling anxiety in her guts. At the previous week's editorial meeting it had been agreed that it would be a front-page story on the first Friday of December—a considerable coup for Jean but one that gave her no pleasure. Now, she was in the counterintuitive position of hoping that the piece would come and go with as little impact as possible.

"It will be good for you—get your name out there," said Duncan.

She gave him a weak smile. "That's what I thought six months ago. A lot has changed since then."

The urge to confide in someone was almost overwhelming. Duncan gave her a quizzical glance. In all their dealings over the years the conversation had never strayed from the job. If the opportunity to share any detail of their private life had arisen, they hadn't taken or even noticed it. The temptation and the moment passed; Jean collected herself and grew distant and professional again.

They settled on the studio portraits for the front page and one of the informal shots of mother and daughter for the continuation of the story on page 6. Duncan marked the contacts.

"Could I have a copy of this to keep?" Jean pointed to the picture of Margaret. "This is exactly how I always want to think of her."

"Gladly," said Duncan, and if he was struck by the sadness in her voice he kept it to himself.

★

It was over a week since she had written to Howard and the spirit of righteousness, which had borne her up as she committed it to the post, was diminishing daily. There had been no word of acknowledgment from him, though her letter had hardly merited one, and she had no way of knowing whether or not he had made contact with Gretchen. Having surrendered all claim to him, she now had to accept that she was no longer entitled to any news and that there was every chance she might not hear from him again.

Having done the right thing was nothing like the consolation she had hoped. Without constant congratulation, virtue was a lonely business. She frequently found herself at her desk, halfway through some task like writing up the week's Household Hints or Marriage Lines, when she would lose concentration and gaze into space, transported by some memory of Howard's goodness to her.

This dream state could go on for ten or fifteen minutes until the sound of a ringing telephone or an interruption from one of her colleagues would bring her back to earth. Sometimes, when feelings of sorrow threatened to tip over into despair, she would leave the office and walk briskly to Willett's Wood, where she would follow the path they had taken together at their last meeting and allow herself to shed some restorative tears.

She knew that she was not doing a good job of disguising her unhappiness at work because, having once treated her as one of the chaps, people were suddenly either avoiding her or being uncharacteristically sensitive. Unpopular work that would normally have come her way was being diverted to other departments; volunteers mysteriously came forward to take on jobs that she had started and failed to follow up.

Instead of cadging a cigarette off her several times a day, Larry would bring her a custard tart from the bakery in Petts Wood on his way into work and leave it on her desk. Even the fearsome Muriel stopped her in the washroom, where Jean had gone to splash cold water on her face, and offered to bring in a pamphlet from the School of Yoga, which promoted dynamic breathing and other rejuvenating techniques. People are kind, Jean told herself. I'm very fortunate.

The evenings were a trial, because it grew dark so early and there was too much time to think, but she was kept busy answering her mother's bell. Misery was tiring, so she went to bed early, but it also stopped her from sleeping, so she woke unrefreshed.

She tried to remember what life was like before she had met the Tilburys, just six months ago. The days had passed without great peaks and valleys of emotion; her job and the domestic rituals that went with each season had been sufficiently varied and rewarding to occupy her. Small pleasures—the first cigarette of the day; a glass of sherry before Sunday lunch; a bar of chocolate parceled out to last a week; a newly published library book, still pristine and untouched by other hands; the first hyacinths of spring; a neatly folded pile of ironing, smelling of summer; the garden under snow; an impulsive purchase of stationery for her drawer—had been encouragement enough.

She wondered how many years—if ever—it would be before the monster of awakened longing was subdued and she could return to placid acceptance of a limited life. The journey into love was so effortless and graceful; the journey out such a long and labored climb.

One evening, when her mother was settled for the night and the walls of the house were pressing in, Jean slipped out and walked up to the church. She was not religious, but she thought of herself as culturally Christian and had accompanied her mother to services on the major festivals, before the falling-out over the knitted dolls.

Choir practice was just finishing and the singers were leaving, buttoning coats against the chilly night and calling farewells to each other, so Jean hung back in the rectory garden until the last of the footsteps had died away. The heavy wooden door was still unlocked, so she let herself into the cool darkness and sat in a pew at the back, as if prepared to make a quick getaway from God, should He appear.

The only light came from a bright moon through the stained-glass windows. The altar gleamed palely; all was peaceful. She had never been in the habit of praying, for herself or other people, and wouldn't stoop to it now just because she was needy. Instead, she sat contemplating the silence, and the smell of polished wood and candle wax and ancient stone. Minutes passed and she felt her eyes filling with tears, which she allowed to flow down her cheeks, gather at the corners of her mouth and drip off her chin unchecked.

There was a sudden noise—shocking in the stillness—and a shaft of light as the door to the vestry opened. Jolted from her trance, Jean hurriedly wiped her face on her coat sleeve as Mrs. Melsom, no less startled, appeared in the doorway.

"Oh my goodness," she said, clutching her chest and peering into the gloom. "I wasn't expecting anyone to be here still."

She was wearing a fur hat that might have done service in the Russian steppes and sheepskin mittens that were somewhat disabling her efforts with the latch.

"Sorry," said Jean, rising. "I was just . . ."

"Oh, it's you, Jean," Mrs. Melsom said. "I didn't mean to alarm you. I stayed behind after choir to sort out the sheet music—it was all in a muddle." She looked closer. "My dear, is something wrong?"

Jean blinked hard. She could take the path of denial and hasty departure, or accept the sympathy that was offered. A memory nudged at her—the downtrodden daughter from the hotel in Lymington, refusing her hand of friendship. She had clung to her proud self-sufficiency and they had both been diminished that night. Insight, overdue but dazzling, opened Jean's eyes to the truth that when help is accepted, both parties are enriched.

She gave Mrs. Melsom a grateful smile. "Nothing serious, but the truth is, I was feeling rather low. When I look at the future everything seems a bit . . . bleak."

A mittened hand rested on her shoulder. "I'm so sorry to hear that. Things must be very hard for you," came the reply. "Why don't we go back into the vestry and I'll put the kettle on."

"Thank you. You're very kind."

This encounter led to one practical improvement to Jean's situation. She had not disclosed the details of her recent sorrows with regard to the Tilburys but had hinted at the ending of a love affair, and her feelings of regret and isolation. Her mother's reduced horizons had also come up in conversation, and Mrs. Melsom had immediately volunteered to come and sit with her on Saturday afternoon so that Jean might enjoy a little freedom. They would play cards, or chat or do their crocheting together in silence— whatever Mrs. Swinney preferred. There were other good sorts at the church who would be happy to do the same on subsequent Saturdays, she was sure. Maybe, by degrees, she might be tempted downstairs again.

For Jean's aching heart, of course, she could offer no remedy and didn't try. There were only the time-honored methods— endurance, distraction, work—of which Jean was well aware, having had recourse to them once before in the matter of Frank, and recalled now without confidence. Previous experience taught her that the pain would not be unending—but neither would it subside smoothly, incrementally, but rather in a series of crashing waves, some of which might still knock her off her feet.

It was the first Tuesday in December, a few days before the *Echo* was to carry the Strange Case of the "Virgin Mother" as its front-page story, when Jean was hit by one of these waves as she tidied her desk and filed away all her correspondence and notes. The personal letters from Howard, which had come to her home address, were not included in this archive but remained in her dressing table drawer, awaiting the day when she felt resilient enough to reread them. The sight of Gretchen's handwriting on that first brief note—*I have always believed my own daughter (now ten) to have been born without the involvement of any man*—made her feel suddenly queasy, and she had to go to the window and press her face against the cool glass.

"I'm just going for a walk," she whispered to Larry, who was talking on the telephone, feet up on the desk, at his end of the office.

He gave her a thumbs-up without any interruption to the flow of his speech.

It was that hour in the late afternoon when the winter sun is just above the horizon but giving no heat. Her shadow stretched the length of the path, long, flared legs scissoring as she walked along, kicking through the last spiny chestnut shells and feeling the crunch of twigs underfoot. She could hear the distant shouts of children, playing, and somewhere deep in the trees a dog barking. Her scarf was still on the hook in the office and the cold air drilled into her ears.

As always, she followed the path she had taken with Howard, and at the point where they had abandoned the walk she turned back. In the gray distance, a figure emerged from the mist, a smudge of hat and coat. It was not so much the silhouette she recognized but his walk, as unique as a fingerprint, and she stopped, fixed to the spot until he raised a hand in greeting, and only then hurried toward him.

"I went to the office. Your colleague said you'd gone for a walk, so I guessed it might be here."

"Why aren't you at work?" Idiotic that this, of all possible questions, was the first to spring to her mind.

"I wanted to see you and I couldn't wait, so I closed the shop. You can do that, you know, when you're the shopkeeper."

They had stopped about a yard apart on the path, hands in pockets, uncertain what kind of greeting was allowed.

"How are you? How's Gretchen?"

"I don't know about Gretchen. I've been miserable. Your letter just about finished me off."

Hope, that treacherous friend, began its jabs and whispers.

"It finished me off to write it."

"I've thought and thought about what you said, and I've tried to see how it could work, because I know you are good and wise, but I can't do it. I can't give you up."

Jean felt joy flowing through her veins, unfreezing her blood. She had tried to be brave and do the good and decent thing, but she couldn't do it for both of them.

"I thought I could. But it's been awful. Worse than I ever imagined."

He pulled her toward him and they clutched each other almost fearfully, it seemed to Jean, as though unseen hands would otherwise pry them apart. But he was solid as a tree; strong enough to withstand anything.

"I drove past your house a couple of times, just in the hope of seeing you at the window."

"I was going to be so strong and dignified, but I've been a wreck."

"All this unhappiness for nothing." He kissed her lips, four, five, six times, until she pulled away, laughing.

"Did you speak to Gretchen?"

"Yes, we talked for a long time. I feel for her, but it's nonsense to think we can 'patch things up' as if a marriage is just a torn pair of trousers. I couldn't touch her and she couldn't touch me."

"What about Margaret?"

"Even if there were a hundred Margarets, it would never work."

"It used to work well enough until Gretchen left."

She wished she could stop arguing against her own interests, but she couldn't be sure until she had heard her case demolished, point by point.

"Yes, and if she hadn't, *I* would never have left *her*. I would have kept my feelings for you in a sealed box and so would you. But she did, and that released me, and now that I've experienced real love—passion—with you, I can't go back. Do you see the difference?"

"I think so."

They dared to loosen their grip so they could look at each other. One advantage of being the same height was that their eyes were always level.

"I know that sex isn't *everything*, but it isn't *nothing*, either. It's a part of married love, perhaps the biggest part. And the idea that Gretchen can suddenly bury her feelings of revulsion, and that I could possibly make love to her again, knowing how she really feels, is complete madness."

"Did you explain this to her?"

"Yes, of course. I think I got through to her in the end."

"And what will she do? Will she stay with Martha?"

"I think so. She has to have someone."

"Did you tell her about me—us?"

"No. I didn't know whether there was an 'us.'" He took off his woolen scarf and wound it around her neck, not needing to be told that without one she must be cold. "And I've agonized over Margaret, I promise you, but the damage, if that's what you'd call it, has already been done. *Of course* she'd be delighted if Gretchen came back and we all lived together again the way we used to. And imagine how much worse it would then be if a few months on it all fell apart again—as it surely would."

"I thought my life was over."

"I know. Everything you felt, I felt, too."

Happiness flowed and was smooth, but reality had rough surfaces and sharp corners.

"How will we ever manage to be together?"

"With patience and determination. Gretchen will have to be told. And Margaret. And your mother. It will be a bumpy ride, Jean."

"Yes."

She quailed at the thought of the turbulence ahead, but he had resolution enough for both of them. The alternative, already sampled, was unendurable. There could be no secrets. Except for that one unsayable thing, which she would keep to herself forever. Let them believe in innocence and miracles and angel voices; it would be her gift to them all.

"I can't leave Mother. You know I can't."

"I know. And I can't leave Margaret. So for the time being we may not be able to be together much. But we can still love each other, and if I can only see you once a week, I'd rather that than not at all."

"Perhaps if I introduced you to Mother it would be easier for her to understand that you're no threat to her."

With Jean alone she would certainly be difficult, but Howard's presence would be sure to disarm her. She had always taken more notice of men, considering them the superior sex.

"I'd like that. When?"

"Tonight. Now?"

Having accepted that it must be done, Jean wanted it over quickly, while she was still powered by euphoria.

"I have to get back for Margaret."

"Of course."

"Tomorrow, though, she's going to the panto with Lizzie, so the evening is my own." He sounded hopeful.

"You could come to dinner? Mother doesn't come downstairs anyway. She eats on a tray in her room, so once I've introduced you and we've had a chat, we can escape and be by ourselves."

It sounded so simple put that way. In reality, however well

behaved her mother was in Howard's presence, recriminations would surely follow when the two of them were alone. To prevail, Jean would have to be resolute, obstinate even. Somehow the knowledge that he was out there, emphatically and eternally on her side, shoring her up, gave her strength. Once her mother realized she held no cards, Jean could be generous.

"I'd like that. You're not going to change your mind between now and tomorrow?"

"No. Never."

She was already there, ahead of him, the anxious hostess in her wondering what she could possibly make that would be worthy of the occasion.

Dusk was falling, a pale lilac glow at the horizon all that remained of the daylight, as they walked back through the woods arm in arm, the trees in their dark suits lining the path on either side.

40

Wednesday, December 4, 1957

Howard stood in the doorway in Bedford Street looking out at a slab of fog. He had been in his workshop all afternoon resizing rings and mending an elegant pocket watch under bright artificial light and had not been aware of its gathering presence. It was thick as custard and glowed a sickly yellow in the lamplight.

On his way into work in the morning visibility had been poor. He had felt a bit congested as he walked along the Strand, but a cigarette had settled his cough, and he had been able to see well enough to pick up some hothouse roses from the market—at an exorbitant price—for Mrs. Swinney. They were now standing in a chipped mug in the washbasin. The florist had told him to stir some cigarette ash into the water to preserve the blooms, but Howard wasn't sure if he was pulling his leg, so decided not to risk it.

He took off his twill overall and hung it on its usual hook. The cash box from the till was locked in the wall safe. His tools were neatly put away on their pegs, the cabinets locked. He put on his ulster overcoat and felt hat, and tied a cleanish handkerchief over his nose and mouth. (Freshly laundered linen had been an early casualty of Gretchen's departure.)

In his pocket was a velvet box containing the silver bracelet with moonstones that Jean had picked out as her favorite on that unexpected visit to the shop with Margaret. Already a little in love with her, he had stored the memory away in case there should ever come a time in some unimaginable future when he might be able to make a gift of it. She wouldn't have forgotten, either; he was sure of it. She had spent a lifetime on the sidelines, observing, noting, learning; the little details that other people missed were not lost on her.

He hesitated on the threshold, shuffling the keys in his hand, before stepping out blindly into the milky mass, surprised to find that it offered no resistance. It seemed substantial enough to be carved into chunks. He drew down and padlocked the metal shutters and turned the key in the door, a nightly ritual, the scrape and rattle of locking up tolling the end of each working day.

Progress down Bedford Street was slow, hampered by fear of near misses with other pedestrians. He could hear approaching footsteps but see nothing until suddenly a figure would be almost upon him, when they would apologize and step around each other and move on. Scattered particles of light and the persistent ringing of a bicycle bell alerted him that he had strayed near the curb, and he stepped back as the cyclist wobbled into view, its headlight combing from side to side.

He was nearly at the Strand, when he remembered the flowers, still in the sink. Damn and blast. He would miss the 5:18 if he went back and that would make him late. He couldn't decide what would be worse—to arrive late or empty-handed. Unpunctuality— especially on an occasion like this—looked thoughtless, but the roses had been so expensive and the gesture so well meant that he couldn't bear to waste them. No, he would go back. Jean would understand—if the weather was anything like as bad at Hayes, she would have had a difficult journey home herself and might well be glad of a little extra time to prepare.

He turned and floundered up the street the way he had come,

holding his arms out in front of him as though warding off an assailant and apologizing to left and right. Now that he had no chance of making the early train there was no point in trying to rush. In spite of his handkerchief mask, the metallic taste of the fog filled his mouth. He was glad to reach the temporary refuge of the shop once more for a few breaths of relatively unpolluted air.

His decision to return was vindicated by the discovery that he had left the tap on at a rapid drip and the plug in the sink. By morning there would have been a flood to deal with.

He put these lapses of concentration down to preoccupation with seeing Jean rather than the absent-mindedness of age. Inside, he felt no different from the young man who had jumped into the Thames at Battersea and swum across to the opposite bank just to impress the sister of one of his school friends. It was only when he was forced to look at his reflection while shaving that he was confronted with evidence of the hungry years.

He wrapped the bouquet of roses in newspaper, forming it into a sealed parcel, to protect the blooms from the murky atmosphere, and restarted his journey, keeping close to the buildings and feeling his way along the wall. On the corner, he passed the pub where he had recently whiled away the evenings with a pint rather than return to the empty house. The windows were lit up, and the interior of polished wood and shining brass was bright and welcoming. A few solitary drinkers were defying the weather, or sitting it out, but Howard pressed on, untempted, thinking only of Jean waiting and wondering as his promised time of arrival came and went.

On the Strand policemen with whistles were attempting to negotiate a safe passage for pedestrians at the traffic lights. Howard could hear rather than see the shuddering bulk of buses and taxis panting out clouds of diesel, and feel their hot breath on his legs as he crossed in a shuffling mass to the other side.

At Charing Cross a great press of people was waiting in the

concourse, weary office workers and Christmas shoppers laden with carrier bags. A group of half a dozen schoolgirls in uniform snaked past arm in arm, shrieking noisily, confident in their little gang. Swirls of ghostly mist had penetrated in here too, through the open archways, giving it a curious atmosphere of being both inside and outside.

He was elated to discover that the 5:18 to Hayes was still on the platform, its departure delayed, congratulating himself on having made the right decision to go back for the flowers and imagining his disgruntlement if he had left them behind for nothing. Sometimes the cards just fell right.

Drawn along with the curious urgency that makes people speed up as they approach a train, Howard hurried through the barrier. A flurry of movement, whistles and the slamming of doors suggested that departure might be imminent, so he jumped on one of the rear carriages and found a space to stand between the seats.

He laid the newspaper parcel of flowers gently in the overhead luggage rack and unwound the handkerchief from his face, grimacing at the sooty particles trapped in its fibers. The train gave a lurch and a tug. Howard's fellow passengers exchanged smiles of relief and raised eyebrows. At last. He patted his pocket, feeling the hard shape of the velvet box, and imagined Jean's look of recognition and pleasure when she opened it. He would not be so very late, after all.

Afterword

The Lewisham train crash of 1957, described in the opening chapter, was at the time the second-worst peacetime rail disaster in British history. (The Harrow and Wealdstone crash five years earlier being the worst.)

A total of 90 people lost their lives and 173 were injured. The driver of the Ramsgate steam locomotive, which had not stopped at the danger signal and collided with the stationary Hayes train, was prosecuted for manslaughter but acquitted after two trials, the original jury having failed to reach a verdict.

In a landmark case—*Chadwick v. British Railways Board, 1967*—which became a precedent for thirty years, the British Railways Board was successfully sued by the widow of a member of the public who had assisted at the scene for damage caused by "nervous shock." Henry Chadwick, who had climbed inside the crippled carriages to help the injured and dying, was unable to work again until his death (from unrelated causes) in 1962.

An unduly observant reader might notice that the account of the crash appears in the (fictional) *North Kent Echo* on Friday, December 6, 1957, thereby knocking Jean's virgin birth story off the front page.

The seed for this book came from an interview broadcast on BBC Radio 4's Woman's Hour toward the end of the last millennium with journalist Audrey Whiting. The *Sunday Pictorial*, for whom she worked in 1955, ran a competition to find a virgin mother, prompted by research by Dr. Helen Spurway, a geneticist at the University of London.

Dr. Spurway had observed that a species of fish (*Lebistes reticulatus*) was capable of spontaneously producing female progeny. It had also proved possible to obtain parthenogenetic development in rabbits by freezing the fallopian tubes. This led to speculation about whether or not spontaneous parthenogenesis might be provable in other mammals—most notably the human female.

The competition was launched, inviting women to present themselves for research. Of the nineteen who came forward, all were gradually ruled out for various reasons—including confusion as to what virginity actually involved—apart from a Mrs. Emmimarie Jones, who had been bedridden in a German hospital at the time of "conception." She and her daughter, Monica, were subjected to various blood and serological tests, which seemed to validate her claim, but the final skin graft test eventually failed in both directions.

Details of the tests and their outcomes were reported in *The Lancet*, Vol. 267, issue 6931, June 30, 1956, pp. 1071–2 and Vol. 268, issue 6934, July 21, 1956, pp. 147–8. Even the doctors running these tests disagreed as to their significance. Their correspondence in *The Lancet* makes interesting reading.

Having caught the tail end of this interview on the radio, I sensed its potential as the basis of a novel but at the time I was writing (in my view, at least) humorous fiction, and this story didn't lend itself to light comedy. I therefore left it hanging at the back of my mind for well over a decade, like a piece of flypaper, to see if anything stuck to it.

I had been living in Hayes, Kent, for more than twenty years and used to commute daily on the Charing Cross line without ever having come across a mention of the Lewisham rail crash. It was only when researching the local history of the area in 2015 to see whether or not it might do as the setting for what I now thought of as the virgin birth novel that I came across a reference to it. This was the fly that stuck.

I have had to do some violence to history to unite these two strands. The facts of the rail crash are, as far as I can manage, accurate; the virgin birth story—apart from the seed described above and the medical tests detailed in *The Lancet*—is fiction. The characters, events and conversations are all mere invention. There is, I understand, a chapter about the case of Mrs. Emmimarie Jones in *Like a Virgin: How Science Is Redesigning the Rules of Sex* by Aarathi Prasad (London: Oneworld Publications, 2012), but I didn't dare to read it in case it contained something that derailed my plot.

All the household hints are taken from issues of the *Hayes Parochial Magazine* and the *Hayes Herald*, published between 1953 and 1959.

I did some enjoyable reading to steep myself in the flavors of a period that I am just too young to have lived through. The novels of the 1950s are too numerous and too well known to need listing here. Of the nonfiction, the most useful were:

The diarists of the mass observation project collected in *Our Hidden Lives: The Everyday Diaries of a Forgotten Britain, 1945–1948*, edited by Simon Garfield (London: Ebury Press, 2005).

Family Britain 1951–1957, David Kynaston (London: Bloomsbury, 2009).

For a frank and illuminating account of extramarital love and sex, long before such things were formally invented in 1963, I was glad to have found *Diary of a Wartime Affair: The True Story of a Surprisingly Modern Romance* by Doreen Bates (London: Viking, 2016).

London: Portrait of a City 1950–1962 by Allan Hailstone (Stroud: Amberley Publishing, 2014) provided photographic inspiration.

For the local history of the Hayes area I am indebted to Jean Wilson and Trevor Woodman's *Hayes: A History of a Kentish Village: Volume 2: 1914 to Modern Times* (J. Wilson, 2012).

Acknowledgments

When I was first published in my twenties, I used to think acknowledgments were a sign of weakness and I pitied those writers who seemed to need a whole village to raise their book. I feel rather differently about the matter now and ashamed that some extremely helpful people went unthanked.

In that spirit, I am indebted to the following: Judith Murray of Greene & Heaton, who is everything a writer could wish for in an agent; Federico Andornino, my editor at W&N—his suggestions have greatly improved the book and it has been no small pleasure working with him; Claire Pickering for thoughtful copyediting.

Thanks are also due to Ken and Sylvia Truss for their encyclopedic knowledge of the era and area in which the book is set, and very much overdue to Esther Whitby, my mentor for the past three decades.

Last in this list, but the first in importance, is my husband, Peter, for his unwavering support.

About the Author

Clare Chambers was born in southeast London in 1966. She studied English at Oxford and after graduating spent the year in New Zealand, where she wrote her first novel, *Uncertain Terms*, published when she was twenty-five. She has since written eight further novels, including *Learning to Swim*, which won the Romantic Novelists' Association best novel award and was adapted as a Radio 4 play, and *In a Good Light*, which was long-listed for the Whitbread best novel prize.

Clare began her career as a secretary at the publisher André Deutsch, when legendary editor Diana Athill was still at the helm. They not only published her first novel, but made her type her own contract. In due course she went on to become an editor there herself, until leaving to raise a family and concentrate on her own writing. Some of the experiences of working for an eccentric, independent publisher in the pre-digital era found their way into her novel *The Editor's Wife*.

She took up a post as Royal Literary Fund Fellow at the University of Kent in September 2020. She lives with her husband in southeast London.